Economics, Evolution and the State

Economics, Evolution and the State

The Governance of Complexity

Edited by

Kurt Dopfer

Professor of Economics, University of St Gallen, Switzerland

Edward Elgar

Cheltenham, UK • Northampton, MA, USA

Published by
Edward Elgar Publishing Limited
Glensanda House
Montpellier Parade
Cheltenham
Glos GL50 1UA
UK

Edward Elgar Publishing, Inc.
136 West Street
Suite 202
Northampton
Massachusetts 01060
USA

A catalogue record for this book
is available from the British Library

ISBN 1 84542 438 7

Printed and bound in Great Britain by MPG Books Ltd, Bodmin, Cornwall

Contents

Contributors

Hans-Peter Brunner, Asian Development Bank, Manila

Uwe Cantner, Friedrich-Schiller-Universität Jena

Kurt Dopfer, Universität St Gallen

Malcolm H. Dunn, Universität Potsdam

Monika Friedrich-Nishio, Institute for Economic Policy Research (IWW), Karlsruhe University

Hariolf Grupp, Fraunhofer Institute for Systems and Innovation Research (ISI) and Karlsruhe University

Horst Hanusch, Universität Augsburg

Reiner Peter Hellbrück, Fachhochschule Würzburg-Schweinfurt

Carsten Herrmann-Pillath, Universität Witten-Herdecke

Wolfgang Kerber, Philipps-Universität Marburg

Matthias Klaes, Keele University

Lambert T. Koch, Bergische Universität Wuppertal

Icíar Dominguez Lacasa, Fraunhofer Institute for Systems and Innovation Research (ISI), Karlsruhe

Andreas Pyka, Universität Augsburg

P. Paolo Saviotti, INRA, Université Pierre Mendes-France, Grenoble

Joachim Schwerin

Gerhard Wegner, Universität Erfurt

Wolfgang Weidlich, Universität Stuttgart

C. Christian von Weizsäcker, Frontier Economics, Köln

Claudia Werker, Max-Planck-Institut für Ökonomik, Jena

Introduction

Kurt Dopfer

A NEW BRANCH: EVOLUTIONARY ECONOMIC GOVERNANCE

The last two decades have seen an explosion of research in evolutionary economics and related fields. There has been an upsurge in the publications addressing evolutionary themes in economics, paralleled by the foundation of new journals, new academic societies and, last but not least, a reorientation of the publication programmes of major publishing houses.

The potential of this knowledge stock with respect to its application to issues of economic governance – in the line of an *evolutionary economic governance* – has as yet received little attention in the literature. Evolutionary economic governance can be defined as the study of the possibilities and consequences of any external intervention into structure and processes of an evolving economic system. Specifically, evolutionary economic policy is the application of evolutionary governance to the economy as a whole.

The notion of '*evolutionary*' acknowledges, on the one hand, that continual change in economic systems is an empirical fact, and it calls, on the other hand, for a theoretical account of this dynamic on the basis of an evolutionary rather than mechanistic explanatory schema. Thus, both explanandum and explanans are evolutionary.

The notion of '*governance*', in turn, means that the analysis is not confined to an economic system in isolation from external instances of mutual or unidirectional influences. Evolving systems can be, and often are, embedded in a hierarchy of decision-making strata. Evolutionary economic policy is a special case of governance that applies to the highest level of aggregation and decision-making authority in an economic system. In its interdisciplinary and long-run perspective evolutionary policy governance resembles much classical political economy.

The 14 contributions to this volume address the issue of evolutionary economic governance at various levels of aggregation and of decision making. Inspired by evolutionary thinking a range of models emerges that highlight the variety and the complexity of evolutionary governance of economic systems.

The contributions were selected from a set of papers presented at two annual conferences of the 'Expert Group for the Study of Evolutionary Economics' (Ausschuss für Evolutorische Ökonomik) devoted to the topics 'Evolutionary Economics: Methodological, Econometric and Mathematical Foundations' and 'Evolutionary Economic Policy'. The complete set of papers of the two conferences was published in the German language as volumes VII and VIII of the series 'Studien zur Evolutorischen Ökonomik' (Dopfer, K.(ed.) (2003, 2004), Berlin: Duncker and Humblot).

INSTITUTIONAL SETTING

Before giving a summary introduction of the various contributions to the volume, a few remarks on the institutional setting in which they came about will be made. The research group mentioned is an institution within the so-called *Verein für Socialpolitik* which is the professional association of German-speaking economists – the *German Economic Association* – with members coming from all over the world, but mostly from Germany, Austria and Switzerland.

> The Verein was founded in the year 1873. The activities of the new association focused on opposing *laissez-faire* in social policy and the revolutionary social ideas of emerging socialism. The founders of the association wanted 'to raise, educate and reconcile the lower classes on the basis of the existing order' as Gustav Schmoller, the chairman of the *Verein* for many years (1890–1917), put it. In Schmoller's time, the *Verein für Socialpolitik* started to develop into a politically neutral, interdisciplinary society. (www.socialpolitik.org)

The *Verein* voluntarily disbanded in 1936 to avoid having to bow to the ruling political party. It was refounded in 1948.

While its over 3000 members discuss their scientific findings at the society's meeting annually (with 700 papers at the 2004 meeting in Dresden), the most concentrated research efforts are probably made in the regular meetings of the expert groups. The *Expert Group for the Study of Evolutionary Economics* has emerged from an unofficial working group organised by Ulrich Witt in 1989 and became an official *Ausschuss* of the *Verein* in 1991. It is the youngest and presently largest and fastest developing of the 23 expert groups of the *Verein*.

The various expert groups reflect the variety of the scientific activities of its members and mirror its history, but the dominant doctrine of the *Verein* (if there is any) revolves around neoclassical economics. The likelihood that a majority of its members may contradict such a statement may signify the particular kind of neoclassical economics that is being followed.

The contributions to this volume are grouped around three major topics:

Economic evolution as open process
Self-organisation and networks
The political economy of complexity.

ECONOMIC EVOLUTION AS OPEN PROCESS

Directedness in Economic Evolution

In their chapter on 'Heterogeneity and evolutionary change – concepts and measurement', Uwe Cantner and Horst Hanusch deal with an empirical approach to heterogeneity as both the force and the result of evolutionary change, that is the result of as well as the source for local technological change. Heterogeneity here is understood as differences in the technological performance of productive units. Those differences are due to the local application and local innovation of specific production techniques resulting in structures of asymmetric productive efficiency and/or in structures of variety in the production technologies in use. Investigating those structures and their development empirically requires a specific measure for technologically heterogeneous performances and a specific methodology which allows the detection of this heterogeneity. With respect to the former the authors propose total factor productivity (TFP) and changes of TFP as measures for technological heterogeneity and its dynamics. From a methodological point of view a non-parametric empirical approach appears appropriate to identify heterogeneous structures and to track them over time. Structures of asymmetric performances as well as of variety can be identified by non-parametric best-practice production or efficiency frontiers. Computing the Malmquist-productivity index allows one to track those structures over time and to identify local changes. Discussing these concepts and procedures the chapter concludes by raising a number of unresolved issues.

C. Christian von Weizsäcker in his chapter is concerned with the question: Is the notion of progress compatible with an evolutionary *view of the economy?* The measuring rod for the performance of an economy is the fulfilment of the needs of its members as evaluated by themselves according to their preferences. Neoclassical economics has developed policy advice making the assumption of exogenously given preferences. This assumption is incompatible with an evolutionary approach to economics. In evolutionary economics it is assumed that preferences 'evolve', hence are endogenously determined. Is then policy advice still possible, if the measuring rod changes with the object to be measured? Von Weizsäcker develops a theory of adaptive preferences which fulfils two requirements at the same time: (1) adaptive preferences can be seen as the 'laws of evolution' of preferences, thereby being compatible with an evolutionary approach in economics; (2) a theorem can be derived which ensures that welfare economics is possible with adaptive preferences, hence endogenously determined preferences. The central idea is to show that normative comparability of different allocations A and B can be obtained consistently by means of 'improvement paths' going from A to B (or vice versa, but not both) even if preferences induced by A would make A preferred to B and preferences induced by B would make B preferred to A, hence would make A and B normatively incomparable.

Gerhard Wegner's contribution to this volume aims at reconciling evolutionary economics with liberalism. Although evolutionary economics highlights the innovation process as the driving force of economic welfare, its political implications are far from being unambiguous and have not resulted in a new conceptualisation of economic policy. It is an open question whether evolutionary economics should stick to the logical structure of deductive normative economics, that is to deduce welfare-promoting policies from a revised 'non-stationary' welfare concept. This chapter casts doubts on such deductivism and advocates a liberal interpretation of evolutionary economics. Namely, economic policy should not be conceptualised to promote welfare directly but to ensure the institutional preconditions for a rise in welfare. It is argued that evolutionary economics supports the view that economic welfare results from experiments which are ultimately based on economic 'world views' or beliefs and lack objectivity; for that reason, their ongoing assessment by a competitive environment is required. Generally, economic policy is well advised to foster economic freedom as well as competition in order to make sure that rival economic ideas cannot outperform each other except through competition. From an epistemological point of view, evolutionary economics denies that a comprehensive description of economic opportunities can be made from the perspective of a theoretical observer. For that reason alone economic policy should desist from 'constructing' superior allocative states in concrete terms.

In 'Historical economics and evolutionary economic policy – Coasean perspectives', Matthias Klaes focuses on evolutionary aspects in Coase's thinking. The recent literature evaluating Coase's work in the light of evolutionary economics has come to distinguish between two Coasean traditions, one appropriated by the economic mainstream, the other identifying a significant heterodox potential. It is the aim of Klaes' paper to take the latter reception of Coase's legacy as the starting point for exploring his contribution in the light of recent debates on an evolutionary approach to economic policy. The author defends the view that contrary to attempts to label Coase as an arch neoliberal, one can identify a commitment to the primacy of institutional direction rather than decentralised allocation of resources across markets as the core building block of his outlook on economic policy. This leads to an interpretation of Coase's approach in terms of a historico-empirical method of comparative institutional analysis, which calls both for a hermeneutical approach to economic policy evaluation, and constitutes a form of historical economics that offers an ambitious research agenda for attempts to move the conceptualisation of history in evolutionary economics beyond affirmations of the relevance of path-dependent processes. What Coase ultimately offers to evolutionary economics is the prospect of a morphological analysis that exhibits interesting parallels to recent developments in evolutionary 'Evo-Devo' biology that have re-established the relevance of ontogenetic approaches to developmental processes.

Self-organisation and Networks

Andreas Pyka and P. Paolo Saviotti in their chapter examine 'The concept of network organisation – biotechnology-based industries as exemplar'. Technological progress in the biological sciences is now advancing across such a wide range and at such a pace that no firm can hope to keep up in all the different areas. Participating in innovation networks offers an alternative to extremely expensive go-it-alone strategies. This imbalance between the rate of growth of the biotechnology knowledge base and the capability of individual firms to access it can explain the persistence of cooperative R&D in the biotechnology-based sectors at the end of the 1990s. Such imbalance is not due any more only to the lack of absorptive capacity of large pharmaceutical firms, because they have meanwhile developed considerable competencies in that field. The authors are proposing that a new role, that of explorers scanning parts of the knowledge space that LDFs (large diversified firms) are capable of exploring but unwilling to commit themselves to in an irreversible way, can be played by DBFs (dedicated biotechnology firms) in innovation networks. The authors' simulation approach attempts to represent the emergence of these two roles as endogenous changes in the motivation for participating in innovation networks, allowing them to become an important and long-lasting organisational device for industrial R&D.

The contribution by Wolfgang Weidlich deals with 'Sociodynamics – an integrated approach to modelling in the social sciences'. Sociodynamics – an important branch of the emergent field of econophysics – aims at providing a general strategy for designing mathematical models for the quantitative description of a broad class of dynamic collective phenomena within human society. These design principles have been applied in the past to models of non-equilibrium economics as well as to those of group dynamics, political opinion formation, migration and urban evolution. Weidlich's contribution highlights the essential formalism of the so-called master-equation, and discusses specifically aspects of the choice of variables, transition rates and the evolution of socioconfigurations. The socioeconomic method is applied to the case of interregional migration of socioculturally different populations and to that of the evolution of a city with hinterland connections. Solutions of the model equations for a range of meaningful trend parameters are offered for both applied models.

Carsten Herrmann-Pillath discusses in his paper 'The concept of space in trade – some evolutionary basics'. Recent research in the theory of international trade shows the serious limitations of its theoretical foundations. The chapter proposes alternative foundations based on the concept of transaction and the proposition that the capabilities of economic agents to realise transactions cannot be priced within a market system. It is thus impossible to include the trading competences of international traders in the general concept of factor, and to apply neoclassical approaches, such as the factor-proportions theory, on the basic endowments of countries and of agents that would enable them to transact successfully across the border. The chapter proposes a totally new concept of factor, based on the properties of storability, non-rivalness of use in time, non-producibility and non-tradability. These factors determine country-specific competences to trade, which are classified in a threefold way as organisational capital, collective human capital, and social capital.

The aim of Lambert T. Koch's 'Economic Policy – A Process of Communication' is to understand and analyse policy and economic policy in particular as an evolutionary process. Agents in this process are by no means only those who are in the public eye as responsible parties for policy and decision making. Every policy has its roots beyond the official political structures, in areas where there is 'private' dissatisfaction, where there is a need seen for action, where this kind of perception is shared with others, where potential policy content is defined and, finally, where critical masses are created which can generate pressure for policy action. The view of the policy-making process to be taken in this chapter goes beyond traditional approaches by emphasising the relevance of cognition and communication. It moves away from the implicit idea currently prevailing, even in well-informed circles, that there are 'born' state tasks, 'right' packages of measures to implement 'objective' aims and scientific methods to find out what 'good' policies are. The basic credo of an evolutionary theory of economic policy according to the author is to see policy as being the product of communicated, related perceptions. These perceptions – which influence evaluations of policy conditions, formulation of objectives and packages of measures – are themselves transformed by the results of running political processes. This doubly recursive structure in itself leads to innovations, giving the phenomenon its evolutionary character.

The chapter by Malcolm H. Dunn, 'Why endogeneity is not enough to explain technological change – a critique of Paul Romer', analyses the inner logic of one of the most prominent models of endogenous growth: Paul Romer's contribution 'Endogenous Technological Change'. Although Romer's model captures important features of technological advance, such as the relevance of externalities and imperfect competition, it also neglects many aspects that are equally important. The paper argues that Romer's growth theory is based on a production function which gives an inadequate account of the dynamics between the existing stock of capital and knowledge on the one hand and the factors leading to the emergence of new products on the other hand. The chapter then attempts to show that technological change can be better interpreted as an open process which is driven by entrepreneurs acting under true uncertainty. Drawing on the rich pool of insights provided by the tradition of evolutionary economics a more complex story behind the emergence of innovation behaviour is suggested. As for the methodology the chapter suggests that more emphasis should be placed on forces which escape an easy formalisation, for instance the achievement motivation and competence of market participants and the system of property rights.

Political Economy of Complexity

In their contribution on 'Innovation and the learning policy maker – an evolutionary approach based on historical experience', Joachim Schwerin and Claudia Werker discuss how to design, implement and perform a learning economic policy approach in line with the principles of evolutionary theory. Socio-economic systems evolve in ways that cannot be fully anticipated. These dynamics pose a challenge to policy makers, who have to devise a framework that needs to co-evolve with the socio-economic system. The knowledge stock on which politicians base their decisions to modify the set of policy rules plays a pivotal role in this process. Here, learning is key to success: Based on past experience, politicians need to constantly improve their knowledge by turning learning into a routine systematically linked with modifications of policy rules. The chapter starts with a methodological analysis that identifies types of rules on which policy should be based to institutionalise learning. On this basis the authors present a practically feasible concept of learning policy built upon the identification of historical invariant patterns. They apply this concept to the analysis of innovation and growth, where they demonstrate that the openness of the set of identified patterns towards a changing environment is a prerequisite for learning. Their results, which lead to some policy guidelines, serve as a reference system for innovation policy that meets evolutionary standards.

'The national German innovation system – its development in different governmental and territorial structures' by Hariolf Grupp, Icíar Dominguez Lacasa and Monika Friedrich-Nishio provides several long time series of R&D indicators bridging more than 100 years of German economic history. The ups and downs are put into perspective and compared to important events in the global innovation system. The pertinence found for the national German innovation system seems to rest in educational, cultural and language traditions rather than in governance and territorial coverage, which changed many times. This is possibly due to path dependence of technological paradigms. The suggested range of indicators on a national or sectorial level gives a detailed impression of both the extent and the contents of innovation activities. The empirical base which evolutionary researchers, interested in innovation and economic history-related questions, can rely on, has been broadened to a large extent, so that there is no longer a serious empirical gap.

Reiner Peter Hellbrück's 'Emergence and diffusion of disastrous innovations – a case study' examines diabetes care in Germany. There is a consensus among all specialists that diabetes care needs to be improved. Hence, there has been steady development, improvement, and implementation of programmes for diabetes care in Germany. In virtually all German lands there is at least one (legal) health insurance fund which is offering a diabetes programme. For this purpose special contracts between at least one health insurance fund and some health care providers have to be signed. These contracts contain an extra budgeting payment to the health care providers. Those contracts have the charm for the health care providers of earning, supplementary to their regular budgets, extra money. Health insurance funds have in turn been hurt by concluding such contracts when evaluated on a regulation ruling from 1993 up to 2000. The chapter tries to answer the following questions: What reasons led to the conclusion of such contracts? Why are these contracts under today's laws, rules, and regulations a hazard to health insurance funds and their business? Why did those disastrous contracts diffuse at all? Which strategies are chosen to reduce the hazard to insurance business? Why are these business-harming innovations not simply stopped?

In his chapter 'Applying evolutionary economics to public policy – the example of competitive federalism in the EU,' Wolfgang Kerber states that due to the Hayekian knowledge problem it seems often to be very difficult to derive positive policy proposals from evolutionary reasoning; he argues in favour of a pragmatic approach, as to how evolutionary argumentation should be used in policy discussions as important complements to other (mainly neoclassical) arguments. Starting with the hotly discussed policy question of centralisation vs decentralisation of public policies in the EU, it is shown that the traditional economic theory of federalism is mainly based upon neoclassical theories, which do not take into account the creation and diffusion of new policies in a satisfactory way. Therefore the theory of federalism should be supplemented by important evolutionary reasoning about the innovation and imitation of public policies. The main evolutionary argument is that decentralised experimentation can lead to more policy innovations and a greater degree of mutual learning from the experiences with public policies (laboratory federalism). Therefore the application of evolutionary (and innovation) economics leads to the conclusion that a more decentralised EU (with a system of competitive federalism) can be expected to lead to more innovation in regard to public goods, legal rules and regulation.

'Can evolutionary economics make a billion $ difference for 60 per cent of the world's poor in Asia?', Hans-Peter Brunner asks in his contribution to this volume. The use of evolutionary and institutional economics in the analysis of increasing returns, transaction costs, and agglomeration and network effects is important because of their determining impacts on the processes of trade, growth and development. Institutional analysis facilitates definition of the role of governments, and of international agencies, in the design of projects and provision of services in sectors such as transport, communications, and financial services. The application of institutional methods and evolutionary models that relate positive externality and linkage effects to actual representations of institutional and physical infrastructures results in a powerful tool for the economic development of financial sectors and trade corridors. The question posed is whether wide application of institutional and evolutionary methods would yield higher payoffs for growth, equity, and poverty reduction. The cases of Nepal's financial sector reform, and of the design of West Bengal's trade and transport corridor, show the huge difference evolutionary economics can make. It is worth the effort. Why then is evolutionary analysis not employed more often? The answer appears to lie in unfamiliarity with the methods and results. The chapter ends with practical suggestions as to how evolutionary and institutional economics could become a household tool for multilateral development institutions.

PART I

Economic evolution as open process

1. Heterogeneity and evolutionary change – concepts and measurement

Uwe Cantner and Horst Hanusch

1. INTRODUCTION

In this chapter we present a methodological discussion on the identification and the tracking of structures over time. In this respect the problem under consideration is central to evolutionary economics, which puts much effort into the explanation of how structures come into existence and how they develop and change over time. The structures we are looking at are based on the heterogeneity of actors – where actors are seen in a rather broadly defined sense including also e.g. countries. To make things more easily accessible we constrain this heterogeneity to that which is closely related to technological and innovative abilities on the one hand, and to imitative behaviour and technological learning on the other. In theoretical work this so-called technological heterogeneity is discussed in a dynamic context focusing on its sources as well as on its consequences for innovative development and technological change. Among other things this work deals mainly with the question of how knowledge spillovers arising out of technologically different actors do influence the direction and intensity of technological change,[1] the structural and competitive development within sectors,[2] and the cross-fertilisation effects between sectors.[3]

This chapter, however, will discuss empirical issues related to heterogeneity and its change over time. The main goal we want to pursue is to coming up with a rather general empirical approach or procedure allowing one to identify and to track technological structures among actors. For this we suggest a three-step procedure:

1. select the variables you consider relevant for identifying technological structures and their change over time;
2. apply a methodology – to be explained below – and identify those structures and their change;
3. test whether the identified structures and their change can be explained by variables related to innovative activities, research output etc.

This chapter will be dealing partly with the first and mainly with the second step. For the third step we refer to the literature.

The methodology suggested is of a rather general character in the sense that it can be applied on several levels of aggregation, i.e. firms, sectors or countries. This rather common conception about technological heterogeneity is applied with respect to the productive structure of a sample of observations under consideration. We suggest that those structures can be dealt with looking at (a) the differences in *total factor productivity* and (b) the differences in *input-intensities, output-intensities* and/or *output coefficients*.

In order to identify such heterogeneous structures and to track their development and their change over time we suggest a specific empirical approach. For this purpose we introduce a two-step analysis consisting of the *non-parametric procedure* to construct production or efficiency frontiers and the *Malmquist-productivity* index to track the change of this structure over time.

The plan of the chapter is as follows. In section 2 we will briefly refer to some theoretical issues describing, firstly, the role heterogeneity plays in the evolutionary framework; secondly, we ask for the criteria to be applied in order to determine the analytically relevant heterogeneity in empirical data and put forward three requirements for the empirical approach to be employed. In section 3 we refer to the measure total factor productivity, distinguish our procedure from the traditional way of computing this measure and briefly introduce the main methodological approach we have chosen in order to detect heterogeneity and to track its development over time. The final section 4 summarises our approach and discusses some as yet unresolved issues and problems.

2. THE CONCEPT OF HETEROGENEITY

In this section, what we attempt to briefly discuss is the concept of heterogeneity both in a more general way and more specifically with respect to the economic theory of technological change and innovation. For the further discussion this initial step allows us to propose a rather well-defined analytical frame constructed on the basis of a conception of heterogeneity which aims at differences in the *technological performance of agents*. This, of course, is an extraction out of all possible sources and instances of heterogeneity, but it enables us to focus on that kind of heterogeneity we consider analytically relevant in the economic theory of technical change.

2.1 Theoretical Issues

Heterogeneity

In economics, there are a number of distinguishing elements of the neoclassical and the evolutionary approach. Probably one of the most important ones is the *heterogeneity* of behaviour, attitudes, characteristics etc. of agents.[4] Thus, what heterogeneity is all about is *asymmetry* among the agents in a set. However, it is not at all obvious whether this asymmetry matters for the description of the state of this set or for its development over time. In neoclassical approaches one would deny this in general with the consequence that the theoretical models suggested are characterised by symmetry of agents or even by a representative agent.[5] All the approaches designed in this way are justified by the attitude that for the final outcome of a certain process the differences in agents' behaviour during this process do not matter – it is just average behaviour which is determining the result and which analytically is relevant and interesting. Hence, heterogeneity is of an only temporary nature and as such it is a phenomenon only showing up during transitory dynamics.

Heterogeneity or asymmetry is a fundamental principle in the theories of economic evolution. S*electionist approaches*, *synergetic approaches* and *developmental approaches* rely on it and discuss how the system's nature or structure as well as how its (structural) dynamics is affected or driven by it. However, in each approach the way heterogeneity affects evolutionary development is quite specific: in the selectionist approach it is heterogeneity which is reduced by competition and generated by innovation. In the synergetic approach it is heterogeneity which brings about specific structural, self-organising features with respect to learning, cooperation etc. In the developmental approach, finally, heterogeneity is a matter of stages of development (to be) passed.

Heterogeneity as asymmetry and variety

Heterogeneity is a concept which refers to *the degree of difference within a population of observations*, be they households, firms, sectors or even regions or countries which differ with respect to their efforts, behaviours and/or success due to – among other things – the artifacts they consume or produce, the modes of production they employ, the direction and intensity of innovative activities they pursue, or the organisational setting they choose. This heterogeneity of agents is, on the one hand, considered the result of technological change, i.e. of different innovative/imitative/adaptive activities and differential innovative/imitative/adaptive success; on the other hand, it also serves as a source for further progress in the sense that this heterogeneity puts pressure on technologically backward actors to improve performance when the gaps become too large and on leaders when the gaps become too close; and that it provides for different kinds of learning processes (imitative and adaptive learning, cross-fertilisation etc.).

In order to account for the heterogeneity of agents driven by and driving technological change one draws on the close relationship between the characteristics and the behaviour of agents, on the one hand, and the kind of inputs which, on the other hand, they transform into outputs. In fact, in the theory of technological change the actors are characterised by the nature, the level and the degree of their innovative activities – either on the input or on the output side.

In this respect heterogeneity can be accounted for by the conception of *variety* (Saviotti 1996). This concept is based on the number of distinguishable elements of a set of artifacts.[6] In this sense Saviotti (1996, p. 94) distinguishes output and input variety, the former being the number of distinguishable outputs and the latter taking account of the number of distinguishable types of processes.

However, heterogeneity in general and within the context of innovativeness in particular is not only a matter of simply counting distinguishable elements. Any innovator attempts to perform better than competitors, and this 'better' may show up in providing goods and services with superior price–quality ratios – compared to those of the competitors. Thus, more often than not one would like to have a conception which allows for a quantification of the differences on which heterogeneity rests. Hence, with respect to output variety one would be interested whether the variety observed is also built upon measurable quality differences (i.e. 'higher' and 'lower' quality) or whether this variety is found within a more narrow or more broad range of the specific characteristic under consideration (i.e. 'more' or 'less' built-in features). Equivalently, with respect to input or production variety we should have an account of whether the several techniques in use are rather similar or far different with respect to their efficiency (i.e. 'more' or 'less' efficient) or their relative input requirements (e.g. 'more' or 'less' capital-intensive).

An appropriate conception in this respect is found in Dosi (1988, pp. 1155–7) who is concerned with the *asymmetry of activities* and distinguishes *variety* as a special case of asymmetry. Both are to be seen in a context where firms engaged in innovative activities are affected differently by technological change in terms of their process technologies and quality (or kind) of output. Whenever firms can be ranked as 'better' or 'worse' according to their distance to some technological frontier he refers to as *asymmetry*. The degree of asymmetry of an industry is then its dispersion of input efficiencies for a given (homogeneous) output and price-weighted performance characteristics of firms' (differentiated) products. For all differences or asymmetries among firms which cannot be ranked as unequivocally better or worse he refers to *variety*. This may be the case when (a) firms producing the same good with identical costs employ different production techniques or (b) when firms search for their product innovations in different product spaces, embodying different product characteristics and aim at different corners of the markets.

The concept of heterogeneity

Based on this discussion, in the following we will be concerned with heterogeneity which is as closely as possible related to technological performances and their differences – thus, heterogeneity is meant to be technological heterogeneity and it is based on the *local application of certain technologies*. As such it, first, includes performances which can be compared directly to each other and by this means be ranked – i.e. producing a certain product with a higher/lower quality or running a specific production process more/less efficiently. Second, this conception comprises also technological performances which cannot be compared to each other directly – i.e. producing different products in the sense of old and new or running quite different production techniques. These latter performances cannot be compared directly (in terms of physical measures) and one has to rely on some other measures such as the comparative economic success of those performances (as measured in terms of profitability, market share, growth rates, etc.).

Technological heterogeneity on higher aggregation levels

Moreover, the technological heterogeneity we are concerned with is not only confined to the technological performance of individual actors. It is also applicable to higher levels of aggregation such as the sectoral, the regional or the national level. By way of aggregation, of course, any sublevel heterogeneity gets covered and only some – here no matter how defined – *average* characterises the higher-level unit. Despite this inevitable loss of information involved here, we nevertheless expect considerable and relevant heterogeneity in technological performance of sectors, regions or economies with respect to the product and quality range produced (e.g. agricultural products, Germany compared to India) and/or the kind and degree of certain production techniques employed (e.g. cotton production, US compared to Pakistan). Accordingly, what we mean by locally applied technologies also – with a loss of specific description – refers in a more aggregate sense to sectors, regions and countries.

Heterogeneity and local progress

Heterogeneity as just introduced can be considered as a snapshot description of a sample of observations. Especially in the context of technological progress it is quite obvious and has to be expected that heterogeneity is subject to change. One could easily think of exogenous forces which quite equally affect all agents. However, for endogenous changes which are provoked by individual action it is just as much obvious that the respective changes are to a considerable degree specific to a certain agent or group of agents – that is the change we are concerned with is *local technological change*.[7] And even if we considered a number of agents as behaving rather similarly, e.g. in catching up to the technology leaders, such progress is local as well in the sense that only a subgroup of the agents under consideration achieved that.

Equivalently to our discussion of heterogeneity the concept of *local technological change* is applicable to several levels of aggregation. In this respect, technological change is specific to a certain country (e.g. the US compared to Togo), to a certain region (e.g. East Asian Tigers compared to Western Europe), or to a certain sector (e.g. in machinery, Germany compared to Japan). Of course, and again equivalent to the above, local change on higher levels of aggregation hides local changes on lower aggregation levels, so that only an 'average' change shows up.

2.2 Empirical Issues

To state the importance of heterogeneity is one side of the coin, the other one is to clearly specify in which unit we should measure or observe heterogeneity and this in a way that it is also analytically relevant.

To identify heterogeneity in empirical work is not an easy and straightforward task at all. In principle, one is facing a similar problem to that the typological approach is confronted with: what is essential for analysing the issue under consideration? Whereas the typological approach searches for some reliable average characteristic, the population perspective is confronted with the task of finding characteristics which are diverse, i.e. heterogeneous, and as such essential for performance and the progress of the population under consideration. Looking for variables which can render this, one more often than not has to be engaged in rather detailed analyses of a nearly case-study type. Although the results are often very illuminating and interesting, it is very often not possible to transfer the methodology and the results of one study to another one; the aggregation of several results is often not possible, because the relevant variables are not of the same type, and so on.

Heterogeneity and innovation

Let us now look more carefully at the theory of technological change and innovation. How can we measure technological performance? To give an answer we start with another question: What does technological progress provoke, how do we distinguish an innovation from a well-known old artifact?

Here it is quite obvious that innovations provide for heterogeneity because something new – a 'new combination' in Schumpeter's (1935/1912) words – is introduced into the market. This may be a better technique of production, a better organisational structure, a better product quality, or an entirely new product. Hence, the innovator introducing this new combination can be distinguished from competitors just by his/her innovation.

Thus, more generally, technological heterogeneity is just the consequence of differential innovative success accumulated up to the present. In a dynamic context, with respect to several features of the process of technological change such as path dependency, cumulativeness etc., this heterogeneity can also serve as an indicator for the direction and success probability of further innovative activities – such as innovation, imitation, adoption etc.

The central question arising out of this is concerned with the measure we should apply in order to account for this innovation and technology related or determined heterogeneity.

Specific versus general measures

Of course, we could have a long list of possible characteristics or features which perform the task of detecting the effects of technological change and innovations. All of the characteristics used in *technometrics* are based on rather technical issues. Look for example at the technological development of helicopters so well studied by Saviotti: technological progress here is represented by the development in technical characteristics such as engine power, rotor diameter, number of engines etc. Or, look at computer chips where we are informed about technological progress by steadily increasing storage capacities. Or, finally look at automobile production where technological progress or organisational progress shows up in the increased number of cars assembled within one hour (Fordism) or in the decreased number of bad quality cars assembled (Toyotism).

However, for all its merits this quite specific and quite exact technical measurement has also its drawbacks:

1. Despite the respective specific characteristics of a technology and despite the fact that its development can be represented relatively exactly, it also brings it about that the more exactly one measures specific features the less a comparison between different observations will be possible and meaningful.
2. Whenever different technologies and their respective progress are analysed, a comparison of the results is less likely to be possible.

3. Any aggregation from the business unit to the firm, to the sector and industry, to the regional or even to the macro-economic level is not possible anymore. The reason for that is quite obvious, because to aggregate the products of different firms in a sector, the products of different sectors in an economy cannot be accomplished when technical attributes are used such as pieces, kg, Mb etc.

On the basis of the following four central requirements we suggest and introduce a measure and empirical procedure which attempts to circumvent the problematic issues just raised and which allows to analyse empirical observations within a theoretical framework aiming at locally applied technologies and local technological change. For each requirement we give a brief suggestion here – a fuller discussion is found in section 3.

Requirement 1 The task therefore is to detect a measure which may help to overcome these problems. Thus, what one has to look for in this context is a measure which on the one hand is exact enough and on the other hand is not that specific so that the above-mentioned deficit will not show up. Hence, what we look for is a measure which serves this purpose and is *applicable to a broad range of innovative phenomena on different levels of aggregation.*[8]

Suggestion 1 In order to show the way for setting up a broadly applicable taxonomy we suggest the *measure of total factor productivity* (TFP) and its *change over time* to play a major or even pivotal role in this endeavour. This suggestion, at first glance, might look somewhat old-fashioned as the concept of total factor productivity has been criticised intensely in the past – mainly in the context of growth-accounting exercises where its construction is based on equilibrium assumption and conditions of traditional production theory combined with the notion of the same production to be applied to all observations. This leads us to a second requirement.

Requirement 2 The way TFP is measured should differ considerably from standard procedures. As such, as a first step, it should allow one to distinguish innovators from imitators and *account for better and for worse technological performance*. Moreover, it should deliver a quantitative account of these differences or *asymmetries.*

Suggestion 2 With respect to requirement 2 we suggest applying a frontier analysis where the *frontier function* or *technology frontier* is set up by the best-performing observations. All worse-performing observations are at some distance from this technology frontier where this distance can be used as a measure for different technological performance.

Requirement 3 Related to the need to distinguish better from worse performance is the requirement that, following the evolutionary approach, the empirical analyses should not be restrictive in the sense that a functional relationship, e.g. a specific production function, is a priori assumed to hold for all observations. One should rather allow for an open number of those relationships and take into account also *variety* in productions functions or output mixes.

Suggestion 3 For satisfying requirement 3 we suggest the computation of TFP measures by a *non-parametric procedure to determine technology frontiers* which – at least compared to the traditional approaches of TFP index numbers, parametric production functions and parametric production frontiers[9] – are rather unrestricted in the functional form employed for the aggregation of inputs and outputs, respectively. In principle, there are as many functional forms allowed for as a sample contains observations.

Requirement 4 The measure applied should be tracked over time. The respective measure of the change in TFP should be able to take account of *local technological change*.

Suggestion 4 In this respect we suggest employing the procedure to compute the Malmquist productivity index which just measures the change in TFP. The important feature of this measure is that it allows one to identify *local technological change* at both the technology frontier as well as the below-best-practice observations.

3. TFP, TECHNOLOGICAL PROCESS AND EVOLUTIONARY THEORY

3.1 TFP as a Measure of Technological Performance

Referring to requirement and suggestion 1 we consider total factor productivity and its change over time as an appropriate measure for technological performance and technological change. This, of course, requires some qualifications.

Generality

As already claimed we are interested in a generally applicable measure which allows one to track technological change on several levels of aggregation and in several fields of application. Thus, what we have to accept is a loss of specificity especially found if one applies the analysis on lower levels of aggregation often coming close to pure case studies. The loss of specificity, however, is counterbalanced (and in our view even overcompensated) by the opportunity to detect more general insights into structure and change whose driving elements are found on the individual level of actors and firms, whose collective outcome then shows up in a characteristic manner on the next level of aggregation and so forth. In this respect the measure of total factor productivity is applicable to all levels and areas of aggregation whenever we have at hand appropriate data on outputs and inputs. The latter we assume to be satisfied – although we are readily aware of the problem of whether the data we use in the analysis are at all the appropriate measures and/or proxies. We do not want to discuss this issue further here.

Construction

Index numbers for total factor productivity (TFP) have found a prominent application in growth-accounting exercises. There it is aggregate output Y, prominently GDP, set into relation to an aggregate I of various input factors, prominently labour and capital:

$$\mathrm{TFP} = \frac{Y}{I}$$

One can easily apply this measure to lower levels of aggregation such as to the sectoral level[10] and to the firm level. Any change in total factor productivity, in the sense that this indicator rises, is considered as the effect of technological progress, i.e. that change in output which cannot be accounted for by a change in aggregate inputs. It is this so-called *residual* which attracted so much research especially in the analysis of economic growth. And it is also this residual that Abramovitz called '*our measure of ignorance*'.

A first question arising in this context refers to whether TFP can be taken as a measure of technological performance and whether a change in total factor productivity can adequately account for technological change. Let us take up this issue accordingly.

TFP as performance indicator

In order to account for the performance of an observation the indicator applied is to be interpreted always as a relative measure, either with respect to some known optimal performance or with respect to the best performance observed. In empirical work it is always the latter relativisation that is employed. For this comparison to work, however, one has to provide for

1. the categories used for measuring inputs and outputs and
2. the respective way of aggregating of inputs and outputs in order to compute the TFP.

being identical among the observations. Otherwise the comparison is inadequate.

To cope with the first problem, one has to look for measures which allow for homogeneous input and output categories. This is certainly not the case, but by some degree of abstraction or cleverly chosen units of measurement – in the sense of real units (e.g. hours worked, kg, etc.) – one might be able to cope with this problem – at least partly.

As to the aggregation functions for inputs and outputs, with respect to inputs it is just the production function that is searched for and which has a number of specific problems. We do not want to go into detail here but only remind the reader that on the theoretically founded perceptions of techniques applied locally and local technological change an aggregation or production function identical for all observations cannot be expected a priori – contrariwise heterogeneity is to be expected.

With respect to outputs the problem is similar whenever we are not in the lucky situation of having to consider only one homogeneous output. Again, this is not the normal case and among the observations we normally have to expect both differences in the quality of the output as well as differences with respect to the number of outputs produced. A common way to deal with this is to accept *product prices* as weights which account for quality differences as well as differences in kind.[11] This leads to output measures such as GDP, sectoral sales or firm sales. Besides this, however, one might also be interested in dealing with output variety in a disaggregated way such as splitting up GDP into the output of various sectors or of firms, sales into the sales of different products. A possible way of performing this is presented below.

Change of TFP as measure of technological change

Interpreting the change of TFP as a measure for technological progress faces the same problems as just stated. Whenever we consider process innovations allowing the given resources to produce more of a homogeneous output, the change in TFP appropriately takes account of this. However, dealing with quality improvements or new products, whenever quantity and price changes account for this in a proper way we can use the aggregate output. But if we were interested in the development beneath the level of aggregation it would be helpful to have the respective TFP change determined on the basis of a disaggregated TFP index.

Other influences on TFP

A final remark here refers to differences in the TFP which are not due to the respective technological performance of the observation. Proper candidates are vintage structures as well as economies of scale.[12] For the change in TFP we should additionally be aware of substitution effects at work. With respect to substitution effects according to Rosenberg (1976) substitution along a traditional isoquant is to be considered as applying a technique not applied yet and this could also be considered as technical change. Moreover one may argue here that even in a purely neoclassical context the distinction between substitution, scale and progress effects is not possible without imposing rather restrictive assumptions.

Having given some justification and qualifications on the TFP measure as a response to requirement 1 we now want to go one step further and introduce a method for taking care of requirements 2 and 3.

3.2 Structure: a Non-parametric Frontier Function Approach

Requirements 2 and 3 ask for a method which allows one to determine TFP in such a way that technological heterogeneity in the sense of asymmetry and variety shows up. For this purpose we suggest a non-parametric frontier function approach.

Unrestricted performance measure

The non-parametric frontier function approach (or DEA for data envelopment analysis) basically relies on index numbers to measure total factor productivity in a fashion similar to the one used in more standard productivity analysis. In a sample of n observations for each observation j ($j = 1, \ldots, n$) a productivity index h_j is given by:

$$h_j = \frac{u^T Y_j}{v^T X_j} \tag{1.1}$$

Here Y_j is a s-vector of outputs ($r = 1, \ldots, s$) and X_j a m-vector of inputs ($i = 1, \ldots, m$) of observation j. The s-vector u and the m-vector v contain the aggregation weights u_r and v_i respectively.

The h_j in (1.1) is nothing else than an index of *total factor productivity*. The respective aggregation functions (for inputs and outputs respectively) are of a linear arithmetic type as also employed in the well-known Kendrick-Ott productivity index.[13] There, however, by special assumptions the aggregations weights, u_r and v_i, are given exogenously. The non-parametric approach does not rely on such assumptions – in particular, it is not assumed that all observations of the sample have a common identical production function. With this – at least to a certain degree – unconstrained way of aggregating both inputs and outputs we are able to account for requirement 3 above. The parameterisation of the aggregation functions and thus the aggregation weights which may be specific to a certain observation are determined endogenously. They are the solution to a specific optimisation problem (as discussed below), and therefore they are dependent on the empirical data of the sample. Critics often argue that a linear arithmetic aggregation nevertheless presupposes at least a special type of production function,[14] such as the Leontief-type production function.[15] However, those arguments do not take into account the following:

1. Since the aggregation weights are determined endogenously and can be different between observations, there ultimately exists a number of parametrically different possible aggregation functions although they are all of the same type.[16]
2. Moreover, the linear aggregation function holds for a Leontief type of production function as well as a linear one.
3. For the input side, moreover, the fact that the Leontief production function fits well into this framework suits well the widely held assumption of short-run limited substitutability of production factors whenever techniques employed are of a local character.
4. The procedure does not have to rely on production functions at all but fits well into a framework dealing with production correspondences. This interpretation is also quite appealing to an evolutionary framework where a neoclassical production function is not considered suitable for an evolutionary analysis.

This unrestricted form of the total factor productivity measure is *central to an application of this method to evolutionary analysis and to detecting heterogeneity in particular*. For computing this index we can include all different kinds of inputs and different types of outputs. This implies also that new products can be taken care of and equivalently new production factors. Since the non-parametric approach does not require all inputs to be employed or outputs to be produced by each observation we are readily able to take into account both product innovations and new techniques of production.

Having found a rather unrestricted mode for measuring the performance of an observation we would like to provide also a comparison of this performance with those of the other observations in the sense that we find statements about 'unequivocally better', or 'unequivocally worse' or even 'not comparable'.

Comparison of performance

For doing this, the basic principle of the non-parametric approach is just to determine the indices h_j in such a way that they can be interpreted as efficiency ratings which implies a comparison of each observation with the best observation(s). The (relatively) most efficient observations of a sample are evaluated by $h=1$, less efficient observations by $h<1$. Hence, by comparing all observations with each other we arrive at an account of different technological performance where the differences are quantified in the measure h – this is just what requirement 2 asked for.

The following constrained maximisation problem is used to determine such an h-value for a particular observation $l, l \in \{1, \ldots, n\}$:

$$\max h_l = \frac{u^T Y_l}{v^T X_l}$$
$$st: \quad \frac{u^T Y_j}{v^T X_j} \leq 1; \quad j = 1, \ldots, n; \qquad (1.2)$$
$$u, v > 0.$$

Problem (1.2) determines h_l of observation l subject to the constraint that the h_j of all observations (including l itself) of the sample are equal or less to 1. The constraints provide that h is indexed on (0,1). Moreover the elements of u and v have to be positive. This requirement is to be interpreted that for all inputs used and outputs obtained there must exist at least a positive efficiency value.[17]

Best-practice or frontier functions

Since we employ linear arithmetic aggregation functions for inputs and outputs, (1.2) is a problem of linear fractional programming.[18] To solve such optimisation problems, there exist a number of methods the best-known of which is Charnes and Cooper (1962). They suggest transforming (1.2) into a standard linear program which then can be solved with the well-known simplex algorithm. Performing this step and transforming the resulting primal to its corresponding dual problem, one arrives at the well-known Charnes/Cooper/Rhodes (1978)[19] envelopment form of the non-parametric approach:

$$\begin{aligned} &\min \theta_l \\ &st: \\ &Y\lambda_l \geq Y_l \\ &\theta_l X_l - X\lambda_l \geq 0 \qquad (1.3) \\ &\lambda_l \geq 0 \end{aligned}$$

Y_l and X_l are the s- and m-vectors of outputs and inputs respectively of observation l, Y and X are the $s \times n$-matrix of outputs and $m \times n$-matrix of inputs of all observations of the sample. The parameter θ_l to be minimised expresses the percentage level to which the inputs of observation l can be reduced proportionally, in order to have this observation producing on the production frontier representing the best practice technologies – it is identical to h_l and is a relative measure of technological performance. With $\theta_l = 1$ the respective observation belongs to the efficient observations on the frontier. Proceeding in this way and solving (1.3) for all observations in the sample, the non-parametric approach determines an *efficiency frontier* or *technology frontier* constructed by the best-practice observations. The efficiency rating of each observation is measured relative to this frontier.

Figure 1.1a states this result for a sample of observations which produce with two inputs, x_1 and x_2, one unit of output y. The technology frontier determined is DAB. The technological performance is the relative distance of an observation from the technology frontier. In the case of observation C, the measure θ_C is given by the ratio OC' to OC.

The n-vector λ_l states the weights of all (efficient) observations which serve as reference for observation l. For the efficient observation l (with $\theta_l = 1$), we obtain 1 for the lth element of λ_l and 0 for all other elements. Grouping all observations according to their respective reference observations allows one to detect regions of similarity. These regions are distinguished by different input intensities, output intensities or input coefficients. In terms of Figure 1.1a, for observation C the reference observations are A and B. Consequently only λ_C^A and λ_C^B are different from 0. The respective values state the degree to which A and B are respectively used to construct C'.

In figure 1.1b we show how the problem looks in output space when one considers more than one output. Here, the observations produce with one

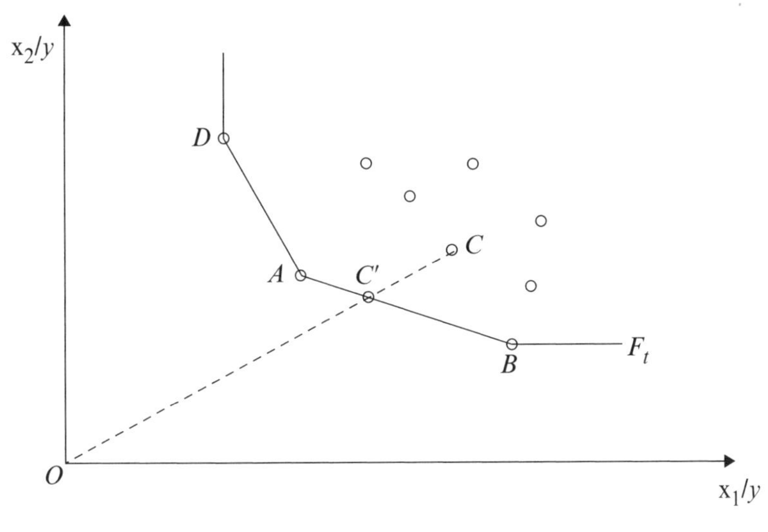

Figure 1.1a Technology frontier and the measure θ_c

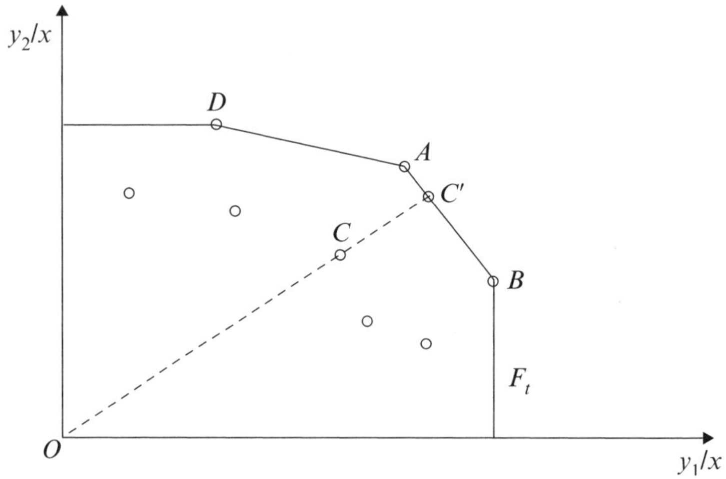

Figure 1.1b Technology frontier in output space

unit of input x two outputs, y_1 and y_2. The frontier function is a transformation curve. The performance of an observation C is again evaluated against this frontier here given by the ratio OC' to OC.[20]

So far, the observations of sample are considered as using all the same categories of inputs and to produce all the same kinds of output – although to a different degree. In addition to that the procedure suggested is readily able to deal also with more diversity such as observations which use an additional type of input or produce an additional kind of output. This latter is appropriate if we deal with product innovations. Figures 1.1c and 1.1d show the kind of technology frontier we get in such cases in the input space (1.1c) and in the output space (1.1d).

A characterisation of the structure of a sample

So far the discussion has delivered an account of a sample which allows one to detect and quantify heterogeneity in productive performance. With program (1.3) we are now readily able to characterise the structure of a sample of observations:

1. θ as a measure of performance indicating and quantifying whether an observation is best practice or below best practice;
2. λ as a measure of structural (dis)similarity (Cantner 1996).

However, modifying program (1.3) some measures can be computed which shed additional light on the structure of a sample.

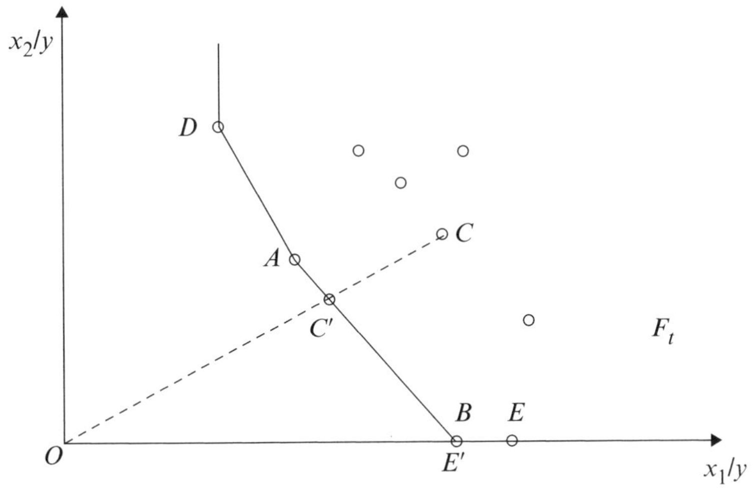

Figure 1.1c Extreme input variety and technology frontier in input space

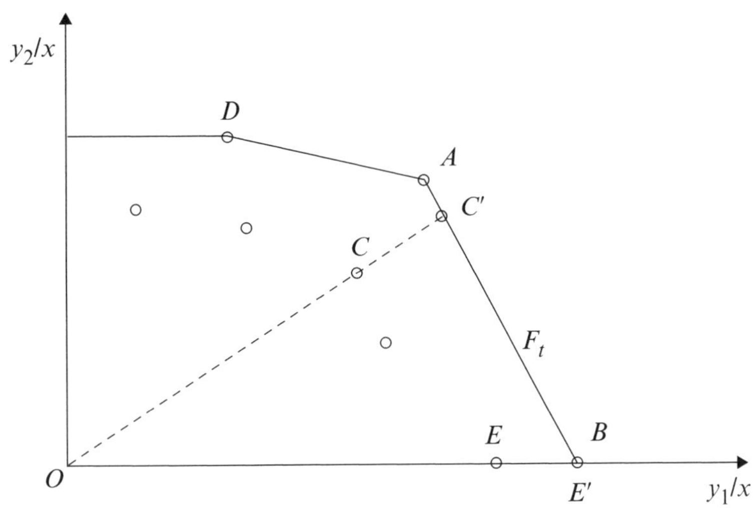

Figure 1.1d Extreme output variety and technology frontier in output space

Comparison of best practice

Since the frontier function is quite regularly constructed by several best-practice observations which cannot be ranked as better or worse, one might additionally be interested in a comparison between them. The following modification of program (1.3) allows for this where now the observation under consideration l is not a member of the reference set:

$$\begin{aligned} &\min \theta_l^* \\ &st: \\ &\quad Y_{-l}\lambda_l \geq Y_l \\ &\quad \theta_l^* X_l - X_{-l}\lambda_l \geq 0 \\ &\quad \lambda_l \geq 0 \end{aligned} \tag{1.4}$$

The matrices Y_{-l} and X_{-l} contain the outputs and inputs of all n observations except observation l. The modified efficiency measure is θ_l^*. For all below-best-practice observations it is identical to θ_l determined by program (1.3). However, for all best-practice observations θ_l^* is different. It holds $\theta_l^* \geq 1$ and the difference $\theta_l^* - 1$ can be interpreted as the buffer or lead observation l holds compared to certain other observations. This θ_l^* is a measure to distinguish observations which with program (1.3) are determined as not comparable (Cantner/Westermann 1998).

Figure 1.2 states the result of program (1.4) for observation A. The respective frontier for A in this case is DB and the θ_A^* is equal to the ratio OA' to OA which is larger than 1.

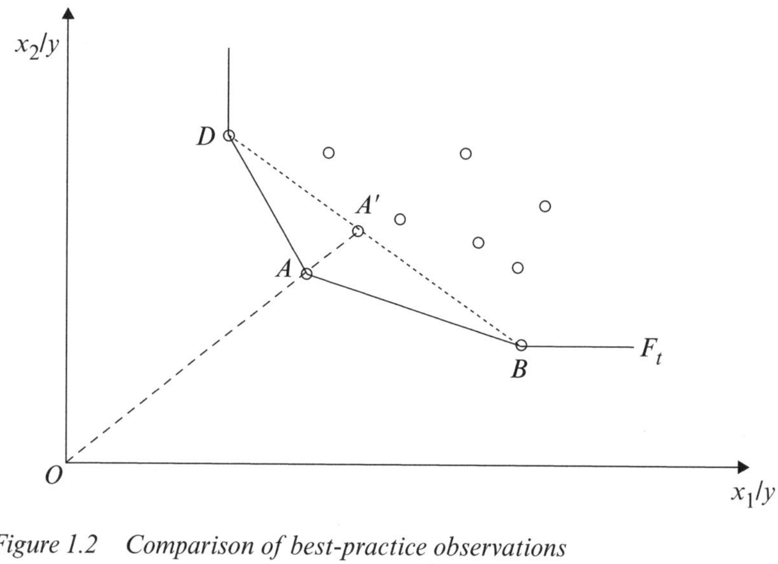

Figure 1.2 Comparison of best-practice observations

Besides this mode of comparing best practice observations an alternative or additional way is to look at the dynamic performance, i.e. their comparative ability to shift the frontier function (by technological progress). This issue will be taken up below.

Accounting for scale effects

Finally, since the programs used so far have been discussed under the assumption of constant returns-to-scale technologies one might be interested in taking into account size effects. This is done by first setting up a program allowing for non-constant returns to scale. This leads to a formulation where the elements of the λ_l vector have to sum up to 1 (e^T is a vector containing only elements 1):

$$\begin{aligned} &\min \theta_l^v \\ &st: \\ Y\lambda_l &\geq Y_l \\ \theta_l^v X_l - X\lambda_l &\geq 0 \\ e^T\lambda_l &= 0 \end{aligned} \tag{1.5}$$

For the efficiency measure determined by program (1.5) we get $\theta_l^v \geq \theta_l$. Taking the ratio of these two measures, $\sigma_l = \theta_l / \theta_l^v$, states the level of efficiency which is due to scale with $1 - \sigma_l$ accounting for that degree of below best practice which is caused by a size different to the minimum efficient scale size.

Besides these measures the non-parametric frontier approach does deliver a number of other measures allowing one to deal with allocative efficiency, non-radial inefficiencies, specific forms of returns to scale etc. These are of minor importance in the context of this chapter. More interesting, however, is the dynamic extension of the analysis.

3.3 Structural Dynamics: Local Technological Change, Catching up and Falling behind

The structures identified so far are of course interesting in their own respect. However, in a dynamic evolutionary context the static performance of observations is only part – probably the minor part – of the whole story. This distinction is rather appealing when one thinks of static and dynamic efficiency (Stiglitz 1987). For this reason a dynamic measure of performance is required.

Therefore, the following discussion refers to requirement 4 asking for an appropriate way of dealing with localised technological change and thus the structural dynamics induced.

Dynamic analysis

In order to track the structure – determined by the measures introduced above – it is by no means sufficient to compare the structural results of consecutive periods because for each period these measures are of an only relative type such a comparison makes no sense. Consequently, consecutive periods have to be set into relation implying that we have to compute relative measures which compare period t with $t+1$ and vice versa. Doing this pairwise for all consecutive periods allows one to track structural change over time. The procedure chosen for this purpose is based on the *Malmquist index* which states a specific observation's change in productivity between two periods. A quite interesting feature of this index is that it can be decomposed into a measure for *technological change* and one for *catch-up* – or, of course, *technological regress* and *falling behind.*

Malmquist index The theoretical basis of the Malmquist productivity index is found in the work of Malmquist (1953), Solow (1957) and Moorsteen (1961). For productivity measurement this index has been applied by Caves/Christensen/Diewert (1982a, 1982b). Färe/Grosskopf/Lindgren/Roos (1994) have shown how the efficiency measure θ above can be used to compute the Malmquist index. We will follow this line of reasoning.

In order to explain what the Malmquist productivity index measures we refer to Figure 1.3 which contains a simple example of two non-parametric production frontiers F_t and F_{t+1} pertaining to period t and $t+1$.

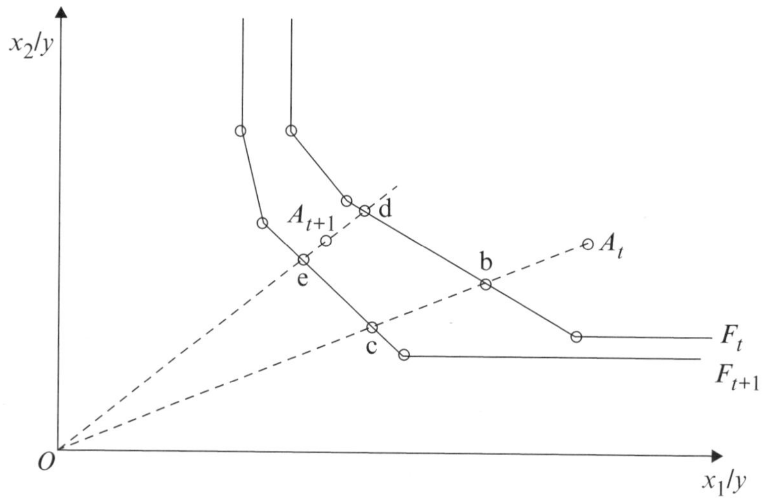

Figure 1.3 Malmquist-productivity index

For measuring the productivity change of observation A from A_t to A_{t+1} consider the following. First evaluate A_t and A_{t+1} towards the frontier F_t and compute the ratio of the two results. For this we get Ob/OA_t divided by Od/OA_{t+1}; if this ratio is less than 1 the productivity of A increased. Second, and in addition to that we could also evaluate A_t and A_{t+1} towards the shifted frontier F_{t+1}; again we determine the ratio, here Oc/OA_t divided by Oe/OA_{t+1}; this ratio less than 1 implies a productivity improvement. In a final step the geometric mean of these two computations is taken.

The resulting index

$$M_A^{t+1} = \left(\frac{Ob/OA_t}{Od/OA_{t+1}} \frac{Oc/OA_t}{Oe/OA_{t+1}} \right)^{0,5}$$

the *Malmquist-productivity index*, states the productivity change of A between t and $t+1$. In a general way, the Malmquist-productivity index M_l^{t+1}measuring the productivity change of observation l from t to $t+1$ is defined as follows:

$$M_l^{t+1} = \left(\frac{\theta_l^{t,t}}{\theta_l^{t+1,t}} \frac{\theta_l^{t,t+1}}{\theta_l^{t+1,t+1}} \right)^{0,5} \tag{1.6}$$

$\theta^{t,s}$, $t,s \in T$, is the efficiency of observation l in period t whenever the frontier function of period s serves as reference measure.[21]

Decomposition of the Malmquist index With some manipulation we can develop (1.6) to the following expression for the Malmquist index:

$$\begin{aligned} M_l^{t+1} &= \left(\frac{\theta_l^{t,t}}{\theta_l^{t+1,t}} \frac{\theta_l^{t,t+1}}{\theta_l^{t+1,t+1}} \right)^{0,5} \\ &= \left(\frac{\theta_l^{t,t}}{\theta_l^{t+1,t+1}} \right) \left(\frac{\theta_l^{t+1,t+1}}{\theta_l^{t+1,t}} \frac{\theta_l^{t,t+1}}{\theta_l^{t,t}} \right)^{0,5} \\ &= \mathrm{MC} \cdot \mathrm{MT}. \end{aligned} \tag{1.7}$$

The second line in (1.7) states the decomposition of the productivity change into *technological progress* MT and *change in the technology gap* MC.

Whenever MC<1 (MC>1) we find catch-up (falling behind). The second term is MT and indicates the movement of the frontier. This is measured twice: first with the factor intensities of l in t, and a second time with those of l in $t+1$. With MT<1 (MT>1) we have technological progress (technological regress) at the frontier. Looking at our example in Figure 1.3 this decomposition is given by the following ratio of distances:

$$M_A^{t+1} = \left(\frac{Ob/OA_t}{Oe/OA_{t+1}}\right)\left(\frac{Oe/OA_{t+1}}{Od/OA_{t+1}}\frac{Oc/OA_t}{Ob/OA_t}\right)^{0.5}$$
$$= MC\ MT.$$

From this, we can state that the first bracket term measures the change in the distance of A towards the frontiers F_t and F_{t+1}. The second term in brackets takes account of the (geometric) mean change of the frontier part pertaining to A. In this example both terms will be smaller than 1 indicating that observation A performed technological progress and was able to catch up to the frontier.

Local change As is readily apparent from Figure 1.3 the productivity change in (1.6) is local in the sense that it is specific to the observation under consideration. In this respect the degree of this local change depends (a) on the observation's ability to shift in direction to the origin and (b) on the behaviour of the frontier. As to (b) the respective change is also local in the sense that for observation l it is only relevant how the respective part of the frontier assigned to l (by the way of the elements of the λ-vector) shifts. The decomposition of the index allows one to distinguish these two movements.

Moreover, the decomposition allows one also to evaluate best-practice observations in a dynamic context by comparing them by the way of the index MT and thus by the ability to locally shift the frontier function.

3.4 Summary of the Issue

In face of the theoretical and empirical requirements stated in section 2 we have suggested measuring total factor productivity by a procedure which is as unconstrained as possible but nevertheless allows one

1. to systematise heterogeneity and
2. to track its change accomplished by technological progress in general and local technological progress in particular.

For this purpose we apply a non-parametric procedure to determine frontier functions. These consist of the best-practice observations in a sample and do not rely on any common a priori parametrically given production function. We thus dispense with any notion of the neoclassical production function and rely entirely on production techniques which in the short run show no substitutability among production factors, i.e. which could be described by a Leontief-type relationship between output and input.

For the dynamics we apply the Malmquist index measuring productivity change by comparing the non-parametric production frontiers and observations of consecutive periods. In this way we dispense with the notion that technological progress shifts the entire production frontier and instead we allow for (a) parts of the frontier to shift and for (b) this shift not to be proportional.

With respect to heterogeneity and its change this two-step procedure performs or detects the following. The first step of this two-step procedure allows one to detect heterogeneity – here technological heterogeneity – and classify the observations into the following categories:

1. heterogeneity in the performance of running a specific technique, class or range of techniques
2. heterogeneity in applying a specific technique out of a larger range of possible techniques.

The second step then tracks this heterogeneity over time and allows for the following:

1. measuring local technological change
2. distinguishing between progress of the best-practice techniques or forging ahead and dynamics of catching up, falling behind

Taken literally, the procedure suggested does classify the observations in a specific way in both a static and a dynamic context. In this way we do not have to rely a priori on restrictive assumptions or constraints which force the observations to behave in a certain way, e.g. to obey to the same parametrically given production function.

4. CONCLUSION

This chapter deals with empirical analysis in evolutionary economics in general and innovation economics as a prominent application of evolutionary ideas in particular. Within the latter, heterogeneity in the sense of different innovative activities, different production processes employed, different qualities or goods produced, is a major analytical element – the more so because innovative actors aim at creating heterogeneity and imitators attempt to reduce it again. This heterogeneity has an additional feature to be accounted for, the performance of the different techniques, activities, goods, etc. under consideration. Thus, it is not only a counting of different elements in a set but also the evaluation of these elements due to their static and their dynamic performances.

The task to be performed by empirical analyses contains three steps or problems: (1) defining the heterogeneity which is analytically relevant; (2) evaluating the performance of the heterogeneous entities; (3) testing whether the structural development of the entities can be explained by evolutionary conceptions.

In this chapter we focus mainly on the two first steps. The third one requires much more space and cannot be presented in an appropriate way here. With respect to steps (1) and (2) we suggest a measure and procedure which are applicable to all levels of aggregation – micro, meso and macro – and which rests on a comparison of total factor productivities of the entities under consideration. The procedure we suggest is as unrestricted as possible: in the static analysis of the non-parametric frontier function approach aiming at the identification of structures there is no restriction on the production technique employed or the output mix produced. In the dynamic analysis performed by the computation of Malmquist-productivity indexes the local character of technological change is allowed to work and to be identified. By this 'twin procedure' the heterogeneity and the differences in performance, so central to innovation, can be accounted for.

Of course, the twin procedure presented provides opportunities for further development; several shortcomings have to be overcome:

1. Stochastic elements could be included or the frontier conception chosen could be switched. An example of the latter is found in Cantner/Hanusch (1996) where we investigate a frontier function in the sense of best practice up to period t.
2. The relations of the aggregated and the disaggregated analyses have to be investigated in much more detail.
3. A major problem is also the rather unrestricted form of the procedure which by definition allows as many production functions or output mixes as observations. Does this imply that a representative sample cannot be used to explain the behaviour of the whole population?
4. Obviously, all the results presented and the future research agenda are dependent on the quality and the number of the data available:
   - The coverage of the data with respect to the time period under consideration is one point.
   - Another one refers to the degree to which the respective variables are an appropriate measure for the technology, the activity the output mix under consideration. Related to this is the problem of

using data which represent economic values – on the output side for example if one uses sales: then we do not measure the effects on technology but the economic evaluation of these effects.
- Measurement errors are of considerable influence on the results as there is no way in which the procedure can deal with this.

5. Finally, the research we attempt to follow aims at shedding some light on the phenomenon of total factor productivity and its development. In many applications this is still a black box or residual. To achieve a better understanding of this residual the procedure suggested might be an promising way to go.

Finally we want to refer to some empirical applications of this approach such as Bernard/Cantner/Westermann (1996), Cantner/Hanusch/Westermann (1997), Bernard/Cantner (1999), Krüger/Cantner/Hanusch (2000). An analysis of how the structural results found are related to technological change is performed in Krüger/Cantner/Hanusch (2000), Bernard/Cantner (1998) and Cantner (1996).

NOTES

1. E.g. Cantner/Hanusch/Pyka (1998).
2. E.g. Cantner/Pyka (1998a, 1998b) Cantner (2000).
3. E.g. Cantner (1996).
4. Other distinguishing features are the different conception of uncertainty, of rationality, etc.
5. Analyses dealing with asymmetric information are an exception to this.
6. An obvious candidate would be this number itself. According to Saviotti (1991, p. 177) in information theory the variety of a set is just the logarithm in base 2 of the number of distinguishable elements.
7. See Atkinson/Stiglitz (1969); a good overview is found in Antonelli (1994).
8. Saviotti (1996, p. 52) states: '. . . a taxonomy at all levels of aggregation in such a way that the relationships of the various units of analysis within and between each level of aggregation can be analysed'.
9. For a discussion and comparison of the non-parametric approach with more traditional methods see Cantner/Krüger (1999).
10. E.g. Wolff (1992).
11. This comes close to what Dosi (1988, pp. 1155–7) claims to be price-weighted performance characteristics of firms' (differentiated) products.
12. Differences might occur also due to scale effects and/or vintage structures (Dosi 1988, p. 1156)
13. See Ott (1959).
14. See also Chang/Guh (1991, p. 217).
15. Leontief (1947) has shown that a linear aggregation exists for a Leontief-type production function. Instead of a Leontief function one could also use a linear production function.
16. Employing parametric methods, e.g. the COLS or the EM-algorithm a specific production function is assumed. The coefficients of this function are estimated using the available data and the resulting production function is used to determine technical (in)efficiencies of all the firms in the sample. This procedure, however, suggests that there

is only one '*best-practice*' technology. With the non-parametric approach a number of '*best-practice*' technologies can be determined.

17. This procedure is also known from activity analysis.
18. An overview of linear fractional programming is given in Böhm (1978).
19. There obviously exists a range of possible model specifications where the one chosen is known as CCR. Applying this one has to keep in mind that possible scale inefficiencies are included in the technical inefficiency measure.
20. Here the efficiency measure is allowed to take values out of $[1,\infty[$ with 1 as best practice. This is due to an output-oriented design of the method which starts not with a productivity index as in (1) but with the inverse ratio.
21. For the respective programs required to compute the several θ-measures see Appendix to this chapter.

REFERENCES

Antonelli, C. (1994), *The Economics of Localized Technological Change and Industrial Dynamics*, Dordrecht et al.: Kluwer Academic Publishers, 1994.

Atkinson, A. and J.E. Stiglitz (1969), 'A new view of technological change', *Economic Journal*, **79**, 573–78.

Bernard, J. and U. Cantner (1998), 'Retombées technologiques, effects de rattrapage et dynamique intra-sectorielle,' in J. Bernard and M. Catin (eds), *Les Conditions Économiques du Changement Technologique*, Paris, Montreal: L'Harmattan, pp. 95–116.

Bernard, J. and U. Cantner (1999), 'French regional performance and variety – A non-parametric frontier approach, in P.Y. Badillo and J.C. Paradi (eds), *La Méthode DEA- Analyse des Performances*, Paris: Hermes Science Publications, pp. 255–73.

Bernard, J., U. Cantner and G. Westermann (1996), 'Technological leadership and variety – a data envelopment analysis for the French machinery industry', *Annals of Operations Research*, **68**, 361–77.

Böhm, K. (1978), *Lineare Quotientenprogrammierung – Rentabilitätsoptimierung*, Frankfurt a.M.: Haag & Herchen Verlag.

Cantner, U. (1996), 'Heterogenität und technologische Spillovers – Grundelemente einer ökonomischen Theorie des technologischen Fortschritts', Habilitationsschrift, Universität Augsburg.

Cantner, U. (2000), 'Heterogenität, technologischer fortschritt und spillovers', in M. Lehmann-Waffenschmidt, *Studien zur Evolutorischen Ökonomik V*, Berlin: Duncker & Humblot, pp. 15–40.

Cantner, U. and H. Hanusch (1996), 'Intrasektorale technologische Dynamik', in E. Helmstädter, G. Poser and H.J. Ramser (eds.), *Beiträge zur angewandten Wirtschaftsforschung, Festschrift K.H. Oppenländer*, Berlin: Duncker & Humblot, pp. 187–216.

Cantner, U. and H. Hanusch (1999), 'Productivity development – a macro-meso approach', mimeo, University of Augsburg.

Cantner, U., H. Hanusch and A. Pyka (1998), 'Pushing technological progress forward: a comparison of firm strategies', in J. Lesourne and A. Orlean (eds), *Advances in Self-organization and Evolutionary Economics*, London, Paris, Geneva: Economica, pp. 114–45.

Cantner U., H. Hanusch and G. Westermann (1997), 'Technological performance and variety – the case of the German electronics industry', in K. Nielsen and

B. Johnson (eds), *Institutions and Change – New Perspectives on Markets, Firms and Technology*, Cheltenham, UK and Lyme, USA: Edward Elgar, pp. 116–40.

Cantner, U. and J. Krüger (1999), 'An empirical account of technological progress on the macrolevel – DEA versus Growth Accounting', mimeo, University of Augsburg.

Cantner, U. and A. Pyka (1998a), 'Absorbing technological spillovers – simulations in an evolutionary framework', *Industrial and Corporate Change*, **7** (2), 369–97.

Cantner, U. and A. Pyka (1998b), 'Technological evolution – an analysis within the knowledge-based approach', *Structural Change and Economic Dynamics*, **9** (1), 85–108.

Cantner, U. and G. Westermann (1998), 'Localized technological progress and industrial dynamics – an empirical approach', *Economics of Innovation and New Technology*, **6**, 121–45.

Caves, D.W., L.R. Christensen and W.E. Diewert (1982a), 'Multilateral comparisions of output, input and productivity using superlative index numbers', *Economic Journal*, **92**, 73–86.

Caves, D.W., L.R. Christensen and W.E. Diewert (1982b), 'The economic theory of index numbers of the measurement of input, output and productivity', *Econometrica*, **50**, 1393–414.

Chang, K.-P. and Y.-Y. Guh (1991), 'Linear production functions and the data envelopment analysis', *European Journal of Operations Research*, **52**, 215–23.

Charnes, A. and W.W. Cooper (1962), 'Programming with linear fractional functionals', *Naval Research Logistics Quarterly*, **9**, 181–6.

Charnes, A., W.W. Cooper and E. Rhodes (1978), 'Measuring the efficiency of decision making units', *European Journal of Operational Research*, **2**, 429–44.

Dosi, G. (1988), 'Sources, procedures, and microeconomic effects of innovation', *Journal of Economic Literature*, **26**, 1120–71.

Färe, R., S. Grosskopf and C.A.K. Lovell (1994), *Production Frontiers*, Cambridge: Cambridge University Press.

Krüger, J., U. Cantner and H. Hanusch (2000), 'Total factor productivity, the East Asian miracle and the world production frontier', *Weltwirtschaftliches Archiv*, **136**, 111–36.

Leontief, W.W. (1947), 'Introduction to a theory of the internal structure of functional relationships', *Econometrica*, **15**, 361–73.

Malmquist, S. (1953), 'Index numbers and indifference surfaces', *Trabajos de Estatística*, **4**, 209–42.

Moorsteen, R.H. (1961), 'On measuring productive potential and relative efficiency', *Quarterly Journal of Economics*, **75**, 451–67.

Ott, A.E. (1959), 'Technischer Fortschritt', in *Handwörterbuch der Sozialwissenschaften*, **10**, Stuttgart, Tübingen, Göttingen: Fischer, Mohr, Vandenhoeck & Ruprecht, pp. 302–16.

Rosenberg, N. (1976), *Perspectives on Technology*, Cambridge: Cambridge University Press.

Saviotti, P.P. (1991), 'The role of variety in economic and technological development', in P.P. Saviotti and J.S. Metcalfe (eds), *Evolutionary Theories of Economic and Technological Change*, Chur: Harwood Academic Publishers, pp. 172–208.

Saviotti, P.P. (1996), *Technological Evolution, Variety and the Economy*, Cheltenham, UK and Brookfield, USA: Edward Elgar.

Schumpeter, J.A. (1935/1912), *Theorie der Wirtschaftlichen Entwicklung*, five volumes, Berlin: Duncker & Humblot.

Solow, R.M. (1957), 'Technical change and the aggregate production function', *Review of Economics and Statistics*, **39**, 312–20.
Stiglitz, J.E. (1987), 'Learning to learn, localized learning and technological progress', in P. Dasgupta and P. Stoneman (eds.), *Economic Policy and Technological Performance*, Cambridge: Cambridge University Press, pp. 125–51.
Wolff, E.N. (1992), 'Productivity growth and capital intensity on the sectoral and industry level: specialization among OECD countries, 1970–1988', working paper, New York University.

APPENDIX

A1 The Enhanced Linear Program of Non-parametric Frontier Analysis

The version of the envelopment form including possible excess inputs and output slacks reads as

$$
\begin{aligned}
\min \theta_l - \varepsilon e^T s_l^+ - \varepsilon e^T s_l^- & \\
s.t.: & \\
Y\lambda_l - s_l^- &= Y_l \\
\theta_l X_l - X\lambda_l - s_l^+ &= 0 \\
\lambda_l, s_l^+, s_l^- &\geq 0
\end{aligned}
\tag{A.1}
$$

A proportional reduction of inputs (as given by θ_l) does not necessarily lead to efficiency in the Pareto-Koopmanns sense. To correct for this the remaining excess inputs (s^+) and output slacks (s^-) are taken into account in the objective function. Vector e^T contains only elements 1. (Of course, one should here distinguish two vectors e^T for inputs and output respectively which contain s and i elements respectively. To ease notation we do not take account of this. The further analysis is not affected.) ε is a positive non-Archimedean small number. Thus, additionally to θ program (A.1) takes into account the remaining output slacks or excess inputs. Only then is a clear-cut selection of efficient and inefficient observations possible.

A2 Linear Programs Required for Computing the Malmquist Index

In computing the Malmquist-productivity index, for each observation l and for each periodical change four different linear programs have to be solved. In the case of $\theta^{t,t}$ and $\theta^{t+1,t+1}$ the programs are just the ones given by (1.3) and we will always get results obeying $\theta \leq 1$. In the case of $\theta^{t,t+1}$ the observation in period t will be compared to the frontier function of period $t+1$; and in the case of $\theta^{t+1,t}$ the observation in $t+1$ will be compared with the frontier in t. In both cases the efficiency values θ are not necessarily constrained to the interval [0,1] but they may be larger than 1. In this case technical progress would be detected.

For these four computations different linear programs are required. They are given as follows with t as the period under consideration and s as the period of the reference frontier:

$$
\begin{aligned}
&\min \theta_l^{t,s} \\
&s.t.: \\
Y^s\lambda_l &\geq Y_l^t \\
\theta_l X_l^t - X^s\lambda_l &\geq 0 \qquad \text{(A.2)} \\
\lambda_l &\geq 0
\end{aligned}
$$

With these programs T-1 index numbers can be computed for all observations, with T being the length of the period under investigation.

2. Is the notion of progress compatible with an evolutionary view of the economy?

C. Christian von Weizsäcker

1. THE NATURALISTIC FALLACY

A hundred years ago G.E. Moore published *Principia Ethica*, dedicated to his teachers and friends at the University of Cambridge.[1] John Maynard Keynes was one of his closest friends[2] in the group who called themselves 'Apostles'. Later on Moore as professor of philosophy at the University of Cambridge was the successor of John Neville Keynes, the father of the economist.

In his *Principia Ethica* Moore criticises Herbert Spencer who had developed an evolutionary ethics.[3] For Spencer evolution has a direction: from the lower to the higher. Spencer derives from this directedness of evolution that acting in accordance with evolution is ethically valuable action. Moore shows that the construction of Spencer is a tautology. The measure of the good with Spencer is identical with the results of evolution. Moore talks of the naturalistic fallacy: by putting certain phenomena of nature (for example that which is successful in the survival of the fittest) as identical with 'the good' one believes oneself able to derive ethical measures from nature; but one obtains those ethical values from nature only because one has put them into nature in the first place.

In the social Darwinism of Spencer social progress is identical with the results of evolution. If we understand this to be a 'naturalistic fallacy' then the concept of progress becomes much more problematical.

2. NORMATIVE INDIVIDUALISM

Neoclassical orthodoxy has developed a welfare economics which can be used to evaluate policy measures. Economics thereby has the theoretical instrument to derive a judgement like the following. The money equivalent of the advantages of this measure with some people is higher (lower) than the money equivalent of the disadvantages of this measure with other people. Hence this measure should (should not) be implemented. I do not want to discuss in this chapter the debate within neoclassical economics concerning compensation principles which, of course, are behind the statement just written down. I have done this elsewhere[4]. The important point is the logical coherence between positive neoclassical theory and neoclassical welfare economics. This coherence is the main reason that economics in the form of neoclassical economics has become the 'Queen of the Social Sciences', that economics has become the valued consultant of politics.

If evolutionary economics wants to compete in earnest with neoclassical economics then it needs a comparable coherence between its positive statements and its normative statements. What evolutionary economics needs is an evolutionary welfare economics. Without this the law makers will simply ignore evolutionary economics.

In traditional economics we have an attitude which has been called 'normative individualism'.[5] Value judgements in society should if possible be derived from value judgements of individuals who are part of this society. There are different variants of this normative individualism which I do not want to discuss here. They result from different approaches to the difficulty of the transition from the level of the individual to the level of society, to the level of the volonté générale, to speak with Rousseau. We have one line of thinking in the tradition of Immanuel Kant. I believe that Rawls[6] as well as perhaps Sen[7] and Buchanan[8] can be associated with this. And then there is a more utilitarian line of thinking which is associated with mainstream economics: authors like Bergson, Samuelson,[9] Arrow,[10] or Mirrlees.[11] Then there is the fundamental scepticism against the concept of justice as it has been proposed by Hayek[12] who of course has been one of the pioneers of modern evolutionary thinking in the social sciences.

The traditional question has been: how do we derive political decisions from individual preferences? In solving this difficult problem authors have used a methodological simplification: the assumption that individual preferences are exogenous. They assume that there is no feedback from the state of society upon the preferences of individuals. Accepting this simplifying assumption and accepting the general norm in social philosophy of the inherent rationality of the desired total process almost by necessity implies the assumption of rational behaviour of individuals. For no cleverly designed social decision process can derive rational social decisions out of irrational individual preferences. Thus we are led to the standard assumption of fixed and transitive preferences, i.e. of homo oeconomicus.

In summary: The program of normative individualism and the assumption of fixed preferences compel us to make the assumption of homo oeconomicus.

3. THE ASSUMPTION OF FIXED PREFERENCES IS ANTI-EVOLUTIONARY

In a sense it is obvious that the assumption of fixed preferences does not fit in an evolutionary theory. But I believe it pays to pursue this topic a little bit further. Obviously biological evolutionary theory in the tradition of Darwin takes certain things as given. These are the basic natural laws, for example those of physics. We can wait as long as we want: nature will never invent the perpetuum mobile because it contradicts basic laws in physics.

But to assume fixed preferences of individuals goes much beyond the assumption of given physical or chemical natural laws. If we follow Darwin then there is a great commonality between the nature of humans and the nature of animals. Behaviour of animals follows certain instincts of those animals which have turned out in the evolutionary process to be fit for the survival of that particular species or the genes of that particular species. Human behaviour in prehistoric times (the 'Stone Age') must have followed the same Darwinian laws. The preferences which have been inherited from this time have been fit for the survival of the species homo sapiens in these prehistoric times.[13]

But one of the conditions for survival of the human species was a certain flexibility of the human individual. Characteristics specific to the human species are their ability to plan forward, to use instruments, to produce instruments, the ability to cooperate on a higher level using developed languages. These characteristics have been the process of a co-evolution together with a rising life expectancy, a longer period of infancy which is characterised by intense learning. From the view of the species as compared to other species the species has invested much more in individuals. The survival of the individual has a higher value for the human species than for most other species because of the substantial investment in this individual. The mental abilities of the human species enabled it to adapt to quite different environmental conditions. They meant a particular flexibility which implied that homo sapiens was able to inhabit a wide variety of climatic zones. All these factors imply that the share of the total adaptability to changed environmental conditions which was borne by the individual rather than by the genes would have to increase. The premium for a higher ability of the individuals to survive after changing circumstances must have increased.

Under these specific conditions of homo sapiens in prehistoric times it is highly implausible that preferences, for example preferences for food, have been fixed once and for all. Much more plausible is the hypothesis that those individuals had a higher survival value whose preferences were able to adapt to the specific circumstances, i.e. individuals whose instincts were sufficiently flexible to adapt behaviour to changed circumstances even beyond the rational capabilities of the individuals. The hypothesis of adaptive preferences is therefore much more plausible in terms of evolutionary biology than the hypothesis of fixed preferences.

I want to repeat the argument in different words to make it clear. We make a distinction between an adaptability to the environment by means of Darwinian evolution of the genes and an adaptability by means of individual behaviour. Plants and animals also have an individual adaptability for given sets of genes. The genes determine the degree to which individuals are flexible. Individual flexibility is a characteristic of the phenotype which in itself is determined by the genotype. That has an evolutionary advantage. Other things being equal a higher individual adaptability helps the survival of the genes of this particular species. But other things are not equal, for a higher adaptability or flexibility pays a price in terms of advantages of specialisation. Therefore in Darwinian evolution there will always be a compromise between individual adaptability and the advantages of specialisation of the species. We can expect that the optimal degree of individual adaptability is positively correlated with the life expectancy of the individuals and with the breadth of the ecological niche which is occupied by that particular species.

Within individual adaptability of humans there is a trade-off between cognitive abilities and will power on the one side and flexibility of preferences on the other side. To obtain a given degree of adaptability an individual with fixed preferences needs a higher intelligence and will power than an individual with adaptive preferences. It is highly implausible that within the range measuring the degree of adaptability of preferences an adaptability degree of zero (i.e. fixed preferences) has an evolutionary advantage over a positive degree of adaptability.

4. ADAPTIVE PREFERENCES: AN ALTERNATIVE TO FIXED PREFERENCES WHILE MAINTAINING THE APPROACH OF NORMATIVE INDIVIDUALISM

I introduce a theory of endogenously changing preferences. It is the theory of adaptive preferences: preferences of economic agents adapt to their environment. To make precise what is meant we need some formal theory. We look at stationary states A, B, C. . . . . There is a preference ordering between these states. But these preferences depend on the state the person is in. By

$$(A; B)\ (>)\ (C; B)$$

we mean: given that the actual state of the past has been B the agent prefers A to C. The preference inequality makes sense, because A and C are compared, given the preferences induced by state B. An inequality like (A; B) (>) (C; D) does not make sense, because in evaluating A preferences are induced by B whereas in evaluating C preferences are induced by D.

Now the axiom of adaptive preferences can be formulated in the following way: Let (B; A) (>) (A; A). Then (B; B) (>) (A; B).

What is ruled out by this axiom is: (B; A) (>) (A; A) and at the same time (A; B) (>) (B; B) the latter would mean: if the agent is adapted to A he/she prefers B and if the agent is adapted to B he/she prefers A. In that case the agent is structurally dissatisfied. It is always better to be where you are not. Note that you can move the agent between A and B and at each move he/she feels improved.

Now we observe that in the inequality defining adaptive preferences there is an asymmetry between A and B. B is preferred to A no matter whether the past was A or B. We then tend to view a move from A to B to be progress for the agent. In terms of progress not every pair of choices may be comparable. We may have (A; A) (>) (B; A) and (B; B) (>) (A; B). Thus it is not automatically ensured that we can define progress consistently.

Here we now develop a theory. In the next two sections I outline a formal theory. For adaptive preferences under certain assumptions we can find a concept of progress which is universally applicable as we are used to it in a world of fixed preferences. The performance of the economy remains measurable even though the measuring rod changes with the state of the economy.

5. THE MODEL[14]

There is one person who is a consumer of commodity baskets x in the positive orthant of the n-dimensional Euclidean space R^N. We work in a continuous time model. At each moment t the consumer maximises an instantaneous utility subject to a budget constraint. But the utility function $U(x)$ itself depends on past experience as expressed by an n-dimensional vector q which stands for past consumption. We formalise this dependence on past consumption in the following way

$$\frac{dq}{dt} \equiv \dot{q} = \alpha(x - q) \tag{2.1}$$

where $\alpha > 0$ is a real number. Thus, if consumption $\bar{x}$ remains constant over time, then q converges towards $\bar{x}$.

The utility function then can be written

$$U = U(x; q)$$

Utilities with different values of q are not comparable; they simply represent different preferences.

We assume that U is continuously differentiable with respect to x and q.

We now consider consumption paths through time. Among paths $x(t)$ which are piecewise continuous we define a subset which we call 'improving paths'. This description is motivated by an axiom, which allows a minimum of comparability between different preferences.

Consider a path of vector x through time such that $x(0) = x^0$ is the starting point, $x(T) = x^T$ is the end point and there is a set J with a finite number of moments of time, called *jump points*, $t_1, t_2, \ldots\ldots t_N$ such that $0 \leq t_1 < t_2 < \ldots\ldots\ldots < t_N \leq T$. Let I_T be the interval $[0, T]$ of real numbers. (We admit the possibility that $T = 0$). Then we consider paths $x(t)$ such that $x(t)$ is continuous in $I_T - J$. We, of course, admit the possibility that the set J of jump points is empty.

For such paths $q(t)$ is well defined by the differential equation (2.1), if $q(0) = q^0$ is given. Indeed we find the unique solution

$$q(t) = e^{-\alpha t}\left[q^0 + \alpha \int_0^t x(z) e^{\alpha z} dz\right]$$

The integral is well defined for piecewise continuous functions $x(z)$.

For any point where the vector $\dot{x}$ exists we can define the following expression

$$\hat{U} \equiv \sum_{i=1}^{n} \frac{\partial U}{\partial x_i} \dot{x}_i$$

Note that this is different from the time derivative of U which is

$$\dot{U} \equiv \sum_{i=1}^{n} \frac{\partial U}{\partial x_i} \dot{x}_i + \sum_{i=1}^{n} \frac{\partial U}{\partial q_i} \dot{q}_i$$

Given that the comparison of utility values for different values of q does not have an economic meaning the expression $\dot{U}$ is economically meaningless. On the other hand the expression $\hat{U}$ does have an economic meaning. If $\hat{U}$ is positive it means that 'real income' increases. For example, if x comes about by maximisation of U with respect to x subject to a budget constraint then $\hat{U} > 0$ implies that either the budget rises or the price index (in terms of the Divisia index) falls, i.e. that real income rises. Therefore it is plausible to talk about an *improvement* if $\hat{U} > 0$.

We use the following notation for piecewise continuous paths $x(t)$. By $\{x(t);\ q^0;\ T\}$ we mean a path of the piecewise continuous consumption vector $x(t)$ in the time interval $[0,T]$ such that preferences are determined by $q(t) = e^{-\alpha t}[q^0 + \alpha \int_0^t x(z)e^{\alpha z}dz]$ with the initial value q^0.

We then can talk of an *improvement path*. It is basically a path in time $\{x(t);\ q^0;\ T\}$ such that $\hat{U} \geq 0$ along the whole path and there are either improvement jumps or there is a subinterval in which $\hat{U} > 0$ is strictly positive. A path is called *weakly improving*, if $\hat{U} \geq 0$, wherever it is defined and utility does not decline at jump points. Note that an improvement path is then weakly improving. But there may be paths which are weakly improving but not improving. One example is a path along which $\hat{U} = 0$.

I now introduce the improvement axiom. Since preferences change through time welfare economics would become impossible unless we had some way of normatively comparing consumption paths that do not have the same preferences. We need some kind of 'metapreferences'. But I want to restrict metapreferences to a minimum. The metapreferences in our case are encapsulated in the following axiom.

Improvement Axiom: Let x^0 be a consumption vector and let preferences be adapted to x^0, i.e. $q^0 = x^0$. Let X^1 be a path such consumption remains constant through time: $x^1(t) = x^0$ and therefore $q^1(t) = q^0$. Let X^2 be a consumption path also starting with preferences $q^0 = x^0$ and starting with the same consumption bundle x^0. Let $x^2(t)$ be such that X^2 is an improving path. Then the person prefers to walk along the improvement path X^2 over walking along the stationary path X^1.

The Improvement Axiom is highly plausible: starting from the same tastes (as represented by q^0) adapted to initial consumption and the same consumption basket x^0 the consumer prefers improvement over constant consumption even if he or she is aware that tastes adapt to the evolving situation through time.

If we accept the Improvement Axiom we can, as will be shown, maintain the concept of progress such that it is consistent with welfare economics – even with endogenously changing preferences.

6. THE MAIN THEOREM

I now report a theorem, which indicates the existence of 'laws of motion' of preferences which are consistent with a reasonable concept of 'progress' in the tradition of welfare economics.

The following notation will be used: $x^*(>)_q x$ means that x^* is preferred over x with preferences corresponding to past consumption vector q. It is equivalent to the expression $U(x^*;q) > U(x;q)$. We will consider price vectors p, which are, as usual, n-dimensional vectors of nonnegative real numbers.

I first introduce a set of five assumptions.

Assumption 1 (Existence of a demand function) Preferences are such that a direct demand function $x = f(p, q)$ exists, where it is always assumed that the budget $p \cdot x = 1$.

Discussion of Assumption 1: by assuming a unique demand vector for each q and each price vector p we restrict our analysis to convex preference structures. We need some such restriction because the process of gradual improvement which we describe with our improvement path only leads to local optimisation. We cannot expect global optimisation in the case of non-convex structures.

Assumption 2 (Non-saturation) If $x^*_i > x_i$ for i = 1, 2, . . . n, then $U(x^*; q) > U(x; q)$ for all q.

Discussion of Assumption 2: it is my guess that this assumption can be weakened. For the time being I find it convenient for my proof. It provides a uniform 'direction' in which to look for improvement.

I now introduce the concept of a *constant budget path*. It is a path which is generated by a constant budget constraint so that changes in the consumption basket are only due to changes in preferences which are induced by changed past consumption.

Assumption 3 (Existence of long run demand) For each budget constraint $p > 0$ there exists a unique convergence point $\bar{x} = F(p)$ of a constant budget path; i.e. the convergence point is independent of the initial value q^0.

Discussion of Assumption 3: the independence of 'asymptotic' behaviour from the initial preferences is unlikely to hold, if the preferences themselves exhibit important non-convexities. Thus, in a sense, Assumption 3 is an extension of Assumption 1. An assumption like Assumption 3 is necessary for a 'global' theorem of the type to be shown here. We cannot expect global optimisation from purely local optimisation procedures as discussed in this chapter, unless we make an assumption like Assumption 3.

Assumption 4 (Continuity) For each triple of vectors $\{x^*; x; q\}$ such that $x^* (>)_q x$ there exist neighbourhoods $M(x^*)$, $M(x)$, $M(q)$ such that $z^* (>)_r z$ for $z^* \in M(x^*)$, $z \in M(x)$, $r \in M(q)$.

Discussion of Assumption 4: it is an extension of the continuity of fixed preferences to changing preferences. The continuity assumption is essential for my proof. This I know from the fact that I cannot simply carry over my theorem to a model where commodity quantities are restricted to integer numbers. The theory of adaptive preferences for non-Euclidean commodity spaces has yet to be developed.

Assumption 5 (Adaptive preferences = non-circularity of improving paths) Let $\{x(t); q^0; T\}$ be an improving path and let $x(0) = q^0$. Then $x(T) \neq x(0)$.

Discussion of Assumption 5: this is the assumption of adaptive preferences. Here it takes a form which is different from the intuitive introduction in section 4. As will be discussed in section 7 the two formulations of adaptive preferences are equivalent.

Definition For any given x^0 let $A(x^0)$ be the set of vectors $\bar{x}$ such that there exists an improving path $\{x(t); q^0; T\}$ with $q^0 = x^0$; $x(0) = x^0$; $x(T) = \bar{x}$.

In other words: the set $A(x^0)$ is the set of vectors, which can be reached from x^0 by an improving path, given that initially the preferences are 'adapted' to x^0.

Remark Obviously, by Assumption 5, it follows that $x^0 \notin A(x^0)$.

Main Theorem 1. Part A The 'long-run demand function' $F(p)$satisfies the strong axiom of revealed preference.

Part B There exists a utility function $V(x)$, which generates the demand function $F(p)$. Let $B(x^0)$ be the set of vectors such that $V(x) > V(x^0)$. Then $B(x^0) = A(x^0)$.

Here I do not give a proof of the theorem. The interested reader is referred to my paper (von Weizsäcker 2004).

The meaning of the Main Theorem is, as has already been said above, that we have an ordering of the commodity space which makes it possible to speak in a consistent manner about progress even though migrations through this space change the preferences which are the measuring rod for the meaning of progress. Indeed, take any two consumption vectors x and z in the n-dimensional space. Then there are three possibilities. Either – with preferences adapted to x – there exists an improvement path from x to z so that we can consider a (perhaps gradual) movement from x to z to be 'progress'. Or the reverse is true: with preferences adapted to z there exists an improvement path from z to x so that we can consider a (perhaps gradual) movement from z to x to be 'progress'. Or there is neither an improvement path from z to x nor from x to z (with initial preferences adapted to the starting point). But then for any vector with equal components $\varepsilon > 0$ we can find an improvement path from $x - \varepsilon$ (with preferences initially adapted to it) to z, and vice versa, so that in a sense x and z are equivalent in a similar sense to that in which two points on the same indifference curve are in the case of fixed preferences.

With adaptive preferences we can avoid the un-evolutionary assumption of fixed preferences and we can avoid at the same time 'welfare chaos'. Welfare economics remains possible.

7. EQUIVALENCE OF THE TWO DEFINITIONS OF ADAPTIVE PREFERENCES

Thus we have shown that there is a chance to develop a welfare economics under the assumption of adaptive preferences. In my Thünen Lecture I have given an example how we can apply such welfare economics.[15] If we want to continue in this direction then we need a deeper understanding of the hypothesis of adaptive preferences. In section 3 above I have already tried to make clear that an adaptation of individual preferences to changed circumstances is a much better hypothesis from the point of view of evolutionary biology than the assumption of fixed preferences.

In the mathematical formulation as developed in sections 5 and 6 the assumption of adaptive preferences takes a form where it is not immediately obvious how it relates to evolutionary biology. Therefore we need to clarify this connection. Intuitively we would say that the adaptability of preferences in a modern market system implies that the long-run demand is more price-elastic than short-run demand. If a good becomes more expensive then demand for it goes down. This reduction in consumption of the good induces a change in preferences such that this good is demanded less at given prices. So this will in the long run amplify the primary effect of the higher price on demand.

A higher price elasticity by means of adaptation of preferences corresponds to a higher elasticity of substitution in traditional theory. But the elasticity of substitution is nothing else but a measure of the adaptability of behaviour to changed circumstances. Adaptive preferences therefore are preferences which adapt in such a way that the substitution effect in the demand function which is induced by a change in relative prices becomes larger than it would be without this change in preferences.

The connection with the assumption of non-circularity of progress paths which was the way in which we formulated adaptive preferences can be made plausible in the following way. The theorem says that the long-run demand under the condition of non-circularity of progress paths is compatible with a utility function $V(x)$. The indifference hyper-surface corresponding to this utility function $V(x)$ which goes through point x^0 is the lower boundary of the area $A(x^0)$ which can be reached from x^0 by means of a progress path. But this area contains the set of all points which according to the short-run adapted preferences are preferred to point x^0, i.e. the set of all points for which the following inequality holds

$$U(x; x^0) > U(x^0; x^0).$$

We may call this area the area $C(x^0)$. For it is obvious that any point in $C(x^0)$ can be reached from x^0 by means of a progress path. The consumer simply must jump from x^0 to x and if x is contained in $C(x^0)$ then obviously this is a progress path. Hence we have $C(x^0)$ is contained in $A(x^0)$. But this means that the curvature of the indifference hyper-surface which is the lower boundary of $A(x^0)$ is less or at most equal to the curvature of the corresponding indifference hyper-surface which is the lower boundary of $C(x^0)$. Therefore the long-run elasticity of substitution is never lower than the short-run elasticity of substitution. Hence the adaptation of the preferences to changed relative prices amplifies the demand reaction for given preferences. Thus we have built a bridge between the assumption of non-circularity and the adaptiveness of preferences.

Another form in which make clear the connection between non-circularity and adaptivity is the following thought experiment. Assume that preferences are the opposite of adaptive; let us call them anti-adaptive. This implies that the long-run reaction to a change in relative prices is lower than the short-run reaction. Take the case of a linear demand function. The price p of a good is raised whereas all other prices remain the same. The consumer is compensated for the price change Δp so that his or her utility level according to the short-run utility function not only remains the same but is raised slightly. The required increase in income ΔY hence is higher by a level ε than the amount which would have been required for keeping utility the same. But due to linearity the compensating ΔY is equal to $\Delta p(x_1 + x_0)/2$ where x_0 is the quantity demanded before the price was raised and x_1 is the quantity demanded after the price was raised. Thus for ΔY we have the following equation $\Delta Y = \Delta p\,(x_1 + x_0)/2 + \varepsilon$. Hence we have a slight rise in utility for this person. If now preferences change but prices remain the same then the resulting change in consumption is an improvement because the consumer has the choice to keep his consumption as before. Let x_2 be the quantity of the good to which consumption converges in the long run after the price has been raised by Δp. Because of the assumption of anti-adaptive preferences we have $x_2 > x_1$. A part of the primary reduction in demand is reversed. If now the consumer is sufficiently close to this convergence point x_2 we make another price change, namely that the price is lowered by Δp so it is again at its original level. Also the income is changed by $\Delta \tilde{Y}$, where $\Delta \tilde{Y}$ is negative. $\Delta \tilde{Y}$ is computed in such a way that it is slightly lower in absolute value (or slightly higher algebraically) than it would be to maintain the utility level. The compensating income reduction can be computed as $\Delta \tilde{Y} = -\Delta p(x_2 + x_3)/2$, where x_3 is the quantity demanded to which the consumer jumps because of the price reduction. Because in the long run the consumer will converge to the original point x_0 and because we have assumed anti-adaptive preferences we know that $x_3 > x_0$. Therefore we have the inequality

$$\Delta\tilde{Y} = -\Delta p(x_2 + x_3)/2 + \varepsilon < -\Delta p(x_1 + x_0)/2 + \varepsilon = -\Delta Y + 2\varepsilon.$$

This means that for a sufficiently small $\varepsilon > 0$ we can obtain the inequality $\Delta Y + \Delta\tilde{Y} < 0$. Thus on an improving path we come into a budget situation which is less favourable than the initial situation. The prices are the same as in the initial situation but the budget is lower. Now we can finish the improving path by now raising the budget to its original level. Then the consumer has the possibility to return by an improving path to the original consumption vector. Hence we have constructed an improving path which is circular. This shows that anti-adaptive preferences do not have the property of non-circularity of improving paths.

8. ADAPTIVE PARETO-OPTIMALITY

Is there a theorem with adaptive preferences which corresponds to the efficiency theorem of Walras equilibria? The traditional efficiency theorem says: a Walras equilibrium is Pareto-optimal. For reasons of simplicity of presentation I take here the case of stationary Walras equilibria. There are m persons in this economy with an infinite life horizon. All these m persons have adaptive preferences. The economy is in a stationary state of a Walras equilibrium. This in particular means that $q = x$ for each person. The rate of interest in this equilibrium is positive.

Now I introduce the following definition:

A stationary state of the economy is called *adaptive Pareto-optimal* if, beginning with the stationary state, there is no implementable path in the economy such that for all persons this path is a weakly improving path and such that there are persons for whom this is an improving path. The traditional concept of Pareto-optimality I denote by 'classic Pareto-optimum'.

Now we can show the following theorem:

Theorem 2: The stationary Walras equilibrium is adaptive Pareto-optimal.

Sketch of the proof: Since we are in a stationary Walras equilibrium our Main Theorem tells us that every person behaves in such a way as would maximize its long utility function $V(x)$. Also according to established theory the stationary equilibrium is classic Pareto-optimal, if we take the long-run utility function as the fixed preferences of this classic Walras equilibrium.

Hence according to traditional theory and using the equilibrium prices the allocation in the equilibrium maximises the present value of the sum of the consumption vectors of the m consumers subject to the constraint that we only look at implementable allocations. Now, because of our Main Theorem a weakly improving path and an improving path for every person only touches consumption vectors for which we have $V(x) \geq V(x^0)$, where x^0 is the equilibrium consumption vector of the stationary equilibrium. For an improving path we even have the strict inequality $V(x) > V(x^0)$. But then in the classical model, with fixed preferences $V(x)$, the total utility of the weakly improving path is greater than or equal to the total utility of the stationary path and the total utility of the improving path is greater than the total utility of the stationary path. But because the stationary equilibrium is classic Pareto-optimal this implies that the total paths consisting of these improving and weakly improving paths cannot be implementable. This shows that the stationary equilibrium is adaptive Pareto-optimal.

Hence we have built a bridge between traditional concepts and theorems of general equilibrium theory and welfare economics on the one side and the concepts and theorems developed with the idea of adaptive preferences on the other side.

9. PATH DEPENDENCE

Our main theorem provides the possibility to define progress even with endogenous preferences as long as these preferences are adaptive. Nevertheless it must be clear that the philosophy of evolution is a different one from the neoclassical philosophy of optimisation, in particular of global optimisation. Our theory of adaptive preferences is a theory of local optimisation with an adaptation of the optimisation criterion to the changed environment. But our theory rests on an assumption (Assumption 2) which implies a convex structure of short-term preferences: for each consumption vector x^0 and each vector q the set of consumption vectors x which are preferred to x^0 is a convex set.

But then there are preferences which do not have this convexity. If I am indifferent between living in Munich and living in Cologne then it does not follow in general that I would prefer to live 50 per cent of the time in Munich and 50 per cent of the time in Cologne over living in one of the two cities exclusively. Is the theory therefore without practical interest? No. For there are large subsets of the commodity space so that within each subset the preferences are indeed convex. Only the theory cannot simply be applied if we want to compare consumption vectors which are in different subsets which are separated by a non-convexity.

But this is what one should expect if one speaks about an evolutionary philosophy. There are such things as evolutionary dead-ends. These are ecological equilibria which under a more general point of view are somewhat unsatisfactory but which nevertheless are the result of a local optimisation. Small mutations and random changes will not lead out of this dead-end. We also have to take into account that speaking of a point of view from a higher level is theoretically not well-founded as long as we don't have a criterion for this higher-level point of view.

But the theory developed here may help us along. The theory is able to distinguish between two kinds of status quo conservatisms or local equilibria. We may have a kind of status quo which, as has been described in section F of my Thünen Lecture,[16] can be criticised and can be explained as the result of a somewhat mistaken institutional arrangement. It is then possible to get out of this equilibrium by means of a progress path and to reach a new equilibrium. The new equilibrium from the point of view of preferences adapted to the old equilibrium is inferior. But it is better in the sense that it can be reached by a progress path and that after adaptation of preferences to the new equilibrium it is preferred to the old equilibrium. Then there is the other kind of equilibrium or local optimum such that two states A and B cannot be compared because of the non-convexities which have been mentioned. Due to these non-convexities there may be neither a progress path from A to B nor a progress path from B to A. In this case we must simply admit that A and B are incomparable. That French people predominantly prefer the French way of life and that Germans predominantly prefer the German way of life does not automatically mean that we can establish a ranking between these two countries by means of our theory.

This chapter adds to my Thünen Lecture on welfare economics with adaptive preferences. In particular I have emphasised the evolutionary character of this theory. I hope to have provided the basis for evolutionary economics to develop valuation criteria so that policy advice becomes possible from the point of view of evolutionary economics. In the long run evolutionary economics may thereby be able to challenge the dominant position of neoclassic economics in policy advice.

NOTES

1. Moore (1903).
2. Keynes (1949).
3. Spencer (1892–93).
4. von Weizsäcker (1998).
5. Vanberg (1986).
6. Rawls (1971).

7. Sen (1970).
8. Buchanan (1974).
9. Samuelson (1947).
10. Arrow (1951).
11. Mirrlees (1971).
12. Hayek (1976).
13. On this topic Witt (2004).
14. This and the following section correspond to parts of a paper of mine: von Weizsäcker (2004). There the reader can find the proof of the Main Theorem.
15. von Weizsäcker (2002).
16. von Weizsäcker (2002).

REFERENCES

Arrow, K. (1951), *Social Choice and Individual Value*, New York.

Buchanan, J. (1974), *The Limits of Liberty*, London.

Hayek, F.A. von (1976), *The Mirage of Social Justice*, London.

Keynes, J.M. (1949), *Two Memoirs*, London.

Mirrlees, J.A. (1971), 'An exploration in the theory of optimal income taxation', *Review of Economic Studies*.

Moore, G.E. (1903), *Principia Ethica*, London.

Rawls, J. (1971), *A Theory of Justice*, Cambridge, MA.

Samuelson, P.A. (1947), *Foundations of Economic Analysis*, Cambridge, MA.

Sen, A.K. (1970), *Collective Choice and Social Welfare*, San Francisco.

Spencer, H. (1892–93), *The Principles of Ethics*, two volumes, London.

Vanberg, V. (1986), 'Individual choice and institutional constraints: the normative element in classical and contractarian liberalism', *Analyse und Kritik*, **8**.

von Weizsäcker, C.C. (1998), 'Das Gerechtigkeitsproblem in der Sozialen Marktwirtschaft', *Zeitschrift für Wirtschaftspolitik*, pp. 257–88.

von Weizsäcker, C.C. (2002), 'Welfare Economics bei endogenen Präferenzen: Thünen-Vorlesung 2001', *PWP, Perspektiven der Wirtschaftspolitik, Eine Zeitschrift des Vereins für Socialpolitik*, **3**, (4, S), 425–46.

von Weizsäcker, C.C. (2004), 'Welfare economics with endogeneous preferences: a beginning', discussion paper, presented at the European Econometric Society Meeting in Madrid, August; available upon request via my e-mail address: ccvwzs@t-online.de.

Witt, U. (2004), 'Beharrung und Wandel – ist wirtschaftliche Evolution theoriefähig', *Erwägen Wissen Ethik (EWE)*, **15**, 33–45.

3. Reconciling evolutionary economics with liberalism

Gerhard Wegner[1]

1. INTRODUCTION

In economic theory it is common to assess new theories by their relevance for economic policy. However, theorists often avoid such an assessment, in particular if new theories are not fully fledged. When theoretical work is in progress, the practical impact of new theories can be ambiguous, something which invites different interpretations as the paradigm undergoes further elaboration. But even if the practical relevance for policy making looms ahead, the political consequences might lack attractiveness for theorists; for the cleavage between economic rationality and political rationality also applies to new economic paradigms so that economic policy is unlikely to change its course in light of new theoretical insights. Such difficulties are commonly taken as an excuse to avoid exploring the political impact of new economic paradigms in advance. Nevertheless, economic theorising is ultimately oriented to welfare and by nature bears political consequences, even if the latter are only indirect and theories do not explicitly identify welfare-promoting policies.

Evolutionary economics is a case in point. So far it has not been linked to one specific political conception, e.g. in terms of interventionism or, alternatively, liberalism, although different scholars tend to adopt one of these interpretations with regard to policy making. But before we enter into a discussion, let us establish that evolutionary economics, even though it represents a very broad field of heterodox research, is oriented to economic policy and thus echoes its stationary rival, that is Walrasian theory. The investigation of novelty and innovation shifts attention to important sources of welfare in society. Furthermore, at least in this respect, evolutionary economics claims superiority to Walrasian theory since innovation is deemed to be of much higher relevance for economic welfare in the long term than welfare maximisation under given constraints in the short term. For that reason alone one should hope for political conclusions deriving from evolutionary economics. Even though only tentative answers have been given so far, a systematic exploration is likely to be within its scope.

If we wish to probe the political consequences of evolutionary economics, we can proceed along different theoretical avenues: first of all, an analogy with Walrasian theory suggests itself. In doing so we would hold on to an overarching goal of economic ends called 'welfare' and derive well-suited political measures to increase or even maximise that goal if markets bring forth welfare deficiencies. The welfare target would, however, undergo revision in order to include innovation as the major driving force of welfare in the long term. The logic behind this concept echoes 'normative economics' in the well-known sense while the conventional welfare concept is revised by an evolutionary update. Although the main problem of this conception derives from the operationalisation of an evolutionary notion of welfare, attempts have followed this way of theorising which would maintain the 'deductivism' of normative economics, that is the deriving of best courses of economic action in a logical sense from an abstract welfare goal.[2]

A second, less ambitious theoretical option would reject a single economic target for the whole society to which the political sphere would have to commit itself. Instead, the concept of welfare could be decomposed and adapted to specific circumstances, which gives politics leeway for defining goals. In so doing, the autonomy of political decision making in a democracy would be acknowledged in a sense which comes closer to Tinbergen's (1952) early conception of a means-ends oriented theory of economic policy. However, evolutionary economic theory could still ask to what extent economic evolution may profit from intervention or even requires it. Furthermore, as we know that political intervention can interfere with economic evolution in terms of unintended side-effects, the political agenda should be carefully checked and broken down if need be, something which is not necessarily at variance with politicians' own interests.

In the following I concentrate on this second theoretical option. But let us mention that the potential of evolutionary economics can also be probed when it comes to further developing a positive theory of economic policy (public choice). By transferring basic ideas into the field of public choice, evolutionary economics may focus on political innovation and its diffusion; in so doing evolutionary economics could analyse preconditions of a change of political preferences instead of taking them as given. As a result evolutionary economics would replace the concept of the political entrepreneur in a sense which comes closer to its market-process analogy, which implies that political action includes aspects of experimenting and learning from failures. Few attempts have been undertaken to further develop an enriched behavioural concept in politics and thus work on this third option of evolutionary political economy is scarce (Wohlgemuth, 2003).[3]

For reasons of space let us concentrate on the prescriptive potential of evolutionary economics. The reasons for our subscription to the second approach instead of the more ambitious first one will be given later. However, let us emphasise that an analysis of the prescriptive aspects of evolutionary economics by no means implies neglecting the discrepancy of political and economic rationality. Evolutionary economists recommending better policies are aware of that built-in imperfection of democracies. However, theoretical reflections on politics may not be pointless if voters are the intended addressees of recommendations. Besides policy makers, the principal in democracy does not attract much theoretical attention although they have an interest in becoming informed about feasible political targets. Otherwise, the principal could pay for ambitious or unfeasible claims addressed to their agents. For the sake of accessibility, prescriptive theories of economic policy could easily be read as recommendations to voters when they shape their political preferences.

2. POLICY NORMS FROM THE PERSPECTIVE OF EVOLUTIONARY ECONOMICS

Any liberal policy norm is strongly linked to normative methodological individualism inasmuch as individual welfare makes up the welfare of society. The standard conception of 'normative economics' operationalises this overarching goal for state activities with a strong version of welfare maximisation in terms of a social welfare function. In order to avoid the difficulties of interpersonal utility comparisons, the standard conception often adopts the criterion of Pareto-superiority. It is usually taken for granted that this conceptualisation of economic policy reflects liberal norms concerning politics, although critics such as Rowley and Peacock (1975) or Cordato (1992) have called this claim into question from an Austrian perspective. Before we assess the adaptiveness of policy norms to a liberal conceptualisation of politics, let us briefly restate the meaning of liberal politics.

According to our understanding of liberal politics,

1. economic policy should concern the welfare of the whole society, which excludes politics acting systematically on behalf of some individuals or groups (classes, ethnical or religious groups etc.);
2. the welfare of society concerns the welfare of its members so that individuals represent the genuine target of state activities;
3. individuals define the criteria of welfare according to their own value judgments which in normal cases should not be overridden by

government (exceptions e.g. in the realm of social policies require good reasons);

4. individuals are deemed to be competent to identify as well as realise welfare gains by entering into co-operation and/or trade relationships with other persons (to be sure, a liberal concept could modify this presumption to some extent, namely with respect to specific groups and their conditions of life).

An implication of this liberal conceptualisation of politics is that individuals need freedom in order to realise mutual gains from trade (freedom of trade; freedom of movement; right of abode). As liberalism, at least in its classical version, is a cosmopolitan idea and has no truck with national priorities, let alone nationalism, it gives strong arguments for opening national borders not only for goods but also for individuals who look for better places in order to make use of their talents and resources.[4] A second implication pertains to the orientation of governmental activities which have to serve individual welfare and are justified only if markets *as well as other forms of non-state collective actions* fail to increase individual welfare. The latter qualification updates the well-known reservations of classical liberalism toward state activities by taking into account a broader concept of institutions as elaborated by New Institutional Economics (NIE). Since institutions can also emerge from voluntary agreements in society (internal institutions as opposed to external institutions), the provision of institutions by the state represents only one possible alternative (Voigt and Kiwit, 1998). Even if an increase of individual welfare requires institutions, safeguards against state activities have to be introduced because mandatory institutions enforced by the state may interfere with individual freedom without justification in terms of welfare.

Even though standard welfare theory claims to be in line with such an understanding of liberal politics, evolutionary market theory shores up liberalism much better and supports doubts about '19th century mechanical liberalism' (Ladeur 2000). Evolutionary market theory does without a theoretical observer who defines the entire ends of economic activities as well as their means in terms of production functions. Productive activities satisfying human wants as well as technologies result from evolutionary processes when individuals make use of their freedom. Determining a transformation curve from the viewpoint of a theoretical observer means fixing the outcome of a process which by definition is open-ended, or, to put it in Hayekian terms, to ignore the discovery procedure inherent in markets (Hayek 1996). For that reason the overall target of productive efficiency from the viewpoint of normative economics gives the impression that freedom is at best only functional for achieving that goal but principally gets second priority. It is no accident that normative economics ignores the notion of freedom.

Compared to this static conception of welfare which points to the satisfaction of given wants under given restrictions in the best way, evolutionary economics stresses the experimental character of identifying welfare. In this regard evolutionary economics differs in the description of welfare and attaches importance to innovation. Innovations are not valued for their own sake from the perspective of evolutionary economics, nor are individual assessments of innovations overridden by a theoretical observer. The importance of innovation from a welfare perspective results from the opportunity given to individuals to reassess their former definition of well-being in view of new alternatives. Hence, it would be a complete 'non-individualistic' misconception to deem innovations as such to be valuable without regard to their consequences. In reality, however, innovations *are* the salient phenomenon in raising welfare in economies. I recommend that we hold on to normative methodological individualism and discard any valuation of technologies made by some outside 'expert'. In consequence, innovation-promoting policies can hardly refer to evolutionary economics without introducing some external and henceforth questionable valuation of innovations (see below). Nothing can be said about the social value of innovation ex ante except that it extends the choice set, leaving their non-acceptance as one alternative which has to be respected by a theoretical observer.

Unlike standard welfare economics, evolutionary economics cannot be concerned with welfare itself but only with the possibility of increasing welfare. This re-orientation of welfare economics is closely connected to the knowledge problem inherent in any evolutionary theory: since novelties and their welfare attributes defy prediction (otherwise they would not be novelties), no 'goal function' (welfare function) for the society can be stated. However, the extension of opportunities to which innovations contribute is desirable from any welfare point of view, whether or not individuals substitute in favour of new (now: better) alternatives. In view of more alternatives, individuals have the chance to check their consumption (and production) plans and to make themselves better off. As a consequence, the premise of normative methodological individualism combined with the experimental nature of identifying welfare strongly corroborates reservations against any public interference with the extension of opportunities; this, in turn, occurs when politics selects innovations which are to be supported and furthered. In so doing, government would supplant the social valuation of innovations by governmental preselection. From the aforementioned normative position there is no justification for such a political privilege. This holds particularly true if innovation policies are accompanied by some crowding-out (distortion) effects in the sense that the promotion of specified innovations implicitly impedes innovations in other technological fields which do not gain public support (any financial support for specified innovations will make for such distortions). The more politics seeks to drive the innovation process in a selective way, the more questionable it becomes from a welfare perspective. This normative conclusion, in turn, derives from the knowledge problem which defies political solution but must be left to competition, that is to the occurrence of parallel 'welfare experiments' to be judged by the demand side of the market. As a precautionary clause one ought to add that policy failure does not represent a logical outcome either, or, put differently, that governments might increase welfare accidentally (our arguments cast severe doubts on innovation policy but, as a matter of logic, cannot *deduce* welfare-impairing effects of policy in a deterministic way).

As a first result one can conclude that evolutionary economics states the welfare problem of society in a more appropriate way than that of normative economics in the ordinary sense: there is no welfare function to be maximised even if the problem of constructing a social welfare function based on individual judgments were amenable to solution. Instead, the *process* of welfare generation comes to the fore. Liberty is a precondition because it gives firms or individuals the option to enter into economic experiments, namely to commercialise novelties and to bear the economic consequences in terms of profits or losses. If neither a theoretical observer nor the public nor politics is privileged to predict the outcome of experimental welfare identification, liberty is the only *political* way to deal with this problem. While liberty by no means guarantees that welfare *will* increase (because such deterministic statements turn out to be an alien element in any evolutionary conception), it establishes one crucial institutional prerequisite of such an increase. By the same token, there is no other feasible way to increase the welfare of society as long as society does not articulate one consistent definition of welfare.

The absence of an objective reference criterion also applies to the supply side of markets. Even if the demand side prefers more innovations to fewer due to the extension of opportunity sets, one cannot conclude that a state of more novelties compared to less should be realised. A possible consequence of this idea would be likewise the public promotion of novelties, e.g. in term of subsidies. Again, such a conclusion suffers from the knowledge problem; since a theoretical observer cannot foresee whether novelties will meet demand, a basis for cost-benefit analysis in order to determine the size and structure of public subsidies for innovation is lacking. Precisely for that reason, to recall a well-known argument given by Hayek, the economic competence should be transferred from some public sphere to the market agents who allocate resources for innovations due to their own profit expectations by making use of their individual assessment of market opportunities.

Innovation decisions are based on beliefs instead of knowledge.[5] Not only can decision making about innovation be erroneous like scientific knowledge; it also entails subjective elements such as world-views or beliefs about human needs which characterise entrepreneurship. Unlike collective decision making which requires the exchange of arguments and good reasons, entrepreneurs can escape this type of rationality and follow their crazy ideas if they are confident of success. Juxtaposing various entrepreneurial ideas in a thought-experiment would hardly lead to a consistent picture of economic opportunities (which the 'ideal socialist planner' (Arrow, 1962) could exploit if private decision making is not optimal). Rather, this picture would display inconsistencies and even contradictory entrepreneurial ideas of how to raise welfare. Nevertheless, this inconsistency does not represent a problem but is the solution to a problem.

Again, the institutional precondition is the non-interference of both public and private actors with individual decision making, to use a different word for liberty. From a welfare point of view, no valid answer can be given to the question whether and what kinds of innovations are desirable for society. This answer must be left to a process of experimentation and, in particular, the constituting institutions which channel the identification of welfare. Hence, no theoretical observer is privileged to offer a solution. However, a political consequence can be drawn as to the institutional setting; those institutions which increase liberty are socially desirable because they ensure the *possibility* of innovations. For the innovation process itself, no benchmark is at hand, once we accept the above-sketched normative position. (If, e.g., one society is late in adopting a particular innovation in comparison with others for reasons which have nothing to do with institutional restrictions, there is no way to disqualify its tardiness or even to term this outcome a welfare loss. Nor does liberal economic policy have the right to force innovations on society because this would contradict the essentials of liberalism).

This welfare conception, of course, deviates from prevalent policy norms attached to standard welfare economics. Neither the Pareto-criterion nor the dead-weight-loss analysis can be adopted without major qualification:

1. The process of market evolution does not lend itself to state-oriented judgments such as the Pareto-criterion. Arguably, the common sense behind the Pareto-criterion appears to be sensible from an evolutionary perspective, too: the statement that the welfare of society has been increased (and the state of the economy is thus preferable to a former state) reasonably demands that no individual undergoes a loss of income when others better their well-being, which includes the possibility that not all individuals participate in the rise of welfare. Although

this normative position makes sense in the medium term, it appears too moral in the short term, as it were. In the process of market evolution, individual assets including human capital are permanently revalued, whereas the creative destructions (Schumpeter) of some assets as a by-product of innovation is one potential outcome. Market evolution, however, is fuelled by the incentive of firms (individuals) to search for new opportunities in order to compensate a loss of income due to a devaluation of their assets. The outlook of some external compensation to be paid by the winners would erode this very mechanism so that the Pareto-criterion may be violated at least in the short term. Applying this norm in a strict sense would suggest negative judgments of any market evolution, which does not seem a sensible normative position from the perspective of evolutionary economics if no other mechanism of raising the welfare of society is feasible.[6] A critical point in particular is the universality of the Pareto-criterion; once accepted, it is a general norm and thus applicable to any comparisons of alternative states concerning welfare positions, no matter whether welfare losses are a temporary phenomenon in the course of market development. In the same vein, no attention is given to the question whether welfare improvements of all individuals need time to materialise. With no such qualifications the 'pure' (in the sense of universal) Pareto-norm must denounce any market process.

2. Innovators create monopolies by definition; monopoly rents prove to be the by-product of market evolution and defy interpretation as dead-weight losses. Again, the transfer of the standard norm 'welfare maximisation' to the market process entails inadequacies as long as the genesis of monopolies escapes attention. Used as a general standard for market deficiencies, dead-weight losses can only be avoided if the market process itself comes to a halt, which amounts to an absurd normative consequence.[7] While the evolutionary conception by no means accepts monopolies in general, it qualifies the analysis of welfare losses from a more general perspective. Whether welfare losses caused by monopolies are a case of market failure now depends on assessments concerning the likelihood of maintaining monopoly profits in view of potential competitors.

3. THE PITFALLS OF ACTIVE ECONOMIC POLICY

In the following I will make a distinction between active economic policy on the one hand and adaptive economic policy on the other. The former may also be termed a production approach of innovation, while the latter is institutional or 'ordnungspolitisch', to refer to a popular term of the German 'Social Market Economy' school. Evolutionary economics has accumulated many insights into the nature of innovation processes, which makes active economic policy a tempting alternative. However, the institutional approach is better prepared to cope with uncertainty, while the production approach is likely to introduce an additional element of uncertainty into society.

By active economic policy I mean a policy which aims to further the innovative process by intervening in the market. Measures for doing so include subsidisation of innovation in general, the subsidisation of selected 'key innovations', the selection of specific paths of innovation, e.g. through public expenditures or the subsidisation of specific patterns of transactions which promise to bring forth new technologies, that is networks. Active economic policy attempts to overcome delays in innovation or the diffusion of innovation in order to attain a first-mover advantage for the economy or, more generally, to exploit 'idle' innovative opportunities. Of particular interest is the contribution to positive externalities which promote specific innovations in regions. I exclude the promotion of basic knowledge gained at universities or publicly financed research institutions from active economic policy because it does not promote commercial innovations directly. Generally active economic policy takes the institutions as given: property rights, regulations or externalities are not changed in order to promote innovations.

Examples of active economic policy can easily be found in many countries and are expected to become even more prevalent in future. The European Union has not only committed itself to this type of policy but also bestows upon it a quasi-constitutional status. In the Maastricht Treaty of the EU, Title XVI (Industry) as well as Title XVIII (Research and technological development) define the promotion of new technologies in the aforementioned sense as one goal of the European Union. Streit and Mussler (1995) express their irritation about the fact that the European Treaty attaches the same importance to the so-called industrial policy (which is identical to active economic policy in our terms) as it does to rules which constitute the economic order in the EU. This implies that the latter can be traded off against industrial policy measures in case of conflict.

Active economic policy might invoke some results of the type described by evolutionary economics.[8] Its various theoretical branches emphasise the contingencies (accidental nature) of market processes and reject a positivistic view of markets which attaches to any outcome some explanation in terms of ex-post rationality. For instance, a multitude of technological opportunities which have not yet filtered out one innovation path can cause the retardation or even the overlooking of profitable innovation; private entrepreneurship by no means guarantees the exploitation of such opportunities based on innovation. The rise in welfare also depends on the early identification of innovative paths, which suggests a more active role for technological policy in order to attain a first-mover advantage for the domestic economy. Additional arguments would stress investment in human capital, learning-curve effects or the gains in reputation of firms when governments promote innovations. Time and again economic history records the tardiness of entrepreneurs who have failed to perceive the importance of key innovations.[9] Other examples point to the importance of technological clusters which can hardly be created by single entrepreneurs but prove to be of great importance for the continuation of innovative processes. Even liberals have to concede that innovative processes are accidental by nature, so that the effect on welfare is uncertain.

Although there is no compelling argument that active economic policy must fail in every case, several arguments militate against the tempting alternative of active political promotion of innovations:

1. Even if we know about the occurrence of various alternative technology paths which make for a window of opportunity, this abstract knowledge does not map onto concrete recommendations for policy makers as long as a theoretical observer is not privileged to identify the most promising innovative path in advance.
2. A wait-and-see strategy by entrepreneurs concerning innovations can be caused by bewildering and inconsistent market signals which do not point to one promising technological path. Active economic policy which promotes the preselection of technological alternatives might suppress the complexity of market signals and bet on the wrong path. The reality of market complexity cannot be ignored by policy makers simply by claiming superiority for political interpretation of market signals.
3. The administrative system proceeds according to its internal requirements (processes) which are difficult to bring into accord with the pace of market developments; in consequence, identifying the precise moment for investment in innovative paths when the window of opportunity is open appears to be a difficult mission for collective decision making in politics.
4. In the same vein doubts can be raised against the learning capacity of the political system once policy failure becomes obvious. Unlike entrepreneurs who act in the private sphere, policy makers have to justify a change of action publicly. Learning from errors offers chances for the opposition in parliament and gives reason to question the competence of government; consequently, policy makers are well-advised to avoid

reactions to changed market signals but hold on to their former course of action as long as possible. Decision making about innovations often requires quick decisions as well as revision of decisions, which is not a proper part of political competence in a democracy; here, policy makers have a stronger incentive to ensure the legitimacy of policies than to reassess them according to benchmarks.

5. Clusters as well as industrial networks play an important role in the (enduring) creation of innovations but are ontologically misunderstood if innovation policy attempts to model them. In Nozick's terms they represent an invisible-hand phenomenon, which in our context means that they emerge as a sum of entrepreneurial decisions but do not derive from one single plan. Their ontological nature is more comparable to Schelling's settlement patterns (ghettos) than to public infrastructure planned by administrations. In consequence, our knowledge about the importance of industrial clusters will not lead us very far in practice because we cannot design what is to emerge spontaneously. Rather, clusters represent an ex-post category for theoretical description but hardly a blueprint for politics.
6. The prospect of public support for innovations changes the incentive structure of the economy and favours those agents who have better access to government; unfortunately, this group is not identical with the most competent agents in the economic sense. A distortion of competition will result which tends to further the capability of communicating with the political system instead of perceiving profitable opportunity. The innovation politics of the EU offers some striking examples of an emerging 'political economy', as it were.[10]
7. The problem of creating new interest groups as an inadvertant side-effect of innovation policy can hardly be by-passed through expertise. Expertise itself creates an incentive to continue a former course of policy, in particular if scientific experts such as economists or engineers become specialised in this field of government consulting and thus create a comparative advantage in the attraction of resources (funds). The chief incentive for scientific advisers and consultants will be oriented to modifications instead of renouncement of innovation policy; only the former offers the chance of receiving further orders from their governmental clients, while the latter amounts to a self-damaging behaviour in the competition for governmental consultive contracts. (Exceptional examples confirm the rules of that game).
8. Public support of innovation runs counter to the rules of a market economy and has to be investigated from that fundamental point of view. Unlike entrepreneurs, policy makers lack liability for erroneous decisions in the field of innovation policy. This very fact calls active

> economic policy into question. In market economies it is difficult to give reasons for compulsory charges to be allocated as risk capital, that is for purposes which are attainable by private decision making, too. If, in addition, failures in innovation policy escape the attention of voters, something which is likely to occur, policy makers can avoid responsibility for their decisions even in political terms. Again, this bespeaks doubts concerning the quality of decision making.

Note that these arguments do not rest on a positivist interpretation of market outcomes; neither reality will become rational nor rationality real, to allude to Hegel's well-known phrase. Rather, contingencies in evolutionary markets are prevalent and so, too, will be deficiencies in the welfare of society. However, this view of markets to which evolutionary economics has contributed does not support active economic policy which rivals private decision making. Chief among the reasons is the experimental nature of decision making concerning innovations which cannot be supplanted by politics without introducing new risks. Implicitly we would presume the supremacy of one theoretical observer (to which politics has access) who is able to identify 'welfare gaps' caused by delays in innovation from his privileged position. Indeed, evolutionary economics denies the existence of such supremacy as long as one takes the notion of novelty seriously and holds onto a liberal concept of welfare.

4. ADAPTIVE ECONOMIC POLICY AS AN ALTERNATIVE

This scepticism towards active economic policy, in turn, does not bespeak the irrelevance of all economic policy with regard to innovations. In the remainder of the chapter, I outline a concept of economic policy which is in line with our above-stated reflections.

The idea of adaptive policy desists from supporting innovations directly. By adaptive policy, I understand policy making which is oriented to the institutional environment alongside the innovative processes. Such institutions concern property rights, competition rules and regulations which affect transaction costs germane to innovations. In the course of the market process institutions can become maladapted and need to be changed.

From a property-rights perspective novelties result from a new combination of resources. As institutions channel the way in which resources are used, they also influence the emergence of novelties, depending on the restrictiveness of institutions. In modern economies these restrictions usually extend those limits identified by economic liberalism, that is the non-interference of economic activities with other private spheres (externalities). In other cases novelties give rise to new cases of externalities and call for new rules which prevent the well-being of other individuals from being impaired by novelties. Both cases represent important examples for adaptive economic policy and sometimes defy easy solution. In the latter case, for instance, the definition of negative externalities can depend on scientific knowledge which confirms or refutes the presumption that novelties such as genetically modified organisms (GMO) or mobile transmitter stations impair the health of human beings. Even if no scientific arguments support the negative impact of novelties so far, the question remains how economic policy should handle the preliminary state of scientific knowledge if irreversible impairments are at least conceivable. From the above-sketched liberal point of view, no reasons support the designing of institutions conducive to novelties without regard to their *potential* negative externalities on others.[11]

If no externalities are involved, the perspective of evolutionary economics can be linked to well-known liberal arguments pointing to welfare impediments of tight regulations which serve the interests of special groups. This criticism holds even though the restrictiveness of regulations is mitigated by the innovativeness of individuals. By making use of their creativity, individuals not only bring forth novelties but also gain the ability to circumvent institutions which restrict their behaviour. Tight regulations, however, are not recommended for the purpose of eliciting innovations in the economy. The welfare of society benefits more if market agents shift their perception directly to opportunities, that means in the absence of such restrictions which have no grounds in the protection of other individuals for economically legitimate reasons (consumer safety, foodstuff regulations, health and safety at work, environmental regulation and similar reasons for regulation). In this regard, deregulation extends liberty and thus has to be put onto the agenda of economic policy which subscribes to evolutionary economics.

Of particular interest for economic policy is the selection mechanism for novelties offered on markets. First of all, evolutionary economics changes the priorities of political targets and attaches more importance to competition policy than to industrial policy. If we stick to the position that the welfare impact of novelties is to be assessed by individuals (firms) on the demand side, there is no room for public interference with the selection process in markets. The support of allegedly efficient global players or mergers and even its toleration through a weakening of merger control are candidates for critique. The achievement of a dominant market position by firms (sometimes with public support such as tax rebates) can hardly be justified on grounds of efficiency when efficiency gets second priority in relation to innovation. From the viewpoint of evolutionary economics, cost savings will not compensate for the weakness of competition if, as a result, innovative entrants are prevented from market entry.

For the same reason large firms which are deemed to be ahead of technological development should not be exempted from competition law. Contrary to EU competition law, which holds out the possibility of a privileged treatment for European global high-tech firms, the distortionary effects of competition should be emphasised. This revision of perspective derives from doubts about the so-called Schumpeter-hypothesis according to which, roughly speaking, innovations depend more on current profits than on competition; one background assumption of this perspective can be seen in what one might call the 'production theory of innovation', which stresses the capability for innovation due to profits but downgrades the necessity to innovate, i.e. the competitive environment of firms. Even if current firms in oligopolistic markets drive technological progress at present, adaptive economic policy refuses to bet on one successful industrial structure for future innovations. What matters is the openness of markets which permanently checks the suitability of industrial structures, whereas a policy of 'picking the winners' orientates itself to the past.[12]

The denial of ends-oriented criteria for market evolution also applies to further instruments of economic policy, namely designing or revising of institutions. North (1990) rightly stresses the potential interference of institutions with market performance. In particular, maladapted innovations turn out to increase transaction costs and thus impede reallocation which is the basic operation of dynamic economies. From that perspective one can follow Engerer and Voigt (2002) who, in accordance with a well-accepted view held by New Institutional Economics, take high transaction costs as an indicator for welfare losses. However, circumspection is required if we draw a clear-cut conclusion concerning institutional policy. In doing so, institutions have to be assessed with respect to their impact on transaction costs, which holds out the possibility of revising institutions accordingly. Such a conclusion would be premature as long as the causes of high transaction costs due to institutions are neglected. As we have seen above, transaction costs will rise if institutions restrict opportunities and induce individuals (firms) to circumvent restrictions in order to realise profitable opportunities. North (1990) made reference to such institutions (instigated by vested interests) which have given rise to a long-term slow-down of economic performance in history, if not a long-term decline of the country in question.

However, transaction costs can also temporarily rise as a result of market evolution which does not encounter such institutional interference. On the micro level, market evolution necessarily makes for intransparency as a result of variation (innovation). Screening innovations on the demand side will increase transaction costs because of informational deficiencies about novelties; for instance, quality attributes of innovations will be unknown in advance and may raise both information and control costs of transactions. If the economy encounters a wave of novelties in a certain period, the total level of transaction costs is supposed to be *higher* in comparison to a more static economy. But this very situation proves to be an impediment to the diffusion of innovations which are held up solely because of a lack of information on the demand side.

On this account it is tempting to revise institutions politically in order to lower transaction costs. This can be done by regulations dealing with quality attributes so that innovators have to fulfil certain characteristics when they intend to commercialise new products. Regulations concerning consumer protection are candidates for the adaptation of institutions to new products; as a consequence, consumers reduce transaction costs and are better prepared to digest the abundance of information about novelties.

Transaction costs, however, do not depend solely on institutions set by authorities (external institutions). Internal institutions also impinge on transaction cost and are formed by market agents who voluntarily agree upon quality requirements in order to promote the emergence of markets. Not least will intransparency in markets encourage new entrepreneurial opportunities, namely for brokers who specialise in the supply of information for customers; as a result, novelties intensify the division of labour and knowledge. These internal capabilities of markets have to be taken into account before economic policy avails itself of the top-down approach to institutional design. Notably, the emergence of better-adapted internal institutions needs time and so will the entrepreneurial discovery of new opportunities dealing with information about new products or services. In this regard we encounter the common characteristics of self-organisation which lends itself to the identification of encompassing market failures.

However, such an external critique implicitly presumes an objective benchmark for competition which is difficult to fix in the process of experimenting with welfare (see above). For that reason adaptive economic policy in our sense should be reluctant to lower transaction costs by (re)designing external institutions. Although governments can create transparency in markets in this way, it is likely to interfere with the welfare-generating process. Regulations can only lower transaction costs by setting new restrictions on economic activities. As long as these restricted activities could meet consumer demands without imposing external effects on others, no intervention should be undertaken. In such circumstances economic policy should attach second priority to the lowering of transaction costs, even if the diffusion of innovations or the emergence of new markets undergoes impediment. Put differently, economic policy should not pursue innovation as an end in itself.[13]

Instead, a more liberal orientation to economic policy is better prepared to cope with the diversity of markets. Priority should be given to the emergence of internal institutions as well as to the discovery of entrepreneurial opportunities dealing with information. Again, policy should identify regulations which impair the emergence of service enterprises. For instance, civil laws which define legal capital requirements for founding a firm may turn out to be maladapted in view of lower capital requirements in the emerging service sector. An example of this kind of potential maladaption of civil law is given by the German economy where entrepreneurs have begun to found 'Limiteds' (limited liability companies) in accordance with British law after the European Court opened up this possibility. In the past, stricter German rules have not impaired the founding of firms in the economy which was dominated by manufacturing; there were good reasons for the legal requirements being in line with the economic requirements to launch a new enterprise. At present, however, these rules turn out to be maladapted and indicate a need of political revision. Although the possibility of adapting the rules of EU member states without relocating offers loopholes and thus mitigates the need for political reform, policy should make use of the latter option.[14] Transaction costs expended in the attempt to become acquainted with foreign rules are avoidable and can be lowered by adapting domestic rules.[15]

5. CONCLUDING REMARKS

Our considerations have been presented in a sketchy way in order to give a flavour of the orientation guided by evolutionary economics. Interestingly, no particular policy recommendations have been devoted to human capital from an evolutionary perspective, although this notion plays an important role in the current debate on economic growth. Two reasons can be given for this omission. Firstly, the public support of scientific knowledge deserves no specific emphasis inasmuch as this type of knowledge represents a public good which has limited chances to be produced by private activities. This type of knowledge defines an indispensable part of economic policy which aims at the promotion of economic evolution. However, evolutionary economics subscribes to standard theory in this respect and so far has no additional theoretical perspective. A second reason is given by the revised perspective on human capital which evolutionary economics takes towards the accumulation of knowledge alongside the market process. Generally, evolutionary economics will not deny the importance of knowledge but questions the possibility of endowing market agents from outside with that specific type of knowledge which drives market evolution. Entrepreneurial activities are based on beliefs about market opportunities which prompt a specific compilation of knowledge in order to pursue their economic ideas. In that respect a theoretical observer lacks the possibility of identifying relevant knowledge which firms can successfully apply. From the evolutionary perspective, knowledge results from entrepreneurial alertness and thus renders more characteristics of economic output than input. What economic policy can influence is the institutional context in which knowledge is accumulated but hardly knowledge itself. The institutional context, in turn, pertains to the competitive environment of market agents.[16]

Our interpretation of evolutionary economics is inspired by Hayek's reflections on market evolution (Hayek 1996). The fundamental idea emanates from the impossibility of describing the economy from the viewpoint of a theoretical observer if welfare generation is conceptionalised as a process of experimenting with welfare. Notably, this perspective leaves the presumptions of normative methodological individualism unchanged but arrives at different political conclusions. Evolutionary economics has good reason to change this perspective in so far as it cannot neglect the role of innovation for economic welfare. However, if individual choice decides on the welfare impact of innovations, evolutionary theories have to desist from supplanting individual choice by outside valuation.

Note that this interpretation of evolutionary economics with regard to politics differs from that of other scholars working in this field who prefer a more active role for the state. However, for reasons stated above I suggest that one reconcile evolutionary economics with economic liberalism. Besides, the evolutionary perspective holds out the possibility of taking a fresh approach to liberalism without repeating its dogmatism. If the elements of welfare are unknown in advance, the whole process of identifying welfare depends on liberty for market agents on both sides of the market. For lack of external benchmarks, economic policy cannot avoid accepting the preliminary results of market evolution but has to open the process for further experiments with welfare. Liberty plays the most important role here in contrast to ends-oriented criteria on which debates on economic policy normally focus: the number of innovations as well as specific technological paths do not represent ends in themselves, even if theorists or policy makers deem them to be of highest importance for the domestic eonomy. From an evolutionary perspective, market outcomes are always imperfect and this very imperfection offers a chance to drive market evolution.

NOTES

1. This contribution has profited from discussions which I had in the Evolutionary Committee of the Verein für Socialpolitik and with my discussant Lambert Koch; I also thank Hans Nutzinger, Sven Meth, and in particular Mark Peacock for discussions and helpful comments.
2. See Vosskamp (2002). An early in-depth criticism of the deductive approach with application to standard welfare economics can be found in Albert (1975).
3. Other attempts have been made by Meier/Slembeck (1998), Slembeck (1997) and Koch (1996).
4. Even the notion of 'liberal nationalism' (Tamir 1993) would contradict to the cosmopolitan conception of liberalism.
5. This statement slightly modifies Hayek who only speaks of knowledge.
6. This insight does not exclude the support of losers in some dramatic cases of income losses. The reader may think of older persons who are simply impeded by their age from reacting to the creative destruction of their human capital, although they might be willing to do so.
7. See Metcalfe (2003).
8. See, for example, Forndahl/Brenner (2003), Lembke (2002) or Pyka/Küppers (2002).
9. In the late 1970s German industrial leaders were criticised for being too late in identifying the market potential of the new generation of consumer electronics. The reader may also recall that even the star of IT, Bill Gates, was late in perceiving the overwhelming importance of the World Wide Web in the early 90s.
10. For a critique see Streit/Mussler (1995).
11. The GMO case is difficult to judge from a liberal point of view: if GMO drive out other plants via offspring which cannot be controlled, individuals lack choice of opportunities no matter what economic policy decides; if, on the other hand, GMO are prohibited, those consumers who prefer this innovation lack choice; in the reverse case, individuals can not buy non-GMO even if they want; then they are forced into a choice and undergo a loss of well-being *compared to the status quo ante*.
12 'Picking the winners and helping the losers' has become the motto of industrial policy referring to the Maastricht Treaty of the EU.
13. For a more detailed investigation of the bottom-up approach to institutional policy, see Wegner (2003).
14. For that reason economic policy is well-advised to accept the New Systems Competition in general; a detailed investigation can be found in Wegner (2004); Sinn (2003) presents a critique from the perspective of equilibrium theory.
15. Another example of adaptive economic policy which investigates the adaptation of property rights to novelties can be found in Hutter (1989).
16. A by-product of this perspective on knowledge is the modification of Arrow's (1962) public-good analogy which has derived a market failure problem too straightforwardly; for an investigation see Metcalfe (2003).

REFERENCES

Albert, H. (ed.), (1975), *Aufklärung und Steuerung*, Hamburg: Rowohlt.

Arrow, K.J. (1962), 'Economic welfare and the allocation of resources for invention', in N. Rosenberg (ed.), *The Economics of Technical Change*, Harmondsworth: Penguin, 1971, pp. 164–81.

Cordato, R.E. (1992), *Welfare Economics and Externalities in an Open Ended Universe: A Modern Austrian Perspective*, Boston: Kluwer Academic Publishers Group.

Engerer, H. and S. Voigt (2002), 'Institutionen und Transformation – Mögliche Politikimplikationen der Neuen Institutionenökonomik'; in K.F. Zimmermann (ed.), *Neue Entwicklungen in der Wirtschaftswissenschaft*, Heidelberg: Physica, pp. 149–215.
Forndahl and Brenner (eds) (2003), *Cooperation, Networks and Institutions in Regional Innovation Systems*, Cheltenham, UK and Northampton, MA, USA: Edward Elgar.
Hayek, F.A. von (1996), *Individualism and Economic Order*, Chicago: Chicago University Press.
Hutter, M. (1989), *Die Produktion von Recht. Eine selbstreferentielle Theorie der Wirtschaft, angewandt auf den Fall des Arzneimittelpatentrechts*, Tübingen: Mohr.
Koch, L.T. (1996), *Evolutorische Wirtschaftspolitik: Eine elementare Analyse mit entwicklungspolitischen Beispielen*, Tübingen: Mohr.
Ladeur, K.-H. (2000), *Negative Freiheitsrechte und gesellschaftliche Selbstorganisation*, Tübingen: Mohr.
Lembke, J. (2002), *Competition for Technological Leadership: EU Policy for High Technology*, Cheltenham, UK and Northampton, MA, USA: Edward Elgar.
Meier, A. and Slembeck, T. (1998), *Wirtschaftspolitik – ein kognitiv-evolutionärer Ansatz*, Munich: Oldenbourg.
Metcalfe, J.S. (2003), 'Equilibrium and evolutionary foundations of competition and technology policy: new perspectives on the division of labour and the innovation process', in P. Pelikan and G. Wegner (eds), *Evolutionary Approaches to Economic Policy*, Cheltenham, UK and Northampton, MA, USA: Edward Elgar, pp. 162–90.
North, D.C. (1990), *Institutions, Institutional Change and Economic Performance*, Cambridge: Cambridge University Press.
Pyka, A. and G. Küppers (eds) (2002), *Innovation Networks. Theory and Practice*, Cheltenham, UK and Northampton, MA, USA: Edward Elgar.
Rowley, C.K. and A.T. Peacock (1975), *Welfare Economics – A Liberal Restatement*, London: Martin Robertson.
Sinn, H.-W. (2003), *The New Systems Competition*, Oxford: Basil Blackwell.
Slembeck, T. (1997), 'The formation of economic policy: a cognitive-evolutionary approach to policy making', *Constitutional Political Economy*, **8**, 225–54.
Streit, M.E. and W. Mussler (1995), 'Wettbewerb der systeme und das binnenmarktprogramm der Europäischen Union' in L. Gerken (ed.), *Europa zwischen Ordnungswettbewerb 96 und Harmonisierung*, Berlin, Heidelberg, New York: Springer, pp. 75–107.
Tinbergen, J. (1952), *On the Theory of Economic Policy*, Amsterdam: North-Holland.
Voigt, S. and D. Kiwit (1998), 'The role and evolution of beliefs, habits, moral norms, and institutions', in H. Giersch (ed.), *Merits and Limits of Markets*, Berlin et al: Springer, pp. 83–108.
Vosskamp, R. (2002), 'Evolutorische Finanzwissenschaft: Problemstellungen und Lösungsansätze', in Lehmann-Waffenschmidt (ed.), *Perspektiven des Wandels – Evolutorische Ökonomik in der Anwendung*, Marburg: Metropolis, pp. 427–56.
Wegner, G. (2003), 'Evolutionary markets and the design of institutional policy', in P. Pelikan and G. Wegner (eds), *The Evolutionary Analysis of Economic Policy*, Cheltenham, UK and Northampton, MA, USA: Edward Elgar, pp. 46–66.

Wegner, G. (2004), *Nationalstaatliche Institutionen im Wettbewerb*, Berlin: de Gruyter.
Wohlgemuth, M. (2003), 'Democracy as an evolutionary method', in P. Pelikan and G. Wegner (eds), *The Evolutionary Analysis of Economic Policy*, Cheltenham, UK and Northampton, MA, USA: Edward Elgar, pp. 96–127.

4. Historical economics and evolutionary economic policy – Coasean perspectives*

Matthias Klaes

INTRODUCTION

The work of Ronald H. Coase is typically discussed in the context of the neoliberal approach of the younger Chicago School, in particular with reference to certain economic policy implications of the Coase Theorem, and to Coase's preference for the market to coordinate economic activity. While Stephen Medema (1996, 1999) and others have drawn attention in the meanwhile to the difference between Coase's work and George Stigler's (1966) 'Coase Theorem', the relationship between Coase's institutional analysis and 'mainstream law and economics' (Kerber 2000, pp. 149–56) has remained less clear. Coase counts as one of the co-founders of this subdiscipline, which seems to suggest a continuity with neoliberal positions such as Richard Posner's. However, this reading would gloss over significant differences (Coase 1993; Williamson 1993). One can observe a similar appropriation of Coase's work by the orthodox wing of the New Institutional Economics (Furubotn 1994). Given this threefold doctrinal canonisation of Coase's work, his reception in evolutionary economics, which has been mostly critical, comes as no surprise.

Not all authors share this critical reading. Nicolai Foss (1994), for example, has begun to speak of two Coasean traditions in order to draw out Coase's potential for evolutionary economics. In the context of present debates on how an economic policy informed by the perspectives offered by evolutionary economics should look (Slembeck 1997, Wegner 1997, Hodgson 1999), this poses the question to what extent a re-evaluation of Coase's work may offer a useful contribution to these ongoing debates.

As a first aim, the present chapter seeks to rebut the predominant neoliberal reading of the Coasean research programme. Coase's neoliberal reputation is largely based on narrow readings of 'The problem of social cost' (Coase 1960, 'SC' from now on). SC sums up and generalises an argument first made in the context of a proposal to allocate the radio frequency spectrum through an auction mechanism rather than administrative decisions of the US Federal Communications Commission (Coase 1959). In contrast to this deregulative and seemingly anti-interventionist potential of SC (see Posner 1975), 'The nature of the firm' (Coase 1937; henceforth 'NF') – the second article responsible for Coase's fame – was written by a self-confessed socialist (Coase 1996, 206; see Campbell and Klaes 2000), setting up a basic tension underlying Coase's work which forms the basis of the reading of SC defended below.

The second and main aim of this chapter is to recover this tension on the level of economic policy and combine it with the historical perspective offered in much of Coase's other – unduly neglected – work in order to clarify important aspects of evolutionary economic policy. Neither is it thus the intention of the following discussion to establish Coase as an evolutionary economist, nor to offer a detailed historical exegesis of his numerous writings. Given the widespread tendency to see his work as a neoliberal institutionalist variation of economic orthodoxy, the present chapter seeks to open up the debate of its evolutionary potential.

Starting out with a discussion of the concept of institutional direction in Coase's work, which is central to its policy dimension, the second section of this chapter looks at the role of the concept of direction in NF, paying particular attention to the context in which it was conceived: the contemporary debate on socialist economic planning. The third section develops this analysis further to establish the primacy of institutional direction as the core proposition of Coase's economic policy perspective. The fourth section demonstrates how this primacy of institutional direction is the direct outgrowth of what will be identified as Coase's historical economics, in which developmental thinking assumes a key role. This leads in the fifth section to a discussion of important parallels to evolutionary economics. The sixth section, finally, draws together the implications of the preceding discussion for an evolutionary economic policy.

THE PRINCIPLE OF DIRECTION

NF counts today as a core contribution to the theory of the firm (Holmström and Tirole 1989). Its main propositions regarding the transaction-cost rationale of the firm are well-known. The crucial economic policy dimension of Coase's early article, by contrast, has attracted much less attention, if it has been noticed at all. Coase was not only concerned with providing a consistent definition of the firm concept, he also actively engaged with the contemporary debate on socialist planning and with

Hayek's position in that debate in particular (Campbell and Klaes 2005). Initially Coase seems to confine his analysis in NF to the relationship between price theory and the economic concept of the firm (NF, 387–9). This discussion is then however translated into the terminology of the planning debate (see Hayek 1935): 'Indeed, it is often considered to be an objection to economic planning that it merely tries to do what is already done by the price mechanism' (NF, 387). Coase counters Hayek's (1933) criticism of central planning as follows: 'Those who object to economic planning on the grounds that the problem is solved by price movements can be answered by pointing out that there is planning within our economic system . . . which is akin to what is normally called economic planning' (NF, 387–8). Coase is thus keen to transfer the full force of his criticism of received price theory to the realm of the planning debate, by suggesting that an entrepreneur runs his business according to the same principles which a central planner would apply to the steering of the whole economy. He refers to this second coordination mechanism, which he holds is different in kind from the price mechanism and should not be confounded with the planning activity of individuals which underlies both, as 'direction' (NF, 399, 404).

NF thus adds support to the socialist position in the planning debate by underlining a fundamental inescapability of regimes of central planning in capitalist economies. What is more, it adds a set of conditions under which planning will be more efficient than economic coordination through prices. This argument comes however with a twist: Coase's transaction-cost argument rests on the premise that ultimately, the optimal mix within the economic system between centralised planning and decentralised prices is determined by the forces of competition.

Therefore, a more detailed look at Coase's views on competition is necessary. When he worked out the main ideas underlying NF in the early 1930s, his knowledge of economics consisted largely of the principles of price theory as he had encountered them in Arnold Plant's seminars of 1931. At the core of this conceptual lens was the emphasis on 'invisible-hand' processes: 'From him [Plant] I learned that producers maximise profits, that producers compete, and therefore that prices tend to equal costs and the composition of output to be that which consumers value most highly' (Coase 1991, p. 37). It is this basic perspective which underlies virtually all of Coase's subsequent major contributions to economics.

As an example, consider Coase's analysis of industry structure (NF, 394–8). Having located the rationale of the firm in the existence of marketing costs and conversely, the rationale of market co-ordination in the existence of intra-firm costs of organising production, Coase initially argues from a partial-equilibrium perspective. Assuming perfect divisibility and homogeneity of transactions, the boundary of the firm is determined by that transaction for which marginal marketing and organising costs are equal.

It is often overlooked that Coase considered this partial analysis only as a preliminary step that needs to be broadened into the kind of multimarket equilibrium analysis typical of early neoclassical economics (see Blaug 1990). In addition, he explicitly considers transactional indivisibility and heterogeneity. In this extended analysis, the size of a firm *F* is determined jointly by the marketing costs of the marginal transaction, by the cost structure of the industry to which the firm belongs, and ultimately, due to the relevance of multiproduct firms (NF, 402–3), by the organising costs across the whole economy. *F* grows to the point where the marginal transaction is more efficiently executed either across the market or within other firms. In the latter case, the market is only superseded completely if *F* is able, through merger, to internalise *all* stages of production previously undertaken elsewhere. Coase sticks thus to the marginal principle, but rather than doing so out of formal considerations his thinking is driven by a concern for realistic analysis. Transactions are not assumed to be perfectly divisible in this form of discrete marginal analysis.

Further qualifications become necessary once the heterogeneity of transactions is taken into account (NF, 396). In general, heterogeneity rules out speaking of the level of marketing or organising costs in general. Instead, the particularities of the relevant marginal transaction under each mode of co-ordination need to be considered. This amounts to the implicit acknowledgement that industries are populated by heterogeneous firms. What is more, the marginal transaction that determines the efficient boundary of firm *F* is not found ex ante, through optimising calculus on the part of the entrepreneur. Rather it emerges out of a process of trial and error by which entrepreneurs across all firms continuously test the limits of profitable expansion.

For our discussion, the following aspects of Coase's analysis of entrepreneurial decision making within an overall context of multimarket moving equilibrium are of particular relevance. First, Coase refused to follow the turn towards the concept of Pareto-efficiency that took hold of the increasingly formalist neoclassical tradition of the early decades of the 20th century. A comparatively understood 'value of production', as the yardstick of economic efficiency that he employed across all levels of analysis, be it the individual firm or the economy as a whole, has kept him firmly grounded in the Marshallian tradition.

Second, Coase did not follow the neoclassical tradition in its assumption of a priori omniscient and faultlessly economising individuals. One can find this commitment unambiguously expressed in the following statement, where Coase distances himself from certain orthodox currents in the new institutional economics: '[T]here is one respect in which I hold a heretical view. Most economists make the assumption that man is a rational utility maximiser. This seems to me both unnecessary and misleading. . . . Let us . . . start with man as he is' (Coase 1984, 231). Given Coase's overall realist commitment (Mäki 1998), this statement can plausibly be taken to express a programmatic orientation that informs all of his work, which largely proceeds on the basis of the multimarket equilibrium analysis discussed above, combined with the assumption of local 'common-sense' rationality of economic agents.

Third, while Coase's analysis is no doubt guided by an overall commitment to equilibrium thinking, the relevant concept is that of moving equilibrium (e.g. NF, 405; see Hayek 1928; Schlicht 1997), within the context of his local rationality concept and the continuous experimentation on the part of economic agents that comes with it. As a fourth point, finally, Coase's extended analysis in the second part of section II of NF, in particular following the assumption of heterogeneous transactions between vertically integrated multiproduct firms, implicitly presumes a heterogeneous population of firms within a given industry.

THE PRIMACY OF INSTITUTIONAL DIRECTION

By pointing to the crucial role played by the debate on economic planning in NF, the previous section laid the ground for placing Coase's binary juxtaposition of direction and market conceptually into an economic policy context. In NF, the tension between these alternative modes of economic coordination is resolved on the basis of Coase's multimarket equilibrium analysis and traditional neoclassical price theory. The present section extends the discussion to SC. It will be argued that SC turns on a more profoundly probing elaboration of the co-ordination problem than NF, by calling attention to the principles of direction that underlie the operation of markets themselves.

The basic starting point of SC is a clarification of the commodity concept, unwittingly taking up a fundamental point most forcefully pressed by Commons (1934). Coase is adamant in stressing that the entities traded in markets are not physical goods and services but bundles of property rights. Importantly, the bundling of rights itself is negotiable and subject to the market process. From this and the basic implications of price theory, what has become known as the Coase Theorem follows immediately. In perfect markets, initial and equilibrium allocation are independent of one another. Therefore, the initial allocation of property rights has no effect on their equilibrium allocation. This straightforward yet somewhat startling result follows from Coase's commitment to a multimarket perspective that already informed NF: the market mechanism allocates resources on the basis of their alternative-use values. They therefore end up in those employments where their contribution to the total value of production – Coase's pre-Paretian efficiency standard – is highest.

Coase's main interest in SC is directed to an economy subject to positive transaction costs (see Medema 1999).[1] Similarly to the analysis in NF, this leads him to embrace a form of comparative institutional analysis that proceeds from the alternatives of directing resources according to some central plan versus their decentral allocation on the basis of market transactions, which are now conceptualised as the result of bilateral negotiations ('Coase mechanism', see Schlicht 1996). SC moves further than NF however by drawing a distinction between direction of resources in firms, and direction by the state as a super-firm (SC, 17). This super-firm stands apart in that it is able to escape competition with other firms (though not necessarily with other states), is not bound to transact solely on the basis of contract law, and has means of enforcement of agreements that go beyond the internal control mechanisms of conventional firms. There are thus two alternative modes of co-ordination to consider now alongside the market, which have to be evaluated according to their relative transaction-cost properties.

Casting the state as a super-firm exposes the central dichotomy of direction and price mechanism most clearly in Coase's thinking. In the context of economic policy considerations, this opens up the question of a potential bias in favour of one of these two modes of co-ordination. Should it turn out that a principled preference for market co-ordination can be identified, one should not hesitate to regard Coase as a neoliberal exponent of the (younger) Chicago School. Yet, '[f]rom these considerations it follows that direct governmental regulation will not necessarily give better results than leaving the problem to be solved by the market or the firm. But equally there is no reason why, on occasion, such governmental administrative regulation should not lead to an improvement in economic efficiency' (SC, 18). As further argued in the next section, Coase assumes an agnostic position in respect of the relative merits of direction and market, rejecting the yardstick of perfect markets that can be found in conventional welfare economics. The nagging 'on occasion' in the above quotation indicates though that Coase's agnosticism is of a methodological kind, leaving room in SC for a prima facie presumption in favour of market co-ordination. Still, the crucial point is that no attempt is made to defend this disposition on dogmatic grounds, allowing only empirical arguments as admissible for comparative considerations.

There is however a further dimension to Coase's discussion of alternative modes of coordination in SC which balances Coase's prima facie disposition towards market exchange with a principled defence of direction, reaching beyond its antithetical position vis-a-vis the price mechanism as expressed in NF. It is the chief concern of SC to demonstrate the relevance of the initial distribution of property rights in an economy subject to positive transaction costs. Due to the differential costs of using the market that result from alternative initial distributions of rights, different distributions will lead to different social products. This means that both legislative processes and court proceedings play a central economic role through the resulting reallocation or rebundling of property rights.

SC addresses therefore a dimension of economic direction that is no longer reducible to market principles. Coase regards the role of direction as more pervasive than the background powers afforded by a libertarian understanding of the state as a 'nightwatchman', which restrict the role of direction to the definition and maintenance of the legal framework within which market exchange operates. On the one hand, centralised direction is operative via the courts, in particular wherever cost-benefit arguments leave room for discretion on the part of judges or juries. On the other hand, the state is not a priori denied the potential to bring about comparatively more efficient solutions than alternative modes of co-ordination. The relevant question in each case is not whether but how markets should be directed.[2]

While those aspects of NF that answer to the debate on economic planning emphasise the principle of direction but keep it ultimately subordinate to the optimality principle of competition, SC develops the argument further in at least two respects. First, as outlined above, market processes themselves rest on the principle of direction. Second, Coase acknowledges implicitly that the optimality principle of competition must in the end be seen as a further aspect of blackboard economics. If the forces of competition were indeed sufficient to bring about an optimal balance between the alternative modes of economic co-ordination, SC itself would beg the question: it would then be futile to point to the diminishing returns of an increasingly centrally administered economy. It is precisely because in economic policy terms, direction is primary to the market that Coase argues for the practical relevance of a case-study based but historically oriented research agenda that allows policy assessment in terms of a comparative analysis of institutional trajectories. Let us explore this unduly neglected aspect of Cosean analysis in a bit more detail.

HISTORICAL ECONOMICS: A DEVELOPMENTAL APPROACH

In a static economy, the role of economic policy is reduced to defining and implementing the preferred institutional framework and the rules according to which market transactions and other economic activity should take place. Following this initial setup, the mandate of economic policy would consist in the monitoring and enforcement of these rules. It would be misguided to speak in this context of the primacy of institutional direction. Coase's approach to economic policy must however be read in the context of his numerous case studies on the economic implications of various communication technologies. These case studies, which notwithstanding Steven Medema's (1994) pioneering contribution have only recently begun to inform the secondary literature on Coase's legacy (e.g. Pratten 2001), clearly exhibit a developmental understanding of economic institutions (e.g. Coase 1939, 1947, 1955, 1961a, 1979). A central recurrent motive is the continuous development of the institutional structure of production in its interaction with technical progress.

Coase explored the development of the British and US telecommunications industry and various forms of technological competition. For example, he looked at inner-city messenger services in the light of emerging broadcasting technologies, or at the competition between wire-based and wireless broadcasting. Each emerging technology prompts existing regulatory regimes to be defended or revised, which the case studies typically portray as a struggle between market co-ordination and state regulation and control. Coase locates the formative factor in each case not in any technological determinants but shows that a detailed historical analysis of the relevant influences is necessary for a thorough institutional appreciation of the situation.[3]

After his emigration to the US, Coase found himself increasingly contributing to contemporary questions of economic policy, notably regarding the allocation of broadcasting frequencies in the US, including testimonies to Congressional hearings (Coase 1959, 14–18, 1961b, 1962). His economic policy recommendations are primarily based on his case-study research prior to the publication of SC and do not draw on transaction-cost arguments at all, being more concerned with the effect of alternative specifications of property rights. The reciprocal nature of harmful side-effects must have become clear to him as a result of his long-standing interest in issues of broadcasting signal interference and its putative relevance for arguments against a marked-based allocation of frequencies. Nevertheless, his doubts regarding the advantages of central allocation of frequencies are primarily based on an empirical assessment of the potential disadvantages such a solution would bring with it.

Coase's historico-empirical method consists of three parts. His case studies typically start out with a historical retrospective on the emergence of a particular communication technology, tracing the economic and institutional effects of the technology in question. At this stage, Coase draws predominantly from secondary historical literature. This step is followed by a more detailed analysis of a controversy centring on the technology. Here, his attention is focused on the motives of stakeholders and other interest groups. His sources at this second stage are often hearing transcripts, court procedings and official reports. The final stage consists of a qualitative comparative evaluation of the various positions that the previous step brought to light. It is mostly only here that economic arguments enter his discussion.

Seen in this light, the historical dimension of Coase's approach takes precedence over economic arguments. It is thus no coincidence that his arguably most successful direct attack on orthodox dogma next to SC (Coase 1974) proceeded almost exclusively on the basis of historical arguments (see Coase 1974). Given that Coase's teacher Arnold Plant had initially read economic history, having been a student of Lilian Knowles, one of the pioneers of the then emerging discipline (see Coase 1986, p. 177; Koot 1987, p. 212 fn. 5), one should not underestimate the influence of the English historical school on the young Coase in this respect.

As we have seen, Coase's method is both historical and of a comparative nature. Hence, it will encounter difficulties when assessing institutional arrangements alternative to the ones that have established themselves. In other words, comparative historical analysis is bound to exhibit a counterfactual dimension when it comes to the assessment of existing arrangements, an issue explicitly recognised and addressed by Coase (1964). Coase applies a largely diachronic analysis of different regimes of economic co-ordination at the subconstitutional level, followed by an evaluation of plausible alternatives. Due to his rejection of the idealised points of reference of conventional welfare analysis, this stage of his analysis is necessarily speculative. One possibility would be to compare an existing constellation in one industry with alternative constellations in other industries. Coase doubts however whether all relevant ceteris paribus conditions would be fulfilled in the practical application of such an approach. His proposed alternative consists in gaining a detailed grasp of existing institutional arrangements in order to arrive at an understanding of the procedural implications of any changes, such as passing of different administrative codes or statutes. 'What is needed is an act of imaginative reconstruction' (Coase 1964, 195).

Coase's empirical method focuses thus on institutional development, both actual and potential. It seeks to gain an understanding of the effect of alternative arrangements by studying these alternatives not in different contemporary industries but in the past of the same industry, therefore exhibiting clear marks of a historico-hermeneutical understanding of economic institutions. This should however not be read as a call towards descriptive economic history at the expense of theoretical insight and explanation. Coase's method is not historical in any historiographic sense. His aim is not to apply standard historiographic methods to unlock the past for its own sake. Quite to the contrary, historical reflection takes the form of what might be regarded as a 'scenario analysis' to establish alternative regimes of economic order, which are motivated in their development and serve as important points of reference for the ensuing comparative institutional analysis.

COASE AND EVOLUTIONARY ECONOMICS

Coase's approach to economics can be characterised in terms of his concept of direction, his process-informed multimarket equilibrium analysis, the resulting principle of the primacy of institutional direction and his historico-empirical comparative analytical framework. Before being able to discuss the implications of this approach for evolutionary economic policy, it is necessary to address the following point head on. Ronald Coase's work is uncontroversial as a classical locus of institutional economic thought. Due to the appropriation of some of his contributions in orthodox quarters, including an important current in the new institutional economics, and the resulting predominantly critical reception in evolutionary economics, one must ask oneself whether Coase may serve as a fruitful source of insight after all, for a research agenda that is diametrically opposed to the economic mainstream.

It is not the aim of the present chapter to establish Ronald Coase as a canonical pillar of evolutionary economics. However, given that the reception of his work has been ripe with misunderstandings of the true thrust of his research in orthodox and heterodox fields of economic research alike, it seems timely to call for a discussion of his contribution as one to evolutionary economics as such (Foss 1994; see also Hodgson 2001, pp. 153, 347), rather than merely regarding him as a proponent of traditions that are related to evolutionary economics but ultimately inextricably bound to the economic mainstream.

To prepare our discussion of the evolutionary dimension of Coase's work, let us first summarise the points of contact that result from the discussion of the preceding sections. While Coase accepts that economic agents have a basic competence of rational decision making, he does not assume perfect knowledge of all contingencies. Instead he suggests we should proceed from 'man as he is'.[4] This proposal not only implies an explicit rejection of the concept of utility maximisation but rests on a sceptical stance towards the concept of utility in the first place. Coase regards this concept as merely ornamental, without any explanatory power in its own right. This assumption of common-sense rationality combines with Plant's price theory into a market-process and competitive rivalry-oriented multimarket analysis, which is ultimately committed to the notion of equilibrium but acknowledges the crucial role played by continuous experimenting on the part of economic agents.

One can see some parallels here to the more elaborate market-process theories in evolutionary economics, notwithstanding the limits that Coase's welfare concept, committed as it remains to early neoclassical price theory, is bound to encounter in any serious process-oriented evolutionary analysis. The entrepreneurs of NF for example are continuously engaged in experiments in how to best allocate transactions, but it is the forces of economy-wide competition that bring about an optimal division of labour and thus an allocation of transactions across firms that ends up minimising transaction costs in that the total value of production achieved through the resulting configuration ensures realisation of the greatest possible value of production. This result is assumed to emerge in a way reminiscent of Alchian's (1950) evolutionary arguments: In the long term, it is not sustainable to buy dearer than one is able to sell (Coase 1998, 577). A similar argument applies to the boundaries of the firm. Lines of production which consistently deliver an operating deficit will be closed down, while productive lines are likely to be expanded.

In the terminology of Ullmann-Margalit (1978), Coase's approach is therefore based on an 'invisible hand explanation of the functional-evolutionary mould' (see Vromen 1995, p. 103). Economic agents may well have the goal to arrive at optimal decisions. However, due to their constitutive incapacity to systematically perform without oversight and miscalculation (Coase 1993, 97), the actual determinants of the results of their behaviour arise from systemic effects.[5] This functionalist theory of selection that forms the basis of Coase's price theory aside, it is also possible to detect more or less clearly expressed aspects of population thinking in his work, most notably in his implicit assumption in NF of a heterogeneous population of firms making up an industry.

The points of contact in Coase's work with evolutionary economic thought mentioned so far should not be accorded too much weight since they are not uncommon within the Marshallian neoclassical tradition of the early 20th century which heavily influenced Coase. A more decisive indication of Coase's position and his intellectual vicinity to current thinking in evolutionary economics may be found in his discussion of the promise of evolutionary theorising for economic purposes (Coase 1978), which, while admittedly not fully elaborated, still resonates with today's discussion (e.g. Witt 1999). In this contribution, Coase underlines the importance of evolutionary thought, but remains sceptical regarding any direct or analogous application of neo-Darwinist approaches in economics. A theory that would be capable of explaining both biological and economic processes risks being formulated at too remote a level of abstraction to be practically relevant in economics. Moreover, economic systems develop much more rapidly than biological systems, not leaving enough time for evolutionary processes to have any significant impact. Finally, economic institutions are, at least in part, the result of intentional action, which cannot be found on the level of genes. For all these reasons, Coase regards the most fruitful application of evolutionary theorising to be in the area of sociobiology, to the extent that it may help furthering our understanding of learning, rule following and the formation of expectations.

Nevertheless, selection provides the basis in a metaphorical sense for Coase's belief that the forces of competition will lead to a distribution of resources that realises the highest achievable social product. This tendency towards optimal outcomes is called into question due to the primacy of institutional direction in the operation of markets. As soon as Coase allows for room for the state as a super-firm to withdraw from competition with other firms, while at the same time according it a role of active direction of markets, competitive pressures cease being able to decentrally balance plan and market co-ordination with each other in optimal proportions. The current extent of central direction becomes to a non-negligible extent the result of the operation of the principle of direction itself, and is criticised by Coase on empirical grounds for having proceeded beyond the efficient scale. It is precisely because he regards direction as primary that he engages in an historico-empirical agenda of comparative institutional analysis that seeks to demonstrate that direction is operating at an inefficient scale in the economy.

In order to come to Coase's main contribution to evolutionary economic policy, however, we first have to address the question of how an evolutionary approach in economics may be meaningfully differentiated from other approaches. One can observe general agreement regarding the object level of evolutionary economics, which has led commentators to speak of an ontological *unité de doctrine* (Dopfer 2001, p. 5). This consensus has so far not led to a comparable level of consensus on conceptual matters. There is presently no commonly agreed set of core concepts or theories of evolutionary economics (see Klaes 2004a for a positive evaluation of this situation). Neo-Darwinist impulses from the biological literature have to date experienced only limited success of a direct or metaphorical transfer of the Darwinist world-view to the social sciences (see Hodgson 1993, Witt 1999). Alongside neo-Darwinist approaches, one also needs to consider parts of the Austrian tradition, 'old' and 'new' institutional economics, non-linear systems theory, synergetics, bioeconomics and other related fields, all of which draw to a significant degree from evolutionary concepts and theories (Witt 2001, pp. 47–8). The boundary between evolutionary economics and related approaches that do not label themselves as 'evolutionary' seems thus to be blurred.

Nevertheless, the following basic distinction has crystallised between economic approaches that draw their inspiration from mechanistic metaphors, and evolutionary approaches (Hodgson 1993, pp. 18ff.; Witt 1993). Conceptually, this distinction can be expressed in terms of the differences between an integral and non-integral algebraic space (Potts 2000). One of the defining characteristics of a non-integral space consists in the fact that processes are non-ergodic. Frequently this gives rise to the catchphrase that 'history matters'. Historical perspectives are therefore of unquestionable importance within the overall programme of evolutionary economics.

Coase would not deny the significance of historical specificity. Nor would he doubt the importance of path-dependent processes for the understanding of institutional developments: 'However fluid an organization may be in its beginning, it must inevitably adopt certain policies and organizational forms which condition its thinking and limit the range of its policies' (Coase 1966, 442). His contribution to evolutionary economics in terms of a historical economics that is based on a developmental understanding of institutions and on a hermeneutic method of 'imaginative reconstruction' however goes further than a mere acknowledgement of the relevance of path-dependent processes. Given the present interest in evolutionary economics in appreciating history as an evolutionary phenomenon in its own right and not just as an epiphenomenon of non-ergodic processes (e.g. Dopfer 1986, Lehmann-Waffenschmidt 1998), Coase's work should be regarded as a key repository of relevant concepts and methods.

In this context, it is useful to draw attention to current debates in evolutionary biology that centre on recent developments in 'Evo-Devo' evolutionary biology (see Goodman and Coughlin 2000). Evo-Devo works towards a synthesis of neo-Darwinist and developmental approaches. Embryology and evolutionary morphology play crucial roles in these debates, notwithstanding their long-standing marginalisation by neo-Darwinist proponents, who regarded these fields as both committed to descriptive data gathering and fundamentally atheoretical.

The integration of phylogenetic and ontogenetic perspectives is all the more plausible and promising in an economic context (Hodgson 1993, p. 50). The crucial difference between the concept of history in Evo-Devo biology and evolutionary economics consists in the fact that in the economic realm, the concept of history must be regarded not just as a category employed by the analysing economist but as an epistemological concept of economic agents themselves (e.g. Fransman 1994, 752ff.). One finds here a promising point of contact for the adoption and further extension of the hermeneutical method that underlies Coase's historical economics into an evolutionary morphology of institutional forms. While historical specificity and developmental thinking have become important co-ordinates within evolutionary economic thought, one can still observe a tendency towards regarding history first and foremost as a path-dependent process. A more deeply probing understanding of institutions and their endogenous development will have to embrace a richer perspective on the ontological status of history.

IMPLICATIONS FOR EVOLUTIONARY ECONOMIC POLICY

Our starting point has been to ask the relevance of the work of Ronald Coase for evolutionary economic policy. The aim was not to portray Coase as an evolutionary economist, but to investigate his contribution in the light of possible points of contact that could inform present debates on evolutionary economic policy. It is a central tenet of the evolutionary approach that economic policy must be regarded as endogenous to economic processes, and this in a way that goes beyond perspectives offered by conventional political economy (e.g. Okruch 2001). There is a clear parallel here to Coase's insistence that any change desirable from the perspective of economic policy must proceed from changes in relevant statute law and the rules on the basis of which government bureaucracy operates and impinges on the economy. Coase's policy proposals rest on the premise that the proper mode of implementation of economic policy is not the blackboard but the legal and administrative rules that govern the operation of markets and the effect of direction in firms: 'In the real world, to influence economic policy, we set up or abolish an agency, amend the law, change the personnel, and so on: we work through institutions' (Coase 1984, 230).

Acknowledging the primacy of institutional direction in the operation of markets entails that every policy measure, even if it is aimed at promoting competition and the setting up and facilitating of market mechanisms, relies on active institutional design efforts. Procedural and developmental thinking promotes an awareness of the difficulties associated with attempts to arrive at institutions that perform better than the existing ones (Coase 1975, p. 60). Not only is clear and detailed understanding of the extant institutional structure required, but also insights into 'how a government organisation does *in fact* carry out the tasks entrusted to it' (Coase 1984, 61; orginal emphasis).

A second point of contact relates to the necessary revision of the traditional interpretation of the framework-setting task of ordo- or neoliberal economic policy. According to this view, the state should ensure that appropriate legal rules and institutional frameworks would be in place to allow free-market exchange to operate smoothly. To refer to one of the lasting metaphors of this strategy of defining an active role of the state that goes beyond being a 'nightwatchman', it would be up to the state to define the rules of the economic game, while the choice of actual moves in the game would be up to economic agents. The design of economic rules on the constitutional level, aimed at ensuring the efficient operation of free markets, would allow the state to largely withdraw from the subconstitutional realm of economic co-ordination and exchange, an argument which side-steps the traditional mutual exclusiveness of central plan and decentral exchange (Pies 2000, p. 349–53).

It was the concern of Coase's contributions right from the beginning to break up this polarity on the subconstitutional level, too. His solution does not however consist of an orthogonal positioning of the two alternative modes according to their mode of operation as done by the German ordoliberals. Market and direction, while seen as alternative and mutually exclusive ways of co-ordinating economic activity, are brought into a complex interplay with each other, interpreting the setting of the rules of the game as a move in the game itself. On this basis, framework setting constitutes at the same time active engagement in the allocation of economic resources, and economic policy remains an endogenous factor to consider.

Finally, Coase's proposal of a historical approach to comparative institutional analysis calls into question attempts to pursue a static comparative analysis that abstracts from the operation of ongoing economic processes. Coase did not turn to qualitative analysis out of incompetence in quantitative methods (e.g. Coase 1935, 1946; Coase and Fowler 1935, 1937). In retrospect, the contributions of SC to economic theory seem to justify his overall inductive approach. Evolutionary economists do not need to be reminded that Coase ultimately shied away from the consequential next step: the development of a theoretical framework to address processes of institutional development themselves. Nevertheless, his historical economics provides a valuable range of avenues to explore in the development of more sophisticated historico-morphological approaches in evolutionary economics. Coase's suggestion of conceiving of institutional change in terms of acts of imaginative reconstruction requires further elaboration, but invites us to try to understand and study economic institutions on a hermeneutical basis that takes seriously the epistemological status of history for human agents.[6]

NOTES

* This chapter refines arguments published earlier (Klaes 2004b). The present version has been streamlined and sharpened up at various points, largely in response to discussions that have taken place since the German paper has been committed to print. I should like to acknowledge in particular recent discussions with Brian Loasby, and ongoing intellectual exchange and collaboration over the past decade with David Campbell on the Coasean tradition in law and economics.

1. For a discussion of the concept of transaction costs as such, see Klaes (2000, 2003).
2. It is worth bearing in mind at this stage that while in principle, one may reject the primacy of direction in the operation of markets with reference to international competition between states and economic systems, the properties of competition in this public sphere are fundamentally different from conventional market competition, to the extent that some commentators regard analogies between the two as 'completely inadmissible' (e.g. Sinn 2004, 30).
3. One should note that some of the historical details of Coase's research have recently attracted some criticism (e.g. Brian Simpson 1996a, 1996b; Coase 1996).
4. In this context, one should also mention the relevance of the concept of radical uncertainty in NF and the resulting role of flexibility and adaptation of transactional agreements (see Foss 1996, 78).
5. See Vromen's (1995, pp. 34–40) discussion of the Becker (1962a, 1962b)–Kirzner (1962) debate, including his criticism of the evolutionary theories of Alchian and Becker, which also applies to Coase's position (at least in the context of global criteria of efficiency).
6. See Herrmann-Pillath (2000) for similar conclusions in a related context.

REFERENCES

Alchian, A.A. (1950), 'Uncertainty, evolution, and economic theory', *Journal of Political Economy*, **58**, 211–21.

Becker, G.S. (1962a), 'Irrational behavior and economic theory', *Journal of Political Economy*, **70**, 1–13.

Becker, G.S. (1962b), 'A reply to I. Kirzner', *Journal of Political Economy*, **70**, 82–3.

Blaug, M. (1990), 'Comment on O'Brien's "Lionel Robbins and the Austrian Connection"', Carl Menger and his Legacy in Economics (Annual Suppl. to *History of Political Economy*, **22**), B.J. Caldwell (ed.), Durham, NC: Duke University Press, pp. 185–8.

Brian Simpson, A. (1996a), 'Coase v. Pigou reexamined', *Journal of Legal Studies*, **25**, 53–97.

Brian Simpson, A. (1996b), 'An addendum', *Journal of Legal Studies*, **25**, 99–101.

Campbell, D. and M. Klaes (2000), 'Ronald Coase's political views at the time he wrote "The Nature of the Firm"', paper presented to EIPE Seminar, 12 April, Rotterdam, Erasmus Institute for Philosophy and Economics, Erasmus University Rotterdam.

Campbell, D. and M. Klaes (2005), 'The principle of institutional direction: Coase's regulatory critique of intervention', *Cambridge Journal of Economics*, **29**, forthcoming.

Coase, R.H. (1935), 'The problem of duopoly reconsidered', *Review of Economic Studies*, **2**, 137–43.

Coase, R.H. (1937), 'The nature of the firm', *Economica*, **4** N.S., 386–405.

Coase, R.H. (1939), 'Rowland Hill and the Penny Post', *Economica*, **6** N.S., 423–35.

Coase, R.H. (1946), 'Monopoly pricing with interrelated costs and demand', *Economica*, **13** N.S., 278–94.
Coase, R.H. (1947), 'The origin of the monopoly of broadcasting in Great Britain', *Economica*, **14**, 189–210.
Coase, R.H. (1955), 'The postal monopoly in Great Britain: an historical survey', in J.K. Eastham (ed.), *Economic Essays in Commemoration of the Dundee School of Economics* 1931–1955, Coupar: Angus, Culross.
Coase, R.H. (1959), 'The federal communications commission', *Journal of Law and Economics*, **2**, 1–40.
Coase, R.H. (1960), 'The problem of social cost', *Journal of Law and Economics*, **3**, 1–44.
Coase, R.H. (1961a), 'The British Post Office and the messenger companies', *Journal of Law and Economics*, **4**, 12–65.
Coase, R.H. (1961b), 'Why not use the pricing system in the broadcasting industry', *The Freeman*, **11**, 52–7.
Coase, R.H. (1962), 'The Interdepartment Radio Advisory Committee', *Journal of Law and Economics*, **5**, 17–47.
Coase, R.H. (1964), 'Discussion', *American Economic Review, Papers and Proceedings*, **54**, 194–7.
Coase, R.H. (1966), 'The economics of broadcasting and government policy', *American Economic Review*, **56**, 440–7.
Coase, R.H. (1974), 'The lighthouse in economics', in R.H. Coase (1988), *The Firm, the Market, and the Law*, Chicago and London: University of Chicago Press, pp. 187–213.
Coase, R.H. (1975), 'Economists and public policy', in R.H. Coase (1994), *Essays on Economics and Economists*, Chicago: University of Chicago Press, pp. 47–63.
Coase, R.H. (1978), 'Economics and biology: discussion', *American Economic Review Papers and Proceedings*, **68**, 244–5.
Coase, R.H. (1979), 'Payola in radio and television broadcasting', *Journal of Law and Economics*, **22**, 269–320.
Coase, R.H (1984), 'The new institutional economics', *Journal of Institutional and Theoretical Economics*, **140**, 229–31.
Coase, R.H (1986), 'Arnold Plant', in R.H Coase (ed.) (1994), *Essays on Economics and Economists*, Chicago: University of Chicago Press, pp. 176–84.
Coase, R.H (1991), 'The nature of the firm: origin', in O. Williamson and S. Winter (eds), *The Nature of the Firm: Origins, Evolution, and Development*, Oxford: Oxford University Press, pp. 3–47.
Coase, R.H (1993), 'Coase on Posner on Coase', *Journal of Institutional and Theoretical Economics*, **149**, 96–8.
Coase, R.H (1996), 'Law and economics and A.W. Brian Simpson', *Journal of Legal Studies*, **25**, 103–19.
Coase, R.H. (1998), 'Comment on Thomas W. Hazlett. "Assigning property rights to radio spectrum use: why did FCC license auctions take 67 Years?" ' *Journal of Law and Economics*, **41**, 577–80.
Coase, R.H and R.F. Fowler (1935), 'Bacon production and the pig-cycle in Great Britain', *Economica*, **2** N.S., 142–67.
Coase, R.H and R.F. Fowler (1937), 'The pig-cycle in Great Britain: an explanation', *Economica*, **4** N.S., 55–82.
Commons, J.R. (1934), *Institutional Economics*, reprinted 1961, two vols, Madison, WI: University of Wisconsin Press.

Dopfer, K. (1986), 'The histonomic approach to economics: beyond pure theory and pure experience', *Journal of Economic Issues*, **20**, 989–1010.
Dopfer, K. (2001), 'Evolutionary economics: framework for analysis', in *Evolutionary Economics: Program and Scope*, Boston, MA: Kluwer, pp. 1–44.
Foss, N. (1994), 'The two Coasian traditions', *Review of Political Economy*, **6**, 37–61.
Foss, N. (1996), 'The "alternative" theories of Knight and Coase, and the modern theory of the firm', *Journal of the History of Economic Thought*, **18**, 76–95.
Fransman, M. (1994), 'Information, knowledge, vision and theories of the firm', *Industrial and Corporate Change*, **3**, 713–57.
Furubotn, E. (1994), 'Future development of the New Institutional Economics: extension of the neoclassical model or new construct?' *Lectiones Jenenses*, **1**, Jena: Max-Planck-Institut zur Erforschung von Wirtschaftssystemen.
Goodman, C.S. and B.C. Coughlin (2000), 'The evolution of Evo-Devo biology', *Proceedings of the National Academy of Sciences of the United States of America*, **97**, 4424–5.
Hayek, F.A. von (1928), 'Das intertemporale Gleichgewichtssytem der Preise und die Bewegungen des "Geldwertes"', *Weltwirtschaftliches Archiv*, **1**, 33–76. Translated in F.A.V. Hayek (1984) *Money, Capital and Fluctuations*, edited by R. McCloughry, Chicago: University of Chicago Press, pp. 71–117.
Hayek, F.A. von (1933), 'The Trend of Economic Thinking', *Economica*, **13**, 121–37.
Hayek, F.A. von (1935), *Collectivist Economic Planning*, London: Routledge.
Herrmann-Pillath, C. (2000), 'Wirtschaftsordnung und Kultur aus evolutorischer Sicht', in H. Leipold and I. Pies (eds), *Ordnungstheorie und Ordnungspolitik*, Stuttgart: Lucius & Lucius, pp. 371–400.
Hodgson, G.M. (1993), *Economics and Evolution*, Cambridge: Polity.
Hodgson, G.M. (1999), *Economics and Utopia*, London: Routledge.
Hodgson, G.M. (2001), *How Economics Forgot History*, London: Routledge.
Holmström, B.R. and J. Tirole (1989), 'The theory of the firm', in R. Schmalensee and R. D. Willig (eds), *Handbook of Industrial Organization*, Amsterdam: North-Holland, vol. 1, pp. 61–133.
Kerber, W. (2000), 'Law and economics: Ein neuer Ansatz zur Analyse institutioneller Rahmenbedingungen', in H. Leipold and I. Pies (eds), *Ordnungstheorie und Ordnungspolitik*, Stuttgart: Lucius & Lucius, pp. 145–170.
Kirzner, I.M. (1962), 'Rational action and economic theory', *Journal of Political Economy*, **70**, 380–5.
Klaes, M. (2000), 'The birth of the concept of transaction costs: issues and controversies', *Industrial and Corporate Change*, **9**, 567–93.
Klaes, M. (2003), 'Residual categories and the evolution of economic knowledge', in H.S. Jensen, L.M. Richter and M.T. Vendelø (eds), *The Evolution of Scientific Knowledge*, Cheltenham, UK and Northampton, MA, USA: Edward Elgar, pp. 37–56.
Klaes, M. (2004a), 'Evolutionary economics: in defence of "vagueness"', *Journal of Economic Methodology*, **11** (3), 359–76.
Klaes, M. (2004b), 'Das wirtschaftspolitische Programm von Ronald H. Coase' in Kurt Dopfer (ed), *Studien zur Evolutorischen Ökronomik VIII*, Berlin: Duncker & Humblot, pp. 185–204.
Koot, G.M. (1987), *English Historical Economics 1870–1926*, Cambridge: Cambridge University Press.
Lehmann-Waffenschmidt, M. (1998), 'Kontingenz und Strukturähnlichkeit als

Charakteristika selbstorganisierter Prozesse in der Ökonomie', in F. Schweitzer and G. Silberberg (eds), *Evolution und Selbstorganisation in der Ökonomie*, Berlin: Duncker and Humblot, pp. 187–208.
Mäki, U. (1998), 'Is Coase a realist?', *Philosophy of the social sciences*, **82** (1), 5–31.
Medema, S.G. (1994), *Ronald H. Coase*, New York: St Martin's Press.
Medema, S.G. (1996), 'More than a caricature: the Coase that nobody knows: a review essay', *Research in the History of Economic Thought and Methodology*, **14**, 373–83.
Medema, S.G. (1999), 'Legal fiction: the place of the Coase Theorem in Law and Economics', *Philosophy and Economics*, **15**, 209–33.
Okruch, S. (2001), 'Ziele, Formen und Verfahren einer evolutorischen Wirtschaftspolitik', paper presented Buchenbach Workshop zur Evolutorischen Ökonomik, 23–26, May.
Pies, I. (2000), 'Institutionenökonomik als Ordnungstheorie: Ein Ansatz für wissenschaftliche Politikberatung in der Demokratie', in H. Leipold and I. Pies (eds), *Ordnungstheorie und Ordnungspolitik*, Stuttgart: Lucius & Lucius, pp. 347–70.
Posner, R. (1975), 'The economic approach to law', *Texas Law Review* **53**, 758.
Potts, J.D. (2000), *The New Evolutionary Microeconomics*, Cheltenham, UK and Northampton, MA, USA: Edward Elgar.
Pratten, S. (2001), 'Coase on broadcasting, advertising and policy', *Cambridge Journal of Economics*, **25**, 617–38.
Schlicht, E. (1996), 'Exploiting the Coase mechanism: the extortion problem', *Kyklos*, **49**, 319–30.
Schlicht, E. (1997), 'The moving equilibrium theorem again', *Economic Modelling*, **14** (2), 271–8.
Sinn, H.-W. (2004), 'The new systems competition', *Perspektiven der Wirtschaftspolitik*, **5**, 23–38.
Slembeck, T. (1997), 'The formation of economic policy: a cognitive-evolutionary approach to policy making', *Constitutional Political Economy*, **8**, 225–54.
Stigler, G.J. (1966), *The Theory of Price*, New York: Macmillan.
Ullmann-Margalit, E. (1978), 'Invisible-hand explanations', *Synthese*, **39**, 263–91.
Vromen, J. (1995), *Economic Evolution*, London: Routledge.
Wegner, G. (1997), 'Economic policy from an evolutionary perspective – a new approach', *Journal of Institutional and Theoretical Economics*, **153**, 485–509.
Williamson, O. (1993), 'Transaction cost economics meets Posnerian Law and Economics', *Journal of Institutional and Theoretical Economics*, **149**, 99–118.
Witt, U. (1993), 'Introduction', in *Evolutionary Economics*, Aldershot, UK and Brookfield, US: Edward Elgar, pp. xiii–xxvii.
Witt, U. (1999), 'Evolutionary economics and evolutionary biology', in P. Koslowski (ed.), *Sociobiology and Bioeconomics*, Berlin: Springer, pp. 279–98.
Witt, U. (2001), 'Evolutionary economics: an interpretative survey', in K. Dopfer (ed.), *Evolutionary Economics: Program and Scope*, Boston, MA: Kluwer, pp. 45–88.

PART II

Self-organisation and networks

5. The concept of network organisation – biotechnology-based industries as exemplar

Andreas Pyka and P. Paolo Saviotti

1. INTRODUCTION

Biotechnology is one of the fields that is at the forefront of the creation of a knowledge-based society. This seems somewhat paradoxical, since it could be maintained that biotechnology is one of the oldest technologies used by mankind. Wine and cheese making constitute two typical examples. However, modern biotechnology has been substantially changed by the advent of molecular biology, a new discipline which was founded in the 1930s based on the attempt to apply to biology the methods of physics. In the mid 1970s two discoveries, recombinant DNA and monoclonal antibodies, transformed a scientific discipline with a brilliant if distant future into a seedbed of industrial applications. Accordingly some authors now call this latest vintage of biotechnology third-generation, to distinguish it from the completely empirical first generation and from the second generation, which began with the production of antibiotics. Second-generation biotechnology used scientific methods but it did not have the knowledge required to change the genetic make-up of organisms. Such knowledge was only provided in a systematic way by molecular biology.

Who were the first actors involved in the development of third-generation modern biotechnology? In the mid 1970s very few research institutions did research in molecular biology and they were mostly in the USA. The industrial firms that in principle could have exploited molecular biology did not have the respective absorptive capacity. Their competencies and knowledge bases were concentrated in more traditional disciplines such as organic chemistry or microbiology. In fact, this lack of knowledge hampered firms' recognition of the opportunities that could have been offered by molecular biology.

With respect to applications and the scope of the research programme, one has to consider that biotechnology is not an industrial sector but a scientific discipline underlying a number of industrial sectors (pharmaceuticals, agriculture, food, environment etc.), here called the biotechnology-based sectors. Very importantly, industrial applications of biotechnology are highly dependent on new scientific developments, even on those that are the result of basic research. Although the lead-times between the discovery of new knowledge and its final embodiment in new products may be very long, the time between the creation of new knowledge and the funding of industrial research aimed at its applications is in general very short. Thus, basic research is not exclusively confined to public research institutions, but is also carried out by firms.

The paradigmatic change in the underlying knowledge-bases, the fast speed of knowledge creation and diffusion processes as well as the great number of different actors involved in these processes necessitate new forms of industrial organisation of research and development. In particular, collaborative arrangements between the different and heterogeneous actors involved seemed to be the form of industrial organisation which emerged in the biotechnology-based industries.

Thus, both in what concerns its intensity of knowledge utilisation and in the mechanisms employed, biotechnology seems to be a very good example of industrial organisation in a knowledge-based society. Of course, the conclusions reached in this chapter will depend on the specificity of biotechnology, but they will also have some general significance for the analysis of a knowledge-based society.

In what follows we first have a look at the developments in the R&D organisation in the biotechnology-based industries since the 1980s. We analyse biotechnology innovation networks with special emphasis on two types of actors, Large Diversified Firms (LDFs) and Dedicated Biotechnology Firms (DBFs). In a numerical model we then analyse the advantages and disadvantages for firms of going-it-alone strategies and of networking strategies, taking into account the environmental factors influencing the formation of links between actors. Network formation will be shown to display a dynamics going beyond a first wave of networks and leading to a re-organisation of the partnerships involved.

2. INNOVATION NETWORKS IN THE BIOTECHNOLOGY-BASED INDUSTRIES

The earliest analyses of innovation networks pointed to the possibility that they are only a temporary form of industrial organisation. Such a temporary character could be the result of discontinuities in knowledge generation, for example of the emergence of a new technological paradigm. It was argued that LDFs were committed to the old paradigm, in which all their competencies were concentrated, and that they could not easily internalise the new knowledge. Alternatively, LDFs did not have the absorptive capacity required to internalise the new paradigm and they were not capable of constructing it rapidly. A new type of industrial actor, small high-technology firms, arose to bridge the institutional gap between public research institutions and LDFs. In the specific case of biotechnology such firms were called Dedicated Biotechnology Firms (DBFs). DBFs were expected to act as intermediaries between LDFs and public research institutions. In the rest of the chapter the DBFs performing this role will be called *translators*. In the course of time by collaborating with DBFs and with public research institutions, LDFs could construct a knowledge-base and an absorptive capacity in biotechnology. Once this happened the role of DBFs would have become superfluous and industrial organisation would return to the traditional dichotomy between the market and hierarchical organisations.

However, the rate of creation of interinstitutional collaborative networks steadily increased all throughout the 1980s and 1990s. In Figure. 5.1 we see e.g. the growth of international collaborations in the biotechnology-based industries including only those cases of new collaborations where the partners come from different countries. The continuous attractiveness of the networking strategy implies the following two alternatives: either LDFs have not internalised the new paradigm constituted by biotechnology or a new role for DBFs has emerged in innovation networks.

The analysis of this problem constitutes one of the main objectives of the present chapter. Looking at Figure 5.2 which shows the number of actors involved in new collaborations in Europe, this clearly suggests the second

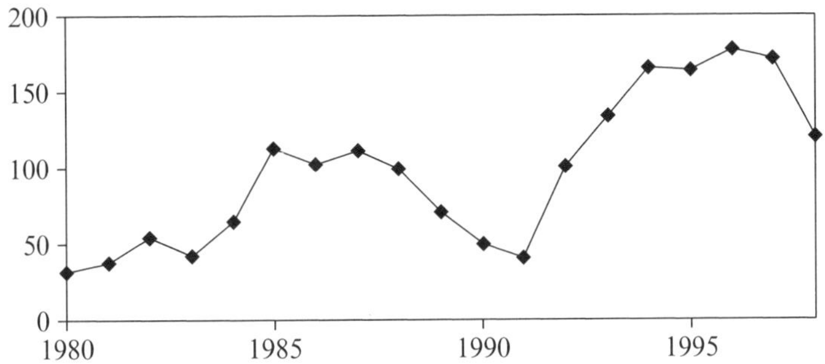

Source: Science and Engineering Indicators 2000

Figure 5.1 *Number of new international strategic biotechnology collaborations*

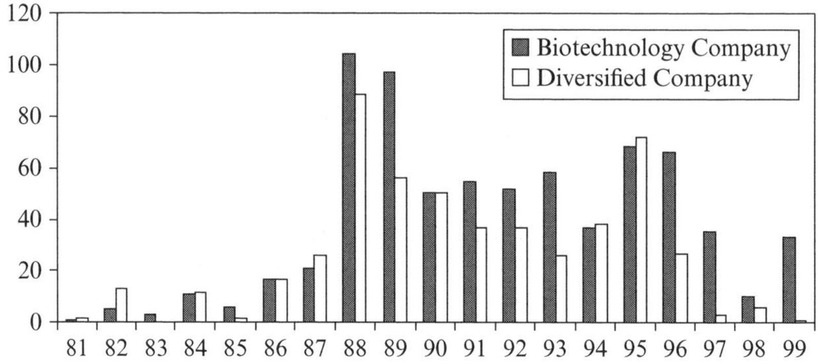

Source: Bioability

Figure 5.2 Types of agents in European biotechnology collaborations

alternative, that a new role for the DBFs has emerged. Since the late 1980s they have clearly dominated the founding of new alliances, often between DBFs only. Furthermore, by the end of the 1980s, of course also the LDFs had acquired a knowledge-base in molecular biology (see for example Grabowski and Vernon 1994) and yet they continued to enter into collaborative agreements with DBFs.

The new role for DBFs we hypothesise in this chapter to be linked to the extremely rapid rate of creation of new knowledge. Even if LDFs have acquired an absorption capacity for it, the sheer rate of advance is such that no LDF could keep up with it all. LDFs might thus use collaborative agreements with DBFs in order to keep abreast of new developments that could turn out to have important economic applications. The alternative course of action for an LDF would be to invest in research in the same fields of biotechnology. However, with a very high rate of growth of knowledge this strategy would involve a very heavy, irreversible and risky commitment. The collaboration with DBFs constitutes a more flexible and reversible strategy. It is to be observed that this role does not involve a qualitative difference in LDFs' ability to understand molecular biology, but only the attempt to reach a better trade-off between readiness for action if promising developments were to emerge in new subsets of the biotechnology knowledge-space and the sunk costs that need to be faced in order to keep these windows open. And, it must be remembered that the competitive advantage of LDFs is not constituted by their ability to understand new knowledge but by their capacity to combine the different competencies and complementary assets required to produce a final product. Furthermore, a rather important share of the new collaborations is occupied by alliances between DBFs only, which underlies the changed trend of collaborations. Whereas in the early 1980s we find a dominance of agreements where knowledge flows from the DBFs to the LDFs in an exchange of R&D funds, since the late 1980s bilateral knowledge-flows play the dominant role in the new collaborations. This second role that can be played by DBFs will be called that of *explorers*.

3. THE MODEL

Before we start explaining the basic structure[1] of our model some remarks with respect to the methodological framework will be helpful. In particular, we are going to use the methodology of the so-called history-friendly models, originally introduced by Malerba, Nelson, Orsenigo and Winter (1999). History-friendly models are designed to capture, in a stylised form, the mechanisms and factors affecting industry evolution, technological advance and institutional change detected by empirical scholars of industrial economics, technological change, business organisation and strategy, and other social scientists. Thus history-friendly models can be considered the natural extension to modelling of qualitative and appreciative theories.

Obviously even in a neo-Schumpeterian approach simulation models have to introduce a certain degree of abstraction and cannot reflect reality in all its complexity. The mechanisms built into the formal model have to be transparent enough, so that the analyst can figure out what the causes are of the observed effects. Therefore, in the first step of our modelling effort we have to carefully single out the relevant actors, bring together variables which are effective in the same direction and combine important developments and possibilities of action. Nevertheless, adopting the neo-Schumpeterian approach allows us to put emphasis on crucial features of innovation processes, such as non-linear dynamics, heterogeneity and true uncertainty, which are beyond the scope of traditional approaches.

In the following the basic building blocks of our modelling framework are introduced. In particular, we focus on the way we present the different agents in our model, the way we capture innovation processes, what we consider to be the prerequisites and consequences of networking as well as the representation of the economic realm in our simulation.

3.1 The Agents

The agents we are considering in our model are Large Diversified Firms (LDFs) and Dedicated Biotechnology Firms (DBFs). They are described in terms of their competencies and capabilities. DBFs possess technological competencies while LDFs possess a mixture of economic and technological competencies.

Competencies

Technological competencies are the components of the knowledge-base required for building up production and innovation capabilities in a specific technology. In other words, before firms are able to develop new marketable outputs they have to develop the respective biotechnological competencies. Furthermore, technological competencies alone are not sufficient to achieve economic success with a new product. Economic competencies are necessary in order to successfully produce and market a new commodity. Examples of these economic competencies are experience in clinical trials, distribution channels and so on. Obviously this representation is somewhat simplified. The full range of competencies required by firms to conceive, develop, produce and market new products is very large and heterogeneous. However, given that most DBFs at the beginning of their life-cycle do not possess any economic competencies and that LDFs in the 1970s were generally unable to acquire the knowledge required to use modern biotechnology, the representation in terms of technological and economic competencies adequately describes the difference between our two main groups of agents. Moreover, we could consider technological competencies as the core competencies (Prahalad and Hamel 1990) of firms and economic competencies as a large part of the complementary assets (Teece 1986) required to produce and market a product.

Figure 5.3 shows the development of technological competencies. In the early phases the building up of the knowledge-base is a difficult process and progress is hard to achieve. However, after having developed a certain knowledge-base it becomes easier to learn even more (threshold effect). Finally, marginal progress becomes progressively more difficult as the knowledge-frontier existing at a given time is approached. A function of this type implies variable returns to investment in the creation of new knowledge within a given field: very low at the beginning, positive and growing in the intermediate phase before diminishing returns set in as the potential of the new field has been exploited. The process of building up a knowledge-base in biotechnology is supported by co-operative arrangements with firms who are already active in this field – an important part of the respective knowledge base is transferred by networking.

The difference between LDFs and DBFs

The two populations of firms which can be observed in the biotechnology-based industries can be distinguished on the basis of their relative technological and economic competencies. The first population of firms is that of

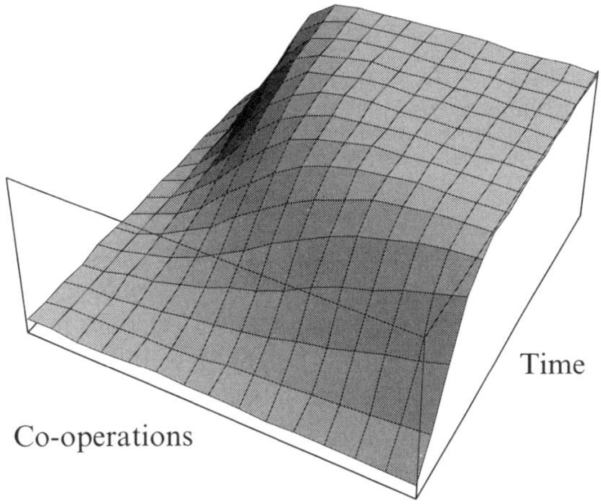

Figure 5.3 Building up of a knowledge-base

LDFs, for example the large established pharmaceutical firms. Until the end of the 70s their research and development was mainly embedded in the paradigm of traditional organic chemistry. The coming up of the new biotechnological paradigm meant a 'competence-destroying technological progress' (Tushman and Anderson 1986) for them, as most of their competencies were threatened by the new ones. In our model this group of agents is represented in the starting distribution with well-developed economic competencies but with almost no technological competencies in biotechnology.

In the second population we find small start-up companies, often university spin-offs specialised in the biotechnology field. This group of agents, the so-called Dedicated Biotechnology Firms or DBFs, by their very nature have highly developed technological competencies, but almost no economic competencies. When they start their existence DBFs depend on external funds for research and development. Accordingly, in our starting distribution they are represented just as having no economic competencies but highly developed technological competencies.

Venture capital firms and universities

In addition to these agents that we are explicitly taking into account, we also consider two further important groups of actors in our model: public research institutes or university labs and venture-capital firms. In order to keep our model simple their behaviour is not explicitly analysed, but they are considered as an important component of the external environment of biotechnology firms. For example, in order to acquire the funds necessary to undertake R&D a DBF can co-operate either with an LDF or with a venture-capital firm; similarly, the cooperation of an LDF with a DBF or with a public research institute leads to almost the same consequences for the LDF etc.

Capabilities

Drawing on their competencies firms can accumulate technological capabilities in specific fields which allow them to explore the technological opportunity-space. The firms in our model act in an environment which continuously forces them to be engaged in such R&D processes. Not to innovate means to fall behind in the competitive environment of biotechnology. In order to increase the probability of an innovation firms accumulate technological capabilities in the course of time.

Together with the technological competencies the technological capabilities determine the probability of an innovation. The relationship is shown in Figure 5.4.

To consider the intrinsic uncertainty of innovation processes the innovation probability of a firm is matched in every period with a Poisson-distributed random number whose mean value is asymptotically reached. A firm is successful in its innovative efforts only if the innovation probability is above the random number.[2]

R&D decision rules

The investment in R&D is no longer guided by an optimisation calculus, but by a routinised behaviour, as innovation goes hand in hand with true uncertainty (e.g. Nelson and Winter 1982, p. 132). Firms adopt certain rules, for example, invest x per cent of your turnover in R&D, retain x per cent of your

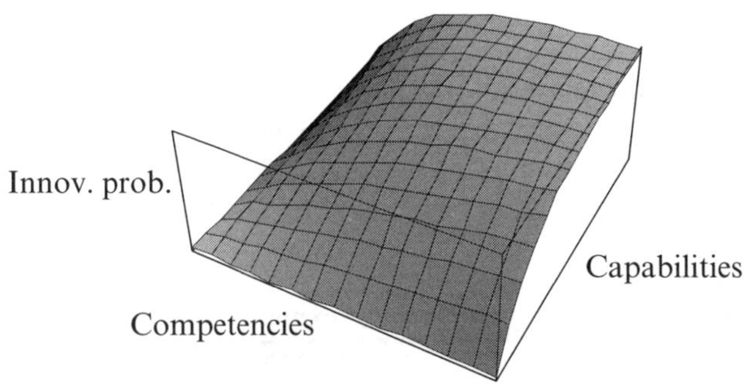

Figure 5.4 Innovation probability as a function of competencies and capabilities

financial support in order to build up your own capital stock etc. In the same way the distribution amongst different activities (e.g. between investing in the building up of technological or economic capabilities) is captured by referring to routines.

3.2 Networking

In order to carry out their innovation processes firms can choose different strategies. They can either decide to go it alone, which means not to draw on external knowledge-sources and not to share their own new know-how with potential competitors, or they can decide to co-operate with other actors and build up collectively the new capabilities necessary for the introduction of a new commodity. Innovation networks emerge through this mutual co-operation, which gives rise to channels for knowledge-flows between the firms participating in the network. In particular, we are considering the evolution of innovation networks at three levels within the model: the environmental conditions favouring or inhibiting the growth of networks, the individual decisions of firms to co-operate or not, and a matching process bringing together firms willing to co-operate. This process creates a population of networks with its own dynamics. The formation of any network constitutes an act of birth or entry into the population. Conversely, the disappearance of a network constitutes an act of death or exit. The dynamics of birth and death of networks will be determined by the specific features of each network and by some features of the external environment.

Environmental conditions for networking

A number of environmental factors increase the probability of the birth of innovation networks. The growing complexity of innovation processes as well as a high degree of technological uncertainty play the most important role. Every time a firm successfully introduces an innovation the number of knowledge fields is assumed to grow. Given the complementary and combinatorial nature (e.g. Staropoli 1998, 15) of biotechnology, the technological space, defined as the number of possible combinations of knowledge-fields, increases in a non-linear way.

Especially in the early phases of a technological life-cycle this increasing complexity is combined with a high technological uncertainty because specific research techniques or heuristics – e.g. how to handle this complexity – are not yet developed. In the model the phase of a technological life-cycle is approximated very roughly by the average age of the different commodities on the product markets.

Additionally, R&D networks are dependent on a number of core technologies or core/central actors who play a crucial role in the establishment of the networks (e.g. Saviotti 1998, pp. 36–7). In our model the population of LDFs is supposed to play this role.

In addition to the previous network-supporting effects, other influences decrease the probability of network formation, thus leading to network death. First, the degree of competition is crucial in this respect. In our model we use as an economic framework a heterogeneous oligopoly. We consider the degree of substitutability of the final products as a measure of the intensity of competition. We use the variance of the variables describing a firm's relative product quality as a measure of product heterogeneity: the higher this variance, the lower is the competitive threat between firms. Furthermore, we can expect demand saturation to decrease the rate of growth of the respective markets and thus the scope of co-operative R&D. In this phase of the industry life-cycle minor improvements of the technology could lead to considerable advantages for a single firm. To capture this influence, we draw again on the life-cycle and assume that in later stages of this life-cycle the rate of growth of demand is likely to decrease. Finally, the techno-economic performance of the network members, again approximated by the relative quality compared to the average performance of all firms, is itself an indicator of the attractiveness of joining a network. In cases where the performance of network members is below the average performance of the whole firm population, the networking strategy significantly loses attractiveness.

Networking decisions

Next, the firms have to decide whether they want to co-operate or not. Generally two forms of co-operation are possible:

1. co-operation focusing on complementary assets, i.e. firms are induced to co-operate to acquire technological or economic competencies that they do not possess but that they judge crucial for their economic success
2. co-operation focusing on general complementarities (i.e. the bundling of R&D efforts in a specific direction) and synergies (i.e. detecting potentials for cross-fertilisation by the combination of different technological capabilities). For example, it is possible to conceive of a division of labour in which firms pursue similar objectives using similar competencies, but they collaborate in order to speed up the innovation process and to spread the relative uncertainty over the network.

In the form of co-operation (1) DBFs play the role of translators, while in form (2) they play the role of explorers. Consequently, the networking decision depends on the respective competencies and capabilities that firms have accumulated. For example, a small start-up DBF in its early phases is not able on its own to raise funds for R&D and necessarily has to look for a partner in order to obtain funding. In the same way established LDFs which want to become active in the promising fields of biotechnology but have no internal technological competencies need collaboration partners experienced in these fields. On the other hand, firms with highly developed capabilities would not run the risk and share their knowledge with potential competitors in the stages immediately preceding the introduction of an innovation.

Matching process

Finally, we have to decide on the mechanism which brings together different firms willing to co-operate. Although different mechanisms are conceivable we think that a mechanism which could be labelled 'success breeds success' is best suited to our purposes. Success breeds success means that firms would tend to pick collaborators with the highest technological and/or economic capabilities. We are here assuming that firms are able to advertise their own capabilities and to evaluate those of potential co-operating partners. This seems to be a realistic assumption, especially in the biotech industry, where firms are ranked on the basis of their technological performance, which is advertised by press announcements, publications, patents and even by the professional standing of the scientists hired by firms, including the Nobel prize winners present on their scientific committee.

3.3 Networking Consequences

After having introduced the way firms get together in innovation networks we now have to focus on the consequences of networking. By entering into a collaboration the agents are exchanging their know-how. This means that firms can benefit from the efforts of other firms in order to build up their own capabilities.

Absorptive capacities

The extent to which a firm can benefit from the knowledge-flow available by co-operation depends on its absorptive capacity (see Cohen and Levinthal 1989 and Cantner and Pyka 1998). In turn, absorptive capacity is expected to increase with the firm's previous experience in co-operation. This means that external knowledge is not easily integrated within their own knowledge-stock, but certain prerequisites have to be fulfilled and a minimum amount of experience is necessary. This also means that the amount of knowledge which flows within the network is severely limited.

Financial flows

Start-up DBFs with missing economic competencies cannot finance their own R&D and are obliged to find a co-operation partner. In this case an LDF co-operating with a DBF is supposed to provide the required research funding. Another possibility for DBFs to acquire R&D money is to apply for venture capital, of which we assume an exogenous supply growing at a constant rate. Access to venture capital is competitive. Amongst the firms applying only those which show the best record in biotechnological capabilities as well as in previous co-operations are funded.

Knowledge-flows

One of the most important advantages of participating in an innovation network is the access to channels of knowledge-flow. External knowledge exerts an impact on the innovation probability function and depends on the amount of absorptive capacities, as well as on the technological capabilities of the co-operating firms. Participating in an innovation network exerts a threefold influence: first, the research budget of a firm is reduced due to co-ordination costs and, in the case of a co-operation with a DBF, by the financial support of this firm. Second, absorptive capacities are positively influenced by entering into a new collaboration as the experience with integrating external knowledge is increasing. Finally, external knowledge becomes available via knowledge-flows between the collaborating firms.

3.4 Competition Processes

The innovative activities of firms are undertaken in an economic environment which is characterised by a certain degree of competition. On the one hand, the firms offering products on the final market compete with each other in attracting demand. Also, those firms whose aim is to offer new technological knowledge compete in a particular way with other firms in acquiring the respective funds. Finally, firms who want to buy the respective knowledge also compete for co-operation with the most attractive research laboratories.

The two levels of competition take place in two different markets: the market for final products and the market for knowledge. Of course, we know that markets for knowledge cannot exist due to their imperfections. However, the existence of DBFs, which very often though not always function as contract research organisations, implies that in particular circumstances such imperfections can be reduced to a level where a market for knowledge, although very imperfect, can exist. In fact, co-operation often exists between firms operating in different markets (e.g. for final goods and for knowledge) and thus having a complementary relationship. Of course, this does not exclude the possibility that firms operating in the same market can co-operate.

On the final markets firms compete in terms of prices and quality which are, in a dynamic context, determined by their innovative success. Generally, one would expect that a successful innovator will be able to attract demand away from its competitors because consumers can choose between several goods. These substitution effects are due to price and quality changes which are the results of the following actions and reactions:

Introducing a new product with improved quality characteristics creates additional demand allowing the innovator to charge higher prices.

1. In the case of an introduction of a new product by two or more vertically integrated firms who co-operated in the R&D stages the increase in demand is divided between the firms involved.
2. As a reaction to this quality-induced substitution effect, non-innovators in related markets lower their prices in order to keep the loss in demand as small as possible.
3. Exploitation of technological opportunities of an already existing technology allows the respective innovator to reduce its price, thereby increasing the demand for his product;
4. As a reaction, non-innovators could fight their loss in demand by also lowering their prices, thereby, however, reducing their profit margin.

Another form of competition takes place in finding the most attractive network partner which is described with the help of the notion of success breeds success (see above). Firms engaged in the search for a co-operation partner will match with those which show either the most developed technological or the most developed economic competencies.

By choosing a heterogeneous multiproduct oligopoly (see Kuenne 1992 and for an application in a simulation model Cantner and Pyka 1998) we allow for the relationships described above. Firms are offering their goods on a heterogeneous product market. Due to an innovation and the introduction of a new commodity on these markets the relative market share of the already existing goods gets eroded. In this way, we also generate the endogenous incentives to the firms to engage in innovation, as they cannot survive in the long run by relying on their original established positions which are continuously threatened by the innovative actions of their competitors.

3.5 The Basic Structure of the Model

The following flow-chart summarises the basic structure of our model. Starting with firms and industry characteristics of the previous round firms

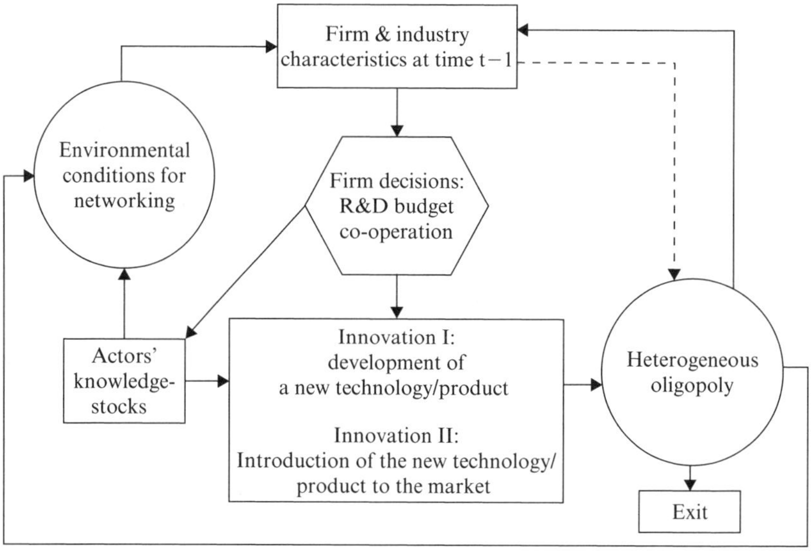

Figure 5.5 Flow chart

have to decide whether to go it alone or to co-operate. They are influenced by environmental conditions either favouring or inhibiting the growth of networks. After having found a co-operation partner in the matching process the firms enter the innovation stages which on the one hand influence the industry and firm characteristics, and on the other hand the market outcomes of the next round.

4. THE MODEL'S RESULTS

In this section we introduce some of the numerical results of the network evolution. These results are then compared in a history-friendly manner with real-world developments in order to see whether our model is able to reproduce some of the developments observed in reality.

Figure 5.6 shows the development of the network density. After a first increase in the density the dynamics of network growth comes to rest after around ten periods, and even starts slightly decreasing until period 45. However, after that period network density starts increasing again, until it begins to oscillate around a value which is twice the average at the beginning. This can already be interpreted as evidence for the changed role of DBFs, which in the first periods find temporary collaboration partners in

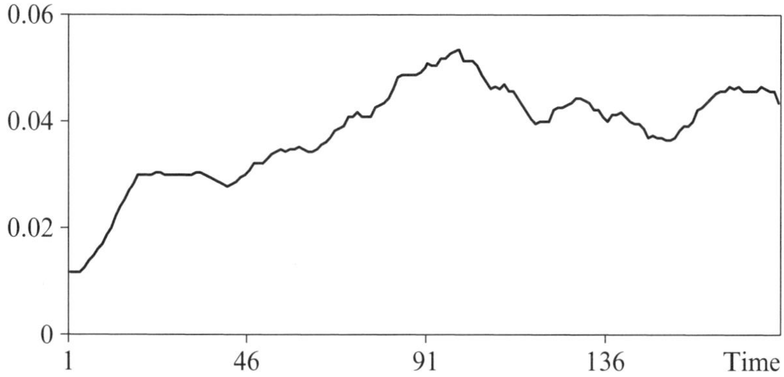

Figure 5.6 Network density (moving averages)

the population of LDFs. These collaborations are mainly oriented towards bridging the gap between the new biotechnologies and the established industry. Later on, however, the DBFs are finally considered as an extension of internal R&D facilities, allowing LDFs to explore a wider opportunity-space. Therefore, collaborations become more frequent and lasting in more advanced states of the industry evolution.

In section 2 we argued that the persistence of innovation networks in the biotechnology-based industries could not be explained by means of only one role played by DBFs. Whereas in early stages the small technology-oriented firms play the role of translators, facilitating the absorption of the new technologies by LDFs, in later stages they become more emancipated as collaboration partners. This means that they no longer serve solely as institutions transferring knowledge between academic and industrial research, but become explorers, allowing LDFs to investigate a broader technological portfolio in an increasing complex technological opportunity-space. This changed role of the DBFs accordingly has to be observed also in the simulation as a development which endogenously takes place within our model's specification. In Figure 5.7 we therefore plot the specific composition of collaborative agreements.

In the first part of the period investigated only co-operative arrangements between LDFs and DBFs are found: DBFs are supposed to support LDFs in building up their biotechnology competencies; and, as a compensation for their R&D efforts, they are funded by LDFs. As soon as some DBFs start to earn their own money they also initiate further collaborations in which they are no longer playing the role of translators but that of explorers. In the simulation we find that these collaborations between DBFs become of increasing importance in later stages. Now, the co-operative

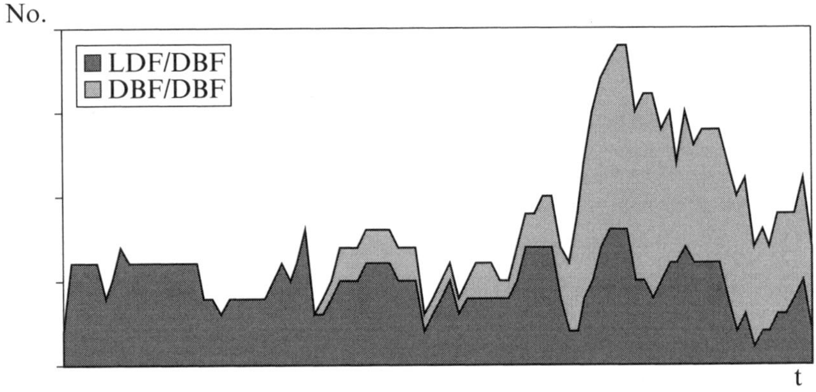

Figure 5.7 Composition of collaborations: LDF/DBF and DBF/DBF

agreements aim at bundling know-how and joint exploration of the technological opportunities. At the end of the period studied the number of agreements between DBFs is becoming comparable to that of agreements between LDFs and DBFs.

This changed role played by DBFs is also mirrored in the decisions made by firms with respect to their collaboration policy. In the model we differ between three strategies: first, the go-it-alone strategy chosen by firms who are either at the technological frontier and do not want to share know-how with followers or by firms which already are engaged in several co-operations. The second strategy aims at attracting research funds; this strategy is adopted by the DBFs in their early phases, when they enter the scene with highly developed technological competencies but they have no economic competencies. Finally, the third strategy aims at the integration of external knowledge in order to build up jointly in a network the capabilities necessary for the introduction of an innovation.

Figure 5.8 shows the share of strategy choices the firms (LDFs and DBFs) make with respect to the specific form of co-operation they want to initiate. This decision, of course, is always influenced by the relative position of the firm, and in particular depends on whether the firm is already engaged in one or more co-operations. Therefore, the white area representing the proportion of firms who do not want to start a new co-operation has to grow with the number of already existing networks because of the increasing co-ordination costs. In the early stages almost all firms wish to start new co-operative relationships according to the translator's type (black shaded area). With the growing diffusion of technological competencies within the population of LDFs and as some successful DBFs

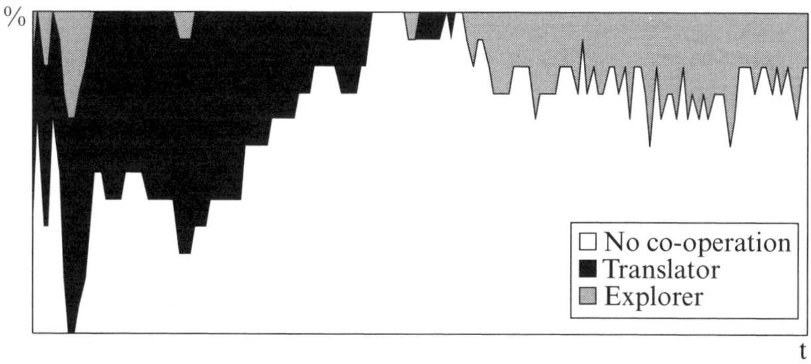

Figure 5.8 *Willingness to start a new collaboration and Strategy choice*

become vertically integrated producers, this decision shifts nearly exclusively to collaborative relationships following the explorer's type (grey shaded area). This also means that the new collaborative agreements to be started in later periods will almost entirely be of this latter type which is in line with the results shown in Figure 5.7.

For an immediate comparison of our artificial world with developments in the real world we use graph theory (e.g. Burt 1980) which offers some measures to compare different networks from a structural perspective. These measures describe, for example, the adjacency, the reachability and the connectivity of a network as well as the centrality of single actors (e.g. Freeman 1979). By comparing these figures we will get some first insights into whether we have caught the basic mechanisms of networking in our industries, or where we have to modify specific components of our model in order to improve our understanding.

The empirical database contains collaborations in the biotechnology-based industries from 1982 to 1998. For more details of the database see Pyka and Saviotti (2002).

In the following we have applied two concepts, in particular the average distance and the degree of centrality in order to compare time-series of artificial networks with real networks. The computations are done with Ucinet (Bogatti et al. 1999), a software tool designed for network analysis.

Figure 5.9 shows the development of the average distance, a measure of the average shortest path between two nodes for our artificial network as well as for our empirical database. This measure can be interpreted as an indicator of the diffusion of information in a network. Both figures show a structural similarity in a sequence of peaks which indicate a qualitative change in the network structure. Whereas these peaks grow in magnitude in

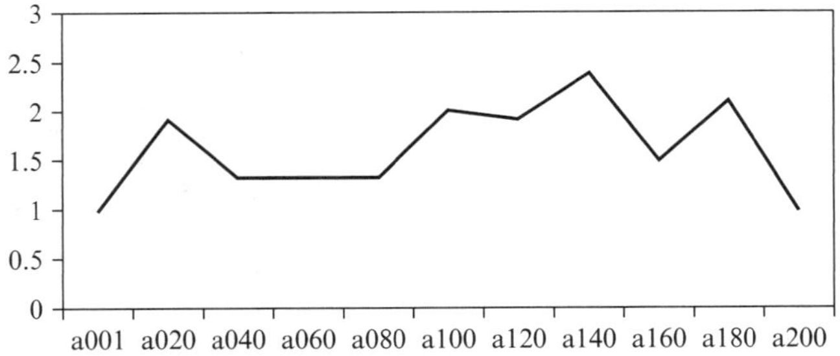

Figure 5.9a *Average distance in the artificial world*

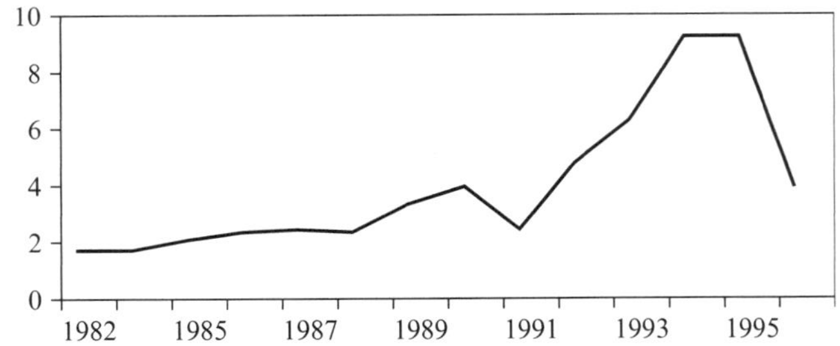

Figure 5.9b *Average distance in the real world*

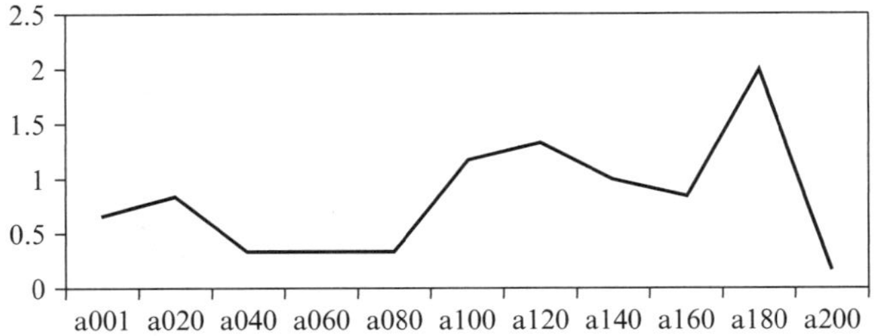

Figure 5.10a *Degree of centrality in the artificial world*

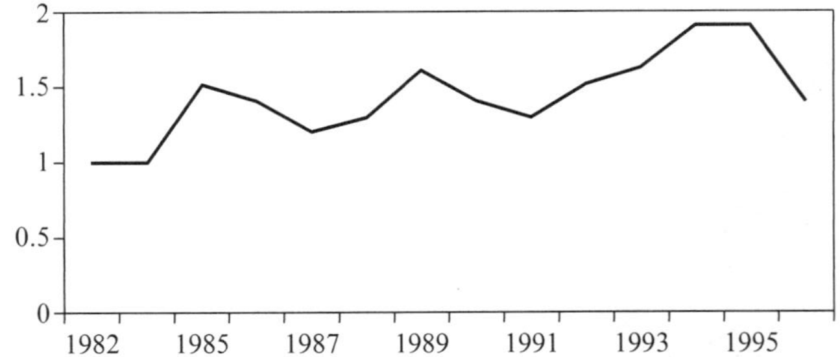

Figure 5.10b *Degree of centrality in the real world*

the real world, their artificial counterpart stays almost on the same level and also the second peak is unimodal in the real world compared to the bimodal peak in the artificial world. This difference is basically caused by the different sizes of the empirical and the artificial populations. The populations in the simulation run are kept smaller due to computational restrictions.

To rule out the influence of network size, index-oriented measures exist. Here we measured and calculated the degree of centrality for both of our worlds shown in Figure 5.10. The degree of centrality measures the asymmetry in the roles played by various actors in a network. For this aspect of network activity we also find a broad correspondence of our artificial and real worlds. The sequence of three peaks can be interpreted as a consequence of the changing role of DBFs in the networking processes. The first peak is caused by DBFs playing the role of translators supporting the LDFs in their efforts to overcome the gap between their dominant knowledge orientation and the upcoming new knowledge-base in biotechnology. The second peak has to be characterised as an intermediate phase, with some DBFs who have already become vertically integrated producers and LDFs still mainly concerned with building up competencies in the new field. The third wave in networking is then caused by a tremendous growth in the technological opportunity-space, where networking is considered to be a strategy to cope with the speed and complexity of technological development. In this phase DBFs play the role of explorers allowing the large and established firms to explore a wider range of technological approaches within biotechnology.

5. CONCLUSIONS

This chapter provides a simulation analysis of the evolution of innovation networks in the biotechnology-based industries. Since this is an applied simulation exercise, great emphasis is placed on the characteristic features of this industry. The results of the simulations are compared to developments in the real world by applying concepts of graph theory which provide us with some measurements of the overall network dynamics. Although there are still some significant differences between the artificial evolution of network structures and the real-world networks, the results look promising as they are able to reproduce at least qualitatively some developments which are observed in reality. The next steps have to be to balance the different mechanisms and to find relative weights in accordance with their specific impacts. Once such weights were attributed, different scenarios could be analysed, showing the influence of different environments as well as of policy measures aiming at the establishment of these new biotechnology-based industries.

One final remark with respect to the stochastic influence of innovation processes on results seems to be necessary. By repeating the simulation experiment several times the Poisson-distributed random number responsible for the innovation event leads to varying relationships between the firms in our sample. However, although collaboration partners change the overall network dynamics do not depend on stochastic influences, but remain rather stable over a large number of simulation experiments performed in a Monte-Carlo-method fashion.

To summarise, in our research we started from the empirical literature and from the existing case studies on the biotechnology-based sectors and developed a formal representation of innovation networks that, while abstract, matched a number of the observed features of innovation in these sectors. Going through this analytical exercise has significantly sharpened our theoretical understanding of the key factors behind the development of networking in the biotechnology-based sectors and contributed to a more general understanding of innovation networks in other sectors.

NOTES

1. The description of the model is given in a non-equation form, not explicitly introducing into details. Interested readers may obtain a comprehensive description of the model by writing to the authors.
2. In this respect, a major methodological advantage of simulation studies shows up in the construction of the innovation processes. Whereas in traditional optimisation models there is no difference between the modeller and the modelled agents, simulation analysis allows programming random numbers whose statistical distribution is unknown to the agents in the model, see Pyka (1999, pp. 189ff.).

REFERENCES

Bogatti, S.P., M.G. Everett and L.C. Freeman (1999), *Ucinet 5 for Windows: Software for Social Network Analysis*, Natick, MA: Analytic Technologies.

Burt, R.S. (1980), 'Models of network structure', *Annual Review of Sociology*, **6**, 79–141.

Cantner, U. and A. Pyka (1998), 'Absorbing technological spillovers: simulations in an evolutionary framework', *Industrial and Corporate Change*, **7**, 369–97.

Cohen, W.M. and D. Levinthal (1989), 'Innovation and learning: the two faces of R&D', *The Economic Journal*, **99**, 569–96.

Freeman, L.C. (1979), 'Centrality in social networks, conceptual clarification', *Social Networks*, **1**, 215–39.

Grabowski, H. and J. Vernon (1994), 'Innovation and structural change in pharmaceuticals and biotechnology', *Industrial and Corporate Change*, **3**, 435–49.

Kuenne, R.E. (1992), *The Economics of Oligopolistic Competition*, Cambridge, MA: Blackwell.

Malerba, F., R.R. Nelson, L. Orsenigo and S.G. Winter (1999), 'History friendly models of industry evolution: the computer industry', *Industrial and Corporate Change*, **8**, 3–40.
Nelson, R.R. and S.G. Winter (1982), *An Evolutionary Theory of Economic Change*, Cambridge: Cambridge University Press.
Prahalad, C.K. and G. Hamel (1990), 'The core competencies of the corporation', *Harvard Business Review*, **90**, 79–91.
Pyka, A. (1999), *Der kollektive Innovationsprozeß – Eine theoretische Analyse absorptiver Fähigkeiten und informeller Netzwerke*, Berlin: Duncker & Humblot.
Pyka, A. and Saviotti, P.-P. (2002), 'Innovation networks in the biotechnology-based sectors', in A. Pyka and G. Küppers (eds), Innovation Networks – Theory and Practice, Cheltenham UK and Northampton, MA, USA: Edward Elgar.
Saviotti, P.-P. (1998), 'Industrial Structure and the Dynamics of Knowledge Generation in Biotechnology', in Jacqueline Senker (ed.), *Biotechnology and Competitive Advantage: Europe's Firms and the US Challenge*, Cheltenham, UK and Northampton, MA, USA: Edward Elgar.
Staropoli, C. (1998), 'Cooperation in R&D in the pharmaceutical industry', *Technovation*, **18**, 13–24.
Teece D. (1986), 'Profiting from technological innovation', *Research Policy*, **15**, 285–305.
Tushman, M.L. and P. Anderson (1986), 'Technological discontinuities and organizational environments', *Administrative Science Quarterly*, **31**, 439–65.

6. Sociodynamics – an integrated approach to modelling in the social sciences

Wolfgang Weidlich

INTRODUCTION

Sociodynamics has the ambitious aim of providing a general strategy, which means a frame of theoretical concepts for designing mathematical models for the quantitative description of a rather broad class of collective dynamical phenomena within human society.

In the meantime these design principles have been applied to models of migration of interacting populations, group dynamics, political opinion formation, non-equilibrium economics and urban evolution.

A full acount of the sociodynamic method and its applications can be found in a recent book of the author (Weidlich 2002).

The present chapter sketches the main ideas and, as an example, their application to problems of migration and urban evolution.

Since sociodynamics provides an *open frame* for model design, it can be expected that previous models will not be the end but rather the beginning of further progress.

1. PRINCIPLES

1.1

Sociodynamics aims at describing the dynamics of processes in human society – i.e. not only stationary states – on the macro level by an overarching mathematical concept of model design.

1.2

The micro level of individuals and the macro level of collective evolution are mutually interdependent. The formalism takes this fact into account.

1.3

Concepts of social science, notably the motivations, decisions and actions of individuals under the influence of collective trends are integrated from the start. Therefore, sociodynamics is not at all a 'physicalism'.

1.4

Transition rates between states in the space of configurations of the social system (e.g. of its demographic, economic, social or political sector) are the central concept of sociodynamics. They comprise individual motivations and collective trends as well and engender the dynamics of the system.

1.5

Equations of evolution for system states are derived starting from the transition rates, either on the probabilistic level (including all fluctuations) or on the deterministic level (for the mean evolution).

1.6

Simulations of scenarios represent possible evolutions according to the models. After appropriately adjusted calibration of trend parameters the real evolution can also be interpreted and forecast in terms of the models.

2 FORMAL FRAME

2.1 State and Variables of State

The state of a society is characterised:
on the one side by a set of personal variables

$$\mathrm{n} = \{\ldots n_i^\alpha \ldots\} \tag{6.1}$$

where the meaning of n_i^α = is the following:

n_i^α = number of members of a subpopulation $\mathcal{P}^\alpha$ having an 'attitude' (i.e. opinion, or kind of activity) '*i*'.

on the other side by a set of material variables

$$\mathrm{m} = \{m_1, \ldots, m_k \ldots m_K\} \tag{6.2}$$

where the meaning of m_k can for instance be: number of produced commodities per unit of time; price of one unit of a commodity; number of buildings on a site of a city; etc. The multiple of variables

$$\mathrm{v} = \{\mathrm{n}; \mathrm{m}\} \tag{6.3}$$

is an element of the space of socioconfigurations. It describes the personal and material state of the society, or of one of its sectors, e.g. of the demographic, urban, economic, sociopolitical sector, respectively.

2.2 Transitions and Transition Rates

The dynamics of the society is described by transitions from any one given initial state v_a to a neighbouring state v_b.

Transition rates (by definition probabilities per unit of time proceeding from state v_a to state v_b) engender the transitions, i.e. they are the 'driving forces' of the transitions. They are induced by the activities of individuals (e.g. on the migratory, social, economic or political sector).

Since transition rates are by definition always positive definite quantities they can be written in the form

$$w_{ba}(\mathrm{v}_b; \mathrm{v}_a) = n_a p_{ba} = n_a \mu_0 \exp\{M_{ba}(\mathrm{v}_b, \mathrm{v}_a)\} \tag{6.4}$$

where n_a is the number of individuals initiating the transition $\mathrm{v}_a \Rightarrow \mathrm{v}_b$. The individual transition rates p_{ba} can be mathematically represented in a standard form:

$$p_{ba}(\mathrm{v}_b; \mathrm{v}_a) = \mu(\mathrm{v}_b, \mathrm{v}_a)\exp\{u_b(\mathrm{v}_b) - u_a(\mathrm{v}_a)\} \tag{6.5}$$

Interpretation of transition rates

From the form of equation (6.5) of the individual transition rates there follows their general sociodynamic meaning:

> The motivation potential $M_{ba}(\mathrm{v}_b, \mathrm{v}_a)$ depends on the motivation of the individuals initiating the transition. Their motivation arises from comparing and evaluating the initial state v_a versus the intended state v_b.

The mobility $\mu(v_b, v_a) = \mu(v_a, v_b)$ is a measure (symmetric in v_a and v_b) of the speed of the transition.

The attractiveness $u_a(v_a)$ and $u_b(v_b)$ is the respective measure of the utility of the initial state v_a and intended state v_b, valuated by the individuals initiating the transition. If $u_b(v_b)$ exceeds $u_a(v_a)$, the transition $v_a \Rightarrow v_b$ is favoured against the inverse transition $v_b \Rightarrow v_a$ according to equation (6.5). The functions $u_a(v_a)$ and $u_b(v_b)$ are also denoted as 'dynamic utility functions' in order to distinguish them from utility functions used in neoclassical modelling concepts.

2.3 Evolution of the Socioconfiguration

The sequence of elementary transitions between neighbouring states eventually leads to the long-term evolution of the social system. The description of this evolution can take place on two levels of exactitude:

If the probabilistic nature of all stepwise actions of individuals is fully taken into account, their composition will also lead to a probabilistic evolution of the collective macrovariables introduced in section 2.1. We thus obtain a probabilistic description of the evolution of the society on the macro level.

If instead only the mean evolution of a bundle of 'stochastic trajectories' is considered one obtains by neglection of fluctuations a deterministic description of the evolution of the society or its sectors in terms of 'quasi-mean values'.

The probabilistic description

This description is based on the master equation, i.e. the central equation for the evolution of the probability distribution over all collective macrovariables of the social system.

Let $P(v; t)$ be the probability of finding realised the configuration v of the social system at time t. Since any one of the – mutually exclusive – configurations must be realised, the total probability of all configurations is equal to one:

$$\sum_{v} P(v; t) = 1 \tag{6.6}$$

The master equation, which is compatible with (6.6), reads in its general form:

$$\begin{aligned} \frac{dP(v_a; t)}{dt} = &-\sum_{v_b} w_{ba}(v_b; v_a)P(v_a; t) \\ &+ \sum_{v_b} w_{ab}(v_a; v_b)P(v_b; t) \end{aligned} \tag{6.7}$$

It can easily be understood that the change with time of the probability v_a, i.e. the l.h.s. of (6.7), comes about by two contraproductive processes, namely:

1. the outflux from probability $P(v_a; t)$ into the probabilities of neighbouring configurations v_b (first term of the r.h.s. of (6.7))
2. the influx from probabilities $P(v_b; t)$ of neighbouring configurations v_b into the probability of configuration v_a (second term of the r.h.s. of (6.7)).

It should be noted that the master equation, in spite of its easy interpretation, is not easily solved!

The deterministic description

The concrete single social system traverses a 'stochastic trajectory'. It is the macroscopic resultant of all accidential, but motivation-guided actions of individuals. Considering, however, a bundle of such trajectories starting – under equal model assumptions – from the configuration $\hat{v}(t_0)$, there results within the small interval of time τ a 'preferred' mean evolution to configuration $\hat{v}(t_0 + \tau)$. If the sequence of 'preferred mean evolutions' is composed, one obtains deterministic differential equations for the 'quasi-mean values' $\hat{v}(t)$.

In the case of $\hat{v} = \{\ldots \hat{n}_i^\alpha \ldots; \ldots \hat{m}_k \ldots\}$, which means of the personal and material variables of the socioconfiguration (3), the quasi-mean value equations have the form:

$$\frac{d\hat{m}_k}{dt} = w_k(\hat{m}_k^+, \hat{m}) - w_k(\hat{m}_k^-, \hat{m}) \tag{6.8}$$

$$\frac{d\hat{n}_i^\alpha}{dt} = \sum_j w_{ij}^\alpha(\hat{n}_{ij}^\alpha, \hat{n}) - \sum_j w_{ji}^\alpha(\hat{n}_{ji}^\alpha, \hat{n}) \tag{6.9}$$

where $\hat{n}_{ij}^\alpha$, $\hat{n}_{ji}^\alpha$ are personal configurations adjacent to $\hat{n}$, and $\hat{m}_k^+$, $\hat{m}_k^-$ are material configurations adjacent to $\hat{m}$. And $w_{ij}^\alpha(\hat{n}_{ij}^\alpha, \hat{n})$, $w_{ji}^\alpha(\hat{n}_{ji}^\alpha, \hat{n})$, $w_k(\hat{m}_k^+, \hat{m})$, $w_k(\hat{m}_k^-, \hat{m})$ are the transition rates for the transitions $\hat{n} \Rightarrow \hat{n}_{ij}^\alpha$; $\hat{n} \Rightarrow \hat{n}_{ji}^\alpha$; $\hat{m} \Rightarrow \hat{m}_k^+$; $\hat{m} \Rightarrow \hat{m}_k^-$, respectively.

3. SCENARIOS OF SELECTED MODELS

We now consider the general procedure for designing selected models and we present some of their results in terms of characteristic scenarios.

3.1 Migration

As a first model we consider the interregional migration of socioculturally differentiated populations.

The procedure of model design consists of the following steps:

1. Introduction of variables: numbers of P 'subpopulations' distributed over L regions
2. Choice of transition rates for migration between regions: by introducing plausible 'dynamic utility functions' taking into account migratory trends
3. Setting up of equations of evolution (master equation; quasi-mean value equations)
4. Calculation of characteristic scenarios after explicit choice of trend-parameters.

The model comprises globally different cases of migratory dynamics:

- the development of a homogeneous mixture
- the development of ghettos
- the development of a 'penetration-evasion dynamics'.

and there exist phase-transitions between these cases, which can be studied in terms of the model.

The simplest case

Two populations 1, 2 migrating between two regions a, b.

We now skip steps 2 and 3 and only present characteristic scenarios, namely solutions of the quasi-mean value equations and the master equation for selected trend-parameters in the two populations–two regions case.

Variables:

$-1 \leq x \leq +1$: Scaled distribution of population 1 over regions a and b.

$-1 \leq y \leq +1$: Scaled distribution of population 2 over regions a and b.

Case. 1 Trend towards homogeneous population mixture for weak internal agglomeration trend within, and weak symmetrical segregation trend between both populations.

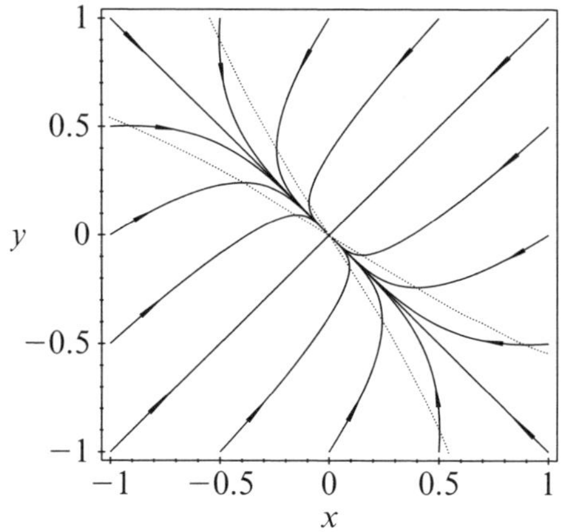

Figure 6.1a Fluxlines of the quasi-mean values
The stable homogeneous population mixture $x=0$; $y=0$ of both populations over both regions is approached.

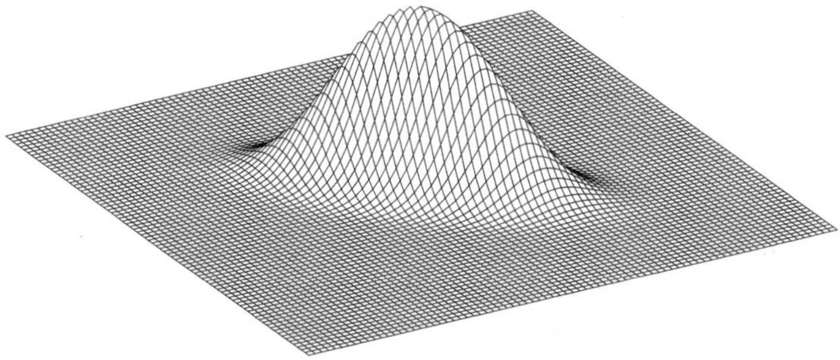

Figure 6.1b The stationary unimodal probability distribution of both populations over both regions
The maximal probability is at $x=0$; $y=0$.

Case. 2 Trend towards ghetto formation for moderate internal agglomeration trend within, but strong symmetrical segregation trend between both populations.

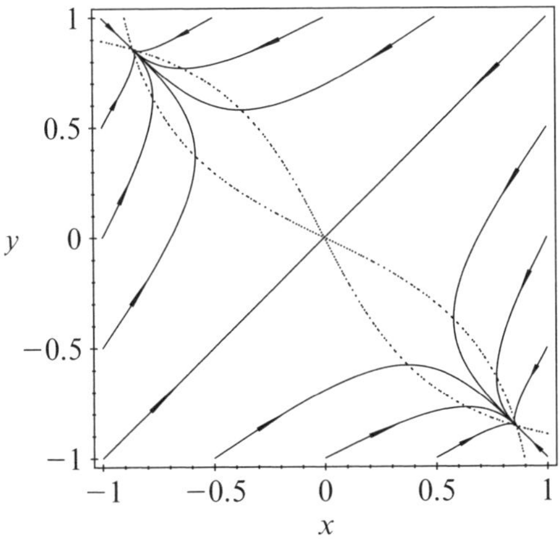

Figure 6.2a Fluxlines of the quasi-mean values
Stable stationary ghetto situations are approached, where either population 1 is concentrated in region *a* and population 2 in region *b*, or vice versa.

Figure 6.2b Bimodal stationary probability distribution with probability peaks at the ghetto situations

Case. 3 Trend towards homogeneous population mixture for moderate internal agglomeration trend within, and strong assymmetric segregation trend between both populations.

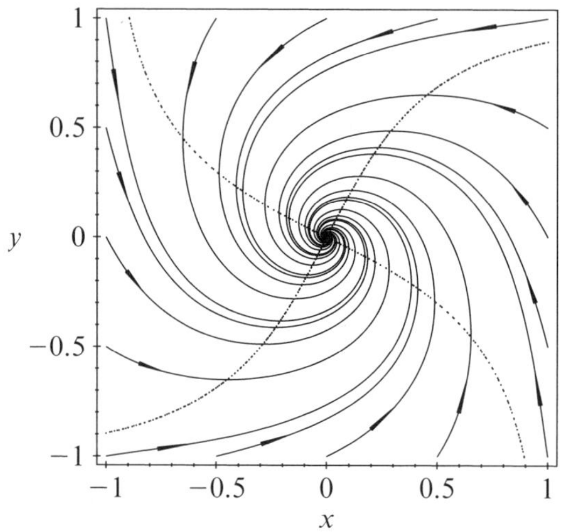

Figure 6.3a Fluxlines of quasi-mean values
They approach the stable focus $x = 0$; $y = 0$ of homogeneous population mixture.

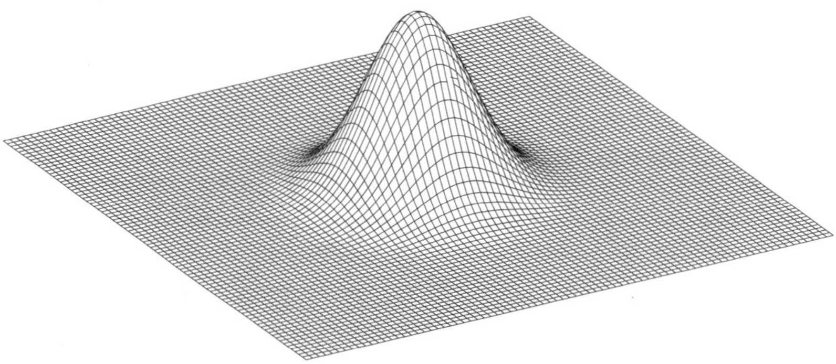

Figure 6.3b The stationary unimodal probability distribution with maximum at x = *0;* y = *0*

Case. 4 Evolution of a penetration-evasion dynamics for strong internal agglomeration trend within, and strong assymmetrical segregation trend between both populations.

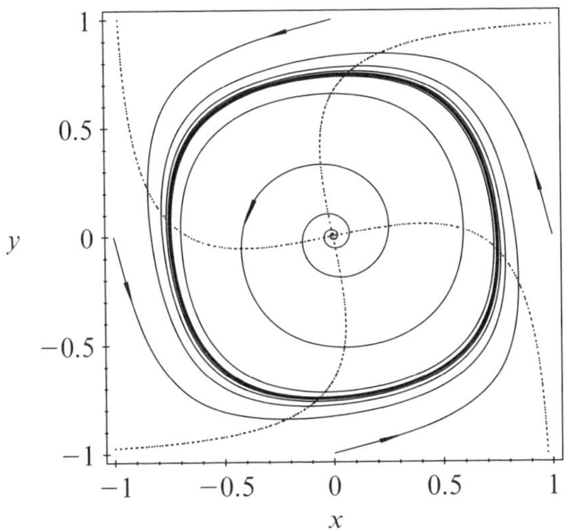

Figure 6.4a Fluxlines of quasi-mean values
They approach a limit-cycle, whereas the point $x=0$, $y=0$ is now an unstable focus.

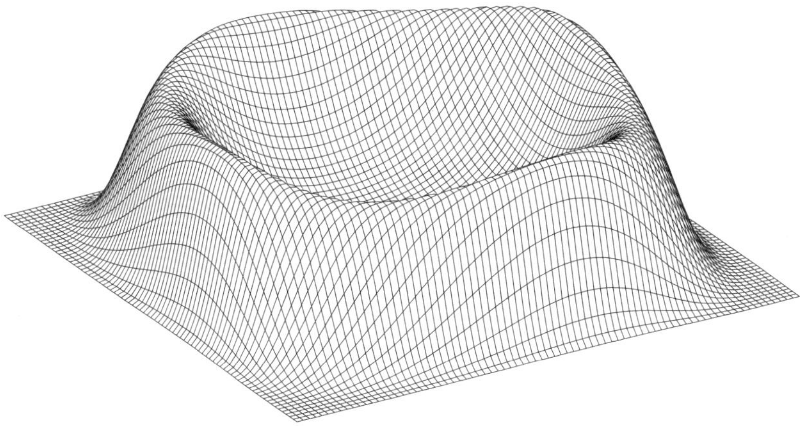

Figure 6.4b Stationary probability distribution with a 'probability ridge' along the limit-cycle of the quasi-mean values

Interregional migration in the Federal Republic of Germany between 1957 and 1983

Another application of the migration model consisted in the comparison and correlation between the model and empirical data for the interregional migration in the Federal Republic of Germany from 1957 to 1983.

For this purpose the following procedure was implemented:

1. The yearly population numbers of the federal states of Germany during the past 25 years were available.
2. The regional utility functions were determined year by year for this period so that the results of the model equations coincided with the real evolution.
3. The correlation of the regional utility functions with regional socio-economic key variables was determined by regression analysis.

The result of the determination of the time-dependent regional utility functions by comparison between model and empirical data is exhibited in Figure 6.5.

The result of the correlation of regional utility functions $ui(t)$ with regional socio-economic key variables by regression analysis is exhibited in Figure 6.6.

3.2 Integrated Evolution of a City and its Population

As a second model we consider the interrelated evolution of a city and its population. The 'sociodynamic' procedure of model design is now more complex and consists of the following steps:

Introduction of variables

The set of variables consists of material and personal variables.

The material variables are formed by first tessellating the area of city c and hinterland h into a lattice of sites with co-ordinates $i(i_1, i_2), j(j_1, j_2); \ldots$. Thereupon on each site 'i' several units $m_i^{(K)}$ of types ... K ... L ... of buildings can be erected until eventually the capacity limit C_i is reached. The multiple

$$\mathrm{m} = \{\ldots m_i^{(K)} \ldots m_i^{(L)} \ldots m_j^{(K)} \ldots m_j^{(L)}\} \tag{6.10}$$

then forms an 'occupation number representation' of a concrete material state of city and hinterland which is an element of the 'space of city and hinterland configurations'.

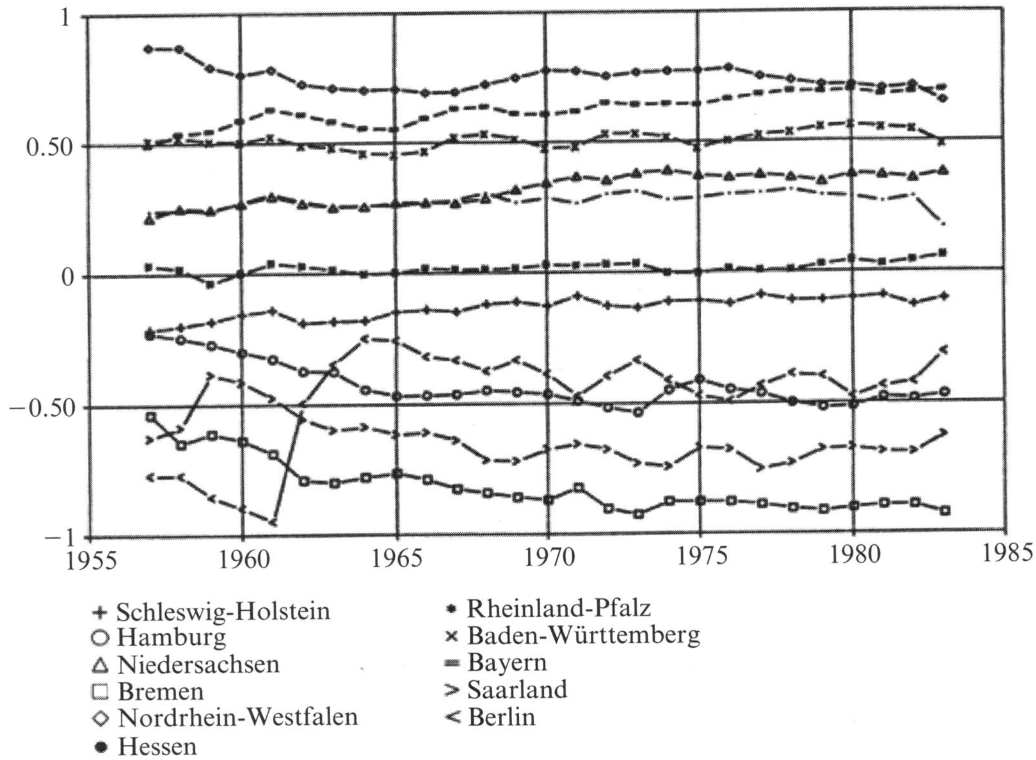

Figure 6.5 The estimated regional utilities $u_i(t)$ *of the Federal Republic of Germany*

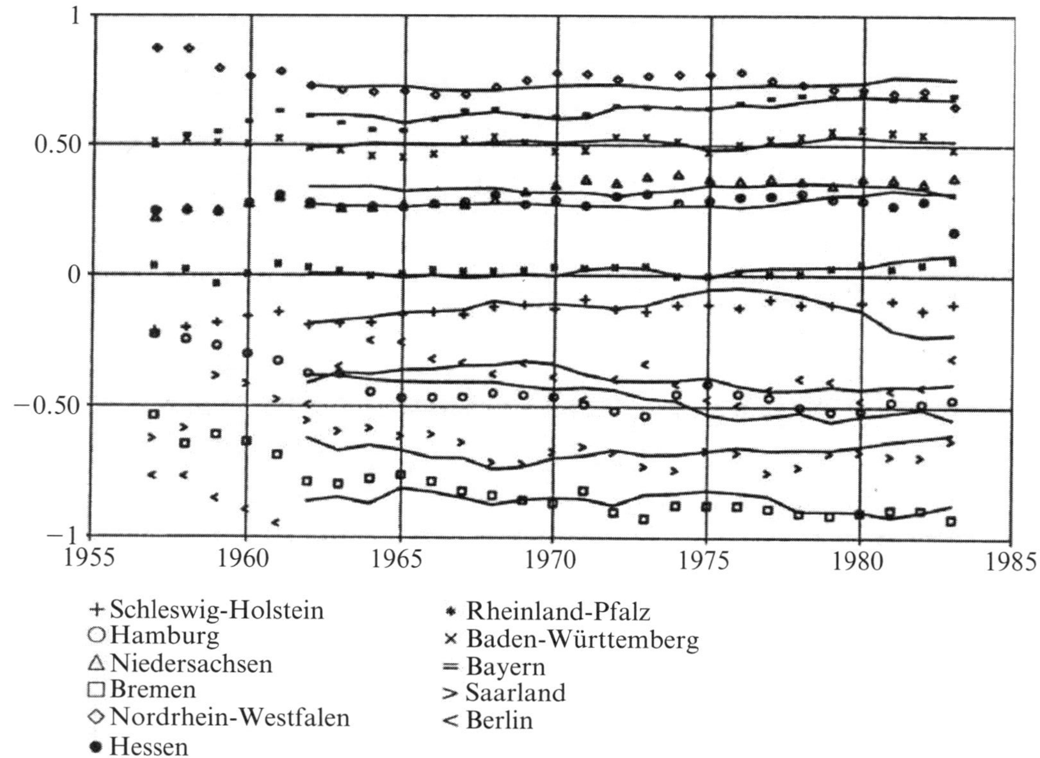

Figure 6.6. Key-factor analysis of the regional utilities of the Federal Republic of Germany

The personal variables describe how several subpopulations $\mathcal{P}^\alpha$ are distributed over the sites 'i', so that N_i^α members of $\mathcal{P}^\alpha$ live on site 'i'. The multiple

$$\mathrm{N} = \{\ldots N_j^\alpha \ldots\} \tag{6.11}$$

then characterises this distribution and is an element of the 'space of population configurations'.

Choice of transitions and transition rates

The integrated material and personal evolution of city and hinterland is engendered by the following elementary transitions:

- construction and tearing down processes of building units of type K on site 'i'

$$\mathrm{m} = \{\ldots m_i^K \ldots\} \Rightarrow \mathrm{m}_{i\pm}^{(K)} = \{\ldots, (m_i^{(K)} \pm 1), \ldots\}. \tag{6.12}$$

- birth-death processes of members of $\mathcal{P}^\alpha$ on site i

$$\mathrm{N} = \{\ldots N_i^\alpha \ldots\} \Rightarrow \mathrm{N}_{i\pm}^\alpha = \{\ldots, (N_i^\alpha \pm 1), \ldots\}. \tag{6.13}$$

- migration of members of $\mathcal{P}^\alpha$ from site 'i' to site 'j'

$$\mathrm{N} = \{\ldots N_j^\alpha \ldots N_i^\alpha \ldots\} \Rightarrow \mathrm{N}_{ji}^\alpha \{\ldots (N_j^\alpha + 1) \ldots, (N_i^\alpha - 1), \ldots\}. \tag{6.14}$$

To these elementary transitions there belong the following transition rates, respectively

$$w_{i\uparrow}^K(\mathrm{m}, \mathrm{N})\,;\, w_{i\downarrow}^K(\mathrm{m}, \mathrm{N}) \tag{6.15}$$

$$w_{i\uparrow}^\alpha(\mathrm{m}, \mathrm{N})\,;\, w_{i\downarrow}^\alpha(\mathrm{m}, \mathrm{N}) \tag{6.16}$$

$$w_{ji}^\alpha(\mathrm{m}, \mathrm{N}) \tag{6.17}$$

According to their standard form (6.4), (6.5), the transition rates can and must be further specified in order to obtain a concrete integrated city and population evolution model. This has been done in the author's book mentioned in the introduction, from which we take the further concrete results.

Setting up of equations of evolution

We restrict further consideration to the quasi-mean value equations which have, according to equation (6.8) and equation (6.9), the following general form:

$$\frac{d\hat{m}_j^{(K)}}{dt} = w_{j\uparrow}^{(K)}(\hat{\mathrm{m}}, \hat{\mathrm{N}}) - w_{j\downarrow}^{(K)}(\hat{\mathrm{m}}, \hat{\mathrm{N}}) \tag{6.18}$$

for the evolution of the material variables, and

$$\frac{d\hat{N}_j^{(\alpha)}}{dt} = \sum_i w_{ji}^{\alpha}(\hat{\mathrm{m}}, \hat{\mathrm{N}}) - \sum_i w_{ij}^{\alpha}(\hat{\mathrm{m}}, \hat{\mathrm{N}}) + w_{j\uparrow}^{\alpha}(\hat{\mathrm{m}}, \hat{\mathrm{N}}) - w_{j\downarrow}^{\alpha}(\hat{\mathrm{m}}, \hat{\mathrm{N}}) \quad (6.19)$$

for the evolution of the personal variables.

Scenarios

Integrated models of course contain several sectors which may be treated separately under simplifying assumptions. In the present model, the interaction between city- and population-evolution essentially depends on how city and hinterland provide capacities C_c and C_h, respectively, for a (perhaps growing) total population.

If on the other hand the capacities C_i of each site i of the city are (formally) kept constant, the evolution of the city configuration must come to an end when all capacities are exhausted. This case is treated in the following scenario.

The first sector: a simple model city

For a simple 'model city' a square lattice of 15×15 sites is assumed with a 'natural' constant capacity distribution over the sites determined by a landscape which contains a river. Only apartments and commerical buildings are assumed to exist and the utility functions in the transition rates take neighbourhood relations between both kinds of buildings into account. Starting from a 'natural' initial condition of a not yet developed city the concrete explicit quasi-mean value equations then eventually lead to a final distribution of 'apartments' and 'commerical buildings' over the sites of the city. (It should be noted that the end configuration depends on some details of the initial configuration. Hence the evolution is 'path-dependent' due to the non-linear structure of the quasi-mean value equations.)

The final distribution of apartments on the lattice of 15×15 sites of a 'model city' is shown in Figure 6.7.

The final distribution of commercial buildings on a lattice of 15×15 sites of a 'model city' is shown in Figure 6.8.

The second sector: migration between hinterland and city

The second sector of the integrated model consists in the migration of the population between hinterland (h) and city (c), which is treated in the next scenario.

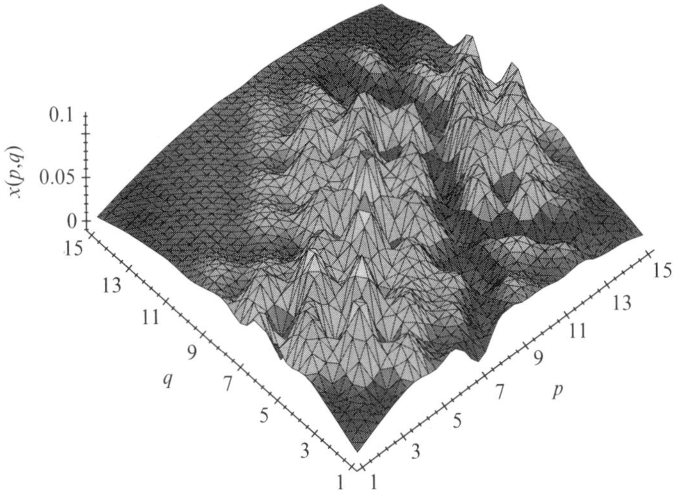

Figure 6.7a Perspective representation of distribution of apartments

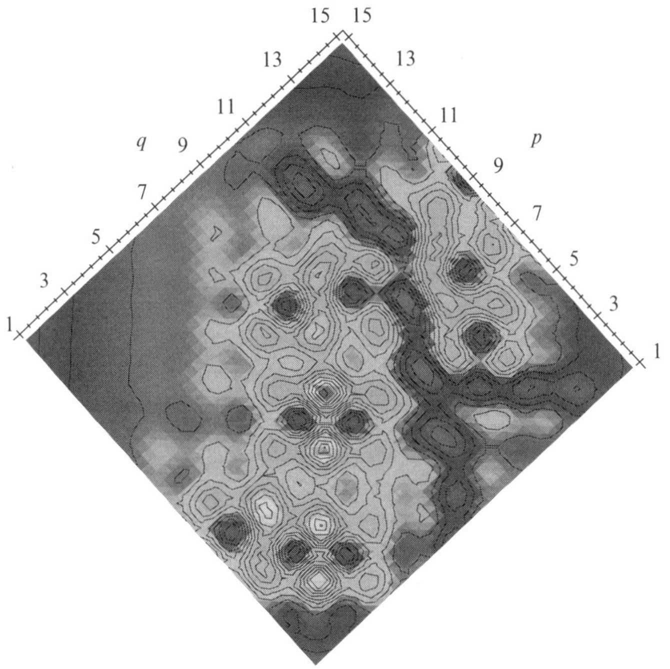

Figure 6.7b Topographic representation of distribution of apartments

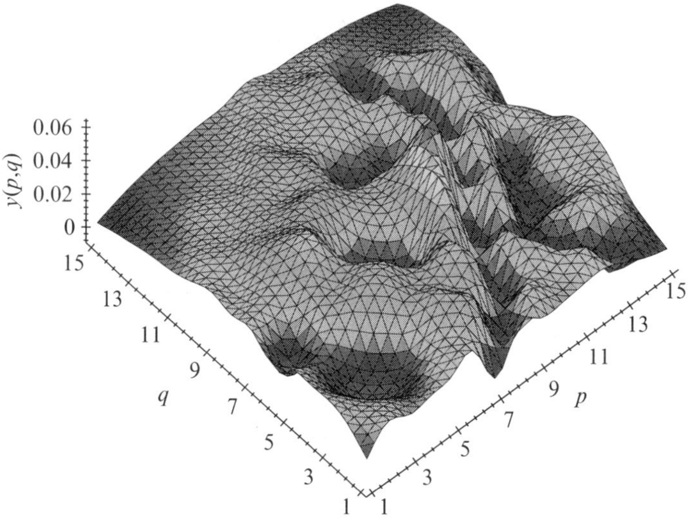

Figure 6.8a Perspective representation of distribution of commercial buildings

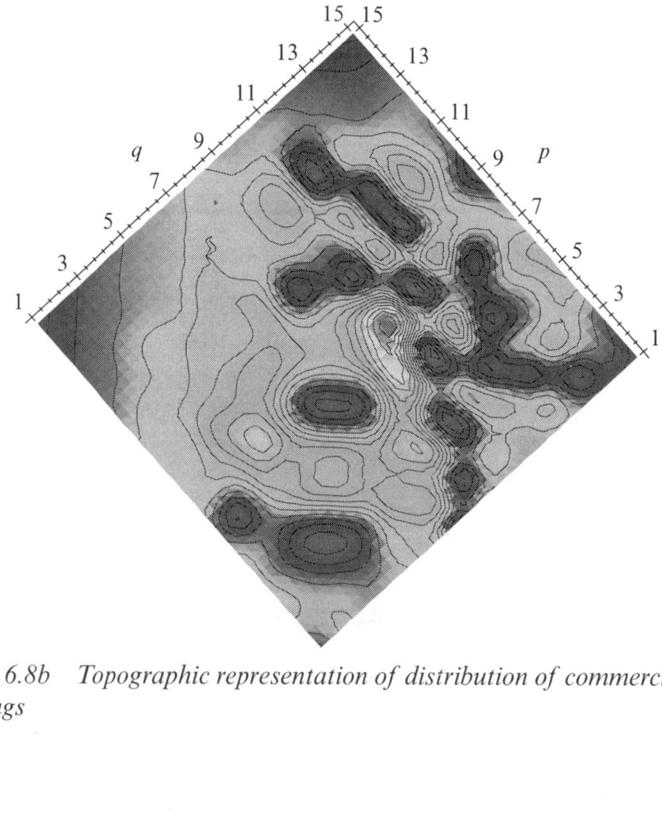

Figure 6.8b Topographic representation of distribution of commercial buildings

In this scenario we let the capacities C_c and C_h of city and hinterland depend on the respective time-dependent population numbers. The model equations are essentially simplified, if only aggregated population numbers are considered as follows:

$$\begin{aligned}
N_c &= n_c P = \text{ city population}\\
N_h &= n_h P = \text{hinterland population}\\
N_c + N_h &= P = \text{ total population}\\
n_c, n_h&: \text{population shares, where } (n_c + n_h) = 1\\
n = (n_c - n_h)&: \text{majority variable, where} -1 \leq n \leq +1
\end{aligned} \tag{6.20}$$

In the – now presumed – case of equal net birth-rates in city and hinterland the population equations (6.19) are decisively simplified to two equations for the population shares n_c, n_h only:

$$\begin{aligned}
\frac{dn_c}{dt} &= -p_{hc}n_c + p_{ch}n_h\\
\frac{dn_h}{dt} &= +p_{hc}n_c - p_{ch}n_h
\end{aligned} \tag{6.21}$$

or, because of $(n_c + n_h) = 1$, to *one equation* for the majority variable $n(t)$ only:

$$\frac{dn}{dt} = (p_{ch} - p_{hc}) - (p_{hc} + p_{ch})n \tag{6.22}$$

The transition rates have the standard form:

$$\begin{aligned}
p_{hc} &= v\exp[v_c - v_h] = v\exp[a(t) + b(t)n]\\
p_{ch} &= v\exp[v_h - v_c] = v\exp[-a(t) - b(t)n]
\end{aligned} \tag{6.23}$$

where v_c and v_h are measures for the attractiveness ('dynamic utility') of city and hinterland, respectively, and where it turns out, according to plausible assumptions of the form of v_c and v_h, that $a(t)$ and $b(t)$ are co-efficients depending on the (in general time-dependent) total population $P(t)$ and on the capacities $C_c(t)$ and $C_h(t)$ provided by city and hinterland.

Equation (6.22) for the evolution of the majority variable can be written in the form

$$\frac{dn}{dt} = -\frac{\partial V(n;t)}{\partial n} \tag{6.24}$$

after introduction of the 'evolution potential'

$$V(n;t) = v\left\{ e^{(a(t)+b(t)n)}\left[\frac{b(t)n-1}{b^2(t)} - \frac{1}{b(t)}\right] - e^{-(a(t)+b(t)n)}\left[\frac{b(t)n+1}{b^2(t)} + \frac{1}{b(t)}\right]\right\} \tag{6.25}$$

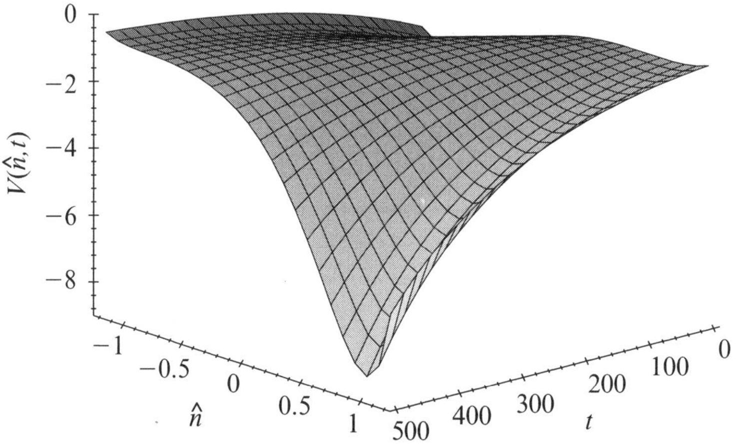

Figure 6.9 Development with time of the evolution potential V(n, t) *for growing total population and worsening balance of capacities between hinterland and city*

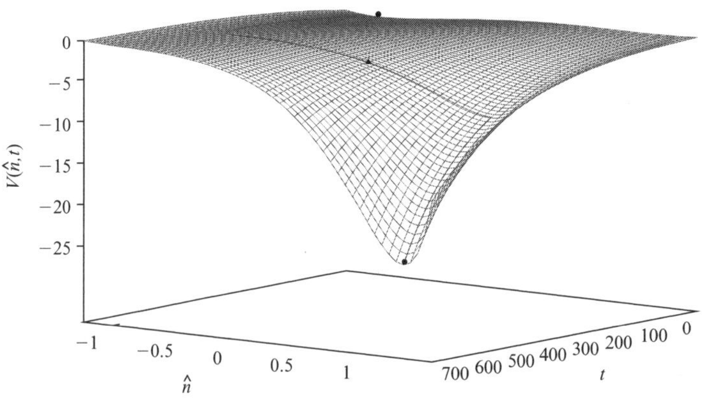

Figure 6.10 Evolution potential V(n, t) *with 'system point', representing the evolution of the majority variable* n(t) *with time*

Among the possible cases we consider the dramatic case of a growing total population and a simultaneously worsening balance of capacities between hinterland and city favouring the city. Then the slowly time-dependent potential $V(n;\ t)$ develops from a two-minima potential into a one-minimum potential. Correspondingly, the majority variable $n(t)$, i.e. the solution of equation (6.24), shows a first slow, then dramatically fast evolution exhibiting a rush of the population from hinterland into the city. Such a 'migratory phase transition' can take place in developing countries with a rural hinterland unable to feed and maintain its growing population which escapes into the neighbouring metropole.

The evolution potential $V(n;\ t)$ and the evolution of the majority variable $n(t)$ are exhibited in Figures 6.9 and 6.10.

REFERENCES

Weidlich, Wolfgang (2002), *Sociodynamics – A Systematic Approach to Mathematical Modelling in the Social Sciences*, London: Taylor & Francis.

7. The concept of space in trade – some evolutionary basics

Carsten Herrmann-Pillath[1]

1. THE CHALLENGE: EXPLAINING THE SPATIAL DIRECTEDNESS OF TRADE

The theory of international trade is one of the most developed contemporary applications of neoclassical equilibrium theory. Its political impact is tremendous, for it provides the intellectual foundation of the free-trade doctrine shaping the so-called 'neoliberal' approach to globalisation. Its academic rank and file obeys a tough intellectual discipline and receives a demanding, high-quality education.[2] The high scholarly appreciation refers to the elegance and coherence of the formal approach as well as to the tremendous efforts in empirical testing and application. The general significance of this strand of research is related to its very strong normative claims and, in particular, to the fact that the basic premise of trade theory, the theory of comparative advantage, is the most cogent demonstration of why markets are beneficial to all participants.

So far, the evolutionary economics of international trade is not a major concern. There are two salient topics, namely the impact of technology on trade (the seminal study is Dosi et al. 1990) and the role of corporate strategies and industrial policies in global competition (for example, see the volume edited by de la Mothe and Paquet 1996). However, there is no systematic attempt at deconstructing the neoclassical approach. Of course, one may hope that both approaches can co-exist, however, as they have fundamentally conflicting foundations, I think that this challenge should not be avoided. One obstacle to a reasonable debate is the fact that the debate is always inextricably linked with the free-trade issue, so that evolutionary approaches, unwillingly or not, are pushed into the corner of potentially protectionist positions.

Facing the impressive record of neoclassical trade theory, deconstructing its theoretical basics is by no means an easy endeavour. The normal scientific way to tackle a task of these dimensions is to focus on unresolved issues and anomalies of a theory in order to accomplish an alternative explanation that, at the same time, includes the mainstream theory as a special case.

1.1 Some Unresolved Issues in Trade Theory

There are two main anomalies in neoclassical trade theory (NTT). First, NTT cannot exhaustively explain the direction of trade in space (or, what the same thing amounts to, the location of production); second, the explanation of the increasing role of multinational corporations in trade remains difficult. The latter issue is linked with the former, because one major research topic is the investigation into the patterns of foreign direct investment, which also involves spatial patterns of economic activity of those firms (e.g. exports of foreign subsidiaries). In the past two decades, investigating these unresolved issues has triggered a burgeoning literature, mostly exploiting synergies between New Trade Theory and (New) Economic Geography (Krugman 1995; Helpman 1998). The trigger for this effort is the recognition of the blatant fact that real space does not actually exist in trade theory (frequently assuming even zero transport costs), which in its mainstream versions is a theory of the international allocation of production as a result of international equilibrium exchange (for a penetrating criticism, see Dunning 1995).

Let me summarise the main facts, beginning with the problem of spatial directedness of trade.

1. The factor-proportions theory leaves a significant share of trade-flows unexplained, i.e. given the current relative endowments of countries in the world, trade-flows should be significantly larger than the observed ones (Trefler 1993); at the same time, the general indeterminacy in multifactor, multigoods models can only be solved by adding exogenous costs of trade to the picture, hence disintegrating parameters in an otherwise perfectly integrated market system (Davis et al. 1997; Bernstein and Weinstein 1998).
2. The atheoretic gravity model is as useful as neoclassical trade theory in explaining trade-flows, however, at the same time this model shows a strong impact of singular spatial determinants on trade (Hummels and Levinsohn 1995; Helliwell 1997).
3. The law of one price is systematically invalid in the long run, including very strong 'border effects' across countries, although neoclassical theory leads to the expectation that violations should be short-run phenomena (Rogers and Jenkins 1995; Haskel and Wolf 1999); this issue is related to the widespread occurrence of 'pricing to market' phenomena in international trade, which renders the purchasing power parity

approach to real exchange rates problematic (Goldberg and Knetter 1997).

If we take a closer look at the arguments that are proposed to resolve these empirical riddles, so far the most important ones are:

1. Taking country-specific productivity differentials into consideration, differences either between observed and factual trade-flows or between expected and factual production structures of countries could be shown to reflect level-effects of the production function whilst still being influenced by relative factor prices (Harrigan 1997; Hanson and Slaughter 1999); in the most general terms, this amounts to an interference among relative and absolute advantages in the determination of trade-flows.
2. The gravity model can be fit into a factor-proportions approach, if it is implemented as a device to identify impediments to trade via the demand side of the model, that is to add multidimensional 'distances' to the neoclassical model, which at the same time reduces the indeterminacy problem in multifactor, multigoods models (Davis and Weinstein 1998).
3. Such kind of generalised 'distances' can also be referred to in order to explain observed deviations from the law of one price in both the gravity model and pricing-to-market models of imperfect competition, with the singular 'Armington bias' as a determinant of directedness serving as an econometric 'catch-all' parameter (Trefler 1995; Deardorff 1998; Engel and Rogers 1999).

Whereas mainstream trade economists interpret these approaches to a solution as supporting the neoclassical model, the particular arguments actually create leeway for switching to other theoretical approaches, simply by means of shifting the emphasis. That is, we could argue, for example, that a technology-based theory of trade is the basic model, which also shows the impact of relative factor endowments, without necessarily including the fully fledged neoclassical equilibrium theory as a reference. Similarly, generalised distances may be regarded as an empirical element of an institutional approach to trade, sticking to the gravity model without trying to adapt it to a general equilibrium framework.

In the 'pricing-to-market' literature, a major focus is the role of corporate strategies and competences in market entry (Clark et al. 1999). Hence, the aformentioned issues are also linked to the phenomenon of the transnational corporation, in the empirical respect at least.

Turning our attention to the second major field of research into open questions in international economics, the main empirical issues are:

1. There is a significantly positive interdependence between trade (goods with factor content) and investment (factor-flows), so that the implied convergence in relative factor-endowments is not reflected in trade-flows, implying that the factor-proportions theory is violated (Collins et al. 1997).
2. Worldwide FDI is mostly among nations on the same level of development and of the horizontal kind, which implies that investment flows cannot be influenced by relative factor-endowments and, hence, factor prices (Braunerhjelm and Lipsey 1998).
3. There is a strong impact of industry-specific determinants as opposed to country-specific determinants, so that countries may not be the relevant units of theorising (Markusen 1995).
4. Intra-industry trade is closely enmeshed with intrafirm trade, which raises the question whether trade-flows are strongly influenced by the institutional determinants of the 'market versus firm' alternative (Klau 1995).

The answers so far proposed by mainstream theory are, amongst others:

1. The factor-proportions approach may be empirically underdetermined because firm-specific knowledge-stocks are neglected, which also implies that observed trade might incompletely reflect intrafirm trade of the respective services ('headquarter services') (Ekholm 1998a; Markusen and Maskus 1999).
2. Equilibrium theory can be modified by including monopolistic competition so that market access becomes an important motive for intra-industry investment-flows, with market access being influenced by the attraction of larger markets as a location of production with increasing returns to scale, and with transport costs as a countervailing force of dispersion of production (Zhang and Markusen 1997; Markusen and Venables 1998).
3. Industry-specific effects may be related to differences in terms of the use of knowledge and human capital, which implies different market structures and firm behaviour, for example in terms of exploiting specific managerial competences (Ray 1995).
4. The 'market versus firm' framework may lead to an enlargement of the equilibrium theory by the neoclassical theory of the firm, so that the firm is a solution to market imperfections, which also impact the direction of trade (Anderson and Marcouiller 1999); hence, observed

patterns of trade and investment reflect the complex interaction of imperfections and costs in the market for goods and the market for direct investment (Ekholm 1998b).

As we see at first glance, these results can also be interpreted in terms of a change of paradigm, with the neoclassical arguments becoming a special case of a knowledge-oriented theory of the transnational corporation. Most of the contributions are useful and significant independently of the general framework of equilibrium theory, so that the naive question can be raised whether it is indeed worth the intellectual effort to fit all this into the Procrustean bed of pure theory. This is the more justified, if we consider the very intricate methodological issues involved in the empirical testing of the models; validity is frequently more dependent on econometric methodology than on sound construction of hypotheses (Leamer 1992). Hence, the door is wide open for entering the evolutionary alternative on the scene.

1.2 Opening the Way for a Change of Paradigm in the Theory of International Trade

On the theoretical level, evolutionary trade theory (ETT) so far emphasises the impact of technology on trade and the role of institutions in the broadest meaning of the term. However, as we have seen, there is no direct contradiction between a technology-based reasoning and the most recent NTT models, because the latter have no difficulties with integrating technology, either as country-specific productivity differentials in labour in trade models or in terms of introducing a special factor component akin to human capital, i.e. a variant of a 'knowledge-stock', in the theory of the transnational firm. In both cases, the ultimate causes of the patterns of trade remain outside the model, however, the mechanics of trade still obey the neoclassical laws. That is, as long as ETT does not directly question the equilibrium framework, even its own empirical results may be easily absorbed by the latter, thereby being re-interpreted as supporting statements of NTT.[3]

At first sight, the same seems to be true for institutional approaches, which may also leave the neoclassical description of the basic mechanisms unchanged, simply because there is an exploding literature on neoclassical institutionalism. However, trying to relate the comparative advantage argument to institutions can result in a major rethinking of the theory of trade proper. The question is whether it is sufficient to separate the NTT from the analysis of the institutional framework, which is then in turn explained via a neoclassical theory, or whether precisely the attempt at establishing an encompassing framework of both the market and its institutions will lead to a crumbling of the theoretical building blocks.

Obviously, transactions in international trade face the same and even more difficult practical problems as all other kinds of transactions, which arise from legal uncertainty, informational asymmetries and so forth. High transaction costs might induce the agents to discover particular institutional solutions, such as for example substituting firms for trade. However, since all these solutions are related to common characteristics of both exporter and importer, it seems to be difficult to reconcile this approach with the comparative-advantage argument in terms of factor endowments, which by definition are exclusive properties of one of the agents. It makes no sense to talk about the relatively 'larger' endowment of one country with institutions, as far as the common transactions are concerned: the real issue is the common institutional framework, or the common capability to co-ordinate transactions successfully. That means, even if the explanation of the institutions rests upon the neoclassical presumptions, difficulties arise from the fact that the impact of institutions on trade falls back on a relational property that cannot be ascribed to either of the sides exclusively. The only way to think about this is to include comparative advantages of pairs of traders as compared to other traders, which, however, explodes the framework of relative characteristics of sets of countries. This difficulty reveals the astonishing fact that trade theory does not explain the transactions of trade proper, which are simply given (Schmidtchen 1984).

There is one important mainstream discourse where these issues gained prominence recently, that is the social-capital debate (for a survey, see Dasgupta and Serageldin 2000). Social capital of countries could be conceived as another factor of production, as far as the effects of internal transaction costs on comparative costs are concerned. But social capital of country A may be completely insignificant for enabling the traders to trade with country B, unless they are able to build new common social capital with traders of this country. This new social capital cannot be simply added to the social capital of country A relative to the endowment of other countries, because it might be insignificant there. This relational property of social capital may also become salient when considering the nonsense argument that countries richly endowed with social capital should specialise in exporting goods with an intensive use of social capital. Although this seems partly reasonable when thinking, for instance, about the importance of social capital for the institutional framework of the production of complex technologies, this would immediately imply that countries with less social capital would stay in this state, specialising in 'lawlessness'. Obviously, lack of social capital is an absolute disadvantage, which might render all other relative advantages useless under any circumstances.

This observation on social capital opens our eyes to a fundamental logical problem of NTT: the basic equilibrium premise in factor-proportions theory is that the impact of factor endowments on trade works via the pricing of factors which in turn affects goods prices, eventually closing the total equilibrium system. This raises the question whether the capabilities of traders to trade can also be treated as a part of that endowment, given the fact that capabilities to trade can only be measured relative to pairs of traders who realise the transaction. This is tantamount to asking whether a relational property of the traders can be priced within the system which comprises that trading relationship, i.e. the market.

The point of departure in the recent literature is the problem of how to distinguish between production cost and transaction cost, because the theory of international trade is exclusively based on the concept of comparative production-cost advantages. We adopt the conceptual distinction between transformation cost and transaction cost introduced by North (1990, pp. 27ff.) who defined the latter as adding up to total production cost. North himself identified the problem that it is very difficult to distinguish neatly between both categories on the theoretical level as well as (and even more so) on the empirical level. The foremost example are the costs associated with measurement problems in transactions where goods characteristics might give rise to transaction costs which could be lowered via an appropriate redesign of the production process, thereby changing transformation costs. Looking at the problem from the opposite angle, Langlois and Foss (1999) complain about the neglect of production cost – transformation costs in North's terms – in the modern theory of the firm based on transaction cost. If the concept of production is rooted in the general concept of putting knowledge to use, there are co-ordination problems in the production sphere that have nothing in common with the behavioural co-ordination problems emphasised by transaction-cost economics, namely opportunism. Therefore, the boundary between the market and the firm cannot be fully explained by transaction costs.

Hence, our problem can be restated in the straightforward question, whether the theory of comparative advantage can include production costs in terms of the sum of transformation costs and transaction costs, which would imply that the capability to trade is a part of general comparative advantage.

2. THE LOGICAL INCONSISTENCY OF PRICING THE CAPABILITY TO TRADE IN AN EQUILIBRIUM TRADE THEORY

Within the neoclassical framework, different capabilities to trade can be treated as being reflected in different transaction costs of the transactions which are realised by different agents. A gifted trader will realise the transactions at lower cost, thereby making higher profit and possibly appropriating the transaction potential of other, less efficient traders (Wegehenkel 1981). Starting out from this, could we think of that capability in terms of a 'factor' in the sense of neoclassical trade theory?

Structurally, to pose the issue in this way is homogeneous with the general Gödel problem in the foundation of formal systems, related to the question whether true statements in a formal language can be decided within that system. This proved to be impossible because of the self-referential structure so that decidability is only possible in new, higher formal language where we can talk about the propositions of the former language. In the same vein, we ask whether pricing of the transactions forming a price is possible in the market, with 'pricing of the transactions' meaning that the underlying institutional quality of the transaction is priced, or the capabilities of the agents to realise the transaction. This is the same as asking whether capabilities to trade can be traded in the market system which is formed by just these trading relations.[4]

In NTT, this problem never arises because equilibrium theory presupposes the successful arrangement of the entire set of transactions outside the system. Traders in NTT act autistically. That this assumption is by no means innocuous becomes immediately obvious when we realise that the inclusion of the capabilities of traders to trade into the equilibrium system leads to severe inconsistencies.

2.1 Non-tradability as a Necessary Condition for Competitive Advantage

Our starting point is the common distinction between comparative and competitive advantage. At any rate, the common ground of NTT and ETT is that both claim to analyse a competitive economy. We elaborate on the simple but fundamental idea that competitive advantage can only rest upon factors that remain exogenous to the market system in the sense of being non-tradable,[5] because otherwise these factors might easily be transferred (imitated, appropriated, purchased etc.) among the competitors, therefore leading toward their erosion.[6] The common example in the evolutionary setting is technology. Competitive advantages in technology would easily erode if the technology can be imitated easily and would therefore diffuse rapidly across all competitors. Apart from the patent system, the maintenance of a competitive lead therefore presupposes the dominant role of technological knowledge that cannot be imitated due to inherent causes, as for example, tacit knowledge in applying the technology. This by definition cannot be traded via the market, and hence cannot be directly priced independently of the entire set of capabilities that make up the technology.

Therefore, it remains exogenous to the market in a fundamental way. The structural evolution of the system of competitive markets and firms will be determined by the degree of separability of the different constituent units of the technology and their respective degree of tradability.

Now we can turn this argument upside down and consider the question whether in the long run the market system will develop toward the withering away of those non-tradable factors, just resulting from the ongoing process of learning and transforming implicit knowledge into explicit. Obviously, this would be possible if there were no novelty. However, the very workings of a competitive market system will foster the re-emergence of new non-tradable entities because only these confer competitive advantages. Whether this happens either unintentionally or by intention does not matter at all. That is, competition and non-tradability, or non-pricibility, are necessary correlates.

As we realise immediately, this is tantamount to a variation-and-selection approach to competitive advantage: Since only non-tradable factors confer sustainable competitive advantages, any structural and behavioural variation leading to the emergence of such advantages will resurrect the strong impact of non-tradable properties on the market system. Hence, the market system itself will always trigger the emergence of forces outside the market driving its own evolution, constantly 'telescoping' minor variations into larger differential pattern formation. As long as these new elements are non-tradable, they cannot be priced and, therefore, do not form an element in the equilibrium system working according to the comparative advantages of agents and countries. That means, if novelty occurs in the system, competition itself produces the incapability of the system to endogenise its driving force, or, the market cannot price the ultimate causes of competitive advantage. Comparative advantage refers to a system where all information has been dispersed across all agents, and where all relevant factors of competitiveness are priced, whereas competitive advantage emerges in a system with exclusive knowledge of single agents, and with essential determinants of competitiveness bearing no price-tag.

Subsequently, I will show that this argument can be made in more detailed and specific terms when analysing the transaction-cost approach as a possible-venue toward pricing the quality of a trading relationship. By this means I wish to show that there is a fundamental distinction between a New Institutional Economics approach to trade and an evolutionary one, and that the problem of making transactions possible necessarily explodes any equilibrium approach to trade. The standard argument to be pondered here is that in equilibrium the difference between the equilibrium level of transaction costs and the disequilibrium level reflects the market-priced value of the efforts of the traders to realise the transaction. The crucial question therefore is what happens in disequilibrium. In disequilibrium, trading opportunities might exist which still await discovery, hence the distinction between tradable and non-tradable goods remains endogenous to the system. To understand sustainable competitive advantages, we must therefore understand the mechanism leading the traders to discover other, more efficient ways to trade.

This is important for the analysis of comparative advantages related to production costs, because there is obviously an interaction between transformation costs and transaction costs. For example, high transaction costs might prevent traders from realising the transaction with traders operating with relatively lower transformation costs, however, production-cost advantages might still prevail for the entire set of activities. The question is, therefore, whether the market process allows traders to compare these two kinds of costs. This step presupposes a separation between transaction costs and transformation costs in the traders' profit calculus.

Here we can apply Buchanan's (1969) classical treatment of opportunity costs, since the opportunity costs of realising a certain transaction are the lost efficiency gains of the possible, yet unaccomplished alternative transaction (i.e. way of organising the transaction) (we follow Kiwit's, 1994, ideas). As we see, the problem is that the trader evidently can only compare their selection with the known alternatives, which might or might not include the most efficient one. This is precisely the meaning of entrepreneurship: the opportunity costs of the entrepreneur are the lost, yet unknown profit opportunities, which, however, might be discovered by other entrepreneurs who thereby make the opportunity costs visible and even calculable for the competitors. Competition is about discovering the value of errors. As Buchanan has therefore argued forcefully, any equation between opportunity costs and costs is only possible in equilibrium where all profit opportunities have been uncovered and exploited, and where there is no longer any difference in the state of knowledge across the agents.[7]

From this we may conclude that observed patterns of comparative advantage will reflect a certain state of knowledge in the economy where entrepreneurs have not yet discovered all the possible ways to transact, and where these undiscovered opportunities remain outside the system, hence being non-tradable. Competitive advantages result from the discovery of these unknown opportunities, and they will only be sustainable as long as they continue to be non-tradable. This, of course, seems to be a tautological statement, yet this statement supports the crucial insight that entrepreneurial capabilities cannot be priced via the market process. Following Buchanan, pricing can only be possible in equilibrium, where, however, the entrepreneurial function has lost any significance. Hence, the question emerges whether such a state can be imagined as arising from an evolutionary market process. This would, at least, presuppose that observers of entrepreneurial action are able to distinguish exactly between the entrepreneurial input and all other inputs.

2.2 The Fundamental Impossibility Theorem on a Unified Price System for Transactions and Transformations

The final sentence in the last paragraph means that we would still assume that the separation between transformation and transaction is viable, so that in equilibrium traders can optimise the mix of transaction and transformation costs. We cast serious doubts on that. Obviously, the separation between transformation and transaction is a transaction in turn. Yet, this new transaction gives rise to transaction costs, too. The difficulties in separating analytically and empirically between transformation costs and transaction costs reflect the transaction costs of just that operation in the real market system. We cannot separate these as observers because the market does not give rise to such a separation.

Obviously, here we are running into the trap of infinite regress. I do not wish to overstretch that point, but this kind of infinite regress is sufficient to conclude that there can be no empirically exact way to measure transaction costs unless the separation already exists in the market, so that there is a price-tag attached to the services needed to realise the transaction. In particular, we are not able to assess the relative role of the transaction costs of the original transaction and the transaction costs preventing the separation between transaction and transformation. That means, for example, that the boundary between firm and market is indeterminate in observational terms, because we cannot identify exactly the differential impact of the relative transaction costs within the firm and across the boundary as compared to the transaction costs linked with the operation of just setting that boundary. Even if we were to believe that there is a clear relation working in reality, we would never be able to observe it unequivocally.

This infinite regress could never be solved if there is a type of transaction that cannot be separated from transformation in principle. In order to find such a kind of transaction, we can start with the most simple case of selling a good. If we leave legal issues aside, the transaction is only complete if the buyer is indeed able to use it. That means, the good actually consists of a good and a service, namely the good proper and the service that leads to the accomplishment of the transaction.[8] This amalgam can be dissected in many ways, as reality demonstrates, displaying a manifold of arrangements, for example, with the separation between logistics, insurance, retail activities and other services from the trading transaction proper. Are there any services complementary to the physical features of the good that cannot be separated from the transfer of the good?

Obviously, this depends on whether there are entrepreneurs who invent a method of separating the service and who are able to sell it profitably. At first sight, again we are back with the problem of infinite regress because selling the service includes the service of organising that transaction, which is by no means a minor issue (for example, the informational asymmetries in both transactions are necessarily different). On a second look we can conclude that the crucial property involved in that process is tradability. In that regard Casson (1997, pp. 81ff., 108ff.) argues that the core property of the firm lies in the fact that the entrepreneur owns a resource that cannot be traded, hence if the service generated from using that resource cannot be separated from the good produced by the entrepreneur, the only viable solution is the establishment of a firm.[9] The most simple unit of a firm therefore is a dyad of one act of production and one related entrepreneurial resource that cannot be traded, which, in our Northian terminology, is the same as saying that *a minimal firm consists of a transformation and a complementary transaction, with the latter being inseparable and, hence, non-tradable*.

There are many possible entrepreneurial resources that cannot be traded, yet there seems to be one common property they can be reduced to: this is the utilisation of contingent, singular and mostly tacit knowledge of the entrepreneur (cf. Hallwood 1997). There is no price aside from the price set by the owner, i.e. the entrepreneur, for the peculiar good they offer. Nobody aside from the owner is able to assess its value which is determined by the subjective opportunity costs of the entrepreneur. Why is this kind of knowledge not tradable, given that at least the entrepreneur might set a price? Since in order to be tradable, buyers must be able to know in advance the possible uses of that knowledge. But if they already knew the possible uses, they would no longer need to buy the service but simply act themselves. Hence the capability to transact would only become an object of market transactions if there were a minimum degree of knowledge about its uses and consequences on the part of the buyer. But precisely that condition would render the service superfluous. Hence, the special core capability to transact must be a non-tradable.

There are many additional arguments supporting this general proof of non-tradability of entrepreneurial core capabilities to transact. Suffice it to mention, first, the relevance of Akerlof's 'lemons' story, given the fact that we think about a state of asymmetric information between seller and buyer. The entrepreneur offering the separate service of realising the transaction would always reap higher profit if he realises the business himself, so that finally a market for that service would collapse. Since possible buyers estimate the entrepreneur's capability according to some average trader's type on the market, true entrepreneurs would decline the buyer's price offer because they know better. Another approach may be to ask whether there is insurance possible for entrepreneurial failure. Obviously, if knowledge underlying the entrepreneurial action is unique, there can be no insurance based on statistical risk and hence no market valuation of entrepreneurial risk, notwithstanding that other entrepreneurs might offer an insurance based on their own singular knowledge.

Leaving those more specific and detailed arguments aside, the essential point is the time asymmetry involved in knowing how to transact and knowing about knowing how to transact (i.e. knowing that).[10] On the part of the hypothetical buyer, there must be fundamental ignorance in terms of the latter if the respective service is of interest for them, because knowing about knowing how means knowing how by knowing that. Yet, if that fundamental ignorance prevails, no market transactions can occur, so that the capability to transact is a non-tradable.

All these arguments lead us to conclude that the market system cannot price the capability to transact, given a state of incomplete and imperfect knowledge about the entire set of possible transactions.[11] Therefore, if competitive advantages rest upon a peculiar mix of transformation and transaction costs, they can never be fully measurable within a market system. We have now demonstrated that this is also true for a hypothetical system where the division of labour would be based on comparative advantages, unless all the transactions had already been arranged outside the system, like, for example, by the Walrasian auctioneer or an omniscient social planner.

This result has direct consequences for the issue of spatial directedness of international trade. If we cannot separate the transaction competences and the related services from the transaction proper, we can never unequivocally reduce the observed transactions on the relative endowments of traders distributed in space, so that neither can we explain the flows via the relative prices of these endowments. There remains always one component that is not priced, although exerting influence on trade-flows. By implication, the observed spatial patterns of trade can never be explained completely by reference to the distribution of pricible factors in space. Hence, the observed violations of the factor proportions theorem are very plausible empirical phenomena, or, the many results of the fundamental role of singular determinants of trade. Similarly, our argument shows that non-separability of transaction and transformaton is the most basic reason why firms exist, which implies that in certain transactions the firm itself must be moved in space to make transactions possible. This is, in principle, the explanation of the rise of the role of the transnational corporation in international trade, and, at the same time, of the difficulties of fitting this phenomenon into the common factor-proportions-framework.

3. A RESTATEMENT OF THE THEORY OF COMPETITIVE ADVANTAGE BASED ON ENDOWMENTS WITH NON-TRADABLE FACTORS

Now we can turn to the positive consequences of our abstract reasoning. A decade ago, Michael Porter (1990, pp. 73ff.) developed the argument that competitive advantage cannot rest on the standard factors of comparative advantage unless they manifest the fundamental property of being singular, non-imitable and immobile. This is directly related to our theoretical point on the non-separability and hence non-tradability of entrepreneurial competences to transact in the market system. When we accept this idea, we reach the conclusion that there is a need to fundamentally restructure the common concept of factor that underlies by far the largest part of mainstream trade theory.[12]

3.1 A New Definition of 'Factor'

For reasons of space, I cannot go into the details. Suffice it to say that the concept of factor belongs to the most elusive categories of economic reasoning, because its use results in the construction of highly aggregate entities that produce 'factor services' which are the real substance of international trade, beyond the surface of the traded goods. If we take the standard Heckscher-Ohlin definition as a starting point, factors are defined as being internationally immobile factors of production. Adding related definitions in the theory of growth, this rather broad definition may be more circumscribed if we add the property of non-producibility (cf. Woodland 1987).

All these definitions, of course, are highly contentious because in many uses of the factor concept other, often contradicting definitions inhere. For example, capital continues to be treated as 'factor' even though it is regarded to be perfectly mobile. Consequently, there is a plethora of possible trade models including, for example, single-factor models if the criterion of immobility is applied strictly (see, for example, 'skills only' models à la Wood 1994), and, on the other extreme, multifactor models which, for example, analyse the impact of sector-specific factors on trade. However, precisely this looseness of definiton results in serious troubles when trying to separate 'factors' from 'goods' analytically, if the latter concept encompasses both final and intermediate goods. This is especially intricate when considering the distinction between 'producer services' in general and 'factors services'.

Furthermore, another conceptual pair becomes relevant here, that is, the distinction between stocks and flows. Obviously, the idea is close to senseless to assume that intermediate goods change their essence when a part of a stock, so that 'capital' would be a different thing when being accumulated and stored as compared to capital being traded. On the other hand, 'services' are frequently treated as being non-storable which implies that no stocks can be built up. Hence, the entire semantic field seems to be in a confused state.

The concept of a stock presupposes the property of storability. If a certain good or service cannot be stored, there is no way to accumulate it. For example, labour in the theory of growth cannot be accumulated per se, because it cannot be stored, so that it is a pure flow. On the other hand, accumulation presupposes the concept of producibility (at least beyond the hunter-gatherer economy), which is a more exact concept than reproducibility. Producibility is related to intentional human action, whereas reproduction can also result from other natural processes. In that sense, producibility is related to the exogenous/endogenous distinction. Producibility is a property that cannot be related to entities which are in principle exogenous to the system and which therefore cannot be influenced by human action at all. Reproducibility can depend on either exogenous or endogenous processes. For example, climate is decisive for the reproductive use of agricultural land and still remains exogenous to the system, i.e. is non-producible, whereas human capital can be regarded as producible today.

If an entity cannot be produced, then the question arises whether the use of it leads to its final consumption. In the classical uses of 'nature' as a factor there is the implicit idea that an eternal reproduction takes place, so that the factor is never consumed. Independent of this idea there is a standard way to assume eternal usability of an entity, namely that the uses are conceived as non-rival in time. This is precisely the property ascribed to knowledge in the most recent theories of trade, especially in the theory of the multinational firm, where the knowledge-stock is treated as a pure public good, whose services, however, can be appropriated within the firm (the related argument is made in the context of country-specific knowledge-bases). Hence, if we regard non-consumability as a necessary property of sustainable competitive advantages, this can be cast into the positive characterisation of non-rival use in time.

Non-producibility entails another twist of the argument if we consider the special role of intention in our definition. We can surmise that non-producibility refers to all unintended results of human action, that is to all external effects which are either unobserved or cannot be avoided by intentional action. Of course, this shows that non-producibility is eventually no property that can be given an empirical meaning a priori, because it depends on the state of knowledge, technology and of the institutional framework. We realise that our ideas begin to close the circle, because unintended consequences are also called 'externalities'. By definition, externalities are phenomena that impact the outcome of the market system, yet cannot be priced via market transactions.

These seemingly scholastic reasonings achieve significance if we link them to the general idea of sustainable competitive advantages. Evidently, if we search for factors that provide the basis for such advantages, this is immediately the case if the relevant entity is non-producible and immobile. This, for example, is the property of land as the most 'classical' factor in international trade because land cannot be moved in space and could only to a very limited extent be produced in those early times of economic theorising. Non-producibility is the basic precondition of non-imitability, because imitation presupposes the capability to produce and generate the respective property intentionally. At the same time, the relevant entity should be storable, so that the distinction between 'stocks' and 'flows' can be applied meaningfully. Finally, the entity should be outside the system in the sense that there is no way to attach a separate price-tag to it, i.e. in our terminology, it is non-tradable.

Drawing all these arguments together, we reach a new and cogent definition of a factor.

A factor is an aggregate stock with the properties of non-producibility, storability and non-tradability, as well as non-rivalness of use in time. Factor uses result in a flow of factor services that inhere in trade in goods.

If we link this definition with our discussion of competitive advantage, we can start our search for factors with the question of which kind of service is the prime source of these advantages. As we have seen, the primordial service is the entrepreneurial making of transactions.

3.2 Three Dimensions of Entrepreneurial Competence as Factor Generating Entrepreneurial Action as Complementary Service to Goods

Which kind of entity might be the stock out of which entrepreneurial services flow? The most simple answer, of course, would point toward the entrepreneurs as a group. However, if we wish to lend more detail to the analysis of the sources of entrepreneurial capabilities, I propose to treat as 'factors' the following three entities, the services of which constitute the flow of entrepreneurial activity that is inseparably linked with the transactions of trade:

- organisational capital
- collective human capital
- social capital.

All these three entities have one structural feature in common, namely the fact that relational patterns in neighbourhoods are involved, with neighbourhoods frequently, but not necessarily, referring to spatially close interactions (closeness can result from 'similarity' in any other respect, for example, kinship). This idea refers to certain arrangements of people in space and time, which are stable and recurrent, and which because of their complexity cannot be straightforwardly imitated ('produced') and transferred ('traded') to another place. This basic insight has already been achieved, amongst others, by Michael Storper (1995), who argued that competitive advantages of locations are rooted in non-traded interdependencies between people at certain places. Our concept broadens this insight to the more abstract structural aspects of social relations between agents, which are regarded as 'capital' that generates entrepreneurial services.[13] This capital is the non-intended result of human action, therefore is non-producible, yet storable, because of its recurrent unintended reproduction, and it also has the property of non-rivalness of use in time.

Organisational capital is the crystallisation of the competences of the firm, that are rooted in certain organisational routines, tacit knowledge, and non-tradable assets which are only reflected in the market value of the firm as compared to the market price of its constituents. Although this is a patterned neighbourhood, obviously the firm as a whole can be traded and transferred in space. However, this presupposes very special competences, too, as is evident from the many failures, for example, of mergers, acquisitions and foreign direct investment. Hence we may speculate that one of the crucial ingredients of organisational capital of the firm is the competence to trade itself, namely to grow into other markets and regions in space-time. Firms, hence, differ in terms of this special competence which can therefore be regarded as especially relevant for international trade.

The concept of organisational capital provides a new foundation for the theory of the multinational corporation, because we regard the stock of firms in an economy as a base of its competitive advantage in trade. This is directly mirrored in the fact that trade and FDI are closely enmeshed, and that intra-firm and intra-industry trade dominate trade the more developed the nations involved, hence the more complex and diversified their stock of firms becomes. The country- or location-specific accumulation of organisational capital is therefore one of the determinants of directedness of trade, and the patterns depend on the special capabilities to transfer organisational capital in space, which is a recursive property of organisational capital. At the same time, that means that the firm drives a logical wedge into the market system, as we have demonstrated in section 2. From this point of view, the violations of the factor-proportions theorem are natural reflections of the existence and the operations of the firm in the international economy.

Collective human capital is a set of competences and knowledge that inheres in networks of agents and not the agents proper (cf. Foss 1999). This, of course, also applies to organisational capital, but we try to distinguish between human capital that is intentionally organised in the firm and another kind that arises from spontaneous interaction both within and beyond the firm. The latter is most salient from the study of industrial districts and other forms of clustering of economic activity (compare Loasby 1999). In other words, collective human capital rests upon stable patterns of spillovers among agents putting their knowledge into use. Stability of patterns presupposes certain social structures which are maintained independently of the specific transaction. This has been called 'embeddedness' in other theoretical contexts. Obviously, these patterns may be highly specific and cannot be directly imitated, because they go back, for example, to historical constellations of social change, or to properties of agents which are not easily imitable, such as religious affiliation. The most salient example is the specific role of 'settings' for certain service industries like entertainment and advertisement (for a penetrating case-study, see Grabher 2001), yet similar considerations may be valid for financial centres. These places are sources of directed flows of services in the world economy, precisely because the complex interaction between lifestyles, professional communication and local organisation of complementary services render those places unique. Traders are attracted to these places even though the costs of entering the hypercompetitive environment are rapidly increasing, yet still being outweighed by the very strong effects on labour productivity. Collective human capital, therefore, stays in the background of the NTT observation that local level-effects play an important role in interregional trade.

Social capital is a property of social networks that is reflected in the effects of transactions on the successful realisation of other transactions, that is, it emerges from chains and networks of transactions that are being perceived and interpreted by agents (Herrmann-Pillath 2000a). Among our three dimensions, social capital most directly refers to the interaction between the two sides of a transaction, hence it is a relational category. However, our concept transcends the simple idea, for example, that both sides belong to the same ethnic network and therefore can lower transactions costs because of higher levels of trust (e.g. Landa 1994). Social capital may also emerge from social structures where indirect channels of communication and social perception are existent, possibly restricting deviant behaviour even without a closer relation between the agents proper. Furthermore, if externalities across transactions are taken into consideration, social capital may be an emergent property of networked transactions, which, however, shows a distinct pattern in space. Those patterns can be self-reinforcing, because there are direct effects on observed transactions costs, so that the externalities are eventually internalised in stable patterns of repetitive transactions.

As we see, all these three forms of capital are to a large extent non-producible in the sense that there is no direct relation between input, output and intentional action. The organisational capital of the firm, for example, is based on tacit knowledge which arises from the accumulation of informal routines. Since this cannot be imitated easily, it provides the foundation of competitive advantages. The same is true for a singular network pattern forming social capital, like particular social relations among traders which cannot be simply rebuilt by other persons who do not have the same personal history.

In what sense are the three kinds of factors related to the phenomenon of directedness? This becomes clear if we distinguish three dimensions of distance that impact on transactions, and if we assign one of the factors to the special capability to overcome the respective distance.

- *Spatial distance* can be overcome (amongst other ways) via the use of organisational capital that enables agents either to shift their focus of activity (direct investment) and/or supports trade relations. Hence we expect the pattern of trade to be strongly influenced by the direction of investment flows and different corporate strategies of market entry. The most salient empirical phenomenon is the growth of intrafirm trade, however, one should also pay attention to networking across firms, like strategic alliances.
- *Technological distance* can be overcome via collective human capital. Here we refer to tacit differences in the use of technologies across locations which imply that trade (especially in intermediate products) will be influenced by these indirect characteristics of space. Technological distance can be measured by comparing absorptive capacities across locations, if this is not simply reduced to 'stocks' of human capital, but is related to qualitative and structural differences between knowledge systems. An important empirical case in point are national systems of innovation which foster the emergence of localised

technological trajectories. These trajectories influence the patterns of trade, for example, via the technological networks implied by the flows of intermediate products.

- *Interpersonal distance* is overcome via the use of social capital. This refers to all kinds of unfamiliarity with the social, legal and institutional environment across locations. The most important empirical example is cultural distinctness, which may induce low levels of trust because of possible misunderstandings. However, social capital allows agents to overcome the impediments caused by cultural distinctness because highly personal relations are developed which include an idiosyncratic environment of the transactions.

If we look back on the list of unresolved issues of NTT, we immediately realise the relevance of our approach. In the most abstract terms, our analysis of factors results in the insight that the directedness of trade can only be explained within a framework that integrates the impact of absolute and relative advantages, the latter working via the price system, and the former working via the singular impact of factors on trade. In empirical terms, these become evident in the strong influence of historical determinants, culture or corporate structures on trade. This by no means precludes the role of prices and relative endowments in trade, however, we expect a complex interaction of the different determinants, just as is being actually observed.

One example of the move of mainstream analysis in this direction is the recent research by Feenstra and associates (1997, 1999) into the role of networks in East Asian trade. They demonstrate how different kinds of networks in Korea, Taiwan and Japan result in different patterns of competitiveness that are reflected in the product composition of their respective exports, because organisation of the markets for intermediate products affects price competitiveness and range of qualities. In our terms, the differences between networks in these countries can be easily described as differences in the structure of organisational capital and different mixes between organisational and social capital. Hence, there is much room for an integration between mainstream and evolutionary arguments, provided that the claim is given up of achieving a complete and full equilibrium system of international trade.

4. PROSPECTS FOR AN EVOLUTIONARY THEORY OF INTERNATIONAL TRADE

We have tried to set up a general and abstract framework for ETT. The main achievement seems to be that we do not reject the empirical insights obtained from NTT, yet put them into a completely different theoretical approach. We also accept one feature of the NTT approach to trade, that is, to analyse trade-flows as surface phenomena of deeper structures. These deep structures refer to properties of locations in space, conventionally treated as 'factor endowments' which generate certain flows of services. These services we interpret either as factor content or as inseparable, complementary services enabling agents to trade. Our main hypothesis, then, is that competitive advantages rely on entrepreneurial inputs that are outside the market system, and which generate the factor contents and services. More specifically, these are related to technology and transactions.

In the most general terms, I wish to pinpoint the difference between ETT and NTT by means of Figure 7.1. The theory of comparative advantage explains trade under the condition of complete knowledge, with the price system endogenising all relevant determinants of trade. The evolutionary theory of competitive advantage explains trade as a process generating knowledge about comparative advantage. This difference is easily illustrated in Figure 7.1.

Circle A–E depicts the circular causation of NTT, which is a closed equilibrium system starting out from points A and B, with the price system directly revealing the complete information about comparative advantages in production of different locations. Via the trading activities, which are basically arbitrage processes, countries are led to further specialise in their

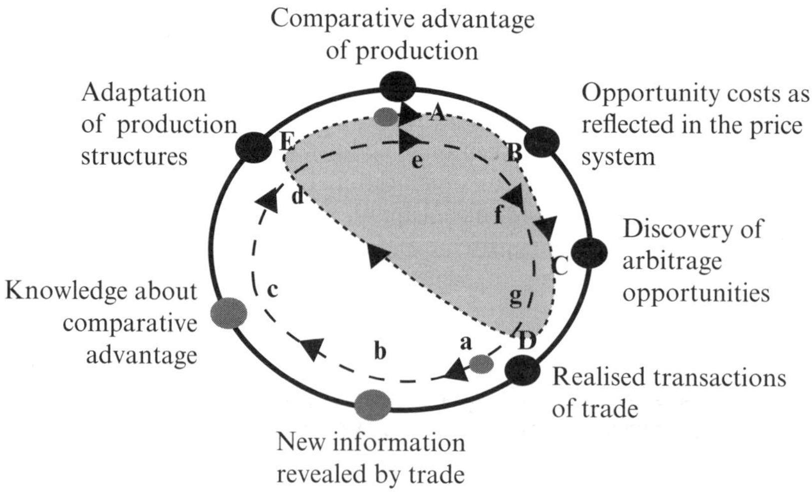

Figure 7.1 Competing patterns of causation in trade theory

comparative advantages, so that in equilibrium optimal production structures are realised. In ETT, there is a wider loop a–g starting at *a*. Here, traders firstly realise transactions that generate information about comparative advantages. That is, the adaptation of the production structure is contingent on the determinants of the transactions.

As we have seen, these determinants lie outside the market system. We have identified organisational, collective human and social capital as theoretical aggregates by which we may grasp and systematise these determinants. If we look at these in more abstract terms, we may imagine tradeflows to follow invisible networks of relations between agents which are rooted in their endowments with the three kinds of capital. These networks become observable via the impact of costs of transactions and costs of co-ordinating knowledge among the agents. This vision is closely related to recent efforts of evolutionary theorists to reformulate the theory of the market as a theory of open, non-integral systems (foremost, Potts 2000). Methodologically, the research strategy of trade theory would move toward the integration of sociology and economics, which is already salient in the recent upsurge of interest in business networks and other forms of nonprice co-ordination in international trade (see the survey by Rauch 2001).

I think that ETT can achieve a similar role as theoretical pinnacle to that which NTT plays with reference to equilibrium theory. Whether there are important policy conclusions beyond the free-trade paradigm, cannot be answered here and remains a task for future work.

NOTES

1. This chapter is based on my German book Herrmann-Pillath (2001a), presenting a condensed version of some crucial theoretical arguments. Related papers in English are Herrmann-Pillath (2000b), (2001b).
2. To get an impression, the reader is recommended to visit the homepage of the 'Academic Consortium on International Trade' (www.spp.umich.edu/rsie/acit/), which reflects the public role of trade economists. The intellectual esprit de corps is reflected in the fact that there is even a 'family tree' of trade economists available in the internet, see www.econ.lsa.umich.edu/~alandear/tree/index.htm
3. I should emphasise that I regard New Trade Theory as a part of the mainstream approach, since it sticks to the equilibrium framework, though achieving, at least partly, an endogenisation of technological change, as in Grossman and Helpman (1991).
4. In economics, Hayek has made the similar point when arguing (1952, see Herrmann-Pillath 1992) that a system with a certain degree of complexity cannot understand itself except via a system of higher complexity that allows one to reproduce the system of lower complexity as well as including at least the additional self-referring relation. Loasby (2001) also stresses the importance of this fundamental insight for constructing economic theories.
5. Our use of 'tradability', 'non-tradable' and related expressions differs a bit from the common use because we refer to the general property of a good being transferable via market transactions, both internal and external. In trade theory, these expressions are

normally restricted to transferability via international markets. In our use, a 'non-tradable' is a good that cannot be sold via any market, whereas in the common use it is a good that can only be sold via internal markets.

6. This is common sense in modern theories of the competitiveness of firms, as in resource-based approaches (e.g. Barney 1991) or competence-based theories (Foss 1993). I should add that in the New Trade Theories, there is also a crucial role of non-tradables in the sense of public goods and externalities, which by definition cannot be priced. In these models, like Grossman and Helpman's (1991) now-classic one, sustainable advantages arise from externally imposed restrictions on the reach and scope of externalities and the use of public goods, such as, for example, national borders.
7. There are exact approaches to this problem within an equilibrium setting. One very interesting one is Greenhut et al. (1987, especially chapter 19) who model an imperfectly competitive economy with endogenous determination of the location of firms (which is a problem closely related to international trade). They introduce a residual return remunerating entrepreneurs for coping with uncertainty. This return accrues to 'non-functional inputs', which cannot be measured with conventional accounting procedures (which, hence, bear no price-tag). Furthermore, they distinguish between 'differential rents for managerial skills' and 'fixed costs of behavioral uncertainty'. Both kinds of rents are conceived as elements of the long-run average cost curve, and they are being determined by the subjective opportunity costs of the entrepreneurs (which is equivalent to Buchanan's point of view). In their model, differences in capabilities will be reflected in different firm sizes, with the zero-profit condition applying. Because of the size differences, the subjective opportunity costs of the entrepreneurs will converge on a common equilibrium value, which, however, is not directly observable in the market, but is only indirectly visible in terms of the size distribution of firms. As we see, if all transaction costs result from uncertainty and lack of information, the Greenhut et al. approach can be applied straightforwardly to demonstrate that transaction costs are in fact imputed rents accruing to differential capabilities to transact.
8. This approach has been proposed by Hirsch (1989) for the analysis of international trade, yet without reference to transaction costs. Hirsch argues that there is always a service component in trading goods, if only the service of trading proper. As is well known, services generally feature a lower degree of international tradability than goods, hence, the international tradability of goods partly depends on the tradability of the complementary services.
9. This argument is related to Barzel's (1989, chapter 4) explanation of the distribution of ownership rights in the firm. In the efficient state, the residual claimant will become that person who affects the variability of the outcome most, and for whom this effect can be measured to the least degree (which, as in Greenhut's approach mentioned in note 7, is the same as saying that it has no price-tag). Only the residual claimant has the incentives to monitor himself, if others cannot monitor him because of the obstacles to measurement.
10. The argument follows the structure of Streit and Wegner (1992) who demonstrate that transaction costs are fundamentally different from transport costs because they result from fundamental uncertainty about the future course of events. If transaction costs result from incomplete information about the future, an optimisation calculus cannot apply because of the information paradox. Hence, transactions need to be realised in order to learn about their costs, and we cannot choose the most efficient one ex ante. On the importance of the knowing how/knowing that distinction for the theory of the firm, firstly proposed by the philosopher Ryle, see Grant (1996).
11. This argument can be stated in other terms without changing its substance. For example, Anderlini and Felli (1998a, b) posit a similar impossibility theorem when analysing the question whether agents can write complete ex ante contracts in which the costs of realising the contract are also included. Obviously, this is impossible to achieve ex ante, without having already realised all the activities necessary to launch the transaction. To conclude a contract, both sides have to incur sunk costs specific to the transaction, and there is no way to reach a sharing agreement ex ante in which, for example, one side

would share its own search costs with the other side. Hence, in a fundamental way contracts can never be complete.

12. In modern writings on international trade, these definitional issues have been shifted into the background, with encompassing monographs like Wong (1995) even doing without any definition of 'factors' in general. There were times when this question received a lot of attention, as, for example, Caves (1967, pp. 93ff.) illustrates. In the early days of formalising the equilibrium trade theory, intellectual giants like Samuelson (1948, 181) raised very serious doubts on the theoretical role of 'factors' in the factor-proportions theory. All this is simply forgotten today.
13. Related ideas have been developed in the most recent foundational research in evolutionary economics, which focuses on the role of networks as embodying knowledge, with the seminal work by Potts (2000, 2001).

REFERENCES

Anderlini, Luca and Leonardo Felli (1998a), 'Costly Coasian contracts', Discussion Paper no. 362, London School of Economics and Political Science.

Anderlini, Luca and Leonardo Felli (1998b), 'Costly bargaining and renegotiation', Discussion Paper no. 361, London School of Economics and Political Science.

Anderson, James E. and Douglas Marcouiller (1999), 'Trade, insecurity, and home bias: an empirical investigation', NBER Working Paper 7000.

Barney, Jay (1991), 'Firm resources and sustained competitive advantage', *Journal of Management*, **17** (1), 99–120.

Barzel, Yoram (1989), *Economic Analysis of Property Rights*, Cambridge: Cambridge University Press.

Bellet, Michel and Corine L'Harmet (eds.) (1999), *Industry, Space and Competition*, Cheltenham, UK and Northampton, MA, USA: Edward Elgar.

Bernstein, Jeffrey R. and David E. Weinstein (1998), 'Do endowments predict the location of production? Evidence from national and international data', NBER Working Paper 6815.

Borchert, Manfred, Ulrich Fehl and Peter Oberender (eds) (1987), *Markt und Wettbewerb. Festschrift für Ernst Heuß zum 65. Geburtstag*, Berne/Stuttgart: Haupt.

Braunerhjelm, Pontus and Karolina Ekholm (eds) (1998), *The Geography of Multinational Firms*, Boston, MA: Kluwer.

Braunerhjelm, Pontus and Robert E. Lipsey (1998), 'Geographical specialization of US and Swedish FDI activity, in Braunerhjelm and Ekholm (1998), pp. 33–58.

Buchanan, James M. (1969), *Cost and Choice. An Inquiry in Economic Theory*, Chicago: University of Chicago Press.

Casson, Mark (1997), *Information and Organization. A New Perspective on the Theory of the Firm*, Oxford: Clarendon.

Caves, Richard E. (1967), *Trade and Economic Structure. Models and Methods*, Cambridge, MA: Harvard University Press.

Clark, Terry, Masaaki Kotabe and Dan Rajaratnam (1999), 'Exchange rate pass-through and international pricing strategy: a conceptual framework and research propositions', *Journal of International Business Studies*, **30** (2), 249–68.

Collins, William J., Kevin H. O'Rourke and Jeffrey G. Williamson (1997), 'Were trade and factor mobility substitutes in history?', NBER Working Paper 6059.

Dasgupta, Partha and Ismail Serageldin (eds) (2000), *Social Capital. A Multifaceted Perspective*, Washington, DC: World Bank.

Davis, Donald R. et al. (1997), 'Using international and Japanese regional data to determine when the factor abundance theory of trade works', *American Economic Review*, **87** (3), 421–46.

Davis, Donald R. and David R. Weinstein (1998), 'An account of global factor trade', NBER Working Paper 6785.

de la Mothe, John and Gilles Paquet (eds) (1996), *Evolutionary Economics and the New International Political Economy*, London/New York: Pinter.

Deardorff, Alan V. (1998), 'Determinants of bilateral trade: Does gravity work in a neoclassical world?', in Frankel (1998), pp. 7–22.

Dosi, Giovanni, Keith Pavitt and Luc Soete (1990), *The Economics of Technical Change and International Trade*, New York: Harvester Wheatsheaf.

Dunning, John H. (1995), 'What's wrong – and right – with trade theory?' *International Trade Journal*, **9** (2), 163–200.

Ekholm, Karolina (1998a), 'Headquarter services and revealed factor abundance', *Review of International Economics*, **6**, 545–53.

Ekholm, Karolina (1998b), 'Proximity advantages, scale economies, and the location of production', in Braunerhjelm and Ekholm (1998), pp. 59–76.

Engel, Charles and John H. Rogers (1999), 'Violating the law of one price: should we make a federal case of it?', NBER Working Paper 7242.

Feenstra, Robert C., Deng-Shing Huang and Gary Hamilton (1997), 'Business groups and trade in East Asia, Part I: Networked equilibria', NBER Working Paper 5886.

Feenstra, Robert C., Maria Yang and Gary G. Hamilton (1997), 'Business groups and trade in East Asia, Part II: Product variety', NBER Working Paper 5887.

Feenstra, Robert C., Tzu-Han Yang and Gary G. Hamilton (1999), 'Business groups and product variety in trade: evidence from South Korea, Taiwan and Japan', *Journal of International Economics*, **48**, 71–100.

Foss, Nicolai J. (1993), 'Theories of the firm: contractual and competence perspectives', *Journal of Evolutionary Economics*, **3**, 127–44.

Foss, Nicolai J. (1999), 'Networks, capabilities, and competitive advantage', *Scandinavian Journal of Management*, **15** (1), 1–15.

Frankel, Jeffrey A. (ed.) (1998), *The Regionalization of the World Economy*, Chicago: University of Chicago Press.

Goldberg, Pinelopi Koujianou and Michael M. Knetter (1997), 'Goods prices and exchange rates: what have we learned?', *Journal of Economic Literature*, **35**, 1243–72.

Grabher, Gernot (2001), 'Ecologies of creativity: the village, the group, and the heterarchic organization of the British advertising industry', *Environment and Planning*, **33**, 351–74.

Grant, Robert M. (1996), 'Toward a knowledge-based theory of the firm', *Strategic Management Journal*, **17** (Winter special issue), 109–22.

Greenhut, Melvin L., George Norman and Chao-shun Hung (1987), *The Economics of Imperfect Competition: A Spatial Approach*, Cambridge: Cambridge University Press.

Grossman, Gene M. and Elhanan Helpman (1991), *Innovation and Growth in the Global Economy*, Cambridge, MA/London: MIT Press.

Grossman, Gene M. and Kenneth Rogoff (eds.) (1995), *Handbook of International Economics*, vol. 3, Amsterdam: Elsevier.

Hallwood, C. Paul (1997), 'Competencies as private information: an efficient capital asset pricing theory of the firm', *Journal of Theoretical and Institutional Economics*, vol. **153**, 532–44.
Hanson, Gordon H. and Matthew J. Slaughter (1999), 'The Rybczynski Theorem, factor-price equalization, and immigration: evidence from U.S. states', NBER Working Paper 7074.
Harrigan, James (1997), 'Technology, factor supplies and international specialization: testing the neoclassical model', *American Economic Review*, **87**, 475–94.
Haskel, Jonathan and Holger Wolf (1999), 'Why does the "law of one price" fail? A case study', CPER Discussion Paper 2187.
Hayek, Friedrich August von (1952), *The Sensory Order*, Chicago: University of Chicago Press.
Helliwell, John F. (1997), 'National borders, trade and migration', NBER Working Paper 6027.
Helpman, Elhanan (1998), 'Explaining the structure of foreign trade: where do we stand?', *Weltwirtschaftliches Archiv*, **134** (4), 573–89.
Herrmann-Pillath, Carsten (1992), 'The brain, its sensory order and the evolutionary concept of mind, on Hayek's contribution to evolutionary epistemology', *Journal for Social and Biological Structures*, **15** (2), 145–87.
Herrmann-Pillath, Carsten (2000a), 'Culture and observation in the study of economic systems,' Discussion Paper 52, Fakultät für Wirtschaftswissenschaft der Universität Witten/Herdecke, March 2000.
Herrmann-Pillath, Carsten (2000b), 'Indeterminacy of international trade: methodological reflections on the impact of non-economic determinants on the direction of trade and absolute advantage,' *Aussenwirtschaft*, **55** (2), 251–89.
Herrmann-Pillath, Carsten (2001a), *Kritik der reinen Theorie des internationalen Handels, Band 1: Transaktionstheoretische Grundlagen*, Marburg: Metropolis.
Herrmann-Pillath, Carsten (2001b), 'A general refutation of the law of one price as empirical hypothesis', in A. Wagner and H. Strecker (eds), *Jahrbücher für Nationalökonomie und Statistik*, **221** (1), pp. 45–67.
Hirsch, Seev (1989), 'Services and service intensity in international trade', *Weltwirtschaftliches Archiv*, **125**, 45–59.
Hummels, David and James Levinsohn (1995), 'Monopolistic competition and international trade: reconsidering the evidence', *Quarterly Journal of Economics*, **110** (3), 799–836.
Kiwit, Daniel (1994), 'Zur Leistungsfähigkeit neoklassisch orientierter Transaktionskostenansätze', ORDO, **45**, 105–35.
Klau, Arne Ragnar (1995), *Firmeninterner Handel: Eine theoretische und empirische Analyse des unternehmensinternen Außenhandels multinationaler Unternehmen*, Berlin: VWF.
Krugman, Paul (1995), 'Increasing returns, imperfect competition and the positive theory of international trade', in Grossman and Rogoff (1995), pp. 1243–77.
Landa, Janet T. (1994), *Trust, Ethnicity, and Identity. Beyond the New Institutional Economics of Ethnic Trading Networks, Contract Law, and Gift-Exchange*, Ann Arbor, MI: Michigan University Press .
Langlois, Richard N. and Nicolai J. Foss (1999), 'Capabilities and governance: the rebirth of production in the theory of economic organization,' *Kyklos*, **52**, 201–18.
Leamer, Edward E. (1992), 'Testing trade theory', NBER Working Paper 3957.

Loasby, Brian (1999), 'Industrial districts as knowledge communities' in M. Bellet and C.P. Harmet (eds), *Industry, Space and Competition*, Cheltenham, UK and Northampton, MA, USA: Edward Elgar, pp. 70–85.

Loasby, Brian (2001) 'Time, knowledge and evolutionary dynamics: why connections matter', *Journal of Evolutionary Economics*, **11** (4), 393–412.

Markusen, James R. (1995), 'The boundaries of multinational enterprises and the theory of international trade', *Journal of Economic Perspectives*, **9** (2), 169–89.

Markusen, James R. and Anthony Venables (1998), 'Multinational firms and the new trade theory', *Journal of International Economics*, **46**, 183–203.

Markusen, James R. and Keith E. Maskus (1999), 'Multinational firms: reconciling theory and evidence', NBER Working Paper 7163.

North, Douglass C. (1990), *Institutions, Institutional Change, and Economic Performance*, Cambridge: Cambridge University Press.

Porter, Michael E. (1990), *The Competitive Advantage of Nations*, London: Macmillan.

Potts, Jason (2000), *The New Evolutionary Microeconomics*, Cheltenham, UK and Northampton, MA, USA: Edward Elgar.

Potts, Jason (2001), 'Knowledge and markets', *Journal of Evolutionary Economics*, **11** (4), 413–32.

Rauch, James E. (2001), 'Business and Social networks in international trade', *Journal of Economic Literature*, **xxxiv**, 1177–1203.

Ray, Edward John (1995), 'Old myths and new realities: foreign direct investment in the United States', *International Trade Journal*, **9** (2), 225–46.

Rogers, John H. and Michael Jenkins (1995), 'Haircuts or hysteresis? Sources of movements in international exchange rates', *Journal of International Economics*, **38**, 339–60.

Samuelson, Paul A. (1948), 'International trade and the equalisation of factor prices', *Economic Journal*, **58**, 163–84.

Schmidtchen, Dieter (1987), 'Unsichtbare-Hand-Erklärung und die Theorie komparativer Kosten', in Borchert et al. (1987), pp. 287–309.

Storper, Michael (1995), 'The resurgence of regional economies, ten years later: the region as a nexus of untraded interdependencies', *European Urban and Regional Studies*, **2** (3), 191–221.

Streit, Manfred and Gerhard Wegner (1992), 'Information, transaction, and catallaxy – reflections on some key concepts of evolutionary market theory', in Witt (1992), pp. 125–49.

Trefler, Daniel (1993), 'International factor price differences: Leontief was right!', *Journal of Political Economy*, **101** (6), 961–87.

Trefler, Daniel (1995), 'The case of missing trade and other mysteries', *American Economic Review*, **85** (5), 1029–46.

Wegehenkel, Lothar (1981), *Gleichgewicht, Transaktionskosten und Evolution. Eine Analyse der Koordinierungseffizienz unterschiedlicher Wirtschaftssysteme*, Tübingen: Mohr Siebeck.

Witt, Ulrich (ed.) (1992), *Explaining Process and Change: Contributions to Evolutionary Economics*, Ann Arbor, MI: Michigan University Press.

Wong, Kar-yiu (1995), *International Trade in Goods and Factor Mobility*, Cambridge, MA/London: MIT Press.

Wood, Adrian (1994), 'Give Heckscher and Ohlin a chance!', *Weltwirtschaftliches Archiv*, **130**, 20–49.

Woodland, A.D. (1987), 'Entry "tradeable and non-tradable commodities"', in John Eatwell, Murray Milgate and Peter Newman (eds), *The New Palgrave. A Dictionary of Economics*, London/New York/Tokyo: Macmillan/Stockton Press/Maruzen.

Zhang, Kevin H. and James R. Markusen (1997), 'Vertical multinationals and host-country characteristics', NBER Working Paper 6203.

8. Economic policy – a process of communication

Lambert T. Koch

1. INTRODUCTION

In the attempt to provide an analytical structure for the process of economic policy making, the literature on the subject often differentiates between three basic categories, i.e. *determining the status quo, setting aims, selecting measures.*[1] Here it is presumed that this three-step process should programmatically guide investigations into economic policy making and that it should thus be the original task of a *positive* theory of economic policy to pose the question as to the most suitable tools for a target-performance comparison on an aggregated level when faced with different types of situations and target constellations. Suitable measures would be those which lead to a corresponding balance in the most efficient way. Doubts about this idea, which is part of the core of orthodox theory on economic policy, are nothing new.[2] Here we are dealing with the basic pattern of a procedure which theorists as far back as Albert already criticised as being *instrumentalistic-technocratic* (cf. Albert 1967, p. 113), seeing the danger of false methodological concepts resulting in excessive expectations of feasibility in economic policy (cf. Homann 1980). An instrumentalistic-technocratic programme suggests that the process of economic policy making can be understood using a *machine model* as described by Heinz von Förster (cf. Förster on 1984). This would mean that sufficient knowledge of an initial situation and of currently valid transformation rules would be enough to deduce the 'right' measures.[3] In this way, planning and forecasting problems in economic policy would to a great extent be reduced to technical-organisational factors – with correspondingly beneficial consequences regarding general control possibilities.

Criticism of this kind of understanding of economic policy in the past few decades goes in many different directions. The difficulties which are created when knowledge necessary for economic policy is to be centralised were dealt with (cf. Hayek 1983). The ideas of 'bounded rationality' of economic agents and the relevance of information costs were introduced, which prevent voters and the elected from including all information relevant in a situation in their decisions (cf. Simon, 1955). And from the perspective of public choice theory, self-interest and the power games that go with it for politicians and interested parties were put forward as grounds for the necessity of changing perspectives; because, independent of their role in the economic policy-making process, the choice and decision-making behaviour of economic subjects does not by any means lead to the preference for continuously 'correct' decisions – quite apart from the fact that the determination of what could be 'correct' is itself confronted with insurmountable theoretical and practical obstacles (cf. e.g. Frey and Kirchgässner 1994, pp. 362ff.).

It is however only recently that a problem area which develops at an earlier stage has increasingly come to the fore. This problem area becomes obvious when moving away from the customary common-knowledge assumption which is an implicit part of the formation of theory and which assumes a predefined econopolitical event or situation. *Before* the situation is assessed and alternatives chosen at a *macro-economic level*, the question as to how an 'econopolitical situation' originates needs to be posed. Here it can be shown that the results gained from determining the situation, setting an aim and selecting measures are very dependent on the individual and societal perception and communication processes which come before them. It is in these processes that certain problem areas crystallise, the contours of which gradually become clear at a later stage. This means, in contrast to the assumptions of many models of economic policy theory, that there are neither 'ready-made' solutions to problems in advance, nor, and this is a particularly important point, are there 'ready-made' problems which just need to be identified by individual politicians or parties and, depending on their political *couleur*, integrated into respective agendas. Very complex phenomena play a role in the complicated interaction process which determines at what point in time and at what 'stage in its development' an *economic* problem which is initially only perceived by a minority actually advances to become a problem of *economic policy*. At the beginning of the problem process, this includes for example the degree of homogeneity of perceptions of reality existing in a society, the individual and collective perception of certain information, the way problems are 'offered', i.e. processed or presented in the media, as well as the effect of historically grounded path dependencies, inponderable events or accelerating/retarding frequency dependency effects in the course of the genesis of a problem.

The contexts mentioned here will be developed in four steps *focusing in particular on cognitive aspects*: firstly, a short look will be taken at the general significance of epistemological factors in the analysis of economic policy, followed by an investigation into the relevance of 'cognitive maps' which guide problems originating at an *individual level*. Then, an attempt will be made to describe and make sense of the problem-diffusion process and the corresponding generation of problems in economic policy making at a *societal level* as an important preliminary phase to the problem *treatment process*. Finally, in the last step, selected cognitive aspects of the process of problem treatment in economic policy will be examined.

2. ECONOMIC POLICY IN THE LIGHT OF THE PROBLEM OF COGNITION

For further analysis the first question which should be asked is why instrumentalistic-technocratic thought patterns have established themselves so firmly in many areas of economics. The idea that we can analytically separate the *possibilities and limitations* of cognition from the *conditions* of action seems to play a role here.[4] Methods based on this regarding the partial analysis of problems will not occasion much criticism. However the same is not true when dealing with such a *complex phenomenon* as the process of economic policy. For this subject matter, the integration of results of modern perception, cognition and communication research seems of the essence, and a central demand of this chapter is to include the construction process of 'econopolitical reality', together with the relevant constructional content, as an issue in a positive theory of economic policy.[5]

To achieve this, first of all a short overview of the mainstream of modern *cognitive sciences*[6] will be given. There has been a clear departure from the idea of a passive, externally determined perception of the environment. Today, it is normally considered as proven that our brain, which processes environmental stimuli, links these external impulses with already existing cognitive structures in an *actively constructive* way. Every piece of incoming information absorbed only receives its specific identity in our brain and mechanisms such as perception, inference, attribution and memory in particular act as mental operations.[7] Cognitive psychology provided sound theoretical and empirical proof for these contexts as early as the sixties and seventies (cf. Neisser 1976) and this later provided strong support for the development of a perspective which was to become known as cognitive constructivism. The following ideas in this chapter are based on this approach, which is present in almost all areas of psychology today (for an overview cf. Nüse et al. 1991). In this epistemological model it is important to understand cognition also as discovery and invention, without having to commit to a decision as to which parts of human perception actually provide information about the existence of an outside world which is subject-independent. Without negating a 'neutral' environment, there is an unavoidable veil of uncertainty surrounding any statements made about it. The main general consequences which result from the integration of these contexts into an analysis of economic policy can be outlined in three points, as follows.

2.1 Subject-specific Reception of Information as a Basic Variable of Economic Policy

First of all, the idea of 'information' as the basic variable of planning in economic policy needs to be rethought. Here, the basic significance of information within this process is not being questioned, however a modification of the way information is understood is required. Modern cognitive sciences emphatically prove that information about facts does not exist independently of individuals and thus cannot simply be passed on to others. Information in the actual sense of the word is created at the moment of reception of external signals in the apparatus of human perception. Thus, in the context of economic policy, the prevailing conditions of this genesis or transformation of information need to be investigated more intensively. Information *transformation* and information *transfer* can be taken as phenomena which belong together and it is of particular importance to realise that each piece of transferred information gains a new identity in the act of being transferred. The main question to be posed here is which factors, either intended or non-intended, influence the process of gaining meaning.

2.2 Individual Information Processing and the Problem of Predictability of Results

Secondly, these aspects throw a different light on the problem of forecasting, both at a scientific and an economic policy level. In information transformation the way our perceptive apparatus functions seems to hinder any use of transformation rules. Research into perceptive physiology has proved that the brain works in a kind of temporal rhythm, always combining several physiological events into one perception, then to be replaced autonomously or spontaneously by another. Here the content of a later perception can be changed even if there has been no change in the sensory data (for an extensive description see Pöppel 1985; Oeser 1987). Suddenly, completely new interpretations of situations can be created, which may then lead to very unexpected and new reactions.[8] This means, ceteris paribus, that it is already for purely cognitive reasons that the possibilities of forecasting economic, social and political cycles decrease with increasing complexity of information networking in a society and between societies (globalisation), especially as there are basic difficulties in connection with the attempt to observe and evaluate internal personal processes (cf. Little 1972; Nisbett and Ross 1980; Witt 1992).

2.3 The Communicative Act in its Significance for the Form of Econopolitical Situation

A third consequence of integrating perception and cognition theories into the formation of a theory on economic policy originates in the central idea that no economic subject thinks, plans and acts against the background of an objective reality, but rather always within the framework of their own subjective reality which only experiences a partial comparison with other individual 'realities' via an act of communication. On the one hand 'cognitive maps' play a role here, a concept which will be dealt with in more detail later. On the other hand the function of social interaction as a reality shaper comes into play. Living together in a society and economic policy are therefore only imaginable if, at least in certain areas, common relevant realities are created by way of communication as described by Berger and Luckmann (1979). This means that, from a cognitive-evolutionary perspective, societal communication has a much more important function than merely the exchange of information, taking the term 'information' here in the traditional, more technical sense (cf. Habermas 1984).

3. ELEMENTS OF AN EVOLUTIONARY THEORY OF ECONOMIC POLICY: ON THE ORIGINS OF PROBLEMS

3.1 The Individual Level

Here, a closer look will be taken at the actual phenomenon, the origin of problems in the context of economic policy. Firstly, in accordance with methodological individualism, what happens on an individual level is of interest – especially considering the fact that there is a deficit in explanation which needs to be dealt with that comes up in well-known attempts at sociological explanations, which are mainly based on collective phenomena in the political process (cf. Scharpf 1991; Searle 1995). To examine the individual level the concept of 'cognitive maps' will be addressed here. This concept, the development of which is linked to Piaget's work (Sugarman 1987), combines the above-mentioned concepts with a series of subphenomena in information processing which have not yet been addressed. For example, an important point is that cognitive maps are highly selective, meaning that pieces of knowledge are linked within them under the same label in the form of terms for characteristics, prototypes, limiting cases and examples. At the same time, so-called tacit knowledge is arranged, knowledge which is constantly developing and being applied, thus changing in action and at the same time influencing the human ability to act without the actor himself or an external observer being able to systematically describe its structure (for an application-based overview see for example Hirschfeld et al. 1994; Vowe 1994).

Cognitive maps which help master the complex range of sensory stimuli play a central role in any cognition and memory process: they form the framework, so to say, into which newly constructed information is inserted, to be then complemented by already-organised pieces of knowledge (cf. Eysenck 1984, p. 324). Thus a referential network is created within which experiences are condensed into patterns, which themselves then shape experiences. All evaluations, expectations, plans and decisions made by actors are based on this interdependent linkage of present and past cognitions (cf. Koch 1996). All economic subjects, whatever role they are playing at any moment in the process of economic policy, are affected by this subjective prestructuring of perception. Politicians, bureaucrats or voters, members of whatever social class, the old or the young: in their reception of information, events and complex situations everyone is subject to the biological restriction of only being able to perceive what their brain offers them on the basis of their personal (stored) 'history'.[9] In contrast to the concept of 'bounded rationality', the concept of 'cognitive maps'[10] thus emphasises not so much the lack of quantity in information gathering as the unavoidability of path-dependent quality changes in the reception of information.

Should there be considerable contradictions to the previous subjective 'reality' in an individual perceptive situation in the face of certain 'information conditions', these cognitive dissonances can at the same time awaken the wish to reduce them. The strength of the stimulus depends on the estimation of the expected costs and benefits of corresponding activities.[11] The costs can be, for example, to analytically structure and then to communicate the initially subjectively defined problem (for example, in discussions or publications), they can express themselves in altered choice behaviour and they can (this option involves the highest costs) imply a triggering of activity in citizens initiatives, parties or government authorities. 'Information conditions' in which cognitive dissonance occurs can on the one hand be newly created. But on the other hand they can also remain unchanged and the ambiguity results solely from a recombination of established consciousness content which is produced by the apparatus of perception.[12] While the latter possibility can occur at any time, the reception of new target parameters (for example ideas or values) or new knowledge about actual parameters (causal contexts and restrictions) must be added for the former.

The discussion so far implies an altered image of the actors in the political process. At first we have the politician in mind as the economic policy maker, but the assumption of the ubiquitous influence of cognitive maps emphasises that any idea of an exogenous controller having a complete catalogue of assumptions about the behaviour of actors in a system is doomed to failure. Their perception and their resulting behaviour are rather inseparably and reflexively coupled with the specific social context which they are a part of. Every economic politician is himself or herself 'just' an endogenous variable in the model of economic policy. In the process of changing cognition, knowledge components and evaluations, their own cognitive maps are just as inconsistent as those of any other individual agent, so that in principle no 'objective' decision-making field can exist in the area of economic policy (cf. Scherer et al. 1988, pp. 803ff.). Concerning the group voters, there are important conclusions to be drawn from the point of view of cognitive science, which are complementary to corresponding reflections in political economics: in the case of democratic votes on actors and programmes in economic policy, for example, it must seem obsolete to look for voting procedures which could represent an 'objective' portrayal of voters' preferences. Also the idea of the 'voters' mandate' which is often diagnosed is nothing more than a point-in-time-based, open structure which changes its importance in a continuous process of reflexive interpretation of reality.[13] Each elected person interprets the 'voters' mandate' just as contextually as the voter evaluates the information available to them concerning a social situation.[14] Voters and the elected will change their ideas of target and performance mutually dependent on each other in the course of a legislative period and will thus also change their interpretation of problem situations, leading to a co-evolution of relevant decision-making fields. These thoughts already show clearly why an evolutionary understanding of economic policy is being supported here and at the same time, they lead to the analysis of the collective level of the process of economic policy.

3.2 The Collective Level

At the level to be discussed here, the question needs to be dealt with as to which kinds of subjectively perceived discontent (problem variation) – for example if faced with an expected under-supply of certain public goods – actually end up becoming a problem of economic policy (problem selection). To explain this, the constitutive function of interaction and communication for societies needs to be examined. When individuals come into contact with each other, they 'automatically', so to speak, alter reality for the person they are interacting with. They observe reactions to their own actions and, if necessary, conceptualise recurrent new experiences together with previous knowledge as cause–effect relationships in new variations or cognitive maps. The fact that in this situation each individual acts according to their own, subjective, schematically coded expectations, aims and purposes is also termed 'double contingency'. As we can assume that within social communities the subjective realities of interactive partners are at least partly synreferential in advance, actors can also always work towards orienting the cognitive area of others towards a certain object (cf. Rusch 1994, p. 63). This point represents an important interface where it is decided whether individually perceived problems at a certain point in time ever become intersubjective or societal problems. The mobilisation resources of individual economic subjects play a decisive role here and there is a wide range of possibilities. Firstly, it depends on the strength of the intrinsic potential, i.e. on the degree of subjectively perceived dissatisfaction and on the will to mobilise. Secondly, there must be sufficient mobilisation abilities such as the correct selection of communication partners and the necessary argumentation skills. Here the social position taken on by the mobiliser is important, as well as the economic and/or political resources and power potential available to them and the experience already had with them in similar situations in the past.

When the spark of problem perception jumps from the individual level to the collective level, a problem subsequently gains a new piece of identity with each further communication, i.e. its quality by no means remains constant during the diffusion process. Nor is there any guarantee that every person concerned will interpret a communicated problem in a similar way. Here the complexity of the subject matter and the quality of the communication process play an essential role. 'The more successful orientation interactions there are and the more reliable they are, the stronger will the actors be convinced of the common and equal nature of reality' (cf. Rusch 1994, p. 71). In other words, depending on the situation there can be a homogenisation of how people interpret reality and problems.

Whether a problem which is perceived and discussed in parts of society actually becomes an issue in economic policy depends in essence on this homogenisation process. The more homogenous the perception of a certain economic target/performance discrepancy and the larger and more powerful the dissatisfied group, the higher the probability, all else being equal, that the problem will be admitted to the political level. In spite of this, no generally valid if-then criteria can be derived for this step. Historical constellations play a role which need to be evaluated according to what kind of macro-economic situation a society is in, what other problems are on the issues list and how urgent they are, and thus what problem perception and problem treatment capacities are still available at that point in time (cf. Meier and Slembeck 1994, p. 75). A further very important point to consider is what institutionally dictated mechanisms facilitate or impede the problem being admitted to the political level (e.g. constitutional requirements for referendum petitions) – a question which will not be dealt with further here. But even if a certain degree of homogeneity is necessary as a kind of minimum 'critical value' for admitting a problem to the level of economic policy, the relativity of this context must be considered. Because in increasingly untransparent, pluralistic and multicultural societies it will become generally more difficult to install homogenous, powerful interpretations of problems which are at the same time stable in time and content. With the acceleration of technological progress and the global diffusion of knowledge (decreasing 'knowledge half-life') as well as the internationalisation of the economic and interjurisdictional competition that goes with it, the relevant problem areas and at the same time the interpretation of individual problem areas are fanning out more and more. However the more heterogeneous the prevailing and competing realities are, the more difficult it is, all else being equal, to make any qualified statement on the course of problem-admittance processes and thus projections about future developments in the process of economic policy as a whole.

In the face of this development, one thing is becoming more and more important: to what extent are initially alien problem areas and interpretations of problems communicated to the other groups in a society in order to create a pool of relevant information in common knowledge (intended reduction of ambiguity)? From the perspective proposed here, such a pool seems to be a conditio sine qua non for constructive sociopolitical discussion on the solution of problems which come up. It combats to a certain extent a 'derationalisation' of the process of economic policy making. In accordance with this, the economic policy-making process would be 'rational' in that what is being communicated about is also what every individual concerned understands as being what they want to express; therefore, the more intensively a theme-based process of mutual orientation gets going, the higher the probability that a problem recognised by many will later be treated 'correctly' or 'rationally' – in the view of many.

Let us now take a closer look at the mechanisms and patterns which play a role in the process of problem diffusion in economic policy. This includes, above all, the observation that cost–benefit relations which economic agents are confronted with, if they want to spread an individual view of a problem, are highly dependent on the established communication structures within a society. These form the 'resonance space' in which problem interpretations have to prove themselves (cf. Siegenthaler 1994, pp. 177ff.).

Here, communication structures should be understood as the total number of valid possibilities and limits of communication between economic subjects in a society. In the modern 'information economy' the various media are of particular importance (cf. Löffelholz and Altmeppen 1994). They do not simply function as 'neutral' communication channels (information transfer), they rather play a decisive controlling role in problem-origination processes by spreading new possibilities for interpretation (information transformation). The abstract object of public opinion as an obstacle or selector for individual models and interpretations is to a great extent a product of the media. A careful evaluation of public opinion can show individuals or groups of actors what costs of mobilisation and thus what level of material and personal resources are to be expected to ensure that a problem actually becomes an issue in economic policy (cf. Merten and Westerbarkey 1994, pp. 200ff.; Kuran 1995).

In this context it can be shown that the problems by no means always originate in the same way. Ideal-typically, there are two basic patterns (cf. Meier and Mettler 1988, pp. 40ff.). The first one, the bottom-up formation of opinion, represents the 'ideal democratic situation': a problem is perceived by a group of individuals relatively homogeneously, and potential supporters – i.e. interest groups, governments and parliamentarians – have to be 'triggered into action' on this basis. The extensive overlapping of individual cognitive maps which is necessary in advance of this[15] means that this type seldom occurs in its purest form, especially considering the fact that there are many structural obstacles which can have an effect. Of particular importance is the fact that as a rule the so-called agenda setters are indispensable, i.e. those who take a problem and make it a political issue, whereby the mobilisation of effective media is potentially very 'expensive' in this case. Therefore a large part of the formation of opinion in society is a more top-down situation, i.e. it is triggered by influential actors. For politicians and representatives of powerful interest groups – for example trade-union functionaries – the access to relevant publicity channels and the focused influence on public opinion that goes with it, mostly incur relatively low transaction costs.[16] 'They have capacity available to them to ensure a media-friendly processing of issues and therefore enjoy good access to the mass media' (Meier and Mettler 1988, p. 41). Thus it is relatively easy for them to produce certain problems or interpretations of problems in a focused way, i.e. to chose the right moment in time, in order to instrumentalise them in the process of economic policy making. This can be observed at the time of writing in the discussion about the introduction of a common European currency or in the debate on the consequences of economic globalisation.

The question as to what events or constellations kick off a problem process and in which economic, social and political context plays an important role here. If there is latent discontent which has been predominant in a larger social group for a long time, the course of problem diffusion will be different than if only a small peripheral societal group sees need for econopolitical action on a certain issue. Based on a categorisation in Bennett (1980, pp. 113ff.), various categories of initiation of econopolitical problems can be differentiated according to the number of people affected and the extent to which they are affected (cf. Meier and Slembeck 1994, pp. 68ff.). According to this, one can speak of an interest-group problem if only a minority in society is affected but this minority organises itself formally on the basis of the high willingness to pay of the individuals concerned. On the basis of the German coal problem in the Ruhr area, the cognitive determinants which are relevant here become clear: normally this concerns groups of economic subjects whose individual realities have a high level of synreferentiality in advance, as they have economic (industry, profession etc.), social (class, ethnicity etc.) and/or geographical (estate community etc.) features in common. This means that the costly setting up of functioning communication structures and the spread of common interpretations of reality are rendered superfluous. In the case of structural problems, however, there is a large number of affected actors but the individual is affected to a lesser degree. Even if the motivation to form a formal organisation is weaker for this reason, this type of problem triggering is still just as significant as the former one. To go back to the planned introduction of the euro, for example, the political significance associated with it becomes clear. In the run-up to the Bundestag elections in 1998, the election campaign strategists of the largest German parties saw an above-average level of uncertainty concerning this issue. From a cognitive-evolutionary point of view, the reason for this was that in the course of the currency debate each potential voter had an opinion, but that these opinions were based on completely different backgrounds concerning knowledge, experience and interest. As a result, it seemed dangerous to commit to a certain strategy at too early a stage, as public opinion was extremely unstable under the circumstances and still is today in connection with this theme.

Only the latter of the ideal types of elite and crisis problems which are less frequent in reality will be looked at here as this is a particularly interesting phenomenon for the context under discussion. A chaotic situation is characteristic, after which a coincidental individual event can very quickly completely change the societal assessment of the situation and thus also the relevance of possible previously existing problems (interest group, structure or elite problems) (cf. Kuran 1995). For example, taking a look at public reaction to a media-effective accident at a chemical production plant, extremely intense 'avalanche-like' protest can be observed in certain cases – especially if there have been no similar accidents in the recent past. It may even happen that all chemical production plants in a country become time bombs in public opinion. The decisive consideration here is that the suddenly altered assessment of the situation can lead to huge pressure on political actors. A social problem is 'born' which results in a political necessity to immediately formulate and implement new aims for a certain area which has been at most a peripheral issue for a long time as regards social interest. It is obvious what kind of economic consequences such coincidental individual events can have, for example, for a whole industry. From a cognitive-evolutionary point of view, the interesting aspect to such an example is that in certain cases the homogenisation of cognitive maps can take place very quickly and unpredictably. When a large majority has swung towards a certain view of reality, decisions can be taken which would never have had a chance of implementation in the past. This is also an aspect which again makes very clear the significance of the factors 'coincidence', evolutionary self-dynamics and path dependency for the results of the process of economic policy – phenomena which are often neglected in traditional approaches.

4. ELEMENTS OF AN EVOLUTIONARY THEORY OF ECONOMIC POLICY: ON THE TREATMENT OF PROBLEMS

The above reflections lead us to an analysis of the phase of problem treatment. In the process of economic policy, this follows the phase of problem origination, provided that this has led to successful admittance of the problem to the political level. The following sketch (figure 8.1) is an attempt to recapitulate on the evolutionary view which forms the basis for this and which has been discussed above. As the arrows indicate, changing private and/or public interpretations accompany the process of economic policy from the first phase of problem origination right up to problem treatment – and indeed throughout all its phases respectively.

As the psychological-cognitive phenomena which occur in the process of problem treatment have already been dealt with to a much greater extent in economic literature than the subject matter discussed here so far (cf. Jones 1984; Kuran 1987; Hutter 1989; Lindenberg 1993; Frey and Eichenberger 1994; Meier and Slembeck 1994), this section will be kept relatively brief. Just a few points will be selected which clarify the cognitive-evolutionary dimension of the context of effect on the level of political action.

In general, current power constellations in the competition of interests and interpretation are also the most important factor in the problem-treatment stage. Even if a problem interpretation has already established

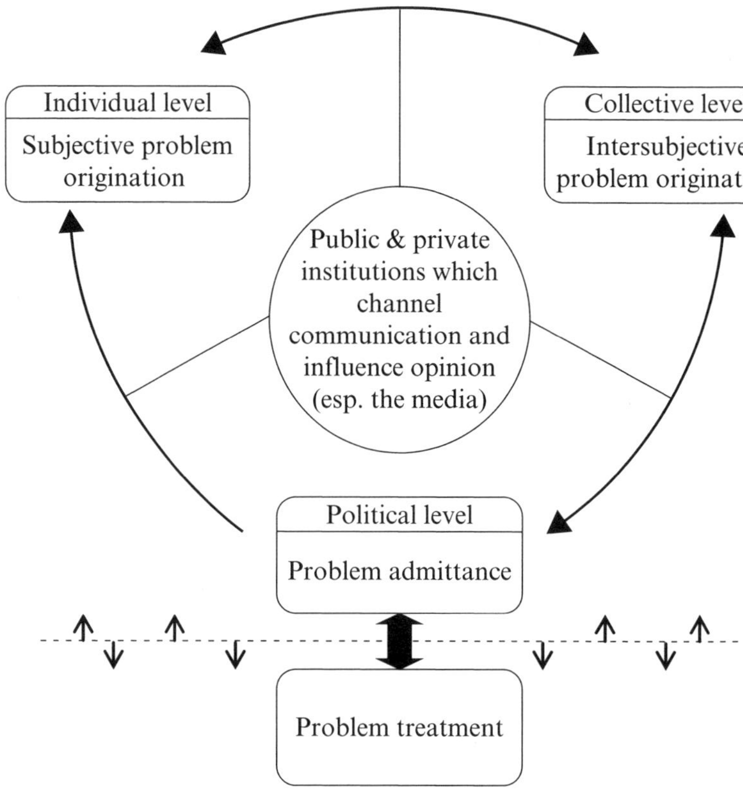

Figure 8.1 From the origins of a problem to its treatment – sketch of the process of economic policy making

itself or become concrete at a collective level to such an extent that it has achieved admittance to economic policy, individuals and groups will continue to attempt to change things to their advantage. Here, there are many different formal and informal options on various decision levels of problem treatment depending on the specific structure of the political system. For example it is well known that the preventive measures taken against the state's abuse of power in the more recent constitutional democracies ('checks and balances'), result in many veto and influence possibilities which do not exist in other systems. However, there are also considerable differences between the various forms of democracy. For example, the British Westminster model or its New Zealand offshoot enable a determined head of government or an ideologically homogenous 'policy conspiracy' to act much faster on the basis of their own interpretation of a problem than is possible in corporatist systems (cf. Wallis 1997).

It should be kept in mind that regardless of to what extent they can influence and affect the situation, actors will attempt up to the last moment to use all their power, resources, and powers of persuasion in order to ensure the success of their own interpretation of a problem and normally also the implementation of their own solution model. This continuous competition between alternative interpretations means that the observer is constantly being offered numerous – prima facie unsystematic or even seemingly contradictory – partial interpretations of the process of economic policy. Such apparent 'irrationalities' can be observed in particular when very different reality models are almost forcibly combined into one perspective in the problem-treatment phase. This is because from this political reality certain aims are formulated and certain measures are chosen solely due to the fact that this 'artificial' current perspective spreads very definite causalities – even if the latter often seem very unsuitable to the external observer (cf. Luhmann 1989). In the background there is an important basic assumption which motivates the political process. This assumption aims at overcoming societal conflicts which hinder action by taking the wide variety of individual realities into consideration.[17] So it is no surprise from a theoretical point of view that in this hither and thither of competing ideas about econopolitical cause-effect contexts, chains of action are created which are difficult to comprehend taken at face value. Furthermore a cognitive-evolutionary approach lends credibility to the assumption that the idea which could be labelled systematical 'muddling through' (cf. Lindblom 1959, 79ff.) is not a contradiction in itself. It should be much more the rule in economic policy – at least in a democratic market-economy system which is conceived as an open and pluralist society.[18] This is because with the institutionally secured admittance of variety, the unavoidable necessity of making compromises on the public level of action is created, implying a loss of logical consistency of the subarguments.

An extensive analysis of different psychocognitive subphenomena of the problem-treatment process in economic policy could now be added to these general reflections, and there are various systematisation methods available for this. For example, the systematics widespread in political economics could be followed and specific 'anomalies' could be worked out for groups of actors (personal differentiation), for voters, politicians, parliamentarians and bureaucrats respectively (cf. Frey and Eichenberger 1994). Another possibility is, as shown below, to differentiate subphenomena according to their occurrence in different phases of political control (temporal differentiation), for diagnosis, prognosis, programming, decision, implementation and evaluation (cf. on this sequence Meier and Slembeck 1994). For this discussion it will, however, suffice to give an example of several selected cognitive factors which play a role in attaching a sometimes 'irrational' character to the real problem-treatment process in economic policy.

4.1 Persistence of the Status Quo as a Result of Diagnosis

Once a problem has become an issue of economic policy, it must then be operationalised. To do this an actual situation must be determined by searching for suitable variables. Depending on the specific subject matter, this can be done quite easily, for example, if it is a routine case to which experience values can be applied. But it could also be a new kind of problem constellation for which there is no solution grid yet and whose cause-effect context is evaluated extremely heterogeneously by the decision makers. In this situation there are two basic possibilities: on the one hand there could be a compromise-led diagnosis result as described above, so that the problem-treatment process can run its course. Or the treatment process is abandoned after the unsuccessful attempt to demarcate the problem in content and form. This possibility is enhanced if the problem has also gradually lost significance in public discussion – whether by force of politics or not. From the point of view of political economics, for example, this form of significance loss could be based on the fact that the problem was instrumentalised solely for election-campaign purposes, the agenda setters lose almost all interest in it after the election and the problem falls victim to the fact that actors and voters forget relatively quickly. From the point of view of cognitive science, and taking an individual perspective, there is the additional aspect that in specific cognitive structures the 'frame goals' change from time to time.[19] This can help 'solve', for example, long-term contradictions; because, as neurologists have proved, our nervous system contains qualitative functions which work as a filter in cognition, so that logical contradictions cannot always or continuously be perceived as cognitive dissonance. Thus this brain function is a kind of protection mechanism for the reduction of environmental complexity and for stabilisation of cognitions (cf. Ciompi 1988). At the collective level these kinds of phenomena can become so strong that in case of a long-lasting ambiguity of problem interpretations which cannot be eliminated by communication, the previously existing conviction, both on the part of politicians and those concerned, that there is a basic need for action is gradually reduced. The result would then be the continuance of the formerly criticised status quo.

4.2 The Inherent Value of Motives in the Prognosis Phase

If on the other hand there is an agreement on a majority ‘political reality’ in the diagnosis phase as a result of a successful reduction in ambiguity as described above, a problem-based target situation needs to be determined. Here there can also be typical ‘irrationalities’, for example when certain individual variables are overvalued in the context of describing the situation. Often the result of this is that an attempt is made to solve an urgent problem in area *A*, but that a new problem is created in area *B* with just as many consequences. This kind of one-sided orientation towards individual variables can easily lead to a long-term process of swinging between different problem situations, a fact which is proved by the well-known example of the political activity-cycle. In addition to established explanations based on public-choice theory (cf. Frey 1983), explanation factors based on cognitive science can also play an important role here: on the one hand, when temporarily overvaluing certain motives in the context of formulating targets, consequential problems may be consciously reckoned with; on the other hand non-intended processes may also be crucial. Again the decisive point is the consideration of the cognitive context of the action situation, from which the dominance of certain ‘frame goals’ with temporary suppression of other motives can be explained. In addition, it seems important that the sometimes dominating motives of economic subjects change at certain intervals, something which is difficult to forecast and observe from the outside. If certain individual ‘frame goals’ assert themselves in the societal communication process, they will also influence the determination of collective aims in the problem treatment process of economic policy. From this perspective, it is very possible that ‘rational’ events form the basis for neglecting motives which ‘make sense’ to the benefit of one-dimensional formulation of aims.

4.3 The ‘Wrong’ Dosage of Measures in the Programming Phase

Once comparable performance and target variables are available as a result of the above-mentioned processes of determining interpretations, the programming of bundles of measures can begin, which then have to be decided on politically and then possibly implemented and tested for effectiveness (evaluation). For the analysis of this phase, cognitive phenomena again play an important role alongside econopolitical phenomena. The cognitive phenomena help to explain the consequences of actions which are basically to be evaluated as failures on the part of political actors. Thus the result is, for example, faulty programming because, due to the make-up of the human perception apparatus, evidently contradictory data are incorporated into established solution patterns. The reason for this is that, against the background of certain cognitive structures, frequency distributions and probabilities are systematically disregarded (cf. Tversky and Kahneman 1982). Other investigations show that the ability to correctly estimate effect mechanisms and reaction-times from the application of the instrument to the intended effect is also very different for different individuals in complex socio-economic systems (cf. Dörner 1991). As already mentioned, no simple input-output prognosis modes can be constructed for these purposes, so the only alternative is to take experience values from comparable situations. Here, intuition plays an important role; from a scientific point of view, we are dealing with implicit heuristics that the perception apparatus offers spontaneously (cf. Six 1987). Typical for the investigation of systematically distorted cognition performance is the incorrect assumption that there are linear cause-effect relations and a disregard of feedback (e.g. self-destroying and self-fulfilling prophecies), regression and contradictory effects as well as the creation of consequential problems in other areas of the system (cf. Dörner 1991; Nisbett and Ross 1980, pp. 124ff.). On the other hand, causal contexts or intentionalities are often searched for where the assumption of coincidence and thus the application of probability concepts would be more suitable (cf. Ross 1977, 175ff.). In the end, time-frames are often wrongly estimated and the present is overvalued in relation to the future.[20] While the above-described 'anomalies' generally lead to wrong dosages when applying instruments, this cognitive failure may explain in particular overdosage in planning measures. This is because the fact that measures take effect at a later stage is often misunderstood and it is assumed that the measure has no effect at all (cf. Dörner 1991, pp. 156ff.). In connection with all of these observations there is empirical evidence that more experienced people systematically act more successfully in complex decision-making situations than the less experienced. However, this is only true under one condition; that both groups of test subjects receive the same initial information on the concrete situation in their respective experiments.

5. RESUMÉ

This quite cursory analysis (for the reasons stated) of the process of problem treatment will now be followed by a summary of the results presented. It was shown that, for an understanding of the process of economic policy, it can be helpful to take a look at the origin of the problem from a cognitive-evolutionary perspective, analytically differentiating between the individual and collective levels, before going over to the treatment of the problem. Phenomena which can be explained from a psychocognitive perspective have the effect that both the process of problem origination as well as the process of problem treatment in economic policy often seem to the observer to be systematically 'unsystematic'. As problem origination and problem treatment are always accompanied by complex competition for influence and power between different interpretations of reality, what is left over as the final result of this process on a collective level can still only be an ambiguous and partially contradictory compromise. This results from the collision of many different ways of thinking, reality models and ideologies whose foundations, even if they seem incommensurable, are set in relation to each other. Because it is the motivation of the decision makers in economic policy to reduce ambiguity on all levels – at least in a democratic system – in order to become or remain able to act. The extent to which the left-over residue of ambiguity or cognitive heterogeneity is present in the phase of problem treatment depends not least on the informal and formal givens of the sociopolitical system of a country. In an individual case analysis, the quality of the installed communication structures and the structure of the democratic involvement and decision-making rules would need to be investigated here.

In addition, it should be kept in mind that the appearance of such problem interpretations born out of the societal communication process and the solution patterns which follow is in no way long-lasting; it rather shifts according to the extent to which certain events, discoveries or power shifts help other or new realities to become temporary 'competitive successes'. Therefore, a positive theory of economic policy must also thematise influential factors of the variability of its categories. It should understand the societal communication process as an all-encompassing medium in which econopolitical interests, models and ideologies are transported, strengthened but also put in their place, thus at the same time sketching again the process-oriented framework concept, within which more light can be shed on the respective individual phenomena.

NOTES

1. Molitor, for example, demands: 'the logic of the econo-political situation entails a division into aim, situation and measure. Whether dealing with political tasks concerning order, stability or distribution, policy should always follow the three steps of interpretation of aim, analysis of situation and programming of measures' Molitor (1988), pp. 29.
2. For an overview of the historical genesis of this programme cf. Albert (1977), pp. 181ff.
3. Here it is of no importance whether the machine is *trivial* or *non-trivial*: in a non-trivial machine the output sequence is not only determined by the input sequence and the transformation rule $f_y(x \rightarrow y)$, it is also determined by the rule (f_z), according to which the transformation function (f_y) is altered. In this way, very complicated input-output sequences of a higher order are conceivable.

4. Or, as Schiepek (1990), p. 199, criticizes common practice: the attempt is often made 'to free scientific descriptions from their cognitive preconditions, i.e. to eliminate the conditions of their feasibility'.
5. Cf. Albert (1977), p. 205, who demands the inclusion of epistemological aspects in a theory of econopolitical action 'which should be taken seriously from a realistic point of view'.
6. 'Cognitive sciences' include all disciplines which deal with the phenomena of perception and cognition, including neurobiology, chemistry, physiology and psychology, other fields of biology and psychology as well as some areas of philosophy.
7. Perception is the absorbtion of stimuli by sensory cells and organs, inference is the formation of implicit conclusions and attribution is the subconscious allocation of cause by the brain.
8. In this context Hesse's reflections on 'cognitive creativity' as a basic variable in the theory of action and economics as well as the consequences of its integration for the explanation of innovation are particularly significant; cf. Hesse (1990). For corresponding consequences in economic policy cf. Koch (1996).
9. In a similar context to the one discussed here, Frey and Eichenberger (1991), p. 75, under the point 'Reference Point Effects', refer to the example of the fear of inflation some Germans have. It seems to actually make a difference in the evaluation of econopolitical scenarios whether actors still have (unpleasant) memories of inflation they experienced themselves or not. People with experience of certain events and developments will subconsciously evaluate situations differently than individuals without the same history.
10. These are sometimes called 'scripts', or 'frames'. In all cases these are special types of complex structural organisations (the terms are also partly synonomous). For example 'frames', which will be dealt with later, normally describe organised knowledge structures that order conventionally determined knowledge of laws and standards which plays a role in social situations. Cf. Dijk (1997).
11. Cognitive assimilation and accommodation processes play a role in connection with the motivation to reduce cognitive dissonance or ambiguity. Cf. Meier and Slembeck (1994), pp. 54ff.
12. In addition to the above-mentioned sources, cf. Pöppel and Edingshaus (1994), pp. 166ff. on the cognitive-scientific preconditions for this possibility.
13. In this context it can be of interest to analyse the mechanisms of reflexive reality modelling, also in advance of elections and votes. Spontaneous actions and institutionalised procedures (cf. Blondel, 1990) ensure that the actual decisions have been made long before the formal election or vote takes place. In spite of this, this cognitive-evolutionary aspect of preparation for votes is often undervalued in expert literature on the subject, an exception being Slembeck, (1997).
14. Kuran (1995), pp. 189ff. analyses in detail the extent to which private preferences for example are in a continuous change process depending on private knowledge and public discussion and the 'preference distortions' which result.
15. The word 'overlapping' here should not be understood from a set theory or homological perspective, but rather in an abstract way which refers back to the above-described reflections on communication theory.
16. Cf. Mueller (1989). The general idea is described that the transaction costs of turning social or political problems into issues (in the widest sense) are basically communication costs, using the example of patent-law production in Hutter (1989), p. 187f, examples for politically motivated 'problem generation' (top-down) can be found, for example, in Scharpf (1991).
17. However this does not exclude the possibility that political oppositions produce ambiguity on purpose to hinder the success of the actions of decision makers or to manipulate society's evaluation of the results of actions.
18. A reference can be made here to Popper's advocacy of a social technique of 'piecemeal social engineering', which he explains on the basis of the characteristics of such a society concept. Cf. Popper (1995).

19. See, for example, Lindenberg (1993) for an explanation of the framing concept which is based on the above-described cognitive-scientific results. From an empirical point of view, Lindenberg refers in particular to investigations carried out by Goffman (1986) as well as by Tversky and Kahneman (1981). The latter proved in experiments that individual decisions for different alternative actions can be extremely dependent on how the respective possibilities are described. In the experiment the descriptions 'objectively' contained the same information, but in some cases the possible profit was emphasised, in others the danger of loss, cf. ibid, 453ff.
20. Here, the elementary human characteristic of setting every action and experience on a time-scale can be counterproductive. Because by constructing action sequences, interaction chains and contexts that 'make sense' from a procedural perspective, thus turning singularities into elements of procedures (cf. Vowe 1994, 438), there is always the possibility that incorrect temporal structures will continue to exist as consequential errors in action planning.

REFERENCES

Albert, H. (1967), *Marktsoziologie und Entscheidungslogik*, Neuwied: Verlag Luchterhand.

Albert, H. (1977), 'Individuelles Handeln und soziale Steuerung. Die ökonomische Tradition und ihr Erkenntnisprogramm', in H. Lenk (eds), *Handlungstheorien – interdisziplinär*, **4**, Munich: Fink, pp. 177–226.

Bennett, W.L. (1980), *Public Opinion in American Politics*, New York: Harcourt Brace Jovanovich.

Berger, P.L. and T. Luckmann (1979), *The Social Construction of Reality: A Treatise in the Sociology of Knowledge*, Harmondsworth: Penguin.

Blondel, J. (1990), *Comparative Government*, Hemel Hempstead: Philip Allan.

Ciompi, L. (1988), *The Psyche and Schizophrenia. The Bond between Affect and Logic*, Cambridge, MA: Harvard University Press.

Dijk, T.A. van (1997), *Discourse Studies: A Multidisciplinary Introduction*, Thousand Oaks, CA, US: Sage Publications, Inc.

Dörner, D. (1991), *Die Logik des Mißlingens. Strategisches Denken in komplexen Situationen*, Reinbek bei Hamburg: Rowohlt.

Eysenck, M.W. (1984), *A Handbook of Cognitive Psychology*, London: Erlbaum.

Förster, H. von (1984), *Observing Systems*, Seaside, CA: Intersystems Publ.

Frey, B.S. (1983), *Democratic Economic Policy: A Theoretical Introduction*, Oxford: Robertson.

Frey, B.S. and R. Eichenberger (1991), 'Anomalies in political economy', *Public Choice*, **68**, 71–89.

Frey, B.S. and R. Eichenberger (1994), 'Economic incentives transform psychological anomalies', *Journal of Economic Behavior and Organization*, **23**, 215–34.

Frey, B.S. and G. Kirchgässner (1994), *Demokratische Wirtschaftspolitik: Theorie und Anwendung*, Munich: Vahlen.

Goffman, E. (1986), *Frame Analysis: An Essay on the Organization of Experience*, Boston, MA: Northeastern University Press.

Habermas, J. (1984), *The Theory of Communicative Action*, London: Heinemann Education.

Hayek, F.A. von (1983), *Knowledge, Evolution, and Society*, London: Adam Smith Institute.

Hesse, G. (1990), 'Evolutorische Ökonomik oder Kreativität in der Theorie', in U. Witt (ed.), *Studien zur evolutorischen Ökonomik I*, Berlin Duncker & Humblot pp. 49–73.
Hirschfeld, L. et al. (eds) (1994), *Mapping the Mind*, New York: Cambridge University Press.
Homann, K. (1980), *Die Interdependenz von Zielen und Mitteln*, Tübingen: Mohr.
Hutter, M. (1989), *Die Produktion von Recht: Eine selbstreferentielle Theorie der Wirtschaft, angewandt auf den Fall des Arzneimittelpatentrechts*, Tübingen: Mohr.
Jones, S.R.G. (1984), *The Economics of Conformism*, Oxford: Blackwell.
Koch, L.T. (1996), *Evolutorische Wirtschaftspolitik: Eine elementare Analyse mit entwicklungspolitischen Beispielen*, Tübingen: Mohr.
Kuran, T. (1987), 'Chameleon voters and public choice', *Public Choice*, **53**, 53–78.
Kuran, T. (1995), *Private Truths, Public Lies: The Social Consequences of Preference Falsification*, Cambridge, MA, US, London, UK: Harvard University Press.
Lindblom, C.E. (1959), 'The science of muddling through', *Public Administration Review*, **19**, 79–98.
Lindenberg, S. (1993), 'Framing, empirical evidence, and applications', in P. Herder-Dorneich et al. (eds), *Jahrbuch für Neue Politische Ökonomie 12: Neue Politische Ökonomie von Normen und Institutionen*, Tübingen: Mohr.
Little, B.R. (1972), 'Psychological man as scientist, humanist and specialist', *Journal of Experimental Research in Personality*, **6**, 95–118.
Löffelholz, M. and K.-D. Altmeppen (1994), 'Kommunikation in der Informationsgesellschaft', in K. Merten, S.J. Schmidt und S. Weischenberg (eds), *Die Wirklichkeit der Medien: Einführung in die Kommunikationswissenschaft*, Opladen, Westdeutscher Verl. pp. 570–91.
Luhmann, N. (1989), 'Politische Steuerung', in H.-H. Hartwich (ed.), *Macht und Ohnmacht politischer Institutionen*, Opladen, Westdeutscher Verl. pp. 12–16.
Meier, A. and D. Mettler (1988), *Wirtschaftspolitik: Kampf um Einfluß und Sinngebung*, Stuttgart: Haupt.
Meier, A. and T. Slembeck (1994), *Wirtschaftspolitik: Ein kognitiv-evolutionärer Ansatz*, Munich: Oldenbourg.
Merten, K. and J. Westerbarkey (1994), 'Public opinion and public relations', in K. Merten, S.J. Schmidt und S. Weischenberg (eds), *Die Wirklichkeit der Medien: Einführung in die Kommunikationswissenschaft*, Opladen, Westdeutscher Verl. pp. 188–211.
Molitor, B. (1988), *Wirtschaftspolitik*, Munich: Oldenbourg.
Mueller, D.C. (1989), *Public Choice II*, Cambridge: Cambridge University Press.
Neisser, U. (1976), *Cognition and Reality*, San Francisco: W.H. Freeman.
Nisbett, R.E. and L. Ross (1980), *Human Inference*, Englewood Cliffs, NJ: Prentice-Hall.
Nüse, R. et al. (1991), *Über die Erfindung/en des radikalen Konstruktivismus: Kritische Gegenargumente aus psychologischer Sicht*, Weinheim: Dt. Studien-Verl.
Oeser, E. (1987), *Psychozoikum*, Berlin: Parey.
Pöppel, E. (1985), *Grenzen des Bewußtseins*, Stuttgart: Dt. Verlagsanst.
Pöppel, E. und A.-L. Edingshaus (1994), *Geheimnisvoller Kosmos Gehirn*, Munich: Bertelsmann.
Popper, K.R. (1995), *The Open Society and its Enemies*, London, New York: Routledge.

Ross, L. (1977), 'The intuitive psychologist and his shortcomings', in: L. Berkowitz (ed.), *Advances in Experimental Social Psychology* **10**, New York: Academic Press, pp. 173–220.

Rusch, G. (1994), 'Kommunikation und Verstehen', in K. Merten, S.J. Schmidt und S. Weischenberg (eds), *Die Wirklichkeit der Medien: Einführung in die Kommunikationswissenschaft*, Opladen: Westdeutscher Verl. pp. 60–78.

Scharpf, F.W. (1991), *Crisis and Choice in European Social Democracy*, Ithaca, NY, London, UK: Cornell University Press.

Scherer, K.R., C. Vogel and K. Immelmann (1988), 'Psychobiologie und Politik', in K. Immelmann, K.R. Scherer, C. Vogel und P. Schmoock. (eds), *Psychobiologie, Grundlagen des Verhaltens*, Stuttgart and New York: Free Press, pp. 803–32.

Schiepek, G. (1990), 'Selbstreferenz in psychischen und sozialen Systemen', in: K.W. Kratky und F. Wallner (eds), *Grundprinzipien der Selbstorganisation*, Darmstadt: Wiss. Buchges.

Searle, J.R. (1995), *The Construction of Social Reality*, London, UK, New York, US: Free Press.

Siegenthaler, H. (1994), 'Wege zum Wohlstand: Das Beispiel der USA, der Schweiz und Brasiliens', in W. Fischer (ed.), *Lebensstandard und Wirtschaftssysteme*, Frankfurt am Main: F. Knapp, pp. 173–212.

Simon, H. A. (1955), 'A behavioral model of rational choice', *Quarterly Journal of Economics*, **69**, 99–118.

Six, B. (1987), 'Attribution', in D. Frey und S. Greif (eds), *Sozialpsychologie*, Munich: Psychologie-Verlags-Union.

Slembeck, T. (1997), 'The formation of economic policy: a cognitive-evolutionary approach to policy-making', *Constitutional Political Economy*, **8**, 225–54.

Sugarman, S. (1987), *Piaget's Construction of the Child's Reality*, Cambridge, New York: Cambridge University Press.

Tversky, A. and D. Kahneman (1981), 'The framing of decisions and the psychology of choice', *Science* **211**, 453–58.

Tversky, A. and D. Kahneman (1982), 'Causal schemas in judgements under uncertainty, in D. Kahneman, P. Slovic und A. Tversky (eds), *Judgement under Uncertainties*, Cambridge: Cambridge University Press, pp. 117–28.

Vowe, G. (1994), 'Politische Kognition: Umrisse eines kognitionsorientierten Ansatzes für die Analyse politischen Handelns', *Politische Vierteljahresschrift*, **35**, 423–47.

Wallis, J. (1997), 'Conspiracy and the policy process: a case study of the New Zealand experiment', *Journal of Public Policy*, **17**, 1–30.

Weick, K.E. (1986), 'Organizations as cognitive maps: charting ways to success and failure', in: H.P. Sims et al. (eds), *The Thinking Organization, Dynamics of Organizational Social Cognition*, San Francisco: Jossey-Bass.

Witt, U. (1992), 'The endogenous public choice theorist', *Public Choice*, **73**, 117–29.

9. Why endogeneity is not enough to explain technological change – a critique of Paul Romer

Malcolm H. Dunn[1]

For ten years now, we have been experiencing a renaissance of growth theories in the form of so-called 'endogenous growth theories'. These claim to supply us with an empirically substantial explanation of the driving forces behind the growth-rate of an economy. On the one hand, proponents argue that, in contrast to the older neoclassical growth theory of the Solow-type, technological change is no longer treated as a residual value, calculated by determining the difference between the growth of inputs to the empirically observed national growth of outputs, i.e. to the social product. Instead of an assumed exogenous rate of technological change, i.e. a rate that is not explicitly explained, we have a rate which is attributed to the intentional actions of profit-maximising agents of an economy, i.e. an endogenous rate.

Another advance, proponents argue, is that endogenous growth theory coincides better with the observable facts than does the older theory. While the older neoclassical theory still concluded that per-capita growth rates had a tendency to converge, explaining this among other things with the public goods character of technical advances, newer theories assume that technical knowledge is not ubiquitous. This is why a stable gap in per-capita growth rates can occur, the closure of which gives rise to the need for economic policy. At least some proponents of endogenous growth theory view their reasoning as a justification for extensive state intervention in the form of industrial and technological policy measures.

There is no doubt that endogenous growth theory is *en vogue* and this not only because one of its founders was awarded the Nobel prize for his work on rational expectations, but also because the deficits in the area of the micro-economic foundations of macro-economics are felt more strongly than was the case 30 or 40 years ago. In spite of or because of the public appreciation of endogenous growth theory, it must be 'permissible' to ask wherein the advancement of endogenous growth theories actually lies. Addressing this question is the objective of this chapter. The present inquiry will be made from the perspective of both evolutionary economics and the very closely related New Institutional Economics, another school of thought which has also experienced a renaissance in the past few years.

The present contribution is structured as follows: the actual inquiry is preceded by a description of technological change from the perspective of evolutionary economics (second section). The purpose here is not to review the already numerous contributions to this school of thought, but rather to develop questions which are important for the ensuing analysis. In the third section one of the models which has received the most attention, namely Romer's growth model, 'Endogenous Technological Change', introduced in 1990, is discussed. Again, the purpose here is not to presume to give an exhaustive account of all endogenous growth theories, but to use the model to illustrate some fundamental problems of endogenous growth theories. In the ensuing fourth section, it will be demonstrated that, in spite of the advances of *this* model in comparison to those of traditional neoclassical growth theory, one cannot speak of an 'endogenisation' in the strict sense of the term, because important aspects of the market, representing the driving forces behind technological change, are ignored. The chapter closes with some deliberations on the conclusions to be drawn from the deficits of the Romerean growth model (fifth section). In this context, brief reference to other endogenous theories of growth will be made.

TECHNOLOGICAL CHANGE FROM THE PERSPECTIVE OF EVOLUTIONARY ECONOMICS

Both the perspective of evolutionary economics and the New Institutional Economics assume 'that the institutional and organisational structure of a national economy and not merely market mechanisms must be considered for resources and income to be distributed effectively' (Grupp 1998, p. 66). In addition to the question of how institutions are formed and how institutional change is to be explained, defendants of the evolutionary paradigm dedicate themselves to explaining technological change. However, instead of taking these contributions as a point of departure, another approach will be chosen here. If it is assumed that technological change, as the growth generator of an economy, is the product of the interaction of various institutions, then it makes sense to first have a look at how these institutions are characterised within the context of evolutionary economics in order to then analyse the extent to which these same institutions are modelled within the framework of newer growth theories.

Institutions, as they are understood here, are defined as a system of deliberate (formal) and indeliberate (informal) rules including the provisions for their enforcement. 'Institutions together with the people taking advantage of them are called organisations . . .' (Furubotn and Richter 2000, p. 7). The most important institutions involved in technological change are no doubt firms, private households and the state as an intervening authority that sets up laws and implements economic policy. How do these organisations come into the field of view of the analysis of technological change?

The way in which institutional economics discusses the firm dates, as we know, back to Coase's contribution 'The nature of the firm' (1937). In this article, Coase pursues the question of how the existence of firms can be explained. On the other hand, firms as producers of technological change are not considered. Coase does, however, introduce the concept of transaction costs, a concept unknown to neoclassical theory. The neglect of transaction costs in neoclassical theory leads, according to Richter and Furubotn (1998, p. 9f.), to the conclusion that the question of how production is organised is unimportant. For this reason, the existence of firms must remain unexplained. Not only this, but it is noteworthy 'that, in the zero-transaction-cost-world of neoclassical economics, the two economic systems . . . , capitalism and socialism, can be modelled by general equilibrium systems' (ibid., p. 14).

This assertion is also important for the explanation of technological change. For it is not at all inconsequential for the explanation of technological change if the economic system in question is characterised by capitalist firms or not. The incentive for technical progress arises from the firm's objective to realise the economic benefit that technical progress affords. The profit motive induces firms to continually reduce their production costs by means of process innovations and to attract the ever limitedly solvent demand to its own supply via product innovations. Both processes take place, not by coincidence, but as a result of deliberate planning. Following Schumpeter's earlier contributions, Freeman, e.g., emphasises that technological change is less something produced by obsessive tinkerers working somewhere in a garage and more the result of the work of professional research teams. Freeman explains the professionalisation of innovation work by pointing to the growing complexity of scientific and technological tasks and the increasing division and specialisation that go with it.

Firms as innovators promote technological change out of self-interest and not because the state demands it of them. Competition, however, does serve as an additional driving force. Due to the fact that at least some firms are actively innovative so that they can attain innovation rents, the question of technical progress becomes, within the context of competition, an existential one: as soon as some firms succeed in minimising their production costs, other firms will be forced to follow. As imitators they contribute to the diffusion of innovations. The process is similar for product innovations. Product innovations will be copied and improved by other firms. Product markets develop which in turn go through a similar cycle (see Heuss 1965).

A constitutive element for the appearance and diffusion of product and process innovations is the uncertainty of market outcomes, as all true incalculable uncertainties are prerequisites for functioning markets.[2] The individual who gives the impetus for a technical innovation does not know beforehand if the new process or product justifies the costs that were incurred for it. Technological change is not the same as economic success, the latter will only make itself felt on the market. This is the point where another economic agent of the market economy is addressed, namely the 'private household'. Just like the firm, the private household appears on the market and decides if a technological advance is also to be considered an economic advance.

Private households are also important in another way. They serve as suppliers of the most important production factor, namely human capital, acquire skills and knowledge during their working life and, by virtue of their work, contribute to a continuous improvement of the implemented technologies and processes. What then happens is what evolutionary economists call *incremental* technical progress: while the technological paradigm as defined by Dosi is a stock of knowledge with public-goods character – examples are provided by the research results of the natural sciences – incremental technical progress is less fundamental. It is related to the specific use of technologies and results mostly from step-by-step improvements in efficiency due to learning effects.[3] For this reason, Dosi also describes this type of change as 'localised technological progress', the pace and direction of which depends on the technical level that has already been reached in the firm.[4] This localised technological progress is important especially because it is based on firm-specific know-how and with this, takes on the characteristics of a private good.[5]

This differentiation of technical progress as a public or a private good bridges the gap to another field of research within the framework of evolutionary economics, namely to property rights-theory and with this, indirectly to the role of government in the innovation process. As Richter confirms: 'Property rights matter!' (1994, p. 13), arguing that control rights are an incentive in a world in which there are latent transaction costs. In connection with technical progress, the question arises as to whether the innovator will also succeed in obtaining the profits of his investment. This is by definition a problem for the type of technical progress which can be viewed as a public good, because the non-rivalry and non-excludability of public goods means that innovators cannot exclude others from using their know-how. It is possible, when competing firms imitate an innovation, that the innovator will find himself deprived of his innovation profit. He even suffers a competitive disadvantage in comparison to the competition, because of the costs he has incurred producing the innovation. In this case, the market provides little or no incentives for innovation. The institutional deficit of the market is only attenuated by the creation of another institution, namely of the government-regulated protection of patents. This may maintain the incentive system for innovations, because it gives the innovator the opportunity to realise monopoly revenues temporarily. However, since externalities cannot be completely excluded by the protection of the patent, many authors see it as the responsibility of the state to intensify its own efforts in the production of new knowledge.

Evolutionary economists were not the first to object to this conclusion concerning industrial policy by noting that technical progress can also take on the characteristics of a private good. Furthermore, it is noted that the existence of positive externalities does not automatically lead to a decrease in the propensity to innovate.[6] On the contrary, technological spillovers can be related to synergy effects which lead to more, and not less, innovation activity.[7] From this it follows that the state's role is not, as industrial policy makers have repeatedly demanded of the state, that of promoting certain technologies and sectors. What really matters is developing networks between firms and public research institutions to promote the diffusion of technical knowledge in a sector or between different sectors. (see Hanusch and Cantner 1993, p. 35).

PAUL ROMER'S GROWTH MODEL (1990) – AN OUTLINE

A common characteristic of the newer growth theories is that they attempt to explain continuous economic growth without having recourse to exogenous values. Instead, growth is explained by market participants' preferences, especially derived from their savings, consumption and investment behaviour and is, in this sense 'endogenised'.

It not difficult to make out where the assumptions of endogenous growth theories come from.[8] First of all, new growth theories assume, just like the older neoclassical ones, profit-maximising economic agents guided by rational expectations. Second, it is also true for the new growth theories that the goods and factor markets' price mechanism perfectly co-ordinates the plans of firms and private households. They are, without exception, equilibrium models. Third, the question of consumers' willingness to forgo consumption and to save is also a relevant question for the new growth theories. This depends, assuming optimisation behaviour, on the profit-rate on investments and the time preference-rate of private households.

A key difference between the older and the newer growth theories is related to the marginal productivity of capital. In traditional growth theory it is assumed that the marginal productivity of the accumulative factor sinks at a constant rate. For this reason, at a certain point it becomes foolish for consumers to continue forgoing consumption. This is why they will reduce their savings, with the consequence that net investments are not made, so that the economy converges towards a zero growth-rate. Only the exogenously introduced technical progress prevents this.[9] In contrast, endogenous growth theories are intent on identifying mechanisms and factors that prevent the continuous decrease of the marginal productivity of the accumulative factor and which in this way create an incentive for market participants to forgo present consumption in favour of future consumption.

The essence of the new growth theory lies therefore in the fact that the marginal productivity of capital must remain constant, so that an endogenous steady-state growth of per-capita income is possible.[10] An endogenisation of the growth-rate takes place in such a way that the factor identified as the respective growth generator is not a given. On the contrary, production factors are considered to be a result of investment decisions made for economic reasons, i.e. the firms produce these themselves.

Figure 9.1 gives us an idea of Romer's multisector model. Technical knowledge is produced in the research sector. Romer calls this kind of knowledge 'designs'. These designs are needed to produce intermediary products. These represent capital goods, necessary for the production of consumption goods. In the centre of Romer's model we have technical knowledge, regarded as a public good with the capacity to grow boundlessly. An example would be natural laws which can be used by different engineers in order to produce innovations. (The private-good character of localised technological progress is still not considered in this model!) Technical knowledge is produced in this sector. In order for this to take place, the costs of producing this knowledge would have to be covered. However, as Schreiter (1997, p. 95) points out, if perfect competition is assumed, there is nothing left for covering the costs of non-rivalling knowledge, unless excludability is possible. Excludability, though, is not compatible with the assumption of perfect competition.

In order to solve the financing problem, Romer makes three assumptions. First it is assumed that the innovators in the research sector receive a patent which is infinitely lived. This makes their knowledge marketable.

$H_Y, L \longrightarrow$

Consumer goods sector

$$Y(H_Y, L, x) = H_Y^{\alpha} L^{\beta} \int_0^{\infty} x(i)^{1-\alpha-\beta} di$$

$$= H_Y^{\alpha} L^{\beta} A_x^{-1-\alpha-\beta}$$

$\longrightarrow Y$

↑↓ Intermediate goods are sold to the consumer goods sector and used there. Consumer goods which were not consumed are at the intermediate goods sector's disposal and can be used as inputs.

$Y \longrightarrow$

Intermediate goods sector

$K_i = x\eta$ or

$x_i = \bar{x} = 1/\eta\, Y(H_Y^i, L^i, x^i)$

$\longrightarrow X_i$

↑↓ The research sector develops designs and sells these to the intermediate goods sector. This enables the research sector to fully cover its costs.

$H_A \longrightarrow$

Research sector

$dA/dt = \delta \cdot H_A A$

$\longrightarrow$ Designs

↑↓ Research enlarges the public stock of knowledge (general knowledge), which represents a production factor of the research sector. This makes research on the whole more productive.

Public stock of knowledge

Notes:
Variables of the model:

A	Quantity of designs, dA/dt increase in designs
H_A	Human capital of the research sector; H_Y of the consumer sector
L	Simple labour
K	Capital, measured in units of the end product
Y	Standard consumer good
$\bar{x}$	Equilibrium quantity on the intermediate goods market
δ	Productivity factor effective in the research sector
η	Quantity of end products 'sacrificed' for an intermediate product

Figure 9.1 Romer's growth model 'Endogenous Technological Change'

Each individual producer in the intermediate-goods sector makes a single payment to purchase exactly one design and produces, using capital, an intermediary good of a certain quality, which he then sells to the consumer-goods sector. The second assumption is that intermediate goods producers exert market power over consumption goods producers. Since the producers of intermediate goods have a monopoly on their products, they can exercise their market power over the consumption market, which is competitive, and realise a monopoly profit. However, they lose this quasi-rent. This is because of the third assumption, namely that a large number of producers of intermediate goods compete with each other to acquire licences from the research sector. The research sector's quasi-rents are spent completely to obtain patent rights from that same sector. In this way, the research sector's costs for the production of knowledge are financed by the sale of usufructuary rights for a discovery.

How do spillovers or positive external effects occur in this model?[11] These occur because in the research sector new knowledge is not only produced in the form of designs but also in the form of general knowledge. In spite of patents, research increases the public stock of knowledge. The research sector produces a factor as a by-product, which it can, in a certain sense, use for free. Due to this, research activity becomes cheaper and, with this, the number of new intermediate goods increases, on which, according to the assumptions of the model, the productivity of the consumer goods sector depends.

PAUL ROMER'S GROWTH MODEL: A CRITIQUE

Richard Nelson (1997) posed, in a widely acclaimed article, the question of how new the new growth theory is. He then proceeded to answer the question by noting that many components of endogenous growth theory can be found in older contributions to growth theory. What appears to be more important than this finding, however, is the criticism he expresses against a degree of formalism these models have. A formalism which rules out, from the onset, being able to take important factors which determine technical progress into account. In the following, this criticism will be discussed using a few leading questions: First: Is technological change modelled in a way suited to production theory? Second: Are market forces identified as the motor behind technological change? Third: How is the endogenisation of technical progress and economic growth achieved? In other words, is the endogenisation successful and, if so, to what degree? Let us begin with the first question.

Is Technological Change Modelled in a Way Suited to Production Theory?

Let us begin with a look at the production function (equation 9.1). The production of consumption goods (Romer, for reasons of simplification, assumes a single consumption good (Y)) takes place using the inputs unskilled labour (L), skilled labour, i.e. human capital (H_Y) and intermediate or capital goods (x).

$$Y(H_Y L, x) = H_Y^{\alpha} L^{\beta} \int_0^{\infty} x(i)^{1-\alpha-\beta} di = H_Y^{\alpha} L^{\beta} A \bar{x}^{1-\alpha-\beta} \quad (9.1)$$

The striking thing about this production function is the assumption that skilled labour (H_Y) remains qualitatively unchanged while the production process undergoes change because of the increase in capital goods input. In other words, the fact is ignored that a change in the quantity of capital goods also implies a qualitative change in the production process, which, in turn, means other skills will be required, skills more appropriate to the changed work process. In this equation, technical progress has no influence on the quality of skilled labour. Progress in productivity takes place, one could say, without so much as touching the human factor of production, even though this same factor becomes more productive due to the increased input of intermediate goods.[12]

Let us look at the last factor in the total economy's production function, capital or intermediate goods (x). It is assumed that every increase in capital or intermediate goods also means an increase in output and that no productivity relation exists between capital or intermediate goods. Both assumptions represent a strange abstraction within the context of an explanation for technical progress, because technical progress does not consist only in the quantitative increase of those intermediate goods used for the production of a consumption good but also in their qualitative change. In addition, technical progress can make an intermediate good superfluous or lead to the replacement of several intermediate goods by a new one. A decreasing number of intermediate goods can therefore be just as much an indicator of technical progress as the development of new intermediate goods (see Hayek 1984).

The fact that – due to technical progress – old products are replaced by new ones is reversed here: every capital good ever made retains its effectiveness regardless of technical progress.[13] In this way, technological change appears as a mere increase of the capital goods that go into the production process, the elimination of technically obsolete capital goods or their replacement with more advanced capital goods does not take place. Thus, a very important factor in technological change is left out.

Another objection refers to how capital goods implemented in the production process come to develop their efficiency. Romer assumes that capital goods are efficient independently. The implementation of a capital good in combination with another or of several capital goods together has, according to the assumption of the model, no effect on efficiency. Again, a surprising assumption, since this means that capital goods are not combined at all, but used separately. The difference between a production process in which technical progress is taken into account and one in which it is not is merely that, in the former case, *more* intermediate goods are implemented.[14]

The qualitative relation between the human capital incorporated in workers on the one hand and the quantitative as well as qualitative composition of capital goods on the other hand, all so important to the understanding of the production relation, are theoretically deleted in the assumed modelling. This is, by the way, also true for the influence that the technically changed production process has on the constitution of the end product. In Romer's model, the quality of the end product remains likewise completely unaffected by technical progress.[15]

Now, one could raise the objection that the production function for the whole economy is not the actual innovation of the Romer model and that the more important thing is the way in which the accumulation and use of technical knowledge is modelled. This addresses the production function of the intermediate or capital-goods sector and the knowledge-production function. The former is expressed in equation (9.2). For the purpose of simplification, it is assumed that the production of the intermediate good proves to be forgone consumption. After a design is purchased from the research sector, a certain amount of the output of good Y can presumably be transformed into a capital-good i. The consumption goods which are not consumed are available to the capital-goods sector. In the corresponding equation (9.2) this is expressed by saying that η units of Y are needed to produce one unit of capital good i.

$$K_i = \bar{x}\eta. \tag{9.2}$$

Let us address the question of how the technical knowledge that goes into intermediate-goods production is produced. This technical knowledge is, in contrast to human capital, the non-rivalling factor. This is justified by the assumption that technical knowledge exists *separately* from *every and any* individual and – as is common in endogenous growth theories – can grow boundlessly. It is assumed, mainly for the purpose of simplifying the model, that each unit of technical knowledge corresponds to exactly one unit of an intermediate good. For this reason, technical knowledge can be described numerically by the number of patents. The production relation behind the production of technical knowledge is contained in equation (9.3).

$$dA/dt = \delta H_A A. \tag{9.3}$$

As can be derived from this equation, a surplus of technical knowledge results from a surplus of human capital working in the research sector, the already available stock of knowledge A and a productivity factor δ, assumed to be constant, and which, when $H_A = 1$, indicates the relation between the new design and the already available ones ($\delta = \dot{A}/A$).

How well does the above cover the process of creating new technical knowledge? If one leaves out the influence of human capital on knowledge production, it follows from equation (9.3) that a 'surplus' of the existing knowledge, regardless of the content, generally increases the production of new knowledge, also regardless of the content. First of all, one must object that technical innovations are, as a rule, path-dependent. They are i.e. dependent on a certain set of scientific findings from the preceding periods: Progress in technical knowledge in the aviation industry has nothing to do with advances in cancer research or the pharmaceutical industry. Second, technical knowledge depreciates constantly and, this, in fact, not only in the economic sense, but also in the technical sense. Advances in the entire stock of knowledge do not consist in a mere 'surplus' of ideas. It is often the case that new ideas replace old ones with regard to their technical relevance. There is also a process of 'creative destruction' of outdated technical knowledge within the natural and engineering sciences, which, by the way, does not exclude the possibility that in individual cases and within the context of a new paradigm, a forgotten concept will be 'rediscovered'.[16]

The simplifying idea of conceiving the production of knowledge as a function of the existing stock of knowledge finds an extension in the way in which human capital is taken into consideration. Connecting the two variables by multiplication means that no advance in technical knowledge can be made without a bearer of that knowledge. Who would want to challenge this? What is striking, however, is the idea that the stock of knowledge exists externally and *separately* from human capital or, expressed in another way, that the stock of knowledge is not at all incorporated *in* human capital:

> According to this specification, a college-educated engineer working today and one working 100 years ago have the same (!) human capital, which is measured in terms of years of forgone participation in the labor market. The engineer working today is more productive because he or she can take advantage of all the additional knowledge accumulated as design problems were solved during the last 100 years. (Romer 1990, p. 84f.; emphasis: M.D.)

Romer's specification contradicts all experience: even a forgotten patent will be grasped by *someone* when its usefulness is rediscovered. In contrast, an engineer's great-grandfather, likewise trained as an engineer, would have, because of his poorer knowledge, great difficulties grasping his great-grandchild's scientific findings because these were gained on the basis of a much broader stock of knowledge. He would be forced to learn new skills in order to understand current patents. In other words, the stock of knowledge is precisely *the* central component of the qualification. One finds oneself asking what the engineer's level of knowledge consists in, if not in the acquired knowledge of his trade?

With the above, we have gathered the elements of Romer's production function: advances in technical knowledge result, as if we were dealing with a recipe, directly from the multiplication of a stock of knowledge with researchers whose qualification does not include this knowledge at all. Regardless of the problem of choosing the factors involved in the achievement of technical knowledge and examining the way they interact, the functional relation is not really of the kind described in Romer's model. The idea that advances in technical knowledge can be represented by a steady monotone production function misses the characteristic feature of technical progress and that of any and every advance in knowledge.[17]

Are Market Forces Identified as the Motor Behind Technological Change?

Process and product innovations increase the welfare of any society. Process innovations make the labour necessary to produce a good cheaper and increase the number and quality of capital goods, while labour remains constant. In addition, they contribute to the creation and satisfaction of new needs. What separates market systems from other systems is the driving force of competition which forces its participants, especially the firms, to constantly lower their prices and to develop new products in order to attract limited solvent demand to their own supply. In this way, innovation and its diffusion become a question of the continuing existence of a firm in competition, an endeavour entailing a number of risks and imponderabilities for market participants. Research has to be done where it crosses the line into a zone of uncertainty, where patents are developed even when their economic use is never realised because better or cheaper solutions exist. Yet other patents make the production of new consumption articles possible but these do not meet with adequate solvent demand.

In short, just like the large supply of goods, patents as well as those consumer and intermediate goods produced with the help of new knowledge are also confronted with competition and have to stand the test of time. It is inevitable that there will also be losers in this process. It is not seldom that production and research costs as well as costs for qualifying employees prove themselves afterwards to be bad investments. On the other hand, it is possible, in other cases, for firms to increase and expand their monopoly position because of technical progress.

One finds very little of this in the Romer model: producers of new knowledge in the research sector develop new designs, which they can, without any apparent complications, sell to the producers of the intermediate- or capital-goods sector. Furthermore, every design obtains the same price. Patents which turn out afterwards to be bad investments or are replaced by other patents do not exist in this model. Future research findings, which cannot be known beforehand, are modelled in such a way as if they were already known. Both in the technical and the economic sense, certainty concerning the production and exploitation of patentable knowledge exists. Capital goods producers who buy individual designs and in this way become exclusive suppliers of a capital good also compete with each other in a surprising way.

The economic incentive to produce capital-goods, i.e. to achieve an extra profit over interest on capital by means of a monopoly price, is completely lost because of the intensive competition of new firms entering the market. At equilibrium, monopoly rents are just enough to finance fix costs, used to purchase designs. The research sector therefore completely assimilates the monopoly profit of the capital-good producers. Finally, conditions of perfect competition in the consumer-goods sector prevail anyway. All firms produce the same consumer good, i.e. they do not compete with each other by diversifying their supply.

The exclusion of the competition of firms that anticipate trends and those that follow suit, i.e. those who take on, imitate or develop innovations and in this manner bring about the diffusion of technological innovations, gives rise to the question of how technical progress can be endogenised. Let us therefore address the third question: How is an endogenisation of technical progress and economic growth achieved in Romer's model in the first place?

How is the Endogenisation of Technical Progress and Economic Growth Achieved?

Growth and technical progress appear in Romer's model in three sectors. Let us have a look at each sector in turn. The growth of consumer goods (Y), with skilled (H_Y) and unskilled labour (L) remaining constant, is exclusively a result of the increased input of intermediate or capital goods. It is assumed in addition that the quantity of intermediate goods of each and every type i is the same. This means: the more qualitatively 'new' intermediate goods, without any change in their quantity, the higher the output of consumer goods. What is striking here is that technical progress in Romer's model is oblivious to the replacement of worn and technically obsolete capital goods. 'New' capital goods are simply placed side by side with 'old' capital goods, which are, by the way, operated by the same number of skilled workers. In a nutshell, both assumptions contradict the essence of technological change: neither does the number and the qualifications of workers remain untouched by technological change, nor does this change consist in constantly adding new intermediate goods to older ones.

Growth in the consumer-goods sector is based on growth in intermediate or capital goods. This requires a production process, with the input of capital goods and specially qualified workers – a process which differs from that of the consumer-goods sector. This is also abstracted from in Romer's model, 'to keep things simple'. Instead, it is assumed that the intermediate-goods sector acquires designs from the research sector and, using the *same* (!) technology used in the consumer-goods sector, produces capital goods.[18] In other words, 'the formal specification here describes the sector that produces capital goods as a black box that takes final output in on one side and gives capital goods out of the other side' (Romer 1990, p. 81).

It is the assumption that the production function of the intermediate-goods sector is equal to that of the consumer-goods sector which makes possible the interpretation of the production of capital goods as forgone consumption. One is reminded of a statement made by Hofmann (1971, p. 269) about the Solowean growth theory when he points out what he calls a peculiarity of that theory. Hofmann comments that one comes to wonder how a loaf of bread as a single good can be invested or, vice versa, how a certain kind of machine is to be consumed.

The objections made in connection with the capital-theory debates of the last decades concerning the 'well-defined' macro-economic production function seem to interest no one at all anymore. For this reason, it is pointed out again here that capital goods and intermediate goods differ in quality, which is why their factor-input ratios differ. Robinson (1953) and Sraffa (1960) pointed this out in their critiques. Thanks to Garegnani (1970 and 1990) we know that, in the light of this objection, a 'well-defined production function' is no longer tenable even when interpreted as a 'parable'.[19]

In the Romer model, the increase in capital goods is due to an increase in the input of designs, which are produced in the research sector. The function decisive for growth in Romer's model is, in fact, the knowledge-accumulation equation (9.3). From this equation it follows that, as a factor of production, the production of designs for one period goes into the production of designs for the subsequent periods. The increase in designs depends on the stock of designs of the preceding periods.[20] The productivity of the research sector, reflected in the increase of designs, increases in proportion to how knowledge was accumulated and more qualified workers were employed in the preceding periods.[21] However this does not suffice to describe equilibrium growth.

Let us assume, e.g., that A in equation (9.3) is replaced by a concave A function. This would mean that the marginal productivity of the human capital in the research sector would not increase in the same proportion as the designs. The larger the number of designs and the stock of knowledge, the more qualified workers would leave the research sector in order to work in the consumer-goods sector. In this way, the economy's growth would be weakened and, eventually, come to a halt. To prevent this in the analysis, Romer assumes a linear relation: qualified workers' marginal product in the consumer-goods sector grows in the same proportion as the increment in designs. This assumption of a linear relation is what makes unbounded growth in this model possible. How is growth achieved in the end? Romer (1990, p. 84) himself gives us the answer:

> Linearity in A is what makes unbounded growth possible, and in this sense, unbounded growth is more like an assumption than a result of the model.

The quote, placed at the end of the critical explanation of the model, is revealing: unbounded growth is not a result of the inherent argumentation of the model, but is simply a result of a scantily justified assumption of linearity. Romer regards the assumption of linearity as 'feasible', 'because there is no evidence from recent history to support the belief that opportunities for research are diminishing' Romer (1990, p. 84). If one compares Romer's model with other endogenous growth models, one will find similar linearity relations.

Linearity, however, is not exactly typical for technological change, as long as the change is path-dependent. New technological paradigms in certain areas of knowledge stimulate an increase in certain areas of research and lead temporarily to a marked increase in patentable knowledge until the paradigm is finally exhausted. Characteristic for technological change are temporary increases in patents on the basis of a technological paradigm, which then slowly decrease in number and importance. In many cases, new paradigms arise to replace the old ones, in turn triggering a new wave of research activities. At the same time, older patents are depreciated, both in the technical and in the economic sense. In yet other cases and because of technical and economic developments, the particular relevance of 'older' patents will be rediscovered. In any case, the assumption that technical knowledge, like every type of knowledge, is infinite, in no way implies linear relations. Even interruptions and periods of less innovation activity cannot be ruled out.

Romer's model then, does not give us an 'endogenisation' of economic growth, in the sense that *proof* is given as to why empirical evidence shows that growth is not weakened and a convergence in the Solowean sense does not occur. Romer admits this himself when he notes: 'Whether opportunities in research are actually petering out, or will eventually do so, is an empirical question that this kind of theory cannot resolve' (1990, p. 84).

But what is left then of the claim to endogenisation, if the explanation of technological change is based on a linear-relations assumption, which has not been tested – what is more, would probably not withstand an empirical test?

CONCLUSIONS OF AN EVOLUTIONARY ECONOMIST

Models of endogenous growth theory are different from Solow-type growth models in many ways, but not in the sense that they do not interpret growth as a deterministic process. They remain deterministic even when, in other endogenous growth models, the role of the 'dynamic entrepreneur' is given more emphasis or the process of innovation is modelled stochastically.[22] More research does not necessarily lead to more innovation.[23] Modelling technological change as a deterministic process ignores the institutional context in which technical progress takes place: competition as an open process which brings forth, and must bring forth, not only winners, but losers as well.[24] However, there is yet another reason why it is incorrect to regard technical progress as a deterministic process. The reason lies in the very nature of technological change: even before the evaluation of the results of research and development is to be given thought to, those same results would already have to be available.[25] Exactly because of their far-reaching informational assumptions, traditional models lead to an erroneous characterisation of technological change.

The institutional deficits of the newer growth theory are of a similar consequence. A definition of a growth equilibrium based on the assumption of a deterministic process of knowledge accumulation is indifferent to the underlying economic system.[26] In actual fact, since market uncertainties have no role to play in neoclassical growth models, these models resemble more the ideal of a planned economy than that of a decentralised market economy.[27] If the whole point of technological change were to 'produce' it with the help of the available stock of knowledge, then, instead of the process of competition, one could have the figure of a central planner who, in order to increase the stock of technical knowledge, would allot the available resources of a society to the research sector. It is not a coincidence that even growth theorists confirm that the steady-state growth-rates of centrally planned economies do not differ substantially from those of market-economy systems.[28]

However, controversy exists concerning the conclusions to be drawn from this criticism. As is generally known, Solow (1991, pp. 15ff.) uses the occurrence of true uncertainty, necessarily connected to technological change, to argue against making technical progress endogenous and to ask 'why I should buy a car with so much horsepower' – meaning the models of endogenous growth theory – 'to drive on such a dark and winding road'. In the same article, Solow points to the fact that there is an 'exogenous element' to technological change in the sense that the result of human decisions and actions have an inherent moment of true and incalculable uncertainty.[29] Does this mean that science should refrain from investigating technological change as an explanation for economic growth? Hardly! Even if it is true that chance represents a constitutive element of technical progress and that neither the technical nor the economic results of a research and development investment are known a priori, this does not mean that we should exclude the investigation of technological change. This is exactly what the contributions of many evolutionary economists make clear.

Characteristic of these works, which stand in the Schumpeterean tradition, is their focus on the entrepreneur as the agent of the innovation process. Instead of the firm as an input/output relation, we have the entrepreneur who recognises and implements new opportunities on the economic plane.[30] Following Röpke (1982), innovative behaviour can be seen as a function of rights of action, competence and entrepreneurial motivation.

Rights of action determine the degree in which one's own actions are permitted to infringe on others. These rights encompass every and any type of normative restriction on action (laws, rules and regulations, norms and sociocultural values). Since innovative possibilities of action do not necessarily represent permissible possibilities of action, transaction costs ensue for the entrepreneur, when they try either to enforce those rights which are propitious for them or have to recompense someone for damages caused by innovations. Both diminish the incentive to carry out innovations. But even when rights of action promote the development and implementation of technical innovations, innovative behaviour requires a certain degree of competence. Innovative behaviour is tied to persons who have to have the capability to develop or imitate new ideas and to carry these new ideas out. These personality traits are both cognitive and non-cognitive. They include abilities, aptitudes, experience, intuition and creativity.

Ability, however, must be paired with inclination, i.e. with 'industry' (Adam Smith). As everyone knows, agents' motivation to act does not only depend on personality traits. Motivation is a cultural phenomenon that is influenced by social environment. As Röpke's work has shown, which causes are attributed to which results is not irrelevant for innovation behaviour. If the probability of an aspired-to goal is not to be influenced by one's own performance, there is no incentive to be innovative. Conversely, one can observe that the incentive for innovative activity is particularly high if carrying out an innovation is perceived to be neither trivial nor extremely difficult. Comparative research on innovation behaviour in different Asian countries supports Röpke's speculation that the environment provides an incentive for innovation behaviour when the challenges are in a middle range of difficulty, i.e. neither too easy nor too difficult with respect to the individual entrepreneurial ability (on this, see Röpke 1982).

Both Röpke's deliberations, as well as those of other evolutionary economists, make clear that more attention has to be paid to qualitative factors which, though not easily formalised, are nevertheless important for understanding the process of technological change.[31] The conclusion which Nelson (1997, 39) draws in his commentary on endogenous growth theory can therefore also serve as the concluding remark to this chapter: 'The general conclusion suggested by this survey of the factors controlling the vigor of enterprise is that a vast deal of emphasis must be placed on forces that, in the ordinary conception of the bounds of economics, would have to be classed as political, psychological, or sociological.'

NOTES

1. I thank Ulrich Fehl, Carsten Schreiter, Rainer Klump and Markus Braun for helpful comments on the German version of this article, which was first published under the title 'Wachstum und endogener technologischer Wandel – Eine Kritik des Wachstumsmodells von Paul Romer aus der Perspektive der Evolutorischen Ökonomik' in *ORDO* (2000), **51**, 277–99.
2. As is generally known, Morgenstern (1972, 1184) pointed out that the firm, as it is presented in the textbooks, could easily be replaced by a computer. The same author makes reference to the fact that the competition of neoclassical equilibrium economics has little to do with the competition firms have to deal with in the real world. On this point, see also Dunn (1998).
3. These learning effects do not always take place on the knowledge frontier. Rosenberg (1994), e.g., confirms that technical progress often only then ensues, when previous knowledge is rediscovered and related to new contexts.
4. Innovation theory speaks in this context of the fact that technological change is path-dependent and develops continually along so-called *natural trajectories*. Hanusch and Cantner (1993, p. 24) point out that the more technological progress is based on firm-specific know-how, the more one may characterise it as a private good and the easier it is to appropriate its (temporarily accrued) rents. As self-enforcing mechanisms that account for the path-dependencies, North (1990, p. 94) following Arthur (1988) mentions: '(1) large setup or fixed costs, which give the advantage of falling unit costs as output increases; (2) learning effects, which improve products or lower their costs as their prevalence increases; (3) coordination effects, which confer advantages to cooperation

with other economic agents taking similar action; and (4) adaptive expectations, where increased prevalence on the market enhances beliefs of further prevalence'.

5. One of the findings of empirical innovation economics is that 'The simple equation of a private stock of intellectual property with total excludability and rivalry, contrasting with a public stock of intellectual property without excludability or rivalry, (with respect to the factor-embodied and disembodied knowledge), only holds in a few instances' (Grupp 1998, p. 462)
6. The occurrence of external effects cannot be equated with market failure. They are rather an ubiquitous characteristic of market economies. On this, see Sälter (1989).
7. This has to do with the fact that technical knowledge, in the form of acquired skills, flows from one firm to the other when employees change their workplace or firms co-operate in R&D projects.
8. See, for a description, Walz (1999).
9. This holds true even when, as in Solow's model, a constant savings rate is assumed. However, if the savings rate is dependent on the interest rate, the growth process will come to a standstill much sooner.
10. As Ramser (1995, p. 238) correctly notes, increasing returns to scale are not necessary for endogenous growth. It is necessary for one or a group of cumulative factors to exist which can be produced with constant returns to scale and without the direct or indirect use of non-reproductive factors. On the same topic, see also Schreiter (1997, p. 89), Klump and La Grandville (2000) as well as Segerstrom (1999).
11. The relation between the introduction of technical knowledge and the occurrence of increasing returns to scale can be illustrated in the following way. Let Y denote the output of any type of good, $\bar{X}$ the input bundle and A the stock of knowledge, then $Y = A\bar{X}$. From this, the relation $aY = aA\bar{X}$ follows, when there is an increase in factor inputs by the incremental factor a. If the stock of knowledge itself also now increases by factor a, we have $Y^* = a^2A\bar{X}$, where $Y^* > aY$. This production function obviously exhibits increasing returns to scale.
12. This also becomes clear when we consider the fact that human capital is treated as a constant. The argument that workers cannot be trained ad infinitum is not valid because the level of human capital is not measured primarily by the duration of training but rather by the content and skills acquired during training.
13. It has to be noted here, however, that there are, in the meantime, endogenous growth theories in which qualitative changes, e.g. in intermediate products, are modelled along a so-called 'quality ladder'. The improvements in quality due to technical progress cause a decrease in the costs of consumer-goods production and an increase in per-capita production (see also Grossman and Helpman 1991, Chapter 4). An endogenous model of growth which treats, following Schumpeter, the case of 'creative destruction', has been developed by Aghion and Howitt (1992).
14. Romer (1990, 81) expresses this as follows: 'Equation (9.1) expresses output as an additively separable function of all the different types of capital goods so that one additional dollar of trucks has no effect on the marginal productivity of computers. . . . The model here considers the case in which all durables have additively separable effects on output. An investigation of complementarity as well as of mixtures of types of substitutability is left for future work.'
15. The remark that the quality of the end product remains unaffected by technological change, does not refer to all endogenous growth models. As has already been mentioned in note 13, the concept of quality ladders is an attempt to formalise the improvement of goods as a result of technical progress. See also Maussner and Klump (1996, pp. 238–41 and 262–68).
16. Equating technical knowledge with patentable designs overlooks the fact that the knowledge process is also based on experimental research *within* firms. Essential impulses for patentable knowledge result precisely from the engineering sciences' analysis of the industrial production process. It is true that Romer indicates that one could model the research sector as a research department of the business sector. This is not enough though, if the knowledge accumulation equation (9.3) is retained.

17. One has to agree with Solow (1991, p. 15f., and 1994, 51ff.), when he expresses criticism aimed at some endogenous growth theories by saying that the scientific research findings, be they patentable or not, are, for the most part, uncertain. Tietzel (1985, pp. 18f.) points out this concept's inconsistency by saying that this would require the predictability of unknown nomological knowledge, which is, even if infinite information costs could be lavished on it, totally illogical and impossible, because we would already have to be in possession of that same knowledge. See also Lachmann (1976, pp. 127f.).
18. 'The resources that would have been used to produce the forgone output are used instead to manufacture capital goods' (Romer 1990, p. 81).
19. Garegnani's criticism (1970 and 1990) is aimed explicitly at Samuelson's (1971) attempt at interpreting the production function as a mere 'parable', in which the possibility of a continual substitution between labour and capital is interpreted as a sign of a change between different production processes for the production of a qualitatively unchanged end product with respectively different capital goods.
20. Romer (1990, p. 84) expresses this in the following way: 'The crucial feature of the specification used here is that knowledge enters into production in two distinct ways. A new design enables the production of a new good that can be used to produce output. A new design also increases the total stock of knowledge and thereby increases the productivity of human capital in the research sector.'
21. As has been mentioned above, this assumption contradicts a characteristic of empirically observable technological change, which does not result from the already accumulated stock of knowledge, particularly because advances in knowledge include the devaluation of former knowledge.
22. In this sense, the already mentioned contribution of Grossman and Helpman (1991) as well as that of Aghion and Howitt (1992), which follow Schumpeter's 'process of creative destruction', must also be described as deterministic. Unfortunately, they cannot be discussed here. A much more positive assessment of those endogenous growth theories which cite Schumpeter is given by Klump (1996).
23. On this topic, see especially Heuss (1965), Röpke (1970 and 1977) and Dosi (1988).
24. Competition means, as Morgenstern (1972) asserts 'struggle with others, . . . fight, . . . attempting to get ahead, or at least to hold one's place'. One feels – according to Morgenstern – absolutely nothing of this true character of competition in equilibrium economics: 'The contrast with reality is striking'.
25. Rosenberg (1994, p. 5) puts it succinctly when he says: 'Instead of proceeding from a natural starting point where firms possess little or no information and acquire information through experience and investment, most economic models of technological change assume that firms are aware of all the technological options available to them (leading to a well-defined production function).' It should be called to mind here that the strong information assumptions are necessary. This is why Tietzel asserts that there can be no surprises in equilibrium and Streissler (1980, p. 40) sums up that neoclassical theory has always been, in principle, a theory of perfect information and certainty.
26. Nelson (1997, 33) expresses himself in a similar way: 'The new neo-classical growth models, . . . treat firms in a highly simplified way and barely address institutions, aside from the "competitive" (or monopolistically competitive) market.' In another contribution, Nelson (1994) himself has proven that organisational structures are relevant for production and distribution.
27. Nelson (1997, 33) sees the continued adherence to the equilibrium approach as the reason why uncertainties play no role in endogenous growth models. On the topic of alternative market processes see also Lachmann (1976), Fehl (1986), Gutmann (1995), and Schreiter (1997).
28. Now and then the necessity of industrial policy interventions is justified with the occurrence of positive externalities, which underlie the assumption of constant marginal returns of capital inputs. However, this justification of the need for government action rings hollow since decision makers are assumed to have doubtful preference structures and an unrealistic information level. Weder and Grubel (1993, 491f.) point out that the use of instruments of industrial policy is often due to particular interests which have

nothing at all to do with the occurrence of positive externalities. In addition, it is possible for private agents to internalise positive externalities without using government intervention. The occurrence of positive externalities does not therefore necessarily justify government intervention (see also Lucas 1988, 12, Ramser 1991; Maussner and Klump 1996, p. 287; Schreiter 1997, p. 105).

29. A. Wagner (1998, p. 244) sees in the quality of innovation behaviour, which he calls other-than-average behaviour of individuals, the reason for the fact that an explanation of technological change and with this, also the explanation of growth caused by technical progress necessarily remain 'insufficient' in macro-economic models. In the same tenor, Krelle (1985, 214) comments that a great part of technical progress is undoubtedly coincidental and can only be taken into account via an exogenous value. Private inventors, he goes on to say, experiment and try this and that, without systematic understanding – this is how the alchemists developed a basic understanding of chemistry, Gutenberg developed the printing press and Lilienthal the airplane. See also H. Wagner (1993, p. 88).
30. Entrepreneurial tasks include recognising the advantage of new combinations, planning the necessary production process thereof, recruitment, training and direction of employees and the securing of funds to finance all of these measures. However, entrepreneurial activity, as defined by Schumpeter, does not require entrepreneurs to do all these tasks themselves – they can also delegate tasks. It is more important for the entrepreneur to succeed in influencing and organising the process of innovation in such a way that a new combination results (see Röpke 1982, p. 33).
31. Nelson's objection to the new growth theories is that they rely on formalisation without being aware of the dangers of an exaggerated formalisation: 'In particular, there is a danger that the goal of formalisation, per se, focuses efforts on understandings that are relatively easy to formalise or on formalisations of these understandings that are relatively easy but miss or deform important parts of those understandings.' (1997, 54)

REFERENCES

Aghion, P. and P. Howitt (1992), 'A model of growth through creative destruction', *Econometrica*, **60**, 324–51.

Arthur, W.B. (1988), 'Self-reinforcing mechanisms in economics', in P.W. Anderson, K.J. Arrow and D. Pines (eds), *The Economy as an Evolving Complex System*, Reading, MA Addison-Wesley: pp. 9–27.

Coase, R.H. (1937), 'The nature of the firm', *Economica*, **4**, 386–405.

Dosi, G. (1988), 'Sources, procedures, and microeconomic effects of innovation', *Journal of Economic Literature*, **26**, 1120–71.

Dunn, M.H. (1998), *Die Unternehmung als ein soziales System: Ein sozialwissenschaftlicher Beitrag zur Neuen Mikroökonomie*, Berlin: Duncker & Humblot.

Fehl, U. (1986), 'Spontaneous order and the subjectivity of expectations: a contribution to the Lachmann-O'Driscoll problem', in I. Kirzner (ed.), *Subjectivism, Intelligibility and Understanding*. Basingstoke, London: pp. 72–86.

Furubotn, E. and R. Richter (2000), *Institutions and Economic Theory. The Contribution of the New Institutional Economics*, Ann Arbor, MI: Michigan University Press.

Garegnani, P. (1970), 'Heterogeneous capital, the production function and the theory of distribution', *Review of Economic Studies*, **37**, 407–36.

Garegnani, P. (1990), 'Quantity of capital', in J. Eatwell, M. Milgate and P. Newman (eds), *The New Palgrave*, Basingstoke: Macmillan, pp. 1–78.

Grossman, G.M. and E. Helpman (1991), *Innovation and Growth in the Global Economy*, Cambridge, MA: MIT Press.

Grupp, H. (1998), *Foundations of the Economics of Innovation Theory. Measurement and Practice*, Cheltenham, UK, and Lyme, USA: Edward Elgar.

Gutmann, G. (1995), 'Wettbewerbstheorie und Wachstumstheorie: Chance für eine Synthese?', *ORDO*, **46**, pp. 149–63.

Hanusch, H. and U. Cantner (1993), 'Neuere Ansätze in der Innovationstheorie und der Theorie des technischen Wandels: Konsequenzen für eine Industrie- und Technologiepolitik', in F.M. Kramer (ed.), *Innovationsökonomie und Technologiepolitik*. Heidelberg: Springer, pp. 11–45.

Hayek, F.A. von (1984), *Der Strom der Güter und Leistungen*. Tübingen: Mohr.

Heuss, E. (1965), *Allgemeine Markttheorie*. Tübingen: Mohr.

Hofmann, W. (1971), *Theorie der Wirtschaftsentwicklung*. Berlin: Duncker & Humblot.

Klump, R. (1996), 'Wachstum und Wandel: Die "neue" Wachstumstheorie als Theorie wirtschaftlicher Entwicklung', *ORDO*, **47**, pp. 101–20.

Klump, R. and O. La Grandeville (2000), 'Economic growth and the elasticity of substitution: two theorems and some suggestions', *American Economic Review*, **90**, 281–91.

Krelle, W. (1985), *Theorie des wirtschaftlichen Wachstums*. Berlin: Duncker & Humblot.

Lachmann, L.M. (1976), 'On the central concept of Austrian economics: market process', in E.G. Dolan (ed.) *The Foundations of Modern Austrian Economics*, New York: University Press, Columbia, pp. 126–32.

Lucas, R.E. (1988), 'On the mechanics of economic development', *Journal of Monetary Economics*, **22**, 3–42.

Maussner, A. and R. Klump (1996), *Wachstumstheorie*. Berlin: Springer.

Morgenstern, O. (1972), 'Thirteen critical points in economic theory: an interpretation', *Journal of Economic Literature*, **10**, 1163–89.

Nelson, R. (1994), 'What has been the matter with neoclassical growth theory?', in G. Silverberg and L. Soete (eds), *The Economics of Growth and Technical Change*, Aldershot: Brookfield, pp. 290–324.

Nelson, R. (1997), 'How new is new growth theory?', *Challenge*, **90** (5), 29–58.

North, D.C. (1990), *Institutions, Institutional Change and Economic Performance*, Cambridge: Cambridge University Press.

Ramser, H.J. (1991), 'Industriepolitik und Wachstumstheorie', in B. Gahlen, H. Hesse and H.J. Ramser (eds), *Wachstumstheorie und Wachstumspolitik: Ein neuer Anlauf*. Schriftenreihe des Wirtschaftswissenschaftlichen Seminars Ottobeuren, **20**, 305–27.

Ramser, H.J. (1995), 'Wachstumstheorie', in N. Berthold (ed.), *Allgemeine Wirtschaftstheorie*, Munich: Vahlen, pp. 235–50.

Richter, Rudolf (1994), *Institutionen ökonomisch analysiert*, Tübingen: Mohr/Siebeck.

Robinson, J. (1953), 'The production function and the theory of capital', *Review of Economic Studies*, **21** (2), 81–106.

Romer, P.M. (1990), 'Endogenous technological change', *Journal of Political Economy*, **98** (5), pp. 71–102.

Röpke, J. (1970), *Primitive Wirtschaft, Kulturwandel und die Diffusion von Neuerungen*, Tübingen: Mohr.

Röpke, J. (1977), *Strategie der Innovation*, Tübingen: Mohr.

Röpke, J. (1982), *Die unterentwickelte Freiheit: Wirtschaftliche Entwicklung und unternehmerisches Handeln in Indonesien*. Göttingen: Vandenhoeck.

Rosenberg, N. (1994), *Exploring the Black Box: Technology, Economics, and History*, Cambridge: Cambridge University Press.

Samuelson, P. (1971), 'Parable and realism in capital theory: the surrogate production function', *Review of Economic Studies*, **29**, 193–206.

Sälter, P.M. (1989), *Externe Effekte: Marktversagen oder Systemmerkmal?* Heidelberg: Physika.

Schreiter, C. (1997), 'Humanvermögen und Wirtschaftsordnung: Konsequenzen der neuen Wachstumstheorie für die Entwicklungsländer?', in S. Paraskewopoulus (ed.), *Wirtschaftsordnung und wirtschaftliche Entwicklung. Schriften zu Ordnungsfragen der Wirtschaft*, **53**, 72–119.

Segerstrom, P.S. (1999), 'Endogenous growth without scale effects', *Amercian Economic Review*, **88** (5), pp. 1290–310.

Solow, R.M. (1991), 'New directions in growth theory', in B. Gahlen, H. Hesse and H.J. Ramser (eds), *Wachstumstheorie und Wachstumspolitik: Ein neuer Anlauf*, Tübingen: Mohr, pp. 3–17.

Solow, R.M. (1994), 'Perspectives on growth', *Journal of Economic Perspectives*, **8**, 45–54.

Sraffa, P. (1960), *Production of Commodities by Means of Commodities*, Cambridge: Cambridge University Press.

Streissler, E. (1980), 'Kritik des neoklassischen Gleichgewichtsansatzes als Rechtfertigung marktwirtschaftlicher Ordnungen', in E. Streissler and C. Watrin (eds), *Zur Theorie marktwirtschaftlicher Ordnungen*, Tübingen: Mohr, pp. 38–69.

Tietzel, M. (1985), *Wirtschaftstheorie und Unwissen*, Tübingen: Mohr.

Wagner, A. (1998), *Makroökonomik*, Stuttgart: Lucius & Lucius.

Wagner, H. (1993), *Wachstum und Entwicklung*, Munich and Vienna: Oldenbourg.

Walz, U. (1999), 'Wissensakkumulation, endogenes Wachstum und Implikationen für Entwicklungstheorie und-politik', in R. Schubert (ed.), *Neue Wachstums und Außenhandelstheorie: Implikationen für die Entwicklungstheorie und-Politik*. Berlin: Duncker & Humblot, pp. 47–62.

Weder, R. and H. Grubel (1993), 'The new growth theory and Cosean economics: institutions to capture externalities', *Weltwirtschaftliches Archiv*, **129**, 488–513.

PART III

The political economy of complexity

10. Innovation and the learning policy maker – an evolutionary approach based on historical experience[1]

Joachim Schwerin and Claudia Werker[2]

1. INTRODUCTION

Economic policy should be based on an appropriate analysis of the economic system it tries to influence and it should be carried out as much as possible in a non-disruptive manner: if one was to propose guiding principles for the conduct of economic policy, these two statements would hardly be contested. In particular the second principle reflects an evolutionary policy approach that adopts a systemic perspective. Rather than disrupting the internal working mechanisms, political actions should build upon existing systemic processes and modify them as little as possible. In practice, however, such 'harmonious' policy making becomes the more difficult to achieve the more turbulent the part of socio-economic life targeted by policy proves to be. Especially in fields characterised by complex dynamics shaped by continuous change and a multitude of overlapping causal factors, sound policy making requires politicians to be able to *learn*. Learning places them in a position to fit their measures to the current state of the evolving socio-economic system at each point in time.

The field of innovation and growth constitutes a prototypical example of such a dynamically changing part of economic life. In this chapter, we will explore the possibility to design, implement and perform a learning innovation policy. We start from the observation that learning cannot occur in a world where everything is the result of pure chance. In such an environment, the past offers no guidance for present and future decisions. Learning requires secured knowledge, and this knowledge depends on the existence of general characteristics of economic and technological change as well as the ability to identify these. This is difficult, as historical processes are not deterministic. However, neither are they purely random. Therefore we will argue that socio-economic change is contingent in the sense that what we call history is the outcome of a complex mixture of regular behaviour based on rules and unpredictable events. If this holds true, economic policy need not be haphazard; instead it can harmoniously build upon those patterns of technological and organisational change that can be identified.[3]

Our analysis will proceed in four steps. We will first discuss in greater detail the dynamically desirable framework for a learning policy from the meta-point of view of the theory of economic policy. These methodological considerations lead to the identification of types of rules on which policy should be based if learning is to be institutionalised (section 2). Building on these results we will then present a practically feasible concept of learning policy. It depends on the identification of invariant patterns within the recorded experience of the past and can be interpreted as a modification of the traditional concept of stylised facts (section 3). In a third step we will apply our method to one particular example, the identification of invariant patterns of innovation and growth. This set of stylised facts serves to describe the 'regular' part of socio-economic change with regard to our concrete topic. In this context we will lay special emphasis on the question how open the set of identified patterns is towards a changing environment or, in other words, what political learning can look like in this context (section 4). These considerations lead to our fourth step, in which we discuss how these results can serve as a reference system for practical innovation policy. We will argue why we view our approach as a sound basis for the conduct of an evolutionary innovation policy, and we will discuss some policy guidelines that encompass the notion of continuous learning (section 5). Short conclusions will serve to highlight aspects for which we see the need for further research (section 6).

2. THE METHODOLOGICAL BASIS OF LEARNING INNOVATION POLICY

Technological and organisational change is a complex phenomenon. It is the outcome of a flow of innovations which overlap, interact and in any case are hardly predictable. In the following it will prove useful to define innovation in a broad way that encompasses its different forms. We will thus define an innovation as the implementation of new combinations, which includes product, process and organisational innovations as well as the new access to markets of suppliers or consumers.[4]

The traditional linear innovation model depicts innovations as the central part of a sequence of steps that follow one another in a linear manner. This sequence starts with an invention resulting from basic research and proceeds with the outcome of applied research, that is results which are then used to market an idea. It is this second step that is usually called innovation. The last step consists of the diffusion of this idea and its adoption by other economic agents.[5]

This linear innovation model is based on the technology-push approach, which assumes that technological change is supply-driven. However, convincing empirical results show that this linear innovation model does not correctly reflect economic reality.[6] The major reason is that the simplifications within this basic model neglect feedback effects between the different stages of this process. This is a severe shortcoming, as such effects are indispensable for understanding the generation and selection of innovations, because the demand side can considerably contribute to both.[7] In particular the problems faced by first-fast adaptors can lead to renewed questions for basic or applied research. As a result innovation processes are much more complex in practice.

This insight raises an important question: How can policy cope with the complexity inherent in processes of technological and organisational change? Answering this question is difficult, even more so in ever-changing environments driven by a multitude of parallel processes. To tackle this problem it seems advisable to first study in greater detail the nature of dynamic change. Most notably one needs to clarify whether such change consists of structural elements which obey general rules, whether it is purely driven by random effects or whether a particular mixture of both elements dominates. The stronger the rule-driven part turns out to be, the more feasible becomes an analytical understanding of these processes, which is a prerequisite for policy making.

In order to assess the characteristics of innovation-driven dynamic change, we apply the concept of 'contingency'. This concept originates from sociology and has recently been introduced into the theory of system dynamics.[8] It is based on an analysis of the dynamic characteristics of evolving socio-economic systems and encapsulates the idea that the complexity of such systems can be reduced by the systematic evaluation of past behaviour. Economic agents do not behave erratically, because selection mechanisms (such as markets) force them to behave in the 'best possible' way. As such selection mechanisms are the same for many individuals and, moreover, prove to be relatively stable in time and space,[9] different individuals tend to behave in similar ways if faced with comparable situations.[10]

Based on these principles one can formulate the hypothesis that similar behaviour of individuals and groups of individuals – 'organisations' such as firms or other decision-making bodies – translates into similar patterns of the evolution of different socio-economic systems. The *extent* to which this holds true is an empirical question. For the moment it suffices to leave this extent open (we will however provide an answer in a specific context;

see section 4). We therefore define contingency as the phenomenon that, at each point in time of a system's evolution, the number of future paths is greater than one but not infinitely large, because it is restricted by the fact that each path must obey the causal logic of socio-economic dynamics.[11]

It follows from these considerations that the concept of contingency replaces the antagonistic concepts of determinism and chance by stating that every economic action which can be observed in reality is a mixture of both. There exists a rule-driven element of behaviour (to whatever extent), but random elements inherent in the concrete historical situation in which this behaviour occurs exert an influence (again to whatever extent). For the analysis of contingent processes it is now essential to understand that the element which is based on rules ('general laws' or 'guiding principles') can be identified by *repeated* observations, but that predictions for any *individual* historical process we encounter in reality are prone to errors, since the element of chance interferes with the invariant part. And yet, as we will demonstrate in sections 3 and 4, the existence of an invariant part offers a good starting point for rule driven (and thus non-erratic) innovation policy.

If one accepts that the conduct of policy based on general rules is in principle possible, one needs to ask what kind of rules should be applied. It is generally conceived that the conduct of economic policy can be based either on per-se rules or on rules of reason.[12] Per-se rules specify causal if-then relations ex-ante. This has the advantage that economic agents know the political reactions to the outcomes of their economic activities in advance. Per-se rules thus create an expectation-stabilising framework of institutions by reducing uncertainty. In addition they allocate economic control in favour of private agents, as they largely reduce the discretionary power of political boards, which have no opportunity to decide on market results ex-post in a discretionary and therefore unpredictable manner. For these reasons per-se rules are often considered as superior to rules of reason. This particularly holds in the context of long-term economic activities such as investment decisions linked to the marketing of innovations. Here, a framework that stabilises entrepreneurial expectations is indispensable.

On the other hand, a general disadvantage of per-se rules consists in their inflexibility: the rules are specified at one moment in time and are then left unaltered for a period during which the economic environment changes, due to the innovation-driven dynamics of socio-economic change.[13] Another problem consists in the complexity of socio-economic relations, which might render impossible the ex-ante specification of all possible outcomes and thus the formulation of government responses towards them. Interpreted in this light a policy based on rules of reason might still be considered as an advantageous alternative, as these rules offer politicians or bureaucratic bodies the opportunity to decide for every individual case anew which market result is 'useful' and thus allowed (given a set of political goals) and which is not.

This view however neglects the information problem. As information is embedded in markets, the substitution of inflexible per-se rules, which put decentralised behaviour centre stage, by discretionary rules of reason, which open the door for ex-post state intervention based on secondhand information at most, loses its appeal. To put this critique of governments' 'Anmaßung von Wissen' in Hayek's words:

> If we can agree that the economic problem of society is mainly one of rapid adaptation to changes in the particular circumstances of time and place, it would seem to follow that the ultimate decisions must be left to the people who are familiar with these circumstances, who know directly of the relevant changes and of the resources immediately available to meet them. We cannot expect that this problem will be solved by first communicating all this knowledge to a central board which, after integrating *all* knowledge, issues its orders. We must solve it by some form of decentralization.[14]

The theory of economic policy further underpinned Hayek's rejection of central planning, especially in the positive theory of regulation. A major result is that even in a neoclassical world information-saving adaptive *central* planning usually fails to establish a social optimum. More importantly, this co-ordination mechanism becomes the less satisfactory the more goods and services are traded and the more changes in the socio-economic environment occur.[15] It follows that although decentralised decision making is far from reaching a social optimum in every case, it becomes the more convincing as an alternative the more dynamic and complex the economic sphere proves to be.

It would however go too far to conclude that this critique based on Hayek's thinking denied any role for policy at all. As in classical economics, the role of policy lies in shaping framework conditions but not in interference with the socio-economic process that emerges and evolves within this framework. This applies for innovation processes as well (see section 5). Here, such a framework is mainly necessitated by the existence of positive externalities in knowledge accumulation and in the importance of publicly financed basic research in the innovation process discussed above.

Evolutionary economics broadly mirrored Hayek's critique and stressed that policy makers operate under constraints of imperfect information and bounded rationality. For this reason they do not reach solutions that are valid once and for all times. Politicians thus share the constraints faced by individual consumers and firms, for instance in the conduct of innovation policy:[16]

> The evolutionary policy maker adapts rather than optimizes, and his central concern is the innovation system, the operation of the set of institutions within which technological capabilities are accumulated. . . . [J]ust as individuals operate under the constraints of localized, imperfect and uncertain information so does the adaptive policy maker.[17]

And yet, while this view on policy making seems appropriate in the light of the information problem, it does not grasp the full story. There is no need to restrict policy making to purely adaptive behaviour in the sense that it should be strictly reactive to socio-economic change. Methodological considerations derived on the basis of Hayek-type arguments in fact primarily serve as a demonstration of the comparative disadvantages of political actions which violate the principle of the superiority of decentralised decision making and selection of economic results. They do not necessitate an adaptive approach. In terms of our discussion of per-se rules versus rules of reason, the implication is that – while both have comparative advantages and disadvantages – from a system perspective the deficiencies of rules of reason seem particularly severe. We will therefore focus on a solution which encompasses a compromise between the two that gives greater relative weight to ex-ante specified per-se rules. In order to address the latter's disadvantages we enrich their application with a dynamic element: in order to avoid the increasing imbalances in time between unchanging, rigid per-se rules and the continuously evolving socio-economic process, we institutionalise a learning routine for policy makers.

Why is the difference between adaptive behaviour and learning so important and what does it imply? The answer is twofold. Firstly, policy making can be interpreted as a transformation of – both old and newly arising – knowledge on socio-economic change into incentives that influence future behaviour of individuals and firms. It thus contains by definition a forward-looking perspective, as it tries to shape future events. Therefore it is backward-looking only to the extent that the accumulation of knowledge (as a prerequisite of policy making) requires the learned analysis of past experience. Secondly, policy is in itself best regarded as a process of trial and error. The stimulation of innovation is subject to great uncertainty, and policy can fail.[18] It thus seems advisable to interpret policy making as part of an experiment, a process of trial and error that serves to accumulate knowledge. As a consequence, policy has an important function even if it fails – as long as politicians learn by their mistakes. 'Learning' refers to improved knowledge about the nature of change in the policy field concerned, which is more than passive observation of change without an understanding of its driving forces.

These considerations do of course not imply that the margin of political error is unimportant. Quite to the contrary, one can hardly contest that the margin for error should be minimised. In the following, we will argue that political learning can achieve this aim if politicians change the set of rules that govern behaviour if and only if scientific progress in economics has advanced enough to enable a better understanding of the mechanisms that drive socio-economic change (it is this 'understanding' that distinguishes learning from adaptation).

In section 3 we suggest a concept of learning policy making that is general enough to be applied in various contexts. Its centrepiece consists of scientific learning by gaining improved knowledge of past experience through the analysis of historical processes. Such analysis could for instance be conducted by a panel of experts, who for the policy field in question continuously evaluate scientific research on past processes for which data exist. These experts then condense their findings into a set of patterns of socio-economic change. This set describes the structured part of socio-economic change outlined earlier in this section. It forms the starting point for policy making, namely the formulation of rules that govern the structured (and thus in principle predictable) part of the behaviour of economic agents. An in-built feedback loop institutionalises learning: If the continuous evaluation of the latest research leads to modifications of the knowledge base by adding new knowledge or falsifying past insights, the existing set of per-se rules needs to be changed as well. This learning process ultimately bases economic policy on the best available knowledge of the socio-economic process to be influenced at every point in time.

3. THE MODIFIED CONCEPT OF STYLISED FACTS AS A BASIS FOR LEARNING INNOVATION POLICY

We will now specify a practically feasible concept of learning policy making that incorporates the preceding methodological considerations. The starting point is the question how the analysis of historical processes can result in new knowledge, which forms the foundation for learning. To answer this question it is useful to assess one of the most commonly used research methods in economics, the concept of stylised facts. It was originally introduced into growth theory by Nicholas Kaldor when he tried to identify invariant patterns between different historical growth processes.[19]

Kaldor postulated that every model should be able to explain the characteristic features of the economic process analysed as observed in reality.[20] The problem of the scientist was to find that kind of abstraction which best explained this observed reality; thus, he faced a problem of choice between different theories. To find a solution Kaldor stated that the researcher had to identify these characteristic features first. In a second step these features could serve as a reference system for the evaluation of competing theories. On this basis he could then choose the 'best' theory in a third and final step. Kaldor summarises what has since become the 'classical' idea of stylised facts as follows:

> [T]he theorist, in choosing a particular theoretical approach, ought to start off with a summary of the facts which he regards as relevant to his problem. Since facts, as recorded by statisticians, are always subject to numerous snags and qualifications, and for that reason are incapable of being accurately summarized, the theorist, in my view, should be free to start off with a 'stylized' view of the facts – i.e. concentrate on broad tendencies, ignoring individual detail, and proceed on the 'as if' method, i.e. construct a hypothesis that could account for these 'stylized' facts, without necessarily committing himself on the historical accuracy, or sufficiency, of the facts or tendencies thus summarized.[21]

Kaldor thus suggests the identification of the invariant part of socio-economic change (' "stylised" facts without . . . committing . . . on the historical accuracy') in the light of historical experience. However he remains opaque on how to achieve this in practice. Even more unsatisfactory is the fact that his concept turns out to be neither methodologically sound nor operational.[22] The main problem is that Kaldor provides no rules that explain how to generate stylised facts. In his own work as well as in the publications of most scientists who used his concept, stylised facts are listed at the very beginning of the analysis, but it is not explained how they were derived.

Such an approach renders stylised facts useless. One of the key problems is that such a way of conducting research offers the researcher (and also any politician who bases his measures on it) broad space for manipulation. Consider a scientist who developed a theory and tries to find out whether it corresponds to the economic process in reality. Based on Kaldor's approach this scientist would formulate a set of stylised facts with which he was to compare his theoretical results. If he did not lay open how he derived these stylised facts, however, there would be no possibility to objectively check whether they are methodologically sound or whether he preselected only those 'historical facts' that fitted to his theory. In the latter case the analysis would obviously become tautological. As there undoubtedly exist incentives for scientists to (deliberately or not) suppress facts that contradict their theories, it is important to ensure that they cannot be exploited, both in theoretical research and for the purposes of policy making.

Based on a detailed critique of Kaldor's approach one of us has therefore constructed a modified concept of stylised facts which offers strict guidelines for the generation of such facts.[23] This new approach for instance emphasises the need to state on what empirical basis stylised facts are derived and what methods are used to analyse the historical data, so that any reader possesses all the pieces of information to reproduce these results independently. Moreover the identification of stylised facts should be systematically based on the broadest accessible amount of other experts' research in the field in question. The scientist checks this research for sufficient consensus. If such consensus on a given hypothesis existed, this hypothesis would qualify as a stylised fact.[24] As stylised facts have to be open to scientific progress, they regularly have to be reassessed in the light of the latest research.

Figure 10.1 summarises the procedure that leads to the identification of a set of stylised facts. It is of particular relevance here that this modified concept can be directly applied by panels of economic advisors, because the use of stylised facts is not restricted to theory evaluation: they can also serve as a foundation for economic policy, as their aim is to give a thorough understanding of economic processes in a condensed yet detailed way. The modified concept of stylised facts thus renders the practical conduct of a learning economic policy possible.

How should a board of policy advisors apply this concept? The process starts with the identification of a practical problem for which policy measures might need to be taken. This problem then has to be transposed into a clear scientific question which is suited for tests on the basis of empirical evidence. As most questions can be tested in various ways based on conflicting theories, the choice of a single test method already includes the implicit use of normative statements. As a matter of consequence one therefore needs to avoid such an approach, which would directly lead to political dispute (given that alternative procedures exist that could lead to alternative results). As a consequence the modified concept of stylised facts takes a different route and starts by using the broadest available amount of experts' knowledge on the relevant question. After the formulation of the scientific question, a panel of scientists systematically collects and assesses all empirical studies which currently exist for a given topic, deliberately including varying approaches.[25] This also implies that the panel bases its analysis on a set of studies that contains all recently discussed variables and hypotheses of the debated question.

The next step marks the core of the concept, the consensus analysis. For all hypotheses put forward in these empirical studies, this analysis reveals

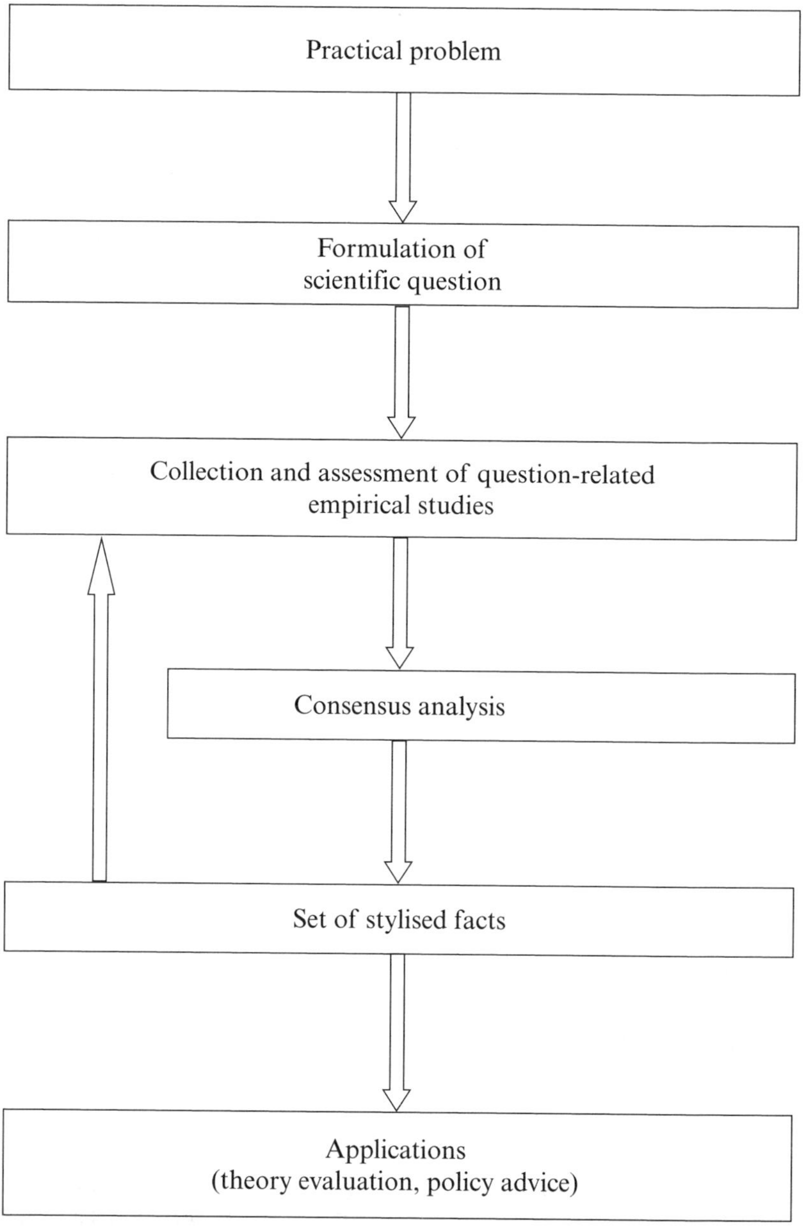

Figure 10.1 The modified concept of stylised facts[26]

the percentage of experts who agree to them. It is important to confine this group of experts to the authors of the empirical studies analysed. In addition only topic-related statements in already-published material qualify as 'opinions'. These requirements minimise observation effects and any direct influence between policy advisors and scientists. Those hypotheses for which a sufficient consensus exists constitute the set of stylised facts for the topic in question.[27] This set of stylised facts then serves as a reference system for theory evaluation and – here the more interesting aspect – as a basis for the guidance of economic policy, most notably the formulation of policy measures.

The upward arrow in Figure 10.1 reflects the crucial aspect for a learning policy: the modified concept of stylised facts is dynamically open in the sense that the facts – and thus the justification for any specific policy measure – have to be regularly reassessed in the light of the latest empirical research. This implies that always if new studies emerge, the question whether a scientific consensus exists or not has to be raised anew. Provided that this process of the generation of stylised facts is institutionalised and will be performed in regular intervals, politicians' learning about the topics they have to decide upon can thus be institutionalised as well.

4. PAVING THE WAY FOR LEARNING INNOVATION POLICY: AN APPLICATION OF THE MODIFIED CONCEPT OF STYLISED FACTS

It is advisable to demonstrate potential strengths and weaknesses of a concept – and any policy based on it – in the context of a concrete application. The modified concept of stylised facts has been applied first in an analysis of the dynamics of growth paths in transition economies.[28] The key results were firstly that this analysis revealed a surprisingly large number of stylised facts on which consensus existed and, secondly, that these results taken in their entirety described a coherent process of innovation-driven growth. It was thus possible to use this analysis not only for theoretical purposes, but also to postulate concrete policy advice that satisfied the methodological desiderata developed in section 2. In the following we will first present the invariant patterns with regard to innovation and change. We will then proceed by discussing how to use these patterns as a reference system for innovation policy (section 5).

The question how long-term growth emerges within economies and what politicians can do to foster this process is an interesting research topic not only because of its political relevance, but also because of the existence of a spectrum of competing theories. These include neoclassical approaches, the factor-accumulation and the innovation-driven models of New Growth Theory, Keynesian models, evolutionary approaches and institutional theory frameworks. From an empirical point of view, numerous works in the tradition of quantitative economic history have recorded historical growth processes and have assessed a set of hypotheses that link potential causes with the effects observed. In order to derive a set of stylised facts by applying the method summarised in section 3, an evaluation based on the use of bibliometric methods evaluated the hypotheses contained in all these works and checked them for sufficient consensus to qualify as a stylised fact.[29] This approach followed the suggestion of Robert Whaples, who defined speaking of a consensus if two thirds of all scientists agree on a certain topic, and added the condition that a sufficient number of diverging methods had been used.[30]

If one applies this method to historical research on growth processes published in refereed journals between 1988 and 1997, the set of stylised facts contains nine results that fulfil the Whaples criterion. This set looks as follows:[31]

1. The generation of growth is a regional phenomenon.
2. Growth is caused by a set of various factors, each of which proves to be a necessary condition.
3. An unspecific accumulation of human capital does not prove to be growth-enhancing. The accumulation of technological knowledge (as a specific variant of human capital) can nevertheless foster growth in the context of the generation of technological progress.
4. The generation and diffusion of technological and organisational progress is a crucial element within this set of factors which cause long-term growth.
5. The increase of demand triggered by geographical market expansion fosters growth at least indirectly by inducing technological and organisational progress.
6. Within the process of technological and organisational progress, the growth effects of innovations are more important than those of inventions.
7. Growth processes are initiated by a clustering of basic innovations and are later maintained by a stream of minor improvements, which especially reflect learning effects.
8. Knowledge networks facilitate the continuation of already existing growth paths. No general statement can be derived for the optimal size of these networks.
9. The emergence of a long-term, self-sustaining growth path within a so-far stagnating economy requires at least three decades.

The first two stylised facts describe general features of growth processes: their regional embeddedness and the fact that they are subject to multiple causality. This second aspect is particularly important for any policy based on these results. Politicians need to avoid the trap of monism[32] and devise a consistent bundle of measures that reflects the interdependencies between the individual causal elements which interact and mutually depend on one another. In order to facilitate a systemic policy approach that takes account of multiple causality, it is important to assess all candidates for such causal elements.

This assessment leads to the third to eighth stylised facts. While no scientific consensus emerged on the role of physical-capital accumulation or labour, the empirical base gave rise to a negative statement on human-capital accumulation. A clear majority of experts refuses the hypothesis that an increase in the rate of human capital accumulation in itself creates a growth effect. They point however towards an indirect effect. An increase in human capital proves important if it is employed in basic or applied research to generate innovation. As a consequence there exists a direct link between structural variables (the stock of human capital) and flow variables (the rate of innovation). It is therefore important to take a closer look at the process of technological and organisational change. This necessity is underpinned by the result (which was achieved independently from the previous one, because it was based on a different empirical basis) that the generation and diffusion of innovation is an indispensable part of the bundle of causal elements that shape growth paths over time.

We stated in section 2 that the demand side played a significant role in the complex process of innovation and change. The fifth stylised fact confirms this view. While a statement that increased demand generally induces growth is too general to be agreed upon by most economists, a more refined hypothesis meets the Whaples criterion: market expansion – notably in geographical terms – fosters innovation, which in turn promotes growth. Here again, as with regard to human capital accumulation, the causal chain leads via the innovation process, which is the actual link between demand and growth.

The following three statements assess this innovation process in greater detail. It turns out that innovation has a bigger impact on growth than invention. This is prima facie not surprising, given that innovation implies the successful marketing of new solutions, whereas invention stresses the technological dimension of novelty. However there is more to this statement than that. A further implication is that transfer of knowledge between regions or enterprises that primarily invent to regions or enterprises that primarily innovate (and imitate) has good chances of success in terms of market results. In other words, for successful innovation to take place it is not a necessary condition that the innovator is the inventor as well.

The seventh stylised fact complements this view. Growth processes evolve in several phases. Firstly, breakthrough innovations pave the way for the emergence of new markets. If several come together a critical mass emerges that pushes the economy on a growth path. This (supply-side) push does not suffice, however, to keep the momentum. The longer the market exists the more important become minor improvements, which are mostly pulled by the demand side, to maintain growth. Radical and incremental innovation, supply-driven push and demand-driven pull effects therefore serve different functions at different points in time, but in essence they are complements, not substitutes.

Knowledge networks support this process in time.[33] Such networks propagate knowledge, and this diffusion seems to be so indispensable that the degree of support for this stylised fact among experts is greater than for any other one: There is virtually full consensus on the fact that a continuous flow of technological and organisational improvements depends on the existence of a full-fledged knowledge network or, in other terms, an innovation system. Only the 'optimal' geographical size of such networks is disputed. Surprisingly, a majority of scientists that conduct historical analyses of innovation systems seem to favour an international dimension compared to a national or regional one.[34] This view is somewhat contradictory to the emphasis within evolutionary economics on national or regional systems of innovation.

The last stylised fact contains an important statement on the time dimension by emphasising the long-term nature of innovation-driven growth processes. This result turns out to be of particular significance for policy making. Processes of technological and organisational change that are to exert macro-economic effects are time-intensive and cannot be artificially accelerated by significant increases of resources. The reasons for this are not fully clear. They can possibly be best explained by taking an institutional approach, that is by analysing the time-frames required for the changes of formal rules and especially informal behaviour. This behavioural aspect would merit further analysis, as it is directly linked to the fact that the accumulation of tacit knowledge is bounded by individuals' limited capabilities, which cannot be substituted by other (political) actions.

If one summarises all these findings by looking at them in their entirety, it is striking that the features of dynamic growth processes described here seem surprisingly consistent. Note that the research question was not to explore the link between innovation and growth, but between any perceivable causal factor – labour, factor accumulation, technological change, infrastructure provided by the government, institutions and others – and growth. It is therefore a strong result that the mechanics of growth processes hinges on a complex yet clearly discernable innovation process, while similar statements cannot be made for alternative factors.

Equally intriguing, the set of stylised facts mirrors recent advances economic thinking and thus underlines the openness of our method. It is impossible to conceive that 30 years ago a bibliometric analysis such as the one described above would have created the same results. Quantitative historical research on growth processes started from scratch in the early 1960s and slowly built up the tools to carry out research that looked inside the 'black box'[35] of endogenous growth generation. This was a prerequisite for the identification of patterns of change as described here. It is thus clear that the modified concept of stylised facts is indeed historically open in the sense that new scientific evidence leads to a reassessment of old knowledge: new research on a given hypothesis can either increase or decrease consensus, and if this affects whether the Whaples criterion is met or not, the set of stylised facts changes as well. If such changes were to occur, it is only logical that any policy that bases itself on these 'facts' would have to be reconsidered as well, and political learning would occur.

From a theoretical perspective, these results highlight the relevance of approaches that endogenously explain the generation and diffusion of knowledge. Such approaches primarily include evolutionary theorising on systems of innovation and the innovation-driven models within New Growth Theory (including neo-Schumpeterian models, which incorporate some principles of evolutionary economics). Furthermore, economic thinking on institutional change provides valuable additional insights. From a political perspective, the stylised facts discussed here provide starting points for an innovation policy approach that bases itself on clear per-se rules whilst using the systemic nature of innovation processes. The following section further explores the possibilities to conduct such policy.

5. IMPLICATIONS FOR INNOVATION POLICY IN PRACTICE

The final step within the flow chart depicted in Figure 10.1 consists of the formulation of policy advice based on the set of stylised facts identified before. As indicated in the previous section, the fact that the patterns of innovation and change are complementary in the sense that they mutually reinforce one another facilitates this task. It is therefore possible to integrate them into a common reference system for a consistent economic policy, which proves to be in line with the systemic approach adopted by evolutionary economists in their analyses of innovation systems. Although this great extent of consistencies is not a prerequisite for the conduct of policy, it is an important asset that increases the likelihood of success.

Before we come to more specific policy implications, we find it instructive to briefly assess the main characteristics of the evolutionary approach. Although evolutionary economics cannot be considered as a well-defined paradigm, a number of features combine to distinguish this approach from theoretical alternatives.[36] First of all, it provides a systemic approach towards innovation and change that builds on the analysis of a population of entities and their interaction among one another as well as with their environment. This approach is aptly summarised as the variation-selection paradigm: it builds on two mechanisms, one of which is the creation of differences (the innovation process) and the other one the choice between the different outcomes on the systemic level.

This emphasis on the differences between economic agents can be considered as a second characteristic of evolutionary economics. Such differences are crucial for competition and change, because heterogeneity spurs innovation in the wake of individuals' attempts at coping with their environment.[37] While many agents will display similar behaviour provided that their sets of objectives do not differ too much, some will deviate from the average and experiment. While their primary goal is survival in their market, that is to fulfil the external constraints imposed upon them by the selection mechanism (thus their behaviour is in line with our discussion of contingency in section 2), there are several reasons why they innovate. These reasons include differences in information, differences in the perception of their relevant environment and how it works and, last not least, the simple fact that the tacit nature of some knowledge leads to individualised solutions to general problems. It is important to endogenise this diversity – and its useful economic function – into any discussion of policy making.

Thirdly, evolutionary economics views endogenous innovation processes as the driving force of change.[38] The fourth, fifth, sixth and seventh stylised facts mirror this perspective as they point at the importance of technological and organisational change for growth and thus fill the 'black box' of growth generation with life. Even more importantly they show that the sources of innovation change in time. Combined with the ninth stylised fact, which reveals that processes of technological and organisational change take several decades to bring about macro-economic effects, these results imply that it is indispensable for policy to take a dynamic, long-term approach. Any short- or medium-term actions can influence the way change occurs, but ultimately not its result. Lasting success requires a lasting, yet not too rigid, approach.

Two other features of evolutionary economics combine to provide further insights. Evolutionary theorising takes into account the institutional and organisational context within which production processes take place,[39] and it focuses on the role of knowledge, as it models the difficulties to find, transfer and store knowledge.[40] Again, the empirical findings on innovation and change support these views. This becomes particularly clear from the eighth and third stylised facts. The interplay between different economic agents needs an institutional framework in which it operates. Knowledge networks provide this framework and can be considered as the core of any innovation system. While stylised facts on the macro-economic level are for the moment too aggregated to allow for a detailed assessment of the working mechanisms within such networks, they point at specific elements. For instance, 'traditional' inputs for growth, such as human capital, need to be embedded in the innovation processes within such networks in order to create effects. This is the essence of the third stylised fact.

The five characteristics of an evolutionary systems approach depicted above provide a foundation for policy making on which more specific policy suggestions can be based. For instance, the lack of empirical support both for monocausal solutions and for unspecified increases in total factor input imply that common government expenditure programmes will not work. Any untargeted increase of demand or supply factors cannot be considered as corresponding to the results of the above analysis. Targeting factors such as human-capital accumulation can only be successful on a sectoral level in the context of knowledge creation. As an example, political measures could foster learning effects by improving on-the-job training. At the same time, targeted support for decentralised information exchange within knowledge networks, for instance through scientific or sectoral engineering societies, access to trade fairs and local or regional gate keepers will complement firm-specific efforts at individual and collective learning.

In this context it is important to note that the sources of knowledge change over time in the evolution of a market. These sources include basic research activities as well as the experience and needs of suppliers of inputs and buyers of output, but also more indirect spillover effects. However not all sources are of equal importance at each point in time. In particular the seventh stylised fact hints at the fact that there exist stages within the dynamics of sectoral change, which are largely caused by the different stages within innovation processes as described in section 2. This finding is in line with the evolutionary product-life-cycle approach, which distinguishes between different market phases. As a consequence policy measures derived from an evolutionary perspective need to mirror these changes in time.[41]

In new markets, for instance, the construction of a suitable institutional framework is of key importance. Because of their greater legitimacy and better co-ordination abilities, policy makers can quickly provide a set of general formal rules that reduce transaction costs.[42] At the same time, policy must not attempt to select market outcomes as long as there do not exist any stylised facts that support specific selection criteria. This means that policy support should not be dependent on strict criteria that can only be met by a limited number of economic agents, such as support only for firms that possess an R&D department.[43] The usual critique of untargeted support does not apply in very early market phases, because the enlargement of technological and organisational variety is a crucial prerequisite for the selection of outcomes by the market later on and thus for change and growth. It therefore reflects the systemic approach described above.

In later stages of market evolution, factors such as increasing returns to scale in production unfold their effects and lead, in connection with the stabilisation of consumer tastes, to the reduction of variety and, ultimately, a certain standardisation of product designs. Routinisation of production processes and greater formalisation of the organisation within firms and their supporting innovation system support this maturation. Here as well these processes need time. Firstly, institutional settings that for instance shape the flow of information within innovation systems depend not only on formal laws, but at least as much on informal conduct based on trust and shared objectives. This process cannot be accelerated without limits, as it is linked to the change of attitudes within the persons involved, which is a slow process. Secondly, minor improvements gain greater relative weight in the innovation process. As their sources differ from those of the bigger innovative steps that usually coincide with the emergence of new sectors, the focus of attention shifts as well, towards the diffusion of best practice and the creation of joint standards.

In the end, markets consolidate and become mature. At this stage, any policy that aims at fostering innovation reaches its limits. Well-established ties between the different market players and relatively low uncertainty may now provide an environment with a functioning market mechanism in theory that in practice becomes prone to collusion. In other words, the focus of political attention shifts from fostering the *ability* to innovate towards fostering *incentives* to innovate, which basically means preventing anticompetitive behaviour. Here, for instance, competition policy might turn into an effective tool. This insight highlights the need for a policy mix that goes beyond the realms of a single policy field and calls for co-operation not only between market players, but also different political bodies within and beyond innovation systems.

And yet, no matter how sophisticated the design of such a dynamic policy mix might be, policy based on this systemic approach can fail, too.[44] What is important to note, however, is the function of such failures within our approach. Failures are in themselves an element of learning policy, because they contribute to the stock of historical experience and, as a matter of consequence, to a better understanding of socio-economic change. This particularly holds true if every policy measure is evaluated independently. Evaluation may accompany the policy measure or may be executed ex post.[45] While we do not focus here on this issue, which goes beyond the basic elements of the concept of learning policy as discussed above, a few words on it will conclude this overview.

The aim of an evaluation is to find out whether the policy measure sets the right incentives or adequately influences more directly the targeted group of economic agents according to the policy aims as specified ex ante. It thus includes an assessment of intended and unintended effects of any policy measure. It also contains an efficiency control of the implementation of the policy measures. The stylised facts derived in section 4 only give hints, but do not provide a full picture, on where policy measures are promising and where not. Current political practice does not base itself on consistent standards for evaluation, and some measures are not evaluated at all. If improvements could be made in this area, for instance through greater international exchange of experience and co-ordination, the results of policy evaluation would turn into a powerful tool for improvements of the empirical basis on which future decisions are based. If innovation policy is performed as a learning policy, even failures may be a part of its success. In such a case, the main requirement for successful innovation policy would not be to exist without any failures, but to identify these failures as soon as possible, avoid them as much as possible in the future and store them in the policy knowledge stock.[46]

6. CONCLUSIONS

This chapter discussed a coherent approach towards the design, implementation and practical conduct of learning policy. Learning policy is a method of conducting policy that intelligently builds upon the best available knowledge at each point in time and uses this knowledge to dynamically modify the set of rules that govern economic behaviour. After an in-depth discussion of the methodological requirements for such a policy approach and the development of a practically feasible concept, we focused our attention on innovation policy to demonstrate how this concept could be applied in practice. We chose the topic of innovation because of its pivotal role for socio-economic change and because it is a truly dynamic process. This particularly enabled us to highlight the openness of our approach towards changes in the knowledge stock of society. Of course, this concept can be applied to other policy fields as well.

We consider this approach as a first step towards improving the conduct of practical policy. However, further steps will have to develop important aspects in greater detail. It seems of particular importance to carefully analyse the incentives and incentive effects that govern the interaction between policy makers and scientific boards. Traditional ways of conducting economic policy often allocate too much discretionary power to politicians, who abuse their powers by putting their private agenda first. Political boards normally tend to facilitate such unproductive behaviour: experts often disagree among themselves to such an extent that politicians have too much room for manoeuvre. One reason results from the fact that an adviser who holds a political function has incentives for expressing his or her views in a way that differs from what he or she would publish in a purely scientific context. Another problem consists in the lack of mechanisms that transform the divergent views of (politically elected) board members into a joint position of the board itself.

The concept of learning policy reduces these problems by providing filters. Firstly, one layer of discretion vanishes as only previously published material that fulfils an objective criterion – publication in refereed journals – is taken into account regardless of who the author is. Secondly, the Whaples criterion offers a clear-cut rule for what can be interpreted as 'knowledge' and what not. As a result the scope of advisors' discretion further decreases. The board of advisors thus becomes enabled to provide a filter in the sense that the current state of knowledge in any particular field is defined as a *scientific* consensus, not a *political* one. This filter takes much discretion out of economic policy and minimises effects of lobbyism – at the very least it will become more difficult for politicians to deviate from such advice than before.

We are totally aware of the fact that boards of advisors already exist in many fields of policy and that their composition and role differs. However, we do not think that it is unfair to state that the working mechanisms of these boards usually do not meet the stringent criteria set above. As a consequence they leave too much room for discretionary political decisions. The way forward we would suggest is therefore not the abolishment of boards of advisors or immense institutional changes, but rather an evolution towards more stringency in the internal working mechanisms of such boards. Indeed, already-existing boards may easily use the modified concept of stylised facts. Whether they have the incentives to do so and whether the ensuing results would meet the expectations are important questions that merit further research.

Last but not least the performance of economic policy in itself needs to be evaluated. By definition policy will have discretion even if our approach is applied – experts can exert pressure by presenting unified and more scientific views, but they cannot force politicians to follow their advice. It thus remains perfectly possible that unintelligent policy prevails, that is policy that fails to learn from past experience. Only the political sovereign, the electorate, could effectively sanction such behaviour. It is a question that still needs to be explored in greater detail which metamechanisms might be introduced to make 'unintelligent' political behaviour, that is the refusal to learn, costly enough for politicians to trigger changes of behaviour.

NOTES

1. We are grateful for helpful comments by Friedrich Breyer, Uwe Cantner and Stan Metcalfe on earlier versions of this paper. The usual disclaimer applies.
2. Corresponding author: Dr Claudia Werker, Max-Planck-Institut für Ökonomik, Abteilung Evolutionsökonomik, Kahlaische Straße 10, D-07745 Jena, Germany; email: werker@econ.mpg.de
3. Economic agents' as well as politicians' expectations of such patterns may turn out to be wrong. However, the concept we propose below takes this into account by means of a feedback loop that translates failed expectations into new knowledge.
4. Cf. Schumpeter (1911/1987), pp. 100f.
5. See, for example, Steinmueller (1994), p. 54, or Fritsch (1991), 198.
6. Cf. e.g. Grupp (1997), pp. 17–20.
7. Cf. Lundvall (1992).
8. See Fulda, Lehmann-Waffenschmidt and Schwerin (1998), pp. 340ff.
9. This statement applies if one takes a functional approach, that is if one does not focus on superficial historically grown differences between different laws, customs and so on that govern behaviour but on the (economic) function these institutions perform.
10. For a profound discussion of the concept of contingency, cf. Schwerin (2001), pp. 75ff. Also note that traditional economics takes this insight to the ahistorical extreme by modelling identical economic agents ('homo oeconomicus'), whereas chaos theory turns out to be blind in the other eye by denying any similarity between different individual actions and the respective outcomes on the system level.
11. Cf. Schwerin (2001), p. 79.
12. Cf. Schmidt (1996), pp. 148ff.
13. A good example is the German antitrust law, which is altered every three to nine years but nevertheless hardly keeps pace with the changes of competitive behaviour in the economy; cf. Schmidt (1996), pp. 155ff.
14. Hayek (1945), 524, emphasis in orginal.
15. See Bernholz and Breyer (1984), chapter. 5.
16. Cf. Hanusch and Cantner (1993); Metcalfe (1995); Metcalfe and Georghiou (1997).
17. Metcalfe (1995), p. 418. See also Teubal (1997).
18. For approaches that discuss such a systemic view of policy; cf. Metcalfe (1995); Lipsey and Carlaw (1996); Metcalfe and Georghiou (1997); and Teubal (1997).
19. Kaldor widely used ideas first developed by Arthur Okun; cf. Kaldor (1985), p. 8.
20. For an introduction into Kaldor's concept, see Kaldor (1968), pp. 177ff.
21. Kaldor (1968), p. 178.
22. See Schwerin (2001), pp. 92ff.
23. Schwerin (2001), pp. 98ff. Parts of the methodological requirements are omitted here in order not to overload this introduction to the new concept.
24. Given that, for a certain topic, several mutually exclusive and contradictory theories exist for which no metacriterion exists which states ex ante what theory is 'true', such

a consensus is the only way to base practical actions on a sound scientific foundation. The absence of such a metacriterion in science is obvious, thus the use of stylised facts as a reference system for theory and policy evaluation serves as a second-best mechanism.

25. The use of quality filters is advisable, as this restricts the studies to those which have been put forward in a period of for instance the last ten years. Such a filter could consist in the exclusive use of publications in top-ranked scientific journals.
26. Cf. Schwerin (2001), p. 114.
27. The consensus analysis becomes even more methodologically sound if it considers only those hypotheses which have been tested in several studies by using different methods.
28. Schwerin (2001), pp. 133ff.
29. On the comparative advantages of bibliometric research compared to questionnaires and other direct means of assessing experts' views, cf. ibid., pp. 118 ff.
30. Cf. Whaples (1995), 139.
31. See Schwerin (2001), p. 179.
32. Landes (1994), 653.
33. For a more detailed discussion of this stylised facts and the implications thereof cf. Schwerin and Werker (2003), 397ff.
34. Cf. Schwerin (2001), p. 174.
35. Cf. the approach taken in Rosenberg (1994).
36. As indicated in section 4, these features may also be part of other theoretical approaches, such as innovation-driven models within New Growth Theory.
37. Cf. Metcalfe (1995), p. 418.
38. Cf. Nelson (1995), 67.
39. Ibid.
40. Cf. for instance Nelson and Winter (1982), pp. 76–82.
41. Cf. the following Werker (2003), pp. 285–90.
42. Cf. Metcalfe and Georghiou (1997), p. 25.
43. Cf. Werker (forthcoming).
44. See Metcalfe and Georghiou (1997), 25.
45. Cf. Kuhlmann (1992), p. 125.
46. Cf. Lipsey and Carlaw (1996), p. 269.

REFERENCES

Bernholz, Peter and Friedrich Breyer (1984), *Grundlagen der Politischen Ökonomie*, second edition, Tübingen: Mohr (Paul Siebeck).

Fritsch, Michael (1991), 'Innovation und Strukturwandel', *Das Wirtschaftsstudium*, **20**, 195–200.

Fulda, Ekkehard, Marco Lehmann-Waffenschmidt and Joachim Schwerin (1998), 'Zwischen Zufall und Notwendigkeit – zur Kontingenz ökonomischer Prozesse aus theoretischer und historischer Sicht', in Gerhard Wegner and Josef Wieland (eds), *Formelle und informelle Institutionen – Genese, Interaktion und Wandel*, Marburg: Metropolis, pp. 327–77.

Grupp, Hariolf (1997), *Messung und Erklärung des technischen Wandels. Grundzüge einer empirischen Innovationsökonomik*, Berlin and Heidelberg: Springer.

Hanusch, Horst and Uwe Cantner (1993), 'Neuere Ansätze in der Innovationstheorie und der Theorie des technischen Wandels – Konsequenzen für eine Industrie- und Technologiepolitik', in Frieder Meyer-Krahmer (ed.), *Innovationsökonomie und Technologiepolitik. Forschungsansätze und politische Konsequenzen*, Heidelberg: Physica, pp. 11–46.

Hayek, Friedrich August von (1945), 'The use of knowledge in society', *American Economic Review*, **35**, 519–30.
Kaldor, Nicholas (1968): 'Capital accumulation and economic growth', in Friedrich A. Lutz and Douglas C. Hague (eds), *The Theory of Capital. Proceedings of a Conference Held by the International Economic Association* [1958], London: Macmillan, pp. 177–222.
Kaldor, Nicholas (1985): *Economics without Equilibrium. The Okun Memorial Lectures at Yale University*, Armons NY: M.E. Sharpe.
Kuhlmann, Stefan (1992), 'Evaluation von Technologiepolitik: Zur Analyse der Wirksamkeit politischer Techniksteuerung', in Klaus Grimmer et al. (eds), *Politische Techniksteuerung, Schriften des Instituts Arbeit und Technik 5*, Opladen: Leske und Budrich, pp. 119–35.
Landes, David S. (1994), 'What room for accident in history? explaining big changes by small events', *Economic History Review*, **47**, 637–56.
Lipsey, Richard G. and Kenneth Carlaw (1996), 'A structuralist view of innovation policy', in Peter Howitt (ed.), *The Implications of Knowledge-Based Growth for Micro-Economic Policies*, Calgary: University of Calgary Press, pp. 255–337.
Lundvall, Bengt-Åke (1992), 'User–producer relationships, national systems of innovaton and internationalisation', in Bengt-Åke Lundvall (ed.), *National Systems of Innovation and Interactive Learning*, London: Pinter Publishers, pp. 45–67.
Metcalfe, J. Stanley (1995), 'The economic foundations of technology policy: equilibrium and evolutionary perspectives', in Paul Stoneman (ed.), *Handbook of the Economics of Innovation and Technological Change*, Oxford and Cambridge, MA: Blackwell, pp. 409–512.
Metcalfe, J. Stanley and Luke Georghiou (1997), 'Equilibrium and evolutionary foundations of technology policy', CRIC Discussion Paper no. 3, University of Manchester.
Nelson, Richard R. (1995), 'Recent evolutionary theorizing about economic change', *Journal of Economic Literature*, **33**, 48–90.
Nelson, Richard R. and Sidney G. Winter (1982), *An Evolutionary Theory of Economic Change*, Cambridge, MA and London: Belknap Press of Harvard University Press.
Rosenberg, Nathan (1994), *Exploring the Black Box. Technology, Economic, and History*, Cambridge, MA: Cambridge University Press.
Schmidt, Ingo (1996), *Wettbewerbspolitik und Kartellrecht*, fifth edition, Stuttgart: Lucius & Lucius.
Schumpeter, Joseph A. (1911/1987), *Theorie der wirtschaftlichen Entwicklung: Eine Untersuchung über Unternehmergewinn, Kapital, Kredit, Zins und den Konjunkturzyklus*, seventh edition, published first in 1911, unchanged reprint of the fourth edition of 1934 Berlin: Duncker & Humblot.
Schwerin, Joachim (2001), *Wachstumsdynamik in Transformationsökonomien. Strukturähnlichkeiten seit der Industriellen Revolution und ihre Bedeutung für Theorie und Politik*, Köln: Böhlau.
Schwerin, Joachim, and Claudia Werker (2003), 'Learning innovation policy based on historical experience', *Structural Change and Economic Dynamics*, **14**, 385–404.
Steinmueller, W. Edward (1994), 'Basic research and industrial innovation', in Mark Dogson and Roy Rothwell (eds), *The Handbook of Industrial Innovation*, Aldershot, UK and Brookfield, US: Edward Elgar, pp. 54–66.

Teubal, Morris (1997), 'A catalytic and evolutionary approach to horizontal technology policies (HTPs)', *Research Policy*, **25**, 1161–88.
Werker, Claudia (2003), 'Market performance and competition: a product life cycle model, *Technovation*, **23**, 281–90.
Werker, Claudia (forthcoming), 'Technologischer Wandel und Innovationspolitik', in Carsten Herrmann-Pillath and Marco Lehmann-Waffenschmidt (eds), *Handbuch zur Evolutorischen Ökonomik, Band II: Evolutorische Ökonomik in der Anwendung*, Heidelberg and New York: Springer.
Whaples, Robert (1995), 'Where is there consensus among American economic historians? The results of a survey on forty propositions', *Journal of Economic History*, **55**, 139–54.

11. The national German innovation system – its development in different governmental and territorial structures

Hariolf Grupp, Icíar Dominguez Lacasa and Monika Friedrich-Nishio[1]

> It is always difficult to record the history of events that have not yet run their course and whose outstanding players are all still living. . . . Events appear different, once they are concluded; different again, while they are still developing. In both instances, the aims of the reporter also differ. Gustav Struve (1849/1980, p. 290)

1. METHODOLOGICAL INTRODUCTION

The general appreciation of innovation corresponds with a typically European method of thinking which is not found in all cultures. 'The positive evaluation of new findings, the esteem for innovation, the idolisation of inventors, as well as inventions and patents, are achievements of the modern world dominated by European-American influence, which, from a historical point of view, are relatively young' (Dohrn-van Rossum 1999, p. 39). However, even in the Christian Occident, the presently predominant emphasis on innovation results from the manifold historical changes of the past centuries. Initially, inventions and discoveries were not considered as an act of creation but only represented the rediscovery of natural phenomena created by God. This change of consciousness – which took place prior to the period investigated by this chapter (1850–2000) – should be dealt with in order to better localise innovation-critical opinions in the present; however, this cannot be done here.

A practicable way to measure innovation could be the elaboration of definitions and measurement methods by starting from a historical point of view, with the objective of recording the enormous change characterising innovation activities. However, this chapter takes the opposite point of departure: starting from today's definitions, an investigation of the comprehensive statistical material including related indicators is carried out, followed by the attempt to trace and complete these back before the foundation of the German Empire. This means that the presently achieved level of theory and methodology serves as a point of departure for the following retrospective.

Consequently, this chapter tries to include a considerable number of quantitative variables, preferentially in the form of time series. Therefore, this analysis can be included in the field of cliometrics, the 'new' kind of economic history, which is based on quantitative methods including econometrics, aimed at reconstructing and interpreting the past (Bannock et al. 1998, p. 61). This method is regularly criticised since *indicators* cannot be *facts*; however, according to some points of view, narrative historiography cannot distinguish facts from interpretation either. According to these, no fundamental difference exists between the description of facts and their interpretation, since every description already represents a certain interpretation which, moreover, depends on the definitions presently available to the describing person (Lorenz 1997, p. 32).[2]

Even if there is no basic cognitive difference between the (widespread) narrative approach and the (less common) quantitative approach, the objective of the quantitative approach is the statement of a relationship between variables, based on many cases, and thus generalisation (Fogel 1964, p. 237 onwards). In contrast, the qualitative approach aims to compare case by case, that is, this contribution has an analytical or holistic character (Lorenz 1997, p. 238). It seems that most historians prefer an approach by case (qualitative approach), whereas most social scientists choose the variable approach, verifying hypotheses for a whole series of cases.

To be provided with variables for many cases on the aggregated level, conceptional ideas are needed which regulate inclusion and exclusion. Whereas, in general, brief experiences can be clearly delimited, the application of specific selection criteria is often difficult, especially in the case of long time series, due to the fact that the individual investigation of all relevant indications is absolutely impossible. Moreover, indicators have a selective rather than objective quality, so their undeniable status only applies to a specific disciplinary context: according to the present status of empirical economic research, more or less ideal indicators are available for theoretical constructs. The process of 'statistical adequation' means the 'tailor-made adaptation' of measurement concepts, the result of which is not entirely satisfactory in view of the theoretical constructs, but which at least corresponds with the descriptive framework used as a basic structure for measurement.[3]

This is aggravated by the fact that the theoretical constructs of innovation research are not clearly defined. Up to the present, rival and irreconcilable innovation theories still exist in several disciplines (Grupp 1998). In addition, linear models are widespread, presuming a sequential succession of innovation-oriented phases, the point of departure of which is an unpredictable serendipity in basic research or exogenous technical progress which falls like manna from heaven. Orthodox approaches have developed, which try to subordinate or marginalise alternative approaches in order to find the 'truth' with the help of their own theory. From an empirical perspective such attempts must be considered with scepticism since modern epistemology actually tries to erase any efforts to find the real truth (Hoyningen-Huene 1999). Therefore, the research on science and technology indicators should ideally begin from a heterogeneous level of theory and definitions in order to find historically solid indicators. Empirical standardisation of theoretically heterogeneous constructs must take the individual contexts into consideration, but it should lead to 'adequate' indicators; for this reason, empirical statistical adaptation often remains incomplete, and yet only a minimum of discrepancy should be left (one only has to refer to the discussion about real and ideal concepts, Machlup 1960/61). Using an economic-historical approach, definitions must be fixed as an orientation structure for both theoretical and empirical analyses; these definitions should stand iterative modification, they should apply on an interdisciplinary level and they should be valid over time.

The standard German textbook for 'businessmen and students' by Roscher (1886), which was reprinted about 20 times by the second half of the 1880s, and which also shaped Schumpeter's theory of economic development (1911/1964), distinguishes six different economic activities, listing *Invention* and *Discovery* first (sic!) – ahead of mining, agriculture, the processing industry, the distribution of goods and the service sector last (excluding wholesale). Based on this, the result-oriented concept by Schumpeter (1942/1975, pp. 136ff.) defines criteria in such a way that innovation represents all that yields a profit for the entrepreneur by being the first, (the so-called quasi-rent or innovation rent). Quasi-rents of innovation tend to be neutralised by time due to the effects of concurrent processes. Innovations can be seen as new goods or services, new methods of production or transportation, new markets or new organisations.

In Germany, the term 'novelty' (Neuerung) was used as a definition of innovation for a long period. The word 'innovation' was unknown for a long time: it only reached the German-speaking regions after Schumpeter's emigration to the United States, where he published English texts; here, the English word 'innovation' was maintained as the Germanised 'Innovation' instead of being translated back to the term 'novelty' originally used by Schumpeter. The definition of innovation was probably adopted around 1960. Consequently, it is evident that the definition of innovation as it is used nowadays cannot be considered as an anchor for the investigation period since 1850. Prior to the 1960s, innovation phenomena were described using other definitions: archives, libraries and research institutions as well as documents from management, personnel departments or production centres show terms which are different from those used according to present standards (for example, 'laboratory' might be described as 'establishment', 'experimental factory').

According to today's view, the concept of a specific research process which leads to measurable innovation and which requires personnel and financial expenditure, is based on Bernal's (1939) farsighted and clearly analysing work. Bernal distinguished the role of public research expenditure from that of civil research and, – as things stood – from that of the war industry. The first statistics on expenditure for 'industrial research' by British companies are found in the annexes to his works. As reported by Freeman (1992, p. 3), the definitions used by Bernal during his lectures at the London School of Economics were brought to international committees (by Freeman himself as well as by others), which, in the 1960s, worked for another standardisation of definitions, which led to a first paper about the measurement of output of research and development (Freeman 1969).

Consequently, the empirical framework underlying this chapter will be determined using the current definitions and concepts. These may have had other meanings in the past, but this 'anachronism' must be accepted. Language is used by any historiography including the hermeneutic one; however, as language develops over time, definitions may arise, disappear, or change their meanings. Consequently and independently of the method applied, any historiography is anachronistic to a certain degree (Lorenz 1997, p. 364). Former innovators were not masters of today's historical knowledge, nor of information about present innovation processes – knowledge and information which we have acquired from our observation post.

Therefore, the definitions found in the leading OECD manuals[4] from the 1990s will be used. Cliometrics are also more concerned with anomalies than with constantly ongoing, inconspicuous processes. If a structural breakage is found in a time series, this could point to a statistical artifact arising from the change of definitions and conventions used. Consequently, structural breakages[5] found must always be interpreted and categorised in a qualitative way. The problem of anachronism – if not avoided – can thus at least be moderated. Intertemporal shifts of emphasis as an explanation of structural breakage are all the more permissible since a functional innovation model serves as an additional basis (see Grupp 1998), working on the assumption that different innovation-oriented processes can be influenced by all types of research and development (R&D).

2. NATIONAL INNOVATION SYSTEM

This chapter is divided into a national (this section) and a sectoral level (see the next section). For the definition of 'national innovation systems', see Grupp 1998, p. 244. From a historical point of view, modifications of the territorial situation (population, and so on) may not be ignored. Therefore, from an empirical point of view it is essential to consider, for example, the size of the Empire or of each federal territory. Not only is the German Democratic Republic considered here, but also Saarland, the Corridor, East Prussia and other areas. Territorial changes which took place can be considered on the basis of today's statistical procedures, so that such data series, *a priori*, do not have to be absolutely consistent with a territory (also refer to Hoffmann 1965, pp. 2 f.). However, it must be pointed out that the omission of smaller districts (such as Alsace-Lorraine from 1871 to 1917) in most cases brings in its train less important errors of estimation than the big variances in the series of the whole territory of the German Reich (Hoffmann 1965, p. 3).

2.1 Public Expenditure for National Science and Technology

Traditionally, the development of science and technology is measured by the number of scholars. In this way, for example, Gascoigne submitted a historical demography (1992) of the scientific community between 1450 and 1900, by listing the nationality and age of all the scientists. According to this study, Italy was the leading scientific country at the beginning of modern times in the late 15th century, representing about half of all the scientists in the world. This had remained almost unchanged during the entire Middle Ages before that century; then exponential growth with a doubling period of approximately 50 years took place.

Detailed and complete statistics are available about scientific staff in Germany since the foundation of the Empire, accessible via today's electronic means. However, generally accessible statistical material about R&D personnel in Germany has only been recorded since the 1960s (in the framework of the Federal Research Report which has been published since 1965).

Another traditional route to the empirical definition of the importance of an innovation system is scientific expenditure (the sum of R&D funds and those for training, teaching, maintenance and diffusion of knowledge). Whereas the evaluation of expenditure for purely educational and R&D institutions is quite simple, this is more complicated in the case of institutions engaged in both research and teaching. Quotas were adopted to cope with the individual fields of specialisation as well as with the individual types of universities. However, it is questionable whether these reflected the right proportions between the percentage of research and that of teaching at all historical points in time; in addition, not only is the historical consideration problematic but also the consideration of the present time. Nevertheless, it is common statistical practice in all OECD countries to work with such quotas (Hetmeier 1990, and Irvine et al. 1990).

Pfetsch (1982) calculated scientific expenditure between 1850 and 1975, so rough estimates of the degree of R&D financing can be derived from this; however, these data records only include public expenditure, disregarding the private sector. Consequently, industrial innovation indicators must be researched separately (see below).

In order to avoid dealing with the difficulty of different currencies, the development of scientific expenditure can be best evaluated by its percentage of the total expenditure of public budgets (Figure 11.1). According to this, scientific expenditure in the German regions prior to the foundation of the Empire was approximately 1 per cent (see Figure 11.1). After this, the percentage reached more than 2 per cent, but dropped to almost 1.5 per cent between the 1880s and the First World War. The Republic of Weimar attained a doubling of scientific financing which, however, was lost again due to the worldwide economic crisis. In West Germany, the support of science was increased dramatically to reach 6.5 per cent of all public

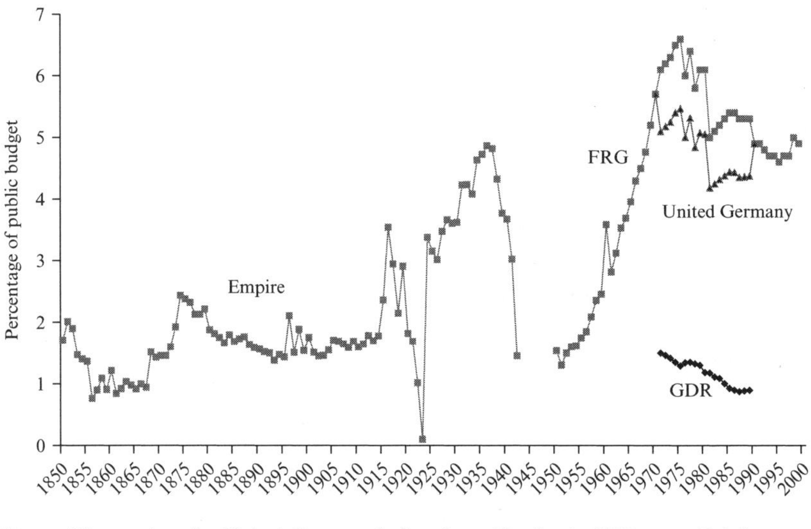

Note: The numbers for United Germany before the unification in 1990 are artificially composed by weighted average values between West Germany and the GDR.

Figure 11.1 *Development of scientific expenditure in proportion to the total expenditure of public budgets(per cent)*

budgets by the 1970s (university expansion), to fall off to approximately 5 per cent by the time of German reunification. Finally, due to reunification, the level dropped even further. These indications are based on the numbers of Empire or Federal institutions and those of regions and states.

Besides the above-mentioned data records, and also based on an analysis of the older part of these, Pfetsch (1974) submitted an extensive analysis of German scientific policy between 1850 and 1914. For example, Pfetsch (1974, p. 60 and p. 171) cannot confirm the thesis that the state spends more money on science and technology in times of increasing economic wealth. In spite of some references to anti-cyclical research policy, overall an irregular economic attitude is shown by government policy.

Surprisingly, expenditures after World War II start at around the same level as at the beginning of the last century (after World War I) which is at the same level as the endpoint of records in the 1940s war years, and increases in a similar way after World War II as after World War I. This points to quite stable and persistent institutional structures underlying the financial totals.

The financial support of Research and Development is typical for post-war Germany. Until 1945, the financing share for R&D only played a subordinate role in total scientific expenditure. Although the research share[6] was 20 to 30 per cent during the first period after the foundation of the Empire, it dropped to less than 20 per cent by the beginning of the first World War (see Figure 11.2). In addition, it is important to know that

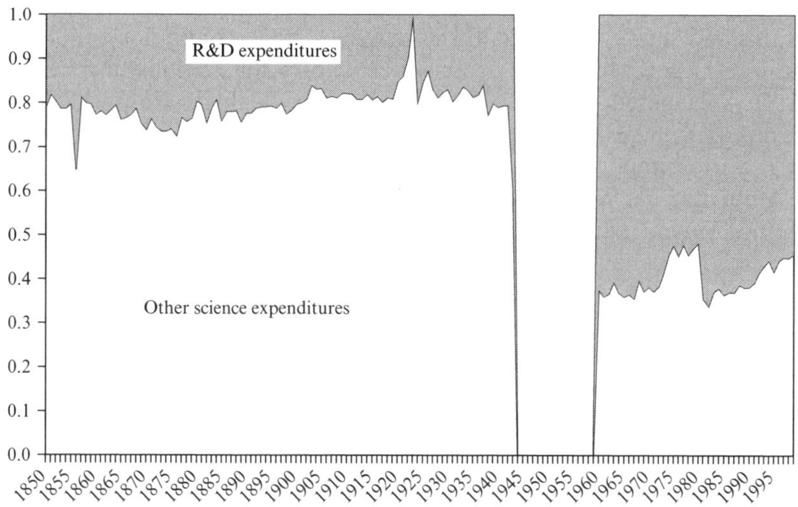

Figure 11.2 Government expenditure for science, divided into the publicly financed R&D share and other scientific tasks

a great deal of scientific expenditure by the Empire was used for defence tasks shortly after the foundation of the Reich. During the Weimar Republic and the Third Empire, the R&D share of the total of scientific expenditure continued to fluctuate at around 20 per cent (industrial research not included).

A quick increase in the R&D share of scientific expenditure occurred when research in certain areas was allowed again in the young Federal Republic, after the signing of the Treaty of Paris in 1955: at times it reached 70 per cent and has only declined due to the recent reunification.

Prior to the Second World War, the relatively insignificant role played by R&D within the scientific world is also shown by the distribution of funds to the different institutions. During the decades preceding and following the foundation of the Empire, the lion's share of approximately 70 per cent of the total public scientific expenditure is accounted for by all types of universities. Empire agencies and other institutions were established over time, so that the universities' share of scientific expenditure decreased to about 35 per cent at the beginning of the 20th century. Now, a little more than 20 to 30 per cent goes to these institutions charged with varied tasks, and almost 10 per cent is accounted for by pure R&D institutions.

During the entire period before and between the two World Wars, a small but significant and strongly varying amount of public expenditure went to functions other than institutional support. The non-institutional support is described as 'project-specific scientific expenditure' by Pfetsch (1982, p. 113); this could be misunderstood, since part of it consisted of public grants and support given to a wide range of projects and not only R&D projects. They ranged from 'Scientific efforts for opening up Central Africa', the publication of archives, international contributions to the surveying of the earth, measures to combat typhoid fever or infant mortality, to financial support for congresses.

Until the First World War more attention was generally given to scientific support on an industrially relevant level, as well as to scientific application (Pfetsch 1974); however, it would be incorrect to conclude that a major part of these funds were granted to private companies, as can be shown for the period following the Second World War. Industry was more interested in a proportional increase in public support of production-relevant branches of science (consequently, in the creation of external effects upon science-based industries, Pfetsch 1974, p. 107) than in the support of their own R&D.

Of course scientific expenditure was borne exclusively by the German states until the foundation of the Empire; afterwards, the central power moderately supported the total public science budget by 20 per cent. Only during the Republic of Weimar did this share grow considerably (see Figure 11.3). After the occupation of Germany at the end of the Second

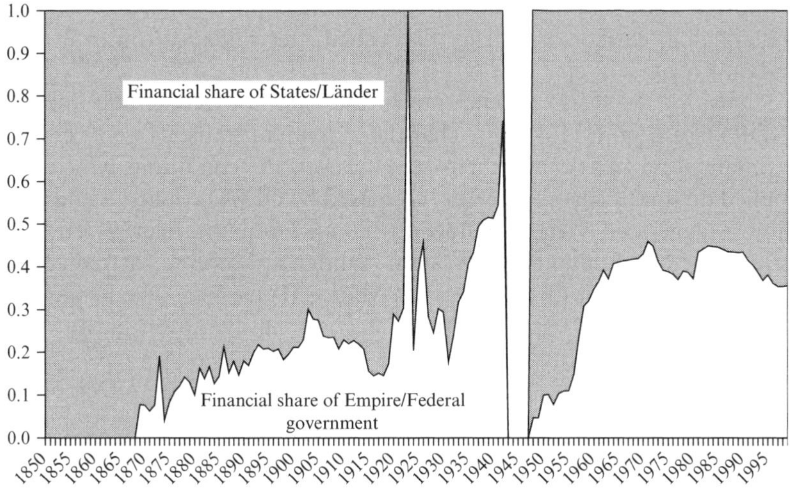

Figure 11.3 Development of the financing of scientific expenditure: the proportion of federal and state financing

World War the Federal Government could not play its prior role again, all the more so since several research areas were prohibited (research in the fields of armament, nuclear science, chemistry and aviation). However, federal institutions systematically increased their influence on science until the level during the Third Reich was reached again. Since the recent reunification, federal administration has been slowly but surely withdrawing from scientific support.

Consequently, it must be noted that, following critical upheavals such as the foundation of the Empire, and the First and the Second World Wars, the Federal states had always begun to take over important tasks of scientific support and were later relieved by the central power. The events following the foundation of the Empire, which were called 'getting empired' by Pfetsch (1974, p. 105), occurred in a hesitant way on complex scientific-political levels. The results were manifold forms of co-operation between private, mixed and individual government institutions and Empire authorities. The same can be observed since 1945 under completely different political circumstances: the Federal Government only slowly became a dominant and central supporter and organizer of the scientific system, its scientific expenditure diminishing both on an absolute and on a relative level only after the reunification. Again this points to persistent basic structures in the national innovation system. The only historical exception is the reunification of 1990: whereas the Federal Government played a dominant role as a central supporter and organiser during the reunification of the two scientific systems, its scientific expenditure diminished afterwards both on an absolute and on a relative level.

Regarding the R&D expenditure of the German Democratic Republic (GDR) (see Figure 11.4), note that the individual statistics were centrally maintained and are comprehensive. However, the conditions which were applied do not fully comply with those used by OECD countries and often show exaggerated values. Following reunification the relevant statistics were revised and adapted to Western standards; however, the conversion problem of the East German Bank's Mark (M) persists. Due to the non-convertibility of this currency the reliable purchasing-power parity values of OECD countries cannot be applied.

Figure 11.4 compares the R&D expenditure of the German Democratic Republic with that of West Germany. In order to be certain, a pessimistic and an optimistic variation can be applied in order to show a range of uncertainty due to conversion. The first possibility is based on the purchasing-power parity (PPP) of so-called baskets of commodities; in the second model the subsidies included in GDR commodity prices are taken into consideration and deducted (anonymous, 1986, pp. 259–268). It is shown in both estimations that the national R&D expenditure of the German Democratic Republic could not equal the West German level (per head of the population) but the general upward trends resemble each other somewhat. This may come as a surprise to those who point to the inefficiencies of the communist part of Germany, but again, the underlying institutional

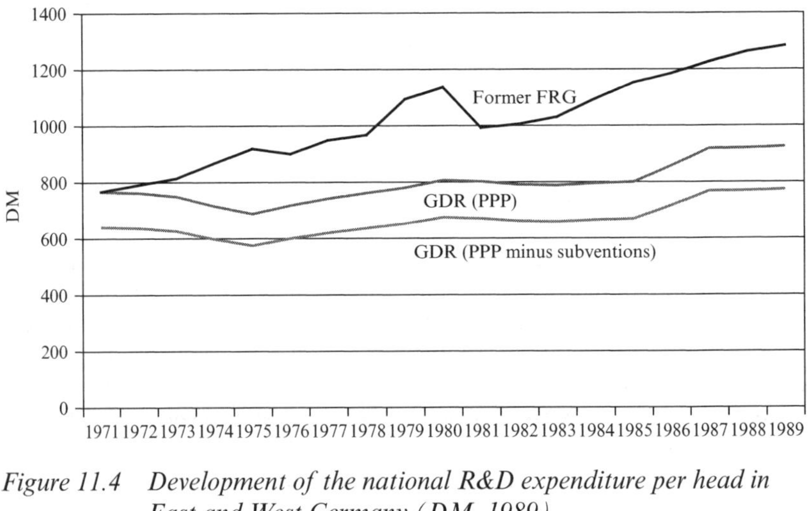

Figure 11.4 Development of the national R&D expenditure per head in East and West Germany (DM, 1989)

structures remained basically the same as before the war, requiring similar amounts of public support.

2.2 Development of Scientific Activities

It is impossible to achieve an insight into the development of non-codified and thus 'tacit' knowledge and experience of the scientific staff. For this reason the historical development of an innovation system is often shown by the personnel statistics, or by statistics showing monetary expenditure. However, only expenditure is measured by this method, instead of the fruit of scientific activities. Efficiency measurements are particularly impossible. Consequently, modern innovation statistics make regular use of yield measures; regarding scientific work, statistics of publications are a typical output indicator. Analyses of the degree of publication activities have been maintained for centuries; however, it must be noted that the publication media chosen by scientists may differ from one faculty to another, as well as over time (Wagner-Döbler and Berg 1996, p. 289). Only during the 19th century did scientific journals achieve the same degree of significance as books, the dominating publication media until then.

Regarding publication activities in selected areas, only a few but informative historical time series for selected areas are available (see below). However totals are studied first. Due to the known difficulties of aggregation, only limited sources of publication activities are available on this level of analysis. An analysis of the Catalogue of Scientific Papers for the 19th century shows that the output of scientific papers had been growing constantly since 1800; and it accelerated tremendously from 1884 onwards (anonymous, 1925). This analysis is not limited to Germany but refers to worldwide publication output.

From 1900 onwards the availability of data improved worldwide. The growth rates of periodicals were evaluated in *Ulrich's Periodical Database* (CD-ROM version) by Mabe and Amin (2001); if one takes the example of peer-reviewed academic journals from this catalogue, a remarkable exponential growth is shown up to the end of the 20th century, which then slightly decreases (Figure 11.5). A detailed statistical analysis covering the period from 1900 until 1944 shows an almost constant increase in the inventory of journals of 3.2 per cent per year, followed by a phase of expansion with an almost constant growth rate of 4.8 per cent per year until 1974, ending with a lower rate of growth of 3.7 per cent per year, similar to the first half of the century ('century standard').

This development seems to be linked with historical structural breakages on a worldwide level. Following its academisation during the 19th century,

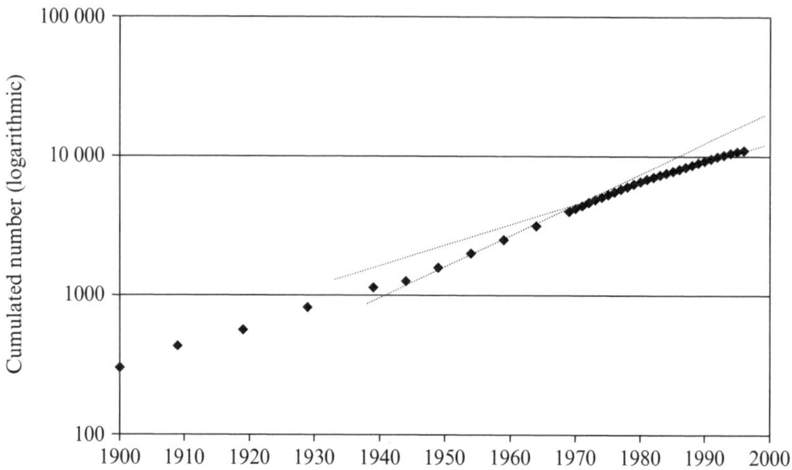

Note: The thin drawn lines represent the exponential growth rates for the main growth periods as explained in the text.

Figure 11.5 Cumulated number of scientific journals peer-reviewed worldwide (shown as a semi-logarithmic figure) from 1900–2000

science was characterised by constant expansion until the Second World War. This can be called the normal development. After the Second World War, the growth rate of scientific output increased and reached almost 5 per cent for almost three decades (the so-called boom phase), due to the economic miracle, the armament race and reinforced industrial research and development activities, as well as an expansion of scientific activities in general. This phase was followed by a normal phase of expansion similar to pre-war conditions; it can be linked to the ending of university expansion and the consequences of a severe recession due to the oil crisis, as well as with a general decrease of economic growth rates ('limits to growth'). Using a completely different timeseries, Maddison (1982, p. 92) found phases showing a high degree of similarity (his phases are 1930–50, 1950–73, after 1973).

Analysing the situation in Germany, the *Bibliography of German Periodicals Literature* represents an alternative regarding historical data. This bibliography covers the German-speaking periodical literature from 1896 until 1964, and the international periodical literature from 1965 onwards. However, no information about the author's nationality or the institute's location is found in this source; probably most of the older records come from German authors, but ratios and changes in these are also unknown.

The *Science Citation Index* (SCI), which was available as an online version as early as 1964 (see below), has a printed version listing the publications from 1945 until 1974. Although no indications are found regarding the authors' nationalities or the institutes' locations, the listing of periodicals is classified by the countries editing and printing them. Since Mabe and Amin (2001) have demonstrated a highly positive correlation between the number of periodicals and the number of journal articles, the number of German-language articles listed in this data record can be counted for the period since 1945. The regular announcement by the SCI that records would be completed back to 1900 was withdrawn,[7] so there is no hope for the early publication of a century's inventory.

Taking into account that the total volume of publications has grown enormously, it is surprising to see that the share of German periodicals has been constant since 1945, that is, it has augmented in line with the worldwide volume. The average proportion of German periodicals, which is 8.9 per cent of the total SCI inventory, shows only minimal fluctuation. Since 1974 an equally constant proportion of German authors is shown in the SCI online version; it is obviously sensible to link these two data records, all the more so since they overlap each other over a long period (from 1975 to 1984) so that the corresponding factor of extrapolation from periodicals to publications can be determined.

The SCI online version shows the nationality, a corresponding field being encoded where a German author or an institute located in Germany are concerned (independently from the medium's language). The strongest growth of the (extrapolated) publication numbers is stated from the middle of the 1960s and during the 1970s (Figure 11.6). This matches perfectly with the observation of a worldwide expansion of the scientific system, even though the German scientific world showed a delay of almost 20 years resulting from the special situation of reconstruction as well as from the Allied Forces' restrictions regarding certain research areas.

At the end of the 1980s the growth rate decreases not only in Germany but on a worldwide level; after 1989 the total number of German articles shows a dramatic decrease. It must be noted that the statistics cover both West and East Germany, and that this decrease in publication activities could principally represent the decay or dissolution of the East German scientific system. The publication level of 1987 was only reached again during the publication year 1993, which was characterised by strong growth anticyclical to the worldwide slowdown. A comparison of research activities both on a disciplinary and on a qualitative level is suggested below. Figure 11.6 also shows a simulation of the course of the three periods when growth rates were constant, which points out the exponential growth.

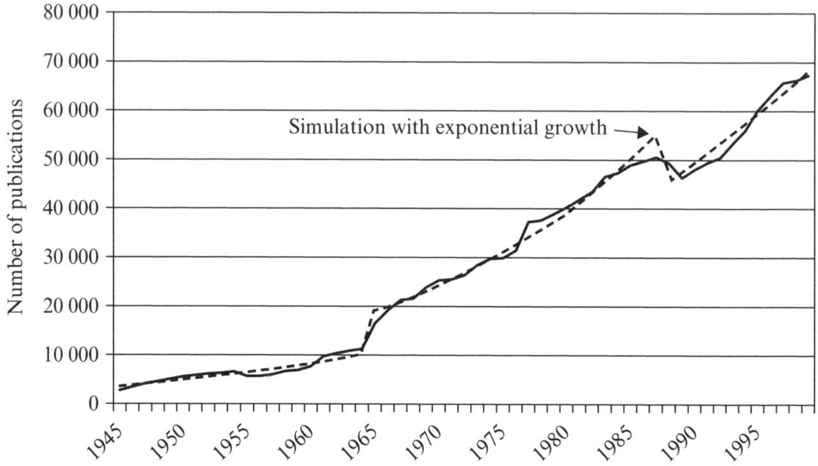

Figure 11.6 Development phases of publication activities in Germany since 1945

From 1974 to 1990, SCI publications from West and East Germany can be compared electronically.[8] This period is characterised by moderate growth of publication activities ('century standard'). In the 1970s, the share of East German publications was approximately 16 to 17 per cent. However, if one compares East and West Germany, both the proportional shares of population and the proportion of R&D staff is almost 30 per cent, so that scientific publications from the German Democratic Republic are less represented in the US-based database. The proportion of East German publications had constantly diminished to reach 13 per cent by the end of the 1980s; and there is no answer to the question as to whether the representation in the database was worse or if the output efficiency of East German research activities continued declining until reunification.

Measured by its publication output, the profile of GDR research resembles that of the former Federal Republic. In proportion to worldwide average shares, researchers of both parts of Germany published much more than a *pro rata* share in the research areas of energy and nuclear technology, chemistry, solid-state physics and microbiology. A weaker level than the worldwide average was shown in information science, engineering, environmental research and public health, as well as in other biomedical subjects. According to our estimation, this structural similarity could be the reason for such a strong diminution of publication activities on an all-German level following reunification. Integration did not affect differently specialised East and West research systems, but only research systems with the same principal orientation, which led to the deplorable 're-allocation and consolidation' process in East Germany. Independently from a political evaluation of the organisation of GDR research institutes, this structural similarity must be pointed out; obviously 40 years of division were not sufficient for a differentiated development of the basic specialisation patterns of research in both parts of Germany. To a great extent, and in the sense of path dependency, research is still based on the (common) preferences which existed prior to the division. This unique historical situation could be understood as an unintended experiment: basic patterns of scientific specialisation change only slowly, even in times of great political system change (Hinze and Grupp 1995, p. 65).[9]

Another method of comparing the two scientific systems is to observe the frequency of citations. More frequently cited scientific studies are considered to be more significant in some way, for example because they include either important methods to which many successive authors return, or especially important results (or errors which are repudiated later). GDR literature shows a lower rate of citations per scientific publication than West German literature; there are two possible reasons for this: on the one hand, the scientific value of GDR publications could have been minor; on the other hand, the periodicals in which these articles appeared were received to a lesser degree on an international level, in particular in the English-speaking realm. This could also be due to the lower circulation figures of the corresponding periodicals (partly of Soviet origin).

In the bibliometric statistics these two effects can be viewed separately, by referring the rate of citations either to the worldwide average or to the average of the individually selected periodicals (Grupp et al. 2001). The following research results emerge: GDR research publications show an almost general lack of worldwide communication of results (particularly in the Anglo-Saxon linguistic area). This explains the low rate of citations. However, a correlation between the frequency of citations and the publication organs (which are typically less read in the Anglo-Saxon area) selected by GDR authors shows that a favourable rate of citations is found in comparison with articles from countries other than the GDR which are also published in these periodicals. Consequently, GDR publications are considered to an above-average degree once the citation ratio due to the lack of international spread is mathematically corrected. The highest regard (ratio of citations) is found in the areas of neuro science and internal medicine, as well as dietetics and agriculture. Following the correction of the ratio of citations, the results of GDR environmental research were the least noticed by the professional world.

A division of science into 27 subsections (Hinze and Grupp 1995) leads to a surprising correlation between the degree of internationalisation and that of attention received: it was found that those research areas which are not internationally spread are significantly more noticed by the professional world than the publications with a higher degree of internationalisation. No such correlation can be found for West German research. It is possible that hierarchy and cadre selection mechanisms played a role regarding access to Western periodicals.

2.3 Industrial Research and Development in Germany

Since the foundation of the Empire, economic growth of industrial countries, in particular in Europe, has increasingly been based on the innovation energy of the knowledge-based industry. 'This is undeniably true for the impulses of growth immediately released by these industries, starting with carbon chemistry and electrical technology' (Wengenroth 1997). There is hardly a clearer and more distinct way to describe the conducive effects of industrial research on the culture and efficiency of innovation.

It is still difficult to demonstrate the companies' increasing R&D expenditure for such an undeniable success. In particular, no complete data records are available about monetary expenditure or research personnel prior to the end of the Second World War, that is, the data record established by Pfetsch (1982) regarding public scientific expenditure has no counterpart for industry. Today's systematic statistics about R&D expenditure and personnel of the Federal Republic start from the year 1962; certain presumptions allow the reconstruction of the corresponding indicators starting from 1948–49 (Figure 11.7). According to this, industry has continuously increased its R&D budgets to a higher degree than government, the share of the latter being at present approximately 35 per cent.

The reconstruction of the corresponding indicators prior to the Second World War is only possible if one starts from the individual companies or branches. This was tried for the areas of chemistry and electrical technology (see the next section). The investigation of the history of R&D in leading companies of two selected industrial branches shows that the execution of case studies in order to represent time series is possible in principle and, moreover, makes sense. During the whole investigation period many large and leading companies in Germany maintained archives which can be considered as complete in spite of difficult conditions at times in German history.

Presently the representativity of company-related R&D time series cannot be plausibly proved for the development of a whole branch and that of all branches for the whole national economy. A more detailed analysis should include other important branches, in particular the metal industry. However, the results found so far show that the existence of different 'cultures' of R&D

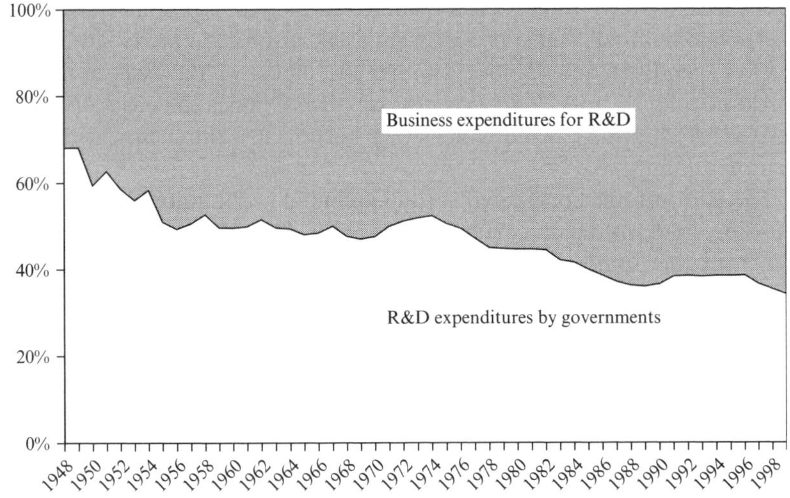

Figure 11.7 Development of government and industrial R&D expenditure in relation to each other from 1948–2000

is possible in the different branches, which influences not only the forms of organisation but also researchers' liberties and practical work.

2.4 Development of Innovation Activity in Germany

The observation of the development of innovation activity is important in itself in order to establish R&D results, mostly on a technological or application level. Adopted methods are statistics on patent applications (a figure representing successful innovation activity seen from the innovators' or applicants' subjective perspective) on the one hand, and, on the other hand, statistics on the number of granted patents (as a figure representing successful innovation activity, seen from the objective perspective of patent examiners). Statistics on patents make even more sense if one takes into consideration that only fragments of industrial R&D expenditure are known prior to the Second World War. Instead of inputs, industrial R&D activities can be measured by their patent outputs, and this even more precisely from a technological perspective than by monetary indicators. This also explains our interest in both patent grants and patent applications: if no patent is granted after verification of the novelty, the inventive step and its commercial usefulness, for example due to a lack of novelty, the applying company had nevertheless invested R&D efforts – even if these led to an objectively already known result. Consequently, the 'subjective' perspective of a successful invention is closely linked to the R&D performance which was in fact realised. Statistics on patent applications as a proxy variable for R&D expenditure may ignore whether the object of the invention was a world novelty or not. R&D expenditure also includes the costs of unsuccessful inventions or those which were belated in comparison with competitors (imitations).

The period to be considered is fully included in the statistics of patents. In some German regions, patents were applied for as early as 1820, starting from the South due to the influence of the Napoleonic legislation. From 1 July 1877, a patent act for the German Empire standardised procedures. Thus, the creation of patent acts in Germany follows the scientific-technological innovation push of the 19th century, at the end of which Germany was one of the leading industrial nations. In about the middle of the century the local, largely secluded markets were dissolved, and the German economy was integrated into the quickly expanding world economy (Ziegler 2000, p. 198, and North 2000b, p. 13).

For several years, patent statistics back to 1879 have been available using machine readable methods. On the one hand, electronic data records since 1970 are more informative than those of former periods, leading to a largely increased importance and use of these patent data records by modern studies in science and technology. On the other hand, if one makes the effort to bring the individually valid patent classifications together, and to link together different patent data records for the appropriate historical sequences, assembled patent statistics can be established for the whole period. Moreover, regarding the assignment of priority years prior to 1969, these must be established according to the reference system of the individual patent authority.

Considering global patent activities in Germany (Figure 11.8), an obvious difference is found between the dynamics of chronological development and that of scientific activities (publication statistics). The strongest growth with an average annual rate above 9 per cent on a low level takes place from 1820 to the foundation of the German Empire; the total growth rate for German regions is shown to be constant except for the setback due to the war of 1870–71. Following the introduction of the countrywide German patent act, the number of applications and grants rises rapidly within a few years, and continues growing at a constant rate, which is lower compared with the period preceding 1870 (annual average rate 6.7 per cent). This growth, which lasted for almost one century, was abruptly stopped by the First World War, the annual patent production being halved. From approximately 1920 to 2000, an eventful development pattern nevertheless shows very little growth. For almost one century the number of annual patent applications is approximately 50000 to 60000. Consequently, German patent productivity per

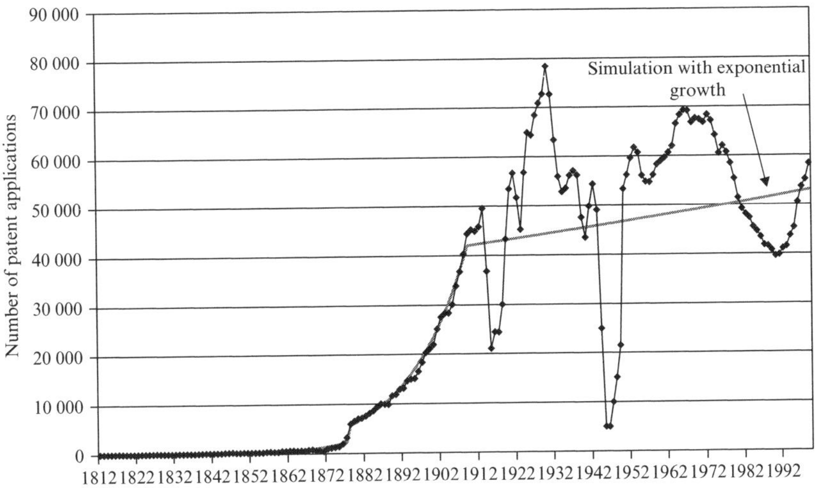

Figure 11.8 Development of patent applications from 1812

person reaches one of the highest levels in comparison with the United States, Japan and the European Union.

Diverging from this rough rule, growth is observed during the Weimar Republic phase until the beginning of the Third Reich, followed by a very deep setback during the Second World War, which is distinctly more serious than that during the First World War, and a return to the average rate by approximately 1960. Another boom follows until 1975 when deep recession takes place which is only overcome in the mid 1990s.

No investigation has yet discovered whether these growth cycles only have economic causes. The economic boom after the foundation of the Empire is well-known (Ziegler 2000, p. 201); the same is true for the serious recession following the oil crisis in 1973 straight after the economic miracle. The question remains as to whether the reduction of innovation activities at the beginning of the Third Reich was only due to economic reasons or to a modified practice of patenting (for example by stronger observance of secrecy due to the early war economy, or by the expulsion or migration of Jewish scientists). Further, the question is asked as to why the growing R&D budgets granted after the Second World War did not lead to an increase in patent activities. Obviously this decrease of patent efficiency is due to an economic calculation which is not exclusively driven by R&D inputs.

Up to now, global indications have been made about patent documents of national and international actors. By international actor it is understood that either the inventors' residence or the applying company is located outside Germany. From 1881 to 1913, the share of foreign patent grants was extremely high, showing an average of 35 per cent: until 1933, Germany's reputation as the leading scientific country attracted many young scientists from abroad. Especially Americans came to the German Empire in order to benefit from practice-oriented education for their degrees, and possibly even to experience some years of active industrial research (Erker 1990 and Smith 1990). After the First World War and the efforts to achieve self-sufficiency in the 1930s, the share of foreigners was reduced by almost 10 per cent but remained a significant figure in spite of all war speculations. Since the reconstruction of the German patent administration following the Second World War, the share of foreign patent grants has constantly increased, reaching more than 60 per cent at this so-called globalisation time.

Although most patent applications originate from industry, universities and other public research institutions are increasingly also involved in patent production. This can be linked to their stronger orientation towards applied research, as well as to their acceptance of outside resources from private industry. Prior to the reunification in 1990, universities attained a share of 3 per cent of all West German patent applications, which grew to more than 4 per cent after reunification. Similar contributions are shown by all other public research institutions and companies, above all the Helmholtz Association (big national labs) and the Fraunhofer Institutes. In view of their limited human resources the patent productivity especially of the Fraunhofer Society must be more highly valued than that of universities (Schmoch et al. 2000).

Compared with Western conditions, certain deviations in the patent law conditions of the former GDR were caused by the socialist spirit of ownership. Consequently, the national patent applications at the former GDR Authority of Invention and Patent Administration (AfEP) can hardly be compared with those submitted in the West (Hinze and Grupp 1995, p. 42 onwards). Therefore another method was chosen for this analysis, which is now based on GDR patent activities in West European foreign countries. With the help of this method all the particularities related to patent law specifications are circumvented, enabling comparison with Western countries. GDR inventors were mostly interested in the economic sector of the former Federal Republic, so that the foreign applications submitted for this target market can be referred to (independently of whether the application was submitted to the German Patent and Trademark Office, to the European Patent Office, or to the International Patent Authority WIPO designating the Federal Republic of Germany).

The basic framework conditions for GDR activities in view of industrial property rights are fixed in the patent law of 6 September 1950

(Albrecht et al. 1991, p. 4). Nevertheless, GDR patent activities according to Western legislation are hard to ascertain during the first years. This is linked to the various forms of recognition of the GDR as an autonomous state by different nations. Some GDR inventors operated from Federal Republic addresses. In spite of these imponderabilities an increase in patent activities by GDR inventors is seen until approximately 1983–84. Then the figures are characterised by stagnation, and since 1987 they have been decreasing. The same tendency is shown on a higher level by national patent applications in the German Democratic Republic, so that the drop of innovation activities prior to reunification is undoubtedly proved (Hinze and Grupp 1995, p. 47). The causal and significant explanation of this development is the fact that since 1981 the share of R&D personnel in the economic sector of the GDR had continuously declined, and financial resources for R&D in the economic sector were also reduced.

A comparison of the specialisation of GDR patent portfolios with those of West Germany is very interesting. According to a division of the whole GDP technology area into 28 fields, particular strength is found in the fields of paper and print, textiles, machine-tool manufacture, handling, optical instruments and metrology. Distinct weakness is shown in the fields of chemistry, electrical technology and electronics and information technology, as well as traffic and transportation. This specialisation profile was constant over time. In particular, the eastern regions' patent profile of the 1990s (including East Berlin) corresponds largely with that of the GDR of the 1980s (Schmoch and Sass 2000). In addition, there is an amazing correlation with that of West Germany. In spite of completely different economic conditions (Stolper et al. 1964), large fields of technology show a correspondence between East and West Germany until reunification (Grupp and Schmoch 1992, p. 118 onwards). This was also found for the area of basic research (publication statistics) and explained by path dependencies and persistent structures in both parts of Germany despite their different political regimes (see above). Since reunification, the new federal regions have expanded their top level technology (semiconductors, biotechnology, surface technology) starting from a low level.

Consequently, the question is whether a similar influence of scientific development on technology can be found in both parts of Germany. An evaluation of the scientific dependency of technology is usually based on the fact that patent specifications include responses to former inventions in the form of citations to patent documents. If an invention is directly based on science which was published but not patented, the patent engineers annotate references to the corresponding scientific literature. It could be shown that the frequency of such scientific hints included in patent specifications is a valid measure of the dependency on science inherent in a field of technology (Grupp and Schmoch 1992).

Regarding the degree to which technology was based on science, the German Democratic Republic remained constantly behind the world average. Although the same is true for West Germany, the gap was distinctly smaller. During the 1980s, both West and East Germany significantly increased their orientation to science-based technology – the GDR on a lower level but with a higher growth rate compared to West Germany. Comparison between the two countries is interesting in that the East-West distance was reduced in this area.

When Germany was reunified in 1990, two almost identically specialised technology systems came together. It was not possible to integrate the strength of one side and the weakness of the other one; instead, the fields characterised by strength were the same on both sides and the weaker fields were equally neglected.

The limited use of science by GDR technology is clear in international comparison; the same is true for the Federal Republic, but on a different level. In view of the extended scientific activities, which were most significant in proportion to the size of the GDR, it is surprising to find that technological development did not benefit from the use of science and therefore remained on a relatively science-poor level.

3. SECTORAL INNOVATION SYSTEMS: ELECTRICAL TECHNOLOGY AND CHEMISTRY

So far, the national German innovation activities have been analysed in the varying territories. In the framework of this article, it is not possible to consider all the university and industrial sectors individually. Therefore, sectoral analysis of the two areas chemistry and electrical technology will be carried out as representative studies. In the literature, chemistry and electrical technology are considered perfect examples of the science-based industries which came into existence in the second half of the 19th century. These industries are characterised by a rapid transfer of research results to production. Due to the intense exchange activities on both sides one can also talk of 'industry-based science' (König 1995, p. 283), since science probably benefits more from industry than inversely in certain phases (for example in the case of the newly emerging academic electrical engineering).

Another motive for the choice of these two specific sectors is the power of innovation in German industry today, which, roughly speaking, is considered as contrasting: chemistry with its brilliant innovation and export performance compares with international standards, and electrical technology (or its subsumption into information technology) is considered as a weak point in the German economy. According to our thesis, an exemplary analysis of these two sectors within the national German innovation system should reveal essential facts to explain their different characters at the end of the 20th century.

3.1 Sectoral Expenditure for Science

Statistics on science expenditure until 1945 include a classification by sectors. However, only natural science and engineering are identified in totals, so that these data records cannot be used for the study of electrical technology and chemistry. The establishment of a data base with sufficient capacity from an institutional level (ministries, universities, and so on) also seems impossible. This has remained unchanged since the Second World War. However, personnel figures from universities are available for selected years in both chemistry and electrical technology.

3.2 Development of Scientific Activities

First, the publication history of the two selected areas, electrical technology and chemistry, will be summarised. One problem is the tracking of publication activities in the fields of electrical technology and chemistry prior to 1974, the period for which no online data base is available. To resolve this problem, the corresponding monographs were submitted to manual analyses, which made the period from approximately 1924 onwards accessible. Because this process was undertaken beyond the year 1974, the manually obtained figures can be extrapolated to the data base level. First analyses support the earlier hypothesis: during the 1960s and early 1970s, the growth of publication activities in chemistry was higher than it was later on, so that a synchronism of scientific publication activities and the economic success of mass chemistry (base) could be confirmed (Figure 11.9).

An extension of the historical period shows a rapid growth of publication activities in the field of electrical technology since the 1950s, reaching its peak from the middle to the end of the 1960s, then again in the mid-seventies. This development is followed by a decrease of publications to reach a relatively low level in 1981, then by another period of growth. Consequently, the present study of data records is substantially supported and completed by manual tracking up to the Weimar Republic. The manual method probably has an even higher explanatory power, since the continuous completion of inventory

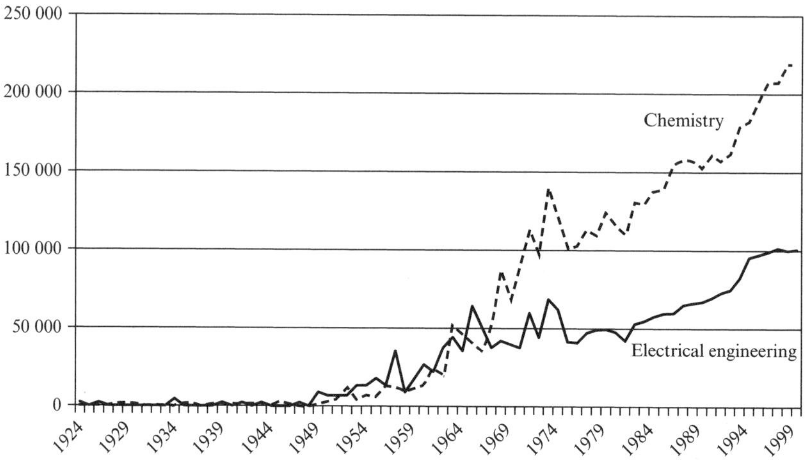

Figure 11.9 Development of German publications in the fields of electrical technology and chemistry, from 1924 to 1999 (early figures extrapolated)

data records (like in the case of the SCI) could lead to artefacts. Although the SCI strives for transparency with the selection procedures of periodicals entering the data base, quantitative conclusions for individual subjects are not always possible (Testa 1997).

Publication activities in the fields of electrical technology and chemistry show interesting subject-specific deviations from the average trends of publication activities in all scientific disciplines in Germany (Figure 11.9). In contrast to the upward development shown by electrical technology prior to and following reunification, which takes an anticyclical course compared with global publication activities, the growth of publication activities in chemistry is reduced synchronously with the publication activities in all scientific fields in the middle of the 1970s. Presumably the anticyclical development of publication activities in the area of chemistry can be linked to the division of basic material chemistry into specialised and fine chemistry which took place in the 1970s, followed by biotechnology. The anticyclic boom of publication activities in the area of electrical technology could be linked to the appearance of the present information and communications technology, and could be interpreted as its scientific predecessor. First analyses of the development of R&D expenditure in chemistry and electrical technology industries support this thesis.

3.3 Industrial R&D Expenditure and R&D Personnel

In the scope of investigations about industrial R&D expenditure, special attention was given to the two industrial branches selected in this analysis. In the fields of chemistry and electrical technology, a small sample of large industrial companies could be personally interviewed regarding the existence of corresponding data records. Sometimes the relevant archives could be accessed. The corresponding industrial federations were involved. Interesting series of figures are available from the federations, but no figures were found regarding R&D expenditure or R&D personnel. In contrast to this, time series can be found relating to the status of memberships, about lectures and other things.

Comprehensive archive material concerning the number of chemists and physicists is available from the successor organisations of IG Farben such as BASF. These indications correlate strikingly with the patents held by these companies; the hypothesis according to which a lack of input figures can be substituted by patent statistics is thus supported. Besides this, employment figures of other technical professions can be constructed. A comparison between the total number of chemists employed by BASF, Hoechst and Bayer, and the chemists employed by universities and technological universities (see Pfetsch 1974, p. 158), shows that, since approximately 1880, the contribution of industry can no longer be ignored. Prior to the foundation of the Empire only a single-digit percentage of all chemists were employed by industry; equality was reached in 1885, and in 1890 the number of industrial personnel exceeded that of university staff. Prior to the beginning of the First World War the three companies already employed three times as many chemists as German universities.

Seen from a quantitative point of view, it is found that even prior to the First World War industrial R&D efforts parallel to public engagement could not be neglected either.

The most important German companies in the electrical technology branch were recorded on the basis of the list of patents granted in 1928, which was established by the German Empire Patent Office (in total 1121 patents, classified by companies). According to this record, the contribution to patents in the area of electrical technology was 20 per cent by the leading company Siemens-Schuckert-Werke, 15 per cent by AEG, 9 per cent by Siemens und Halske and 5 per cent by the subsidiary of the latter, Telefunken. However, the large scale to which electrical technology was embodied in the German economy during this period is shown by the fact that the ten most important patent assignees produced only little more than 60 per cent of all patents; almost 40 per cent is accounted for by other companies. Such a limited degree of concentration means that it would be almost hopeless to register complete R&D input figures by individually interviewing all companies of this branch. Since 80 per cent of all patents are attained by the 50 most 'patent-active' companies the number which were also involved in R&D could have exceeded 100 according to a rough estimate.[10]

The number of scientists employed in research institutes by the above-mentioned large companies can be ascertained; however, no indications about monetary expenditure for R&D are found in the business reports. Even the annual reports of the research institutes were not fertile. In the area of electrical technology it seems almost impossible to take an inventory of relevant R&D input indicators, covering both the broad industry structure and the corresponding period of time. However, as in the case of chemistry, a study based on a selection of companies could be carried out to find a possible correlation between personnel data and patent data. In any case, statistics on patents will serve as a significant method of investigation.

3.4 Development of Sectoral Invention Activities

Due to very detailed patent classifications, the inventory of patents in the area of electrical technology and chemistry can easily be recorded. Although partly contestable delimitations are necessary for this investigation, these can be documented; moreover, a study based on different delimitations is possible.

It is shown that high-voltage technology (electricity, electrical energy) and low-voltage technology (audio-visual technology and telecommunications or communication engineering) can be distinguished for the whole period. On an analytical level, a strong growth of high-voltage engineering is shown since approximately 1900 (the more modern subject in times of electrification), as well as its stagnation after 1950, whereas low-voltage engineering shows moderate growth until 1944, and becomes stronger after 1950 (Figure 11.10).

In total, the very different development dynamics are reflected in global statistics by a 4 per cent share of all German patents held by electrical technology until approximately the end of the 19th century; then the share shows an almost exponential growth to more than 20 per cent during the Second World War (Figure 11.11). In spite of an increased growth of low-voltage engineering, the sum of patent shares is reduced from almost 20 per cent (1958) to approximately 13 per cent (1998); this is in accordance with the internationally common image of a lack of specialisation in the area of German information technology.

At the beginning of the observation period, chemistry had already achieved a patent share of 10 per cent, which remained almost unchanged until 1945 (except for short-term cyclical fluctuations over a few years).

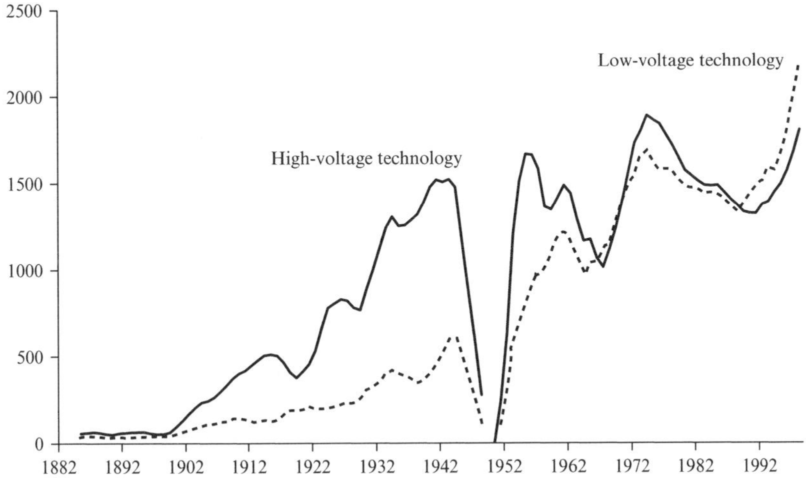

Figure 11.10 Moving average line of the first publications of national patent applications submitted to the German or European Patent Office (with destination Germany)

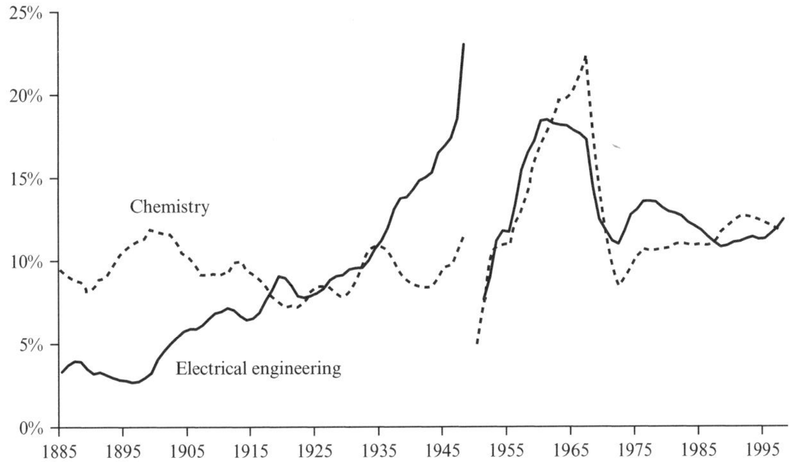

Note: For Patent Offices and averaging see Figure 11.10.

Figure 11.11 Share of the total patent publications about national patent applications held by electrical technology and chemistry

During the period of reconstruction after World War II, the number of patents in the area of chemistry increased, reaching more than 20 per cent, but was hit by a severe crisis following 1967. Since approximately 1970 – when the proportion had dropped to less than 10 per cent – the share of the total number of patents held showed moderate growth to approximately 12 per cent. These high shares of national patent inventory reveal that the fields of electrical engineering and chemistry were and remain leading industrial sectors. They show above-average expansion, and their global economic importance is characterised by continuous growth (Ziegler 2000, p. 240).

Analogous with electrical technology, chemistry can also be divided into patent-statistical classifications (for example organic chemistry, plastics, pharmaceutical substances, biochemistry, detergents and agrarian chemistry. Innovation activities in these six fields show extremely different degrees of development. Both of the first two fields show a continuous increase in the total number of chemistry patents (in spite of cyclical differences in detail), whereas the smaller fields of chemistry, described in the category 'other fields', which was very significant from approximately 1880, started to grow from about 1970 (Figures 11.12 and 11.13). This only points to different definitions concerning 'other fields'.

An attempt to subdivide these 'other fields' shows the spectacularly high share of biochemistry in the total number of chemistry patent applications prior to the turn of the century. This surprising development is explained

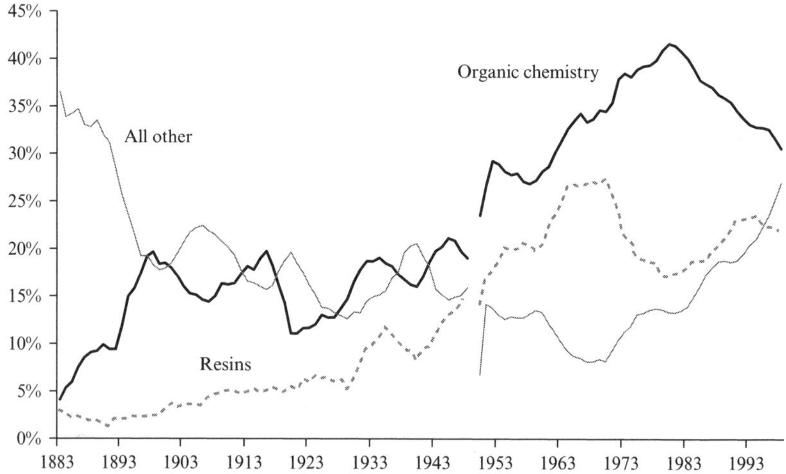

Note: For sources and averaging see Figure 11.10.

Figure 11.12 A selection of patent shares of the whole field of chemistry

by a comparison of patent classes included in the definition biochemistry in the years 1900 and 1998: according to our definition, biochemistry was dedicated to the food industry in 1900. Between the turn of the century and the First World War, the food industry based on biochemistry reached its peak: living organisms were used in the most varied ways. At that time, biotechnological procedures competed with chemical-synthetic procedures in the field of production.

According to Marschall (1999, p. 280), prior to the First World War a 'path dependency' arose in German chemistry, which supported the evolutionary choice for chemical synthesis. This path dependency was based on subsidised investments in high pressure technology, as well as on its use by the chemical industry. Therefore, inventions in biochemistry were repressed. Nevertheless, it must be noted that brewing beer accounted for almost 50 per cent of all inventions in the area of biochemistry around 1900 (only a few per cent today), whereas second place was held by the extraction, refining and conservation of fat (today, also only a few per cent). In 1998, however, the dominating area included devices for enzymology or microbiology, and second place was held by microorganisms or enzymes (Figure 11.14).

The difference between electrical technology and chemistry also comes from the significance of foreign inventors. According to the same criteria as above, patents can also be classified according to their country of origin.

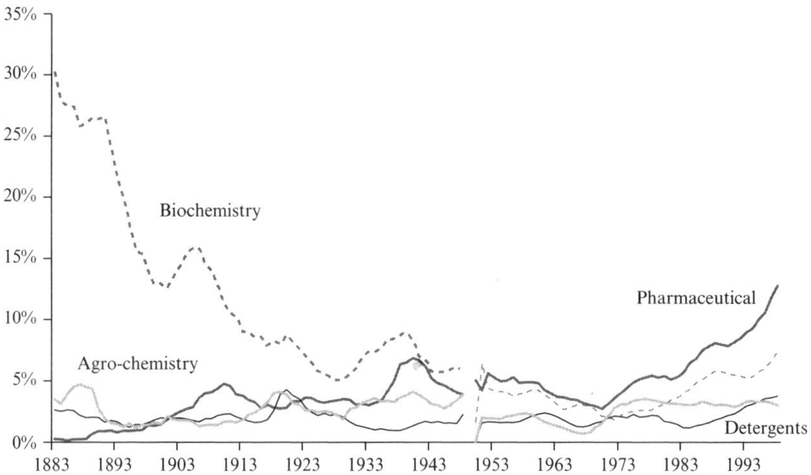

Note: For sources and averaging see Figure 11.10.

Figure 11.13 *Breakdown of the 'other fields' in the total number of patent publications in the area of chemistry*

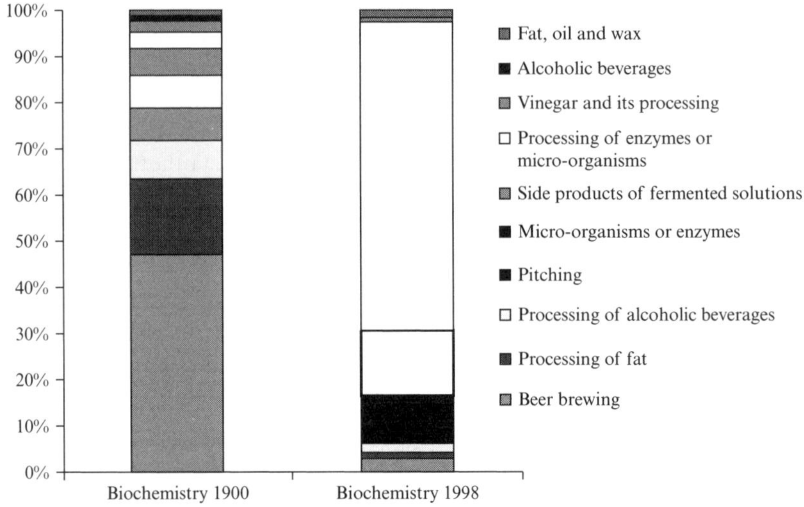

Figure 11.14 Breakdown of patent shares within biochemistry in 1900 and 1998

The results show that more important foreign inventions were realised in the area of electrical technology than in chemistry. The proportion of foreign inventors in the area of electrical technology corresponds approximately with the average of all technical areas; that is, it regressed from more than 35 per cent (1902) to approximately 20 per cent by 1928 and to 10 per cent by 1942. In the area of chemistry, the situation is different: foreign inventors always played a minor role (1902: 20 per cent), however, this ratio was slightly reduced (1942: 13 per cent).

Regarding the historical statistics of the selected sectors, it is concluded that, under conditions of a relatively low level of knowledge exchange with foreign countries, a branch suffers less from periods of crises and autarky and that, on the other hand, intense knowledge exchange with foreign countries leads to correspondingly sensible change. This will certainly have important effects on the organisation of innovation activities, which should be analysed on the level of individual institutions (companies as well as research institutes).

The patent statistics of the German Democratic Republic can also be divided both on a technical and on an institutional level. For example, studies exist showing the extent to which the Humboldt University of East Berlin applied for patents in the areas of chemistry and electrical technology. According to this, chemistry had become one of the most prominent research areas of the GDR in approximately 1990, whereas electrical technology lost significance (Albrecht et al. 1991, p. 107). Identical analyses were submitted for central institutes, other centres and companies (Albrecht 1991, Hinze and Grupp 1995, p. 59). The function of universities in relation to technological development was very important not only for West Germany but also in the GDR.

4. DISCUSSION AND CONCLUSIONS

This look back into the historical times of innovation reveals many interesting perspectives: for instance the present globalisation trends in R&D may now be interpreted as a renaissance of the times around 1900: before the autarky and war situations in national socialist Germany the innovation system was internationalised in a similar way as today but possibly not to the same quantitative extent. Yet the logistic and travel possibilities for exchange of knowledge are much better today than a hundred years ago.

Most astonishingly the German innovation system was very stable although it witnessed several political system changes in the past century. The total amount of government spending on science and innovation followed similar quantitative tracks after its formation in the 19th century, after the First World War and after the Second World War. The respective central powers were no strong pillars in science and technology. On the contrary, the science and technology operation was maintained and reconstructed by the German states before the central power found ways to establish itself as dominating. However, considerable differences are observed when regarding the strong role of enterprises in innovation after the Second World War which was – in pecuniary terms – not as visible before. Only after reunification in 1990 was the acting power the federal government at a time when enterprises were largely dominating the financing of R&D. This was definitely different a hundred years ago.

In terms of the basic sectoral structures in science and technology, the strong and the weak sides were almost the same whatever regime and territorial boundaries existed. This persistence of the innovation system points to a resistant innovation culture in and around Germany which may not be influenced too much by external shocks or incentives be it in monetary or institutional form. If technology and innovation policy intends to change the German innovation culture in its basics one probably needs other government methods than those being used up to today. Even the isolation of the former GDR and its subjection under the communist regime could not change much.

There seems to be a specific German understanding of the opening and development of technology trajectories. The industrial research system in

Germany was one of the first in the world to be formed and developed. Other countries followed that pattern more or less closely. Yet the subjects of research seemed to be different between the countries and remained largely constant over long periods. Obviously the technical and scientific elites in Germany succeeded in following their interests in any political system collectively. For the research and education policy this means that soft factors like group identity, schools of thought and personal exchange are more reliable and more efficient government instruments than the traditional monetary incentive systems. This sustainable culture imprint can only be analysed and detected in historical time series.

Innovation is no 'reality' whatsoever, and it is not considered as existing 'in itself'; instead, innovation activities are only constituted by the specific method of scientific approach. An historical object of investigation about innovation activities is not 'given', instead, it is 'imposed' on the researcher, that is, he/she must establish a measurement concept. An operationalisation considered as ideal could lead to an exorbitant cost of collection, whereas a less adequate method could have favourable effects on both the process and the results of measurement. This applies particularly to evolutionary innovation research, where results are not always shown by a formal mathematical model. Here, the keyword of an 'appreciative' theory was created. Based on such an approach, absolutely no immediate, constituent measuring directives can be derived either. Consequently, it is necessary to construct corresponding indicators for insufficient 'tailor-made' theoretical constructs. Although this procedure could be considered wearisome, there is no other option.

The suggested range of indicators on a national or sectoral level gives a detailed impression of both the extent and the contents of innovation activities during more than the past hundred years. The empirical base which evolutionary researchers interested in innovation and economic history-related questions can rely on, was broadened to a large extent, so that there is no longer the possibility of a serious empirical gap. On the one hand, many of the questions raised by evolutionary theory cannot yet be studied on an empirical level. On the other hand, however, the inverse is equally correct: empirical findings have become available, discovering structures which could be picked up by the theoretical side for further construction of theoretical thought.

On the future research agenda should be many more such longitudinal studies of innovation systems. The basic findings for Germany should be compared to other countries which possibly suffered less from territorial and political changes. The data used in this article should exist in other countries as well and may be brought to the surface. Also we need more sectoral studies in order to work out typologies of innovation development over long periods. Altogether results achieved so far should encourage more cliometric research all over the world.

NOTES

1. This chapter was drafted and presented to the International Joseph A. Schumpeter Conference in April 2002. An earlier abridged version was published in Shavinina (2003). The chapter is based on a much more detailed volume by the same authors in German language (Grupp et al. 2002).
2. See also the contributions included in Müller and Rüsen (1997).
3. Cf. Machlup (1960/61), Grohmann (1988) and Grupp (1998).
4. According to these (OECD 1992, 1993), technological innovations comprise new products and processes and significant technological changes of products and processes.
5. Maddison (1982, p. 2 and p. 83) talks about system shocks. Gerschenkron (1943) points to the pervasive institutional powers that may overcome external shocks for decades.
6. More precisely, 'research share' means the 'R&D share' of the total expenditure for science and technology.
7. Personal communication Dr. Eugene Garfield, founder of the Institute for Scientific Information, Philadelphia, 14 October 2000.
8. Due to the delay in appearance of scientific publications following submission, no quantitative cutback in literature production by the researchers of German Democratic Republic institutes can be perceived until the end of 1990 (Weingart et al. 1991, p. 4).
9. Recently, surprisingly similar results were also found using other methods.
10. In 1928, 358 member companies were registered in the central association of electrical technology and electrical industry (Zentralverband Elektrotechnik- und Elektroindustrie, ZVEI).

REFERENCES

Albrecht, E., O. Dohnert, M. Schneider and H. Bourcevet (1991). 'DDR-forschung im internationalen vergleich unter zugrundelegung der patentstatistik', Report for the Science Council, Sektion Wissenschaftstheorie und Wissenschaftsorganisation, Berlin: Humboldt University.

Anonymous (E. W. H.) (1925). 'Output of scientific papers', *Nature* **116** (2908), pp. 129–30.

Anonymous (1986). 'Das kaufkraftverhältnis zwischen d-mark und mark in der DDR 1985', *DIW-Wochenbericht* 21/86, **53**, pp. 259–68.

Bannock, G., R.E. Baxter, and E. Davis (1998). *Dictionary of Economics*, 6th edition, London: Penguin.

Bernal, J.D. (1939). *The Social Function of Science*, London: George Routledge & Sons.

Boch, R. (ed.) (1999). *Patentschutz und Innovation in Geschichte und Gegenwart*, Frankfurt a. M.: Peter Lang.

Dohrn-van Rossum, G. (1999). 'Erfinder und erfinderschutz im spätmittelalter und in der frühen neuzeit', in Boch (1999), pp. 39–50.

Erker, P. (1990). 'Die verwissenschaftlichung der industrie: zur geschichte der industrieforschung in den europäischen und amerikanischen elektrokonzernen 1890–1930', *Zeitschrift für Unternehmensgeschichte* **35**, pp. 73–94.

Fogel, R.W. (1964). *Railroads and American Economic Growth*, Baltimore: The Johns Hopkins Press.
Freeman, C. (1969). 'Measurement of output of research and experimental development', Statistical Reports and Studies, Paris: UNESCO.
Freeman, C. (1992). *The Economics of Hope*, London: Pinter Publishers.
Freimann, K.-D. and A.E. Ott (eds) (1988). *Theorie und Empirie in der Wirtschaftsforschung*, Tübingen: J.C.B. Mohr.
Gascoigne, R. (1992). 'The historical demography of the scientific community', 1450–1900, *Social Studies of Science*, **22**, pp. 545–73.
Gerschenkron, A. (1943). *Bread and Democracy in Germany*, Ithaca: Cornell University Press.
Grohmann, H. (1998). 'Die statistische Adäquation als Postulat einer sachgerechten Abstimmung zwischen Theorie und Empirie', in Freimann und Ott (1988), pp. 25–42.
Grupp, H. (1998). *Foundations of the Economics of Innovation – Theory, Measurement and Practice*, Cheltenham, UK and Lyme, USA: Edward Elgar.
Grupp, H. and U. Schmoch (1992). *Wissenschaftsbindung der Technik*, Heidelberg: Physica-Verlag.
Grupp, H., U. Schmoch and S. Hinze (2001). 'International alignment and scientific regard as macroindicators for international comparisons of publications', *Scientometrics* **51**(2), 359–80.
Grupp, H., I. Domínguez Lacasa and M. Fredrich–Nishio (2002), *Das Deutsch Innovationssystem seit der Reichsgründung*, Heidelberg: Springer–Physica Publishers.
Hetmeier, H.-W. (1990). 'Öffentliche ausgaben für forschung und experimentelle entwicklung 1987', *Wirtschaft und Statistik* 2/1990, pp. 123–29.
Hinze, S. and H. Grupp (1995). 'Ein rückblick auf wissenschaft und technik in der ehemaligen DDR: ostdeutschlands forschungs- und entwicklungspotential', in Holland and Kuhlmann (1995), pp. 41–86.
Hoffmann, W.G. (1965). *Das Wachstum der Deutschen Wirtschaft seit der Mitte des 19. Jahrhunderts*, Berlin: Springer.
Holland, D. and S. Kuhlmann (1995). *Systemwandel und industrielle Innovation*, Heidelberg: Physica.
Hoyningen-Huene, P. (1999). 'Kommt die physik der wahrheit immer näher?' *Physikalische Blätter* **55**(3), 56–8.
Irvine, J., B.R. Martin, and A. Isard, Ph. (1990). *Investing in the Future*, Aldershot, UK and Brookfield, US: Edward Elgar.
König, W. (1995). *Technikwissenschaften – Die Entstehung der Elektrotechnik aus Industrie und Wissenschaft zwischen 1880 und 1914*, Chur: G+B Verlag Fakultas.
Lorenz, Ch. (1997). *Konstruktion der Vergangenheit*, Köln: Böhlau.
Mabe, M. and M. Amin (2001). 'Growth dynamics of scholarly and scientific journals', *Scientometrics* **51**(1), 147–62.
Machlup, F. (1960/61). 'Idealtypus, wirklichkeit und konstruktion', *Ordo – Jahrbuch für die Ordnung von Wirtschaft und Gesellschaft* **12**, 21–57.
Maddison, A. (1982). *Phases of Capitalist Development*, Oxford: Oxford University Press.
Marschall, L. (1999). 'Industrielle Biotechnologie im 20. Jahrhundert – Technologische Alternative oder Nischentechnologie?' *Technikgeschichte* **66**, (4), 277–93.

Müller, K.E. and J. Rüsen, (eds.) (1997). *Historische Sinnbildung*, Reinbek: Rowohlt.
North, M. (ed.) (2000a). *Deutsche Wirtschaftsgeschichte*, München: C.H. Beck.
North, M. (2000b) Einleitung, in North (2000a), pp. 11–14.
OECD (1992). *Oslo Manual: Proposed Guidelines for Collecting and Interpreting Technological Innovation Data*, Paris: OECD.
OECD (1993). *Frascati Manual 1992*. 5th Revision, Paris: OECD.
Pfetsch, F.R. (1974). *Zur Entwicklung der Wissenschaftspolitik in Deutschland 1750–1914*, Berlin: Duncker & Humblot.
Pfetsch, F.R. (1982). *Datenhandbuch zur Wissenschaftsentwicklung*, Köln: Zentrum für historische Sozialforschung.
Roscher, W. (1886). *Grundlagen der Nationalökonomie*, 18th ed., Stuttgart: J.G. Cotta'sche Buchhandlung.
Schmoch, U., G. Licht, and M. Reinhard (2000). *Wissens- und Technologietransfer in Deutschland*, Stuttgart: Fraunhofer IRB Verlag.
Schmoch, U. and U. Sass (2000). 'Erfassung der technologischen Leistungsfähigkeit der östlichen Bundesländer mit Hilfe von Patentindikatoren', Report for the Federal Ministry BMBF, Karlsruhe: FhG-ISI.
Schumpeter, J.A. (1911/1964). *Theorie der wirtschaftlichen Entwicklung*, München and Leipzig, quoted from the 6th edition, Berlin: Duncker & Humblot.
Schumpeter, J.A. (1942/1975). *Capitalism, Socialism and Democracy*, New York, quoted from the German translation, 4th edition, München: Francke.
Shannina, L.V. (2003) (ed). *International Handbook on Innovation*, New York: Pergamon–Elsevier, pp. 1018–43.
Smith, J.K. jr (1990). The Scientific Tradition in American Industrial Research, *Technology & Culture* **31**, 121–31.
Stolper, G., K. Häuser, and K. Borchardt (1964). *Deutsche Wirtschaft seit 1870*, Tübingen: J.C.B. Mohr.
Struve, G. (1849/1980). *Geschichte der drei Volkserhebungen in Baden 1848/1849*, Bern: von Jenni; quoted from the revised reprint, Freiburg: Rombach.
Testa, J. (1997). *The ISI Database: The Journal Selection Process*, Essay No. 1, Philadelphia, Institute of Scientific Information.
Wagner-Döbler, R. and J. Berg (1996). 'Nineteenth-century mathematics in the mirror of its literature: a quantitative approach', *Historia Mathematica* **23**, 288–318.
Weingart, P., Strate, J. and M. Winterhager (1991). *Bibliometrisches Profil der DDR*, Report for the Science Council, Universitätsschwerpunkt Wissenschaftsforschung, University of Bielefeld.
Wengenroth, U. (1997). *Der Beitrag des Staates zu Forschung und Entwicklung in Deutschland seit der Reichsgründung*, Manuscript.
Ziegler, D. (2000). *Das Zeitalter der Industrialisierung*, in North (2000a), pp. 102–281.

12. Emergence and diffusion of disastrous innovations – a case study

Reiner Peter Hellbrück[1]

INTRODUCTION

The central statements are the following: (a) If the 'circumstances correspond with each other', then and only then there can be innovations.[2] Thesis (a) says that there have to be various conditions present and met so that their combination is sufficient for an innovation. The following conditions are met in the case study: (b) the increase of knowledge is essential, nonetheless it is not yet sufficient to explain the emergence and diffusion of the organisational innovation; (c) the organisational innovation corresponds to the preferences of decision makers and supporters; (d) the danger of disastrous consequences for competing firms adopting an organisational innovation are not sufficient to prevent its diffusion; (e) regarding the broader consensus about the societal advantages of an organisational innovation, the potential harm to business can be neutralised and moreover transformed into a competitive edge.

Case studies are only rare in economics. Usually the method of the participating observation is chosen. This case is different; it relates to the author's own personal work experience in the German health-care system. This working experience relates to the years 1998 until 2000 and the author also participated actively in some projects. The time-frame before July 1998, which is the main focus of this analysis, has neither been actively influenced nor affected by the author.

The focus is an organisational innovation and accompanying improvement innovations in diabetes care in Germany between the years 1993 and 2000. This care needs, according to experts' opinion, to be improved (Mehl, Becker-Berke und Müller-de-Cornejo 2000, p. 6 and Bertram 1999). An impression of problems caused by diabetes shows the following facts: approximately 1800 persons become blind annually, 9000 diabetes patients need to undergo enduring dialysis, 28 000 patients need amputations, and there is a three to four times higher risk of coronary heart diseases. Eighty per cent of the people with diabetes receive orally administered antidiabetic medical treatment (Laschet 1998).

Due to the problems of diabetes, in early 1993 contracts concerning diabetes patients were concluded between some health insurance funds and Regional Associations of Statutory Health Insurance Physicians (Kassenärztliche Vereinigung) which can be seen as precursors of rules and regulations to the current contracts (Mehl, Becker-Berke und Müller-de-Cornejo 2000, p. 9). Nowadays, contracts concerning better supply for diabetes patients can be found in each of Germany's federal states: between the years 1993 and 1998, 23 diabetes contracts were counted (Landgraf et al. 1999, ii). However, contracts can be distinguished between old and new types where the latter cover more knowledge about the long-run problems and consequences of diabetes. Information about the disease diabetes as well as the characteristics of different kinds of diabetes contracts will be summed up in the upcoming section 'Diabetes Contracts'.

In the year 1997, additional regulations were introduced by the Statutory Health Insurance Reorganisation laws (GKV[3]-Neuordnungsgesetze, GKV-NOG1 and GKV-NOG2). These revisions particularly concerned the so-called 'Modellvorhaben' (model projects) and 'Strukturverträge' (structure contracts) whereby health insurance funds and Regional Associations of Statutory Health Insurance Physicians were permitted projects to try new organisational forms which were not allowed under the regular law. These changes did not however trigger the new diabetes contracts. These changes in regulation will be described later on in the 'Regulation' section of the chapter.

Surprisingly, the organisational innovation was not introduced by the Allgemeine Ortskrankenkasse (AOK) (a big health insurance fund) which had the main influence in the development and introduction of the 'second-generation' diabetes contracts. The model was brought up first by an AOK competitor, the Barmer Ersatzkasse (BEK). The introduction of this new idea will be further discussed and explained in the 'Emergence' section. Additional health insurance funds, the innovator health insurance fund AOK included, are still practising in the 'second-generation' diabetes contracts. In the 'Diffusion' section the question of why the diabetes contracts were disastrous will be discussed and why those types of contracts still diffused. The section 'Continuation' is dedicated to the question why the diabetes contracts were not simply cancelled and which strategies were adopted to avoid harmful consequences or even to switch the disadvantage into a competitive edge. The most important insights are summed up in the section 'Conclusions'.

DIABETES CONTRACTS

Diabetes is an illness present in virtually every family. Approximately 5 per cent of the German population suffers from diabetes. Diverse illness patterns are the reason for distinguishing at least two types of diabetes: insulin-dependent diabetes mellitus (IDDM,) and non-insulin-dependent diabetes mellitus (NIDDM). The last mentioned is the most common type of diabetes and generally known as 'diabetes of the ageing' because this type emerges at about 35 years of age. In this case the disproportionate level of needed and available insulin usually has its reason in patients being overweight. One treatment is the reduction of the overweight condition.

IDDM has its origin in the malfunction of the human pancreas. This means that the demolished pancreas does not produce any insulin at all and it is speculated that this is caused by an auto-immune reaction. Accordingly, diabetes patients are dependent on the supply of insulin. It could be that a person with NIDDM becomes dependent on insulin as well but this person will not be filed as IDDM.

In general, IDDM is mostly diagnosed in the younger years: from childhood age up to 40 years; NIDDM manifests between the ages of 35 and older. Around 20 per cent of the population between the ages of 65 and 75 have diabetes. Diabetes is a chronic sickness which is correlated with the following diseases: cerebral apoplexy, cardiac infarct, blindness, kidney failure and amputation of toes, feet, and legs. For example, the most common main diagnosis of the AOK Magdeburg (a health insurance fund belonging to the community AOK)[4] is diabetes mellitus with approximately 3 per cent of all hospital cases (Robra et al. 1996). Diabetes mellitus is seen as an illness where methods for an effective treatment are available to delay or to avoid the expensive treatment of subsequent diseases. This is one reason why competing health insurance funds trying to cut costs are interested in improving diabetes care.

In the beginning, diabetes contracts contained only additional services of local doctors and/or hospitals, which were concluded between Regional Associations of Statutory Health Insurance Physicians (Kassenärzlichen Vereinigungen) and health insurance funds. The reason for this kind of contract was the insight concerning NIDDM patients that there is an inequality between needed and produced insulin. Hence, programmes were developed to improve the metabolism of diabetic patients (first-generation diabetes contracts). Usually, in these contracts, an additional amount had to be paid for such services.

Occasionally, so-called transfer fees were negotiated as well which means that in the case of a patient's transfer to a diabetes specialist, the referring family doctor will receive an additional compensation. Transfer lump sums were negotiated because family doctors feared to lose patients to specialists which would result in income losses. To compensate this fear, transfer fees were paid.

Second-generation diabetes contracts have the following characteristics. Additionally to the transfer fees of family doctors, return transfer fees for diabetes specialists have been negotiated. As the fear of family doctors was revealed to be real, return transfer fees should give diabetes specialists the incentive to refer back to the family doctor. On the other side, these fees should only be paid if certain transfer criteria, defined in the diabetes contract, were achieved. The transfer of a diabetes patient from the family doctor to a specialist in case of further vital treatment (training and examinations of the patient) should be obligatory. For example, it should be immediate as soon as the HbA/1c ratio shows a higher rate than 7.5 per cent within two or three sequential three-month periods or if the blood pressure exceeds certain limits determined in the diabetes contract. On the other side, there should also be a transferral of the patient from the specialist back to the family doctor as soon as the indispensable treatment was completed. Furthermore, criteria and instructions for treatment by family doctors and diabetes specialists respectively were contractually determined, so-called treatment instructions, which corresponded with the transfer criteria. Transfer criteria and treatment instructions created the treatment corridors (Scherbaum 1997, p. 45 presents a version differing considerably from the ones actually used). First-generation and second-generation diabetes contracts differ from each other in two factors. First, return transfer fees which should secure the patient's return from the specialist to the family doctor. The other factor is the definition of the treatment corridors.

REGULATION

The organisation of health insurance funds and health-care providers, the claims of the insured, as well as the relationships between insured, health insurance fund, and health-care provider are regulated by law and additional contracts. Health insurance funds, Regional Associations of Statutory Health Insurance Physicians and licensed hospitals are only allowed to close contracts based on laws and degrees (Verordnungen) as well as skeleton agreements (Rahmenvereinbarungen) concluded between their federal or regional associations. The most important source is the fifth book of the social legislation (i.e. Sozialgesetzbuch V, abbreviated by SGB V); for in-patient treatment additional legislation being relevant: the hospital financing law (Krankenhausfinanzierungsgesetz (KHG)) and the decree to regulate hospital financing in detail (Bundespflegeversatzordnung (BpflV)), especially the regulation of hospital budgets and fees.

Within the last few years, the most important rules and regulations in relation to diabetes contracts are the health-structure law (Gesundheitsstrukturgesetz (GStruktG)) of 12 December 1992,[5] the first Statutory Health Insurance Reorganisation law (GKV-NOG1) of 23 June 1997, the second Statutory Health Insurance Reorganisation law (GKV-NOG2) of 23 June 1997, the Statutory Health Insurance Solidarity Stabilisation Law (GKV-Solidaritsstärkungsgesetz) of 19 December 1998, as well as the Statutory Health Insurance Health reform law 2000 (GKV-Gesundheitsreformgesetz) of 22 December 1999. Especially the sections §§63–65 and §73a SGB V 1997 were the pillars for concluding diabetes contracts. Starting from 1 January 2000, a new type of contracts was made possible with paragraphs §§140a–h SGB V 2001. Since this change does not lie in the inspection period, this chapter will not further explain this voluminous regulation.

As early as 1993, health insurance funds had the opportunity to try new models and research.

> To improve and develop statutory health insurance, health insurance funds can examine benefits, measures, and procedures (even as models) based on the regulation of this section. Its goal should be to implement incentives to supply benefits at a reasonable price and not to waste scarce resources. (§63, SGB V 1993)

For the most part, the legislator had the implementation of elements of private health insurance in mind. For example, according to §65 SGB V 1993, an opportunity for health insurance funds was given, saying they could choose reimbursement of expenses instead of benefits in kind[6] to their insured.

Sections §§63 to 64 of the SGB V were completely restated in 1997 by the GKV-NOG2. In particular, the objective had changed through this legal amendment.

> To improve the quality of care and the economical supply of health care, health insurance funds and their associations can either carry out or arrange models according to §64 concerning procedures, organisation, financing, and reimbursement within the framework of its legal task. (§63 SGB V 1997)

In contracts which were concluded on the basis of §§63 and/or 64 SGB V 1997 deviations from Chapter 4 SGB V 1997, the hospital financing law and all regulations based on them were allowed. The financing of out-patient treatment as well as the medication area are regulated in Chapter 4 SGB V

1997. Compensation of in-patient treatment is also regulated in Chapter 4 SGB V 1997, the hospital financing law (KHG 2000), and in a decree called 'Bundespflegesatzverordnung' (BpflV 2000).

However, section §§63 SGB V 1997 is linked to contribution-rate stability (Beitragsatzstabilität) which had its validity in models based on §§63 and 64 SGB V 1997. The principle of contribution-rate stability states that:

> Concerted action gives recommendations to the treatment sectors and also to the variation of compensation. Recommendations can be given for the duration of one year and for a longer period too. The recommendations have to be formed such that an increase of the contribution rate will be avoided except where the necessary medical care cannot be guaranteed even if scarce resources are being used effectively (principle of contribution-rate stability). (§141, 2 SGB V 1997)

An additional characteristic of regulation §§63 and 64 SGB V 1997 was that models were limited to a time-frame of eight years. On the other side, structure contracts (Strukturverträge) introduced by the GKV-NOG2 1997 opened the possibility to restructure out-patient medical care permanently.

> Regional Associations of Statutory Health Insurance Physicians are able to agree upon supply and compensation structures with Regional Associations of Health Insurance Funds and Associations of Statutory Substitution Health Insurance Funds (Verbände der Ersatzkassen) with the aim to give the family doctor who was chosen by the patient responsibility for the quality of medical care and economical supply as well as responsibility for prescribed and disposed services. . . ., ... (§73a SGB V 1997)

This paragraph was included in the SGB V 1997 due to some activities of the Federal Association of Health Insurance Funds BKK (BKK means firm health insurance fund). In the mid 90s, this association set up a 'physician network with combined budgets' (Müller, Richard, and Schönbach 1999). Its aim was the realisation of cost savings through the co-ordination of medical activities.

In 1993, the health-structure law brought an additional important reform for health insurance funds. The responsibilities of health insurance funds and members' voting rights were changed so that future competition between health insurance funds became more and more fierce. However, this competition between health insurance funds did not take place until the year 1997. Without additional regulation it was feared that health insurance funds would compete for insurants with low risk of sickness. To prevent this, the Risk Structure Compensation Scheme (Risikostrukturausgleich abbreviated by RSA) was introduced (§266 SGB V 1993). No matter what characteristics a person admissible to the German Statutory Health System has, health insurance funds should have no incentive to prefer low-risk insurants.

With the GKV-NOG2, competition among health insurance funds has intensified. Regulation §175, 4 sentence 3 SGB V was changed into the following: 'If a health insurance fund increases its contribution rate or changes benefits as part of its conduct, a termination of the membership for the following month is possible, . . ., with a time period of a month beginning with the end of the following month of the day of the increase or the service change'(SGB V 1997). Moreover, if a health insurance fund increased its contribution rate, their insurants had to pay higher co-payments too. However, the legislator also defined that co-payments of the insurant would shrink, if their health insurance fund was going to reduce its contribution rate (§221 SGB V 1997). Regulation §221 SGB V 1997 was cancelled by the Solidarity Stabilisation Law of 19 December 1998.

Anyway, due to fierce competition among health insurance funds, the contribution rate became the most important decision variable for them. Nevertheless, migrations from health insurance funds with high contribution rates to those with low contribution rates appeared and took place very quickly. Some persons of the Federal Association of Health Insurance Funds AOK and others (Andersen and Schwarze 1999) feared to attract bad risks as a result of managed care.

EMERGENCE

Diabetes contracts of the first generation were signed and closed before and after the year 1997, when competition between health insurance funds intensified considerably (Meierjürgen 1994). Mehl, Becker-Berke and Müller de Cornejo (2000) talk about the precursor of the second-generation diabetes contracts: diabetes contracts in Brandenburg and Saxonia for the year 1993. These contracts already included extra budgeting payments to furnish diabetic services and training achievements. The first diabetes contract of the second generation took effect in 1998; it was concluded between the BEK (innovator health insurance fund) and the Associations of Statutory Health Insurance Physicians in Westphalia-Lip. Shortly after that, the innovator fund AOK concluded a second-generation diabetes contract with a minor health insurance fund (agricultural health insurance company) and the Associations of Statutory Health Insurance Physicians in Thuringia.

However, why did the diabetes contracts come into existence at all? There were several reasons. First of all, diabetes was back in everyone's mind and interest due to the St Vincent Declaration. Moreover, through the fall of the Berlin Wall in East Germany a development was unleashed which led to the first-generation diabetes contracts. Insufficiencies and inefficiencies of first-generation diabetes contracts gave enough reasons to revise the contracts. The new contracts were founded on evidence-based medicine (EbM), which means medical treatment upon medical, economic and scientific evidence. The basic idea of the second-generation diabetes contracts cannot be assigned retroactively to a certain person, but individual concern was a strong stimulus for the great personal engagement in the development process of diabetes contracts. The origin of those contracts can be described in detail as follows.

1. In 1989 the so-called 'St Vincent Declaration' was published. In this declaration goals were formulated to be achieved within five years for improving diabetes care. The goals were discussed, accepted and published by European government representatives, diabetes physicians, and representatives of patient associations in the town of St Vincent, Italy in 1989. For example, this proclamation demanded that within five years late consequences of diabetes should decline by one-third. These demands were supported by the World Health Organisation (WHO) and in Germany were also included in political discussions concerning health issues (Hellbrück 1997, pp. 27–8).
2. In former East Germany, the care of diabetic patients took place in special medical units, called 'Dispensaires' (not to be confused with dispensaries); family doctors were not involved in diabetes care. In the old states of West Germany, diabetes care was and still is a common task of local family doctors. After the fall of the Berlin Wall, the Western health-care system was spread over the new German states; now diabetes care were also delivered by family doctors and not any more by Dispensaires. Due to the introduction of this new system, health insurance funds feared a decline in quality of diabetes care in the new lands. This fear led to the first-generation diabetes contracts between the AOK and Associations of Statutory Health Insurance Physicians in the states of Brandenburg and Saxonia in 1993. The structure of diabetes care of the former East Germany was copied and additional diabetes centres were established.
3. However, a lack of co-operation between family physicians and specialists for diabetes care as well as between the out-patient and in-patient area was found (Mehl, Becker-Berke und Müller-de-Cornejo 2000). One reason for this lack of collaboration between the two kinds of physicians lay in the fear of the family doctor to lose patients through a transferral to a speciality physician which could result in a permanent income loss for the family doctor. To avoid this, family doctors referred diabetic patients to hospitals if patients' metabolic attitude visibly deteriorated or because of illnesses complications or for

pure economic reasons. Then, family doctors felt certain not to lose patients for long periods to more highly qualified persons (specialist physicians).

4. Parallel to this development, alternatives for NIDDM treatment were internationally examined for years in a long-term study (especially in Great Britain) in the framework of the famous UKPDS (start of the recruiting of test persons in 1977). This study showed that a better metabolism leads automatically to a significant reduction of subsequent diabetes diseases. For example, with the exception of cataracts it showed that diabetes-dependent complications could be decreased as a result of a person's lower blood pressure (Adler, Stratton, Neil and Yudkin 2000). This study confirmed hypotheses held for a long time and based on epidemiological studies (Ärzte-Zeitung 1998). In 1993, a guideline for the treatment of IDDM and a standard for the treatment of NIDDM already existed. At the beginning of the 90s and based on requests by a board of experts (Sachverständigenrat für die konzertierte Aktion im Gesundheitswesen) this progress was handed to German scientific-medical research institutes (AWMF) to develop medical guidelines. Since then, the AWMFs have already published several hundred guidelines. Due to the diverse quality of the established AWMF guidelines, the Federal Medical Association (Bundesärztekammer) and the Federal Association of Statutory Health Insurance Physicians (Kassenärztliche Bundesvereinigung) founded the Centre for Quality Assurance (Ärztliche Zentralstelle Qualitätssicherung) in the mid 90s to ensure the quality of medical guidelines (Ärztliche Zentralstelle Qualitätssicherung 1998). This health-political development resulted in an increasing interest by German physicians in assuring quality care (see also Hellbrück 1997 for additional information concerning quality assurance from an economic point of view).
5. On the initiative of the Federal Association of Health Insurance Funds AOK (AOK-BV) the Medical Advisory Council on Diabetes (Wissenschaftsrat Diabetes) was founded. However, a National Association of Health Insurance Funds may not become active without legal permission. According to §217 SGB V 2000, a National Association of Health Insurance Funds has to fulfil its legal tasks. The legislator firmly determined in §73, 1c SGB V 1993 that the content and extent of the medical care of family doctors is to be defined by the Federal Associations of Health Insurance Funds and the Federal Association of Statutory Health Insurance Physicians. This was the basis for the Federal Association of Health Insurance Funds AOK for defining family doctors' competencies. This paragraph was not only

used as an acting base but also as an essential impulse for the foundation of the Medical Advisory Council on Diabetes whereby the Federal Association of Statutory Health Insurance Physicians became, controversially to the legal order, not directly involved.

To found the Medical Advisory Council on Diabetes, some preparatory work started in 1996. Representatives of self-help groups, the president and additional representatives of the German Diabetes Society, the president of the Scientific Society of Family Doctors, representatives of Associations of Statutory Health Insurance Physicians, representatives of hospitals and family doctors and diabetes experts, and representatives of the AOK formed the Medical Advisory Council on Diabetes. Other health insurance companies were not represented. With this composition it is still active today, i.e. the organisations mentioned send further representatives, however it came to personnel changes. In January 1997 the Advisory Council on Diabetes began with the definition of the treatment corridors. The definition of the treatment corridors, which first included the family doctors and diabetic specialists and which were expanded to the the in-patient sector in 1999, were based on insights of EbM.

6. Without the large stake of the persons involved, the development and diffusion of the diabetes contracts of the second generation would not have been possible. In the AOK there were personalities who, due to personal concern, made the improvement of diabetes care their task. As diabetes is present in virtually every family, the same incentive may be present in other organisations too. For many years a representative of a Health Insurance Fund AOK strove for the improvement of diabetes care. For training a representative of the Federal Association of Health Insurance Funds AOK was sent into the Health Insurance Fund AOK and made subordinate to the representative mentioned. Both representatives laid claim to 'copyright' in the diabetes agreements of the second generation. From this co-operation and/or from co-operation of the Federal Association of Health Insurance Funds AOK with representatives of the Eastern Health Insurance Funds AOK, the philosophy of the second-generation diabetes contracts was developed. Hesse's (1990) idea according to which the emergence of knowledge passes several selection stages, thus approaches reality.
7. Within the Federal Association of Health Insurance Funds AOK the diabetes contracts were disputed. The department manager responsible refused the conclusion of the diabetes contracts of the second-generation, however without success. How is this to be explained? The governing board of the Federal Association of Health Insurance Funds AOK (Verwaltungsrat des AOK Bundesverbandes) had taken

an unequivocal stand on intensified efforts to improve prevention (on the self-understanding of members of the governing board, see Henkel (1999) and Becker (1999)). The diabetes contracts, in particular the diabetes contracts of the second-generation, were welcomed on the part of the governing board (Nachtigall 1997, p. 18). The managing committee of the Federal Association of Health Insurance Funds AOK as well as the managing committee of the Regional Association of Health Insurance Funds AOK are elected by their respective governing boards AOK (§§215, 209, 209a SGB V 2000 and §35a, 5 SGB IV 2000).

In particular the governing board has to make all decisions which are of fundamental importance for its health insurance fund. Additionally, it has to represent the health insurance fund in relation to the managing committee. Furthermore, as the members of the governing board are representatives of the employer or of the employee side, they have an incentive to represent the interests of the insurants which explains the preference of the governing board for prevention. Due to this preference, it is clear why the department manager responsible did not gain a hearing at the managing committee AOK. The governing board of the Federal Association of Health Insurance Funds AOK consists of representatives of the governing boards of all Regional Associations of Health Insurance Funds AOKs. Thus it may be speculated that the influence of the governing boards on the managing committees of their regional AOKs was similar to that on the federal level.

Besides, the responsible employee of the Federal Association of Health Insurance Funds AOK also electioneered outside of his regular work-time for the diabetes contracts of the second generation. In the end, virtually all relevant health politicians at federal level and almost all influential persons in the German Health Care System were informed about and unusually interested in the new possibilities in health-care management.

8. As the foundation of the Medical Advisory Council on Diabetes started in 1996, that is about one year before the Statutory Health Insurance Reorganisation laws passed in the parliament, it can fairly be alleged that legal conditions changed, but these changes cannot be regarded as the cause of the emergence of the diabetes contracts of the second generation. In 1996 the persons participating in the development process of the second-generation diabetes contracts could not know the concrete contents of the amendment happening one year later. However the amendment, the so-called third stage of the German health-care reform, was expected, so that the BKK could operate its

'physician network with combined budgets' beyond its testing phase. As the diabetes contracts can be understood as a special physician network, that is a diagnosis-specific practice network, justified hope existed of being able to implement the organisational innovation.

The reasons leading to the emergence of the diabetes contracts of the second generation can be summarised as follows. Calling attention to a problem of great importance (St Vincent Declaration, fear of a deterioration of diabetes care in the new lands of Germany); development of a solution with consideration of existing structures (diabetes agreement of the first-generation); discovery of the weak points of this solution and efforts to solve the problems; infusion of new knowledge (new scientific insights and foundation of the Medical Advisory Council on Diabetes); large stake of persons concerned with diabetes care and similar preferences of decision makers, whereby it may be that the preferences of the decision makers were affected by the efforts of some few persons. Though the changing law was surely a necessary condition for the innovation, it can hardly be regarded as its cause.

DIFFUSION

Now the diffusion of the second-generation diabetes contracts is outlined without laying claim to completeness. In 1998 in Thuringia (AOK and Agricultural Health Insurance Fund), Suedwuerttemberg (AOK, other health insurance funds are not known), in Westphalia Lip (BEK), North Rhine (BKK, later joined by the AOK), Saxonia and Bavaria (all health insurance funds) second-generation diabetes contracts were concluded.

Why did the innovation diffuse at such a great speed? The fast propagation within the AOK community is due to the short information paths and due to the problems of diabetes care in the new lands of Germany. Every health insurance fund is a public corporation (§4 SGB V 2000), furthermore it is however, due to §207 SGB V 2000, a conscripted member of a Regional Association of Health Insurance Funds, and this is in turn an obligatory member of a Federal Association of Health Insurance Funds (§212 SGB V 2000). One task of the federal associations is, among others, consultation with and information to its members (§217 SGB V 2000). To fulfil these obligations, work meetings regularly took place in federal associations, in which representatives of the federal and regional associations participated, whereby the information about the organisational innovation spread fast.

How could the information about the new type of diabetes contracts arrive at other health insurance funds? The innovation could not remain hidden. In the Medical Advisory Council on Diabetes there were beside scientists and representatives of the AOK also representatives of the Regional Associations of Statutory Health Insurance Physicians, who were the only contracting parties of health insurance funds at that time in out-patient treatment. Furthermore, representatives of family doctors were on the Medical Advisory Council on Diabetes, and they had expressed a great interest in a demarcation of the family doctors from medical specialists.

On what legal basis were diabetes agreements concluded? A playing field was opened to the health insurance funds by allowing model projects in order to accomplish such projects or to conclude contracts with Associations of Statutory Health Insurance Physicians for supplying benefits, for example prevention programmes, which were not statutory benefits (§63, 2 SGB V 1997). Diabetes contracts of the second generation were usually concluded on this legal basis. There were two reasons for this: (1) the financing risks of the health insurance funds were limited to eight years by law (this rule based on the GKV-NOG2 in 1997); (2) additionally, without extra budgeting payments, the conclusion of diabetes contracts would not have been possible and §63 SGB V (1997) created this very possibility.

Nevertheless contribution-rate stability was to be considered. This meant that health insurance funds and Regional Associations of Statutory Health Insurance Physicians had to shape their agreements about remuneration in such a way that a rise of the contribution rate was usually excluded. If necessary medical supply was not possible even after 'exhaustion of economic reserves', increasing contribution rates were however allowed. The reason for this rule was increasing contribution rates in the past (i.e. before 1997) which, as regards the policy, were sometimes dammed up by drastic means (for example by the strict budgeting of the in-patient sector by the Health Structure Law (Tuschen and Quaas 1995). Contribution-rate stability was however not violated, if there were 'additional expenses caused by a model project being balanced by savings due to that model project. This balance has to be proven' (§63, 3 sentence 2 SGB V 1997). This formulation permits two interpretations: (a) increasing expenses and savings temporarily fallen apart or (b) increasing expenses and savings taking place at the same time. Since the primary reason for the diabetes contracts was to avoid subsequent diseases, it was to be assumed that additional expenses result today and possible savings arise tomorrow.

The conclusion of contracts based on §§63–65 SGB V 1997 with extra budgeting payments would not have been possible with a strict interpretation of the legal basis. The contracting parties (in particular the health insurance funds) had despite the possibility of the cancellation of regulations laid down in Chapter 4 SGB V 1997 to consider contribution-rate stability. But the formulation in §63, 3 sentence 2 SGB V 1997 left open whether savings have to be proven ex post or ex ante. In the diabetes contracts extra budgeting payments were agreed upon that were to be disbursed during the run-time of the model projects. Thus the financing risk of the diabetes contracts had to be borne by the contracting health insurance funds.

On the other hand, to convince their member physicians, the Associations of Statutory Health Insurance Physicians had to insist on extra budgeting payments, otherwise the conclusion of second-generation diabetes contracts would have not been possible. As in 1998 health insurance funds could only conclude diabetes contracts with Associations of Statutory Health Insurance Physicians on the basis of §§63–65 and 73a SGB V (1997), extra budgeting payments were inevitable for the conclusion of diabetes contracts. Though §64, 2 SGB V 1997 permitted the conclusion of model projects between health insurance funds and contract physicians (i.e. physicians allowed to treat insurants of health insurance funds) without participation of of the Associations of Statutory Health Insurance Physicians (the so-called quorum regulation), the condition for this was the definition of the principles for executing model projects between Federal Associations of Statutory Health Insurance Funds and the Federal Association of Statutory Health Insurance Physicians (§64, 2 sentence 1 SGB V 1997) which was never realised.

Why, however, were diabetes contracts concluded at all although the financing risk was borne exclusively by the contracting health insurance funds? It was referred to the large amount of diabetic persons (5 to 6 million are diagnosed in Germany) and the associated treatment costs as well as on the associated savings potentials (Mehl, Becker-Berke und Müller-de-Cornejo 2000, p. 5 and Ahrens 1997). As early as in November 1997, before the negotiations of the AOK for diabetes contracts in Thuringia were finished, the chairman of the managing committee of the Federal Association of Health Insurance Funds AOK did not leave any doubt during a public event that the AOK would conclude diabetes contracts of the second-generation (Ahrens 1997, p. 51).

Were the diabetes contracts of the second generation disastrous at all if evaluated from the viewpoint of the Health Insurance Funds as announced in the heading of this contribution? The answer to this question is simplified by defining the term 'disastrous'. Disastrous innovations are in our context business-damaging. Being business-damaging has two dimensions: on the one hand the competition of health insurance funds into private health insurance companies and on the other hand the competition within the group of health insurance funds are affected. A health insurance fund behaves in a business-damaging way, if its competition position worsens compared to other health insurance funds or to private health insurance companies.

In order to discover what is business-damaging, it is worthwhile to differentiate strictly between costs and expenditures. Additionally, it is necessary to make clear, who incurs costs, who has cost-cuts, whose expenditures increase and whose expenditures are reduced. Diabetes is a costly illness because of associated subsequent costs. As explained earlier in the chapter, the most important subsequent diseases are diabetic feet, kidney failure, cardiac infarct, going blind and cerebral apoplexy. These subsequent diseases develop within ten years due to bad metabolic adjustment and were often treated in hospitals. If a second-generation diabetes contract was to be successful, the improvement of the metabolic adjustment and accompanying reduction of subsequent diseases and in-patient costs would take place after several years.

Second-generation diabetes contracts are a means to strengthen prevention to either avoid subsequent diseases or to postpone their development. Prevention is part of out-patient treatment. Diabetes contracts of the second generation not only consist of a job-sharing idea between home doctor and diabetes specialist, they comprise also quality management (Hellbrück 2000). The development of the necessary structures requires extensive settlements which haven't been concluded yet. The settlements bear on the development of a new database, the implementation of necessary software in medical practices, the compatibility of the software used, and changes in the working organisation in doctors' offices. An improved metabolism causes additional costs in the drugs area. Because of this doctors, Associations of Statutory Health Insurance Physicians, and Health Insurance Funds today face costs.

Associations of Statutory Health Insurance Physicians are often ready to bear a part of the costs for their internal reorganisation, but these costs are usually not accompanied by expenses. In addition, extra budgeting payments lead today to higher expenses and costs for the Health Insurance Funds. Though in-patient costs will be reduced by diabetes contracts, the existing regulation does not allow health insurance funds to change these cost savings into expense reductions for health insurance funds. As a result, diabetes contracts lead to higher contribution rates, worsening their competition position: these contracts are disastrous. This is especially true for health insurance funds in the new lands; their financial situation between 1997 and 2000 was very fraught.

A prerequisite for the implementation of model projects was the alteration of the statute of health insurance funds, i.e. benefits supplied by model projects were so-called 'statute benefits'. Expenses for statute benefits, as well as for such benefits for which patients have no right to claim, are left out in the Risk Structure Compensation Scheme. This means additional expenses from diabetes contracts not being balanced by the Risk

Structure Compensation Scheme which make it even harder to compete with others.

Furthermore, from the perspective of a health insurance fund a diabetic person represents a high risk even if he/she has a good metabolism; that is the amount of coverage of diabetic persons is negative. Nevertheless, the diabetes contracts were published in the form of press briefings, press statements and brochures. It is however not known to what extent diabetic persons were attracted by those contracts.

The attraction of bad risks by diabetes contracts is related to the number and the contribution rate of the participating insurance companies. If an insurance company makes a contract in a particular area without the participation of another insurance company, it has to carry all the risk by itself. If all insurance companies from one area are contracting partners in a diabetes contract, the competition doesn't change within this group but in relation to private health insurance companies; nevertheless, a good marketing campaign for the diabetes contract by a health insurance fund with high contribution rates can leave health insurance funds with low contribution rates much affected by diabetic insurants.

CONTINUATION

At the end there is still the question, why diabetes contracts were not cancelled by health insurance funds as the negative effects were identified. The answer to that question cannot be given with complete certainty. It is possible that the harm to the companies hasn't been recognised. Against this interpretation is the fact, that within the Federal Association of Health Insurance Funds AOK and BEK criticism arose, which included the effects of diabetes contracts on competition.

The following interpretation is more likely. The Regional Associations of Statutory Health Insurance Physicians were, without any doubts, interested in continuing these contracts. If a diabetes contract had been cancelled by the Health Insurance Funds, a public éclat initiated by the Regional Associations of Statutory Health Insurance Physicians would certainly have happened. Additionally, the personal interests of the decision makers were not negatively affected, and/or the harm to the business was evaluated as too small.

This point of view is supported by the fact that the first AOK diabetes contract of the second generation in Thuringia was over on 31 March 2001. An ensuing contract is being negotiated and till its conclusion the existing contract will be used. Another fact is that diabetes contracts of the second generation in general replaced diabetes contracts of the first generation. It looks as though existing extra-budgeting payments paid for first-generation diabetes contracts were replaced by higher-quality second-generation diabetes contracts. The Regional Associations of Statutory Health Insurance Physicians secure extra payments and the representatives of health insurance funds could justify the continuation of extra budgeting payments by higher-quality care. This explains also why there was no limitation on some regions, for example the new German states, within the AOK community.

It also needs to be stated that the damaging of business has a time dimension: what does damage in the short run, might not impair in the long run. Health insurance funds concluding diabetes contracts damage their business in the short run, as it has to afford extra-budgeting payments nowadays, without getting them paid back at the next day. Contracts based on §§63–65 SGB V will not be considered in the Risk Structure Compensation Scheme and the danger of additional bad risks and of accompanying increasing contribution rates is possible. Any health insurance fund taking part in a diabetes contract has to face these consequences. Subject to the relative number of diabetic patients participating in a diabetes contract, the market position of the contracting health insurance funds changes even within this group. The Federal Insurance Office (Bundesversicherungsamt) makes it clear: 'A health insurance fund which has an excellent quality management of expensive diseases could economically commit suicide' (quoted according to Jacobs et al. 2001, p. 46, footnote 2).

Health insurance funds have more possibilities than cancelling a contract. One strategy is to keep up a good relationship with the legislator, for example acting on behalf of insurants with chronic diseases. To build a good relationship with state institutions is very important for health insurance funds insuring a lot of bad risks compared to their competitors, e.g. health insurance funds AOK, BEK. Moreover, some persons who developed the second-generation diabetes contracts as representatives of health insurance funds changed their job in 1998/99 and obtained new jobs as representatives of physicians' organisations. For example, one person became managing director of an association of physicians, another gained an executive position at the Federal Association of Statutory Health Insurance Physicians. Though these job changes changed their arguments, they tried furthermore to improve diabetes care but with significant room for manoeuvre. Sometimes it takes some time until important views are accepted by health politicians and decision makers. Once in a while they need to be pushed to revise their old convictions.

This push came from experts' opinions on the Risk Structure Compensation Scheme. One advisory opinion was commissioned by the Federal Government (Jacobs et al. 2001), the other (Lauterbach and Wille 2001) from Federal Associations of Health Insurance Funds (that is

AOK-BV, VDAK/VEK, and IKK-BV) whose insurants represent bad risks. Both statements complain about insufficient quality management of chronic diseases, especially the advisory opinion commissioned by some Federal Associations of Health Insurance Funds who point out the deficits in this particular area.

Because of these statements a revision of the Risk Structure Compensation Scheme was required (Ahrens 2001). Those demands and the advisory opinions induced the government to revise the Risk Structure Compensation Scheme. The Ministry of Health wanted to open the possibility of chronic disease-management programmes. Since 1 January 2002, 30 per cent of the costs should be borne by the health insurance fund which insures the person (that is a 'co-payment' of the health insurance fund) and the other 70 per cent of the treatment costs should be paid by the 'Solidarity Community' (that is all health insurance funds). All these disease-management programmes have to be certified by a neutral, nationwide certification institution and all participating patients must register in the programmes. In the long run the introduction of a morbidity oriented Risk Structure Compensation Scheme is wanted.

To evaluate forthcoming disease-management programmes based on the new regulation of the Risk Structure Compensation Scheme is not yet possible, as there is too little information about this. We can however say that the Risk Structure Compensation Scheme may turn out to be an expenditure compensation scheme; all the better will morbidity be mapped (Rürup 2001). Three possible scenarios can be distinguished: (a) health insurance funds insuring especially bad risks get a competitive edge, other health insurance funds are the losers; (b) the opposite of case (a) will happen; (c) the competition between health insurance funds does not change. In the long run it turns out that only in the borderline case (c) could the harmful effects on health insurance funds be avoided. It is however unclear whether extra budgeting payments will pay for themselves and thus the position in the competition process of contracting health insurance funds improve compared to private health insurance.

CONCLUSIONS

Altogether we can say, firstly, that the knowledge increase was not sufficient for the innovation (thesis (b)). Secondly, the changing legal conditions in the Statutory Health Insurance Reorganisation laws in 1997 cannot be regarded as the cause either for the emergence or the diffusion of the second-generation diabetes contracts as these changes were after the first developments of the second-generation diabetes contracts. On the contrary the existing first-generation contracts caused the Regional Associations of Statutory Health Insurance Physicians to take an interest in continuing the contracts, which was not contrary to the personal interests of the decision makers in health insurance funds. If someone would like to see some kind of path dependency, it could be accepted.

Thirdly, to argue that these diabetes contracts were initiated as part of a general strategy of some health insurance funds to change the Risk Structure Compensation Scheme is not convincing. Diabetes contracts were developed and implemented to avoid subsequent diseases and their costs, however, without differentiating between costs and expenditures. These goals have not changed since the statements of Lauterbach and Wille (2001). Besides that the first-generation diabetes contracts were concluded before the Risk Structure Compensation Scheme were invented and implemented at all. The immense improvements to these contracts realised by the second-generation contracts were a nice possibility to continue the old contracts. An even fiercer competition between the health insurance funds who competed for good risks made necessary a revision of the legal conditions, especially of the Risk Structure Compensation Scheme. Additionally, the change in the German government in 1999 and the accompanying shift in health politics (especially the wish to improve quality medical care, see Bundesministerium für Gesundheit 2000) could not be foreseen some years ago.

Fourthly, every contract partner of diabetes contracts usually had the alternative to cancel the contract even during running-time. The short-term business-damaging effects would thus have been avoided. In public discussions which would most likely have taken place, the companies could have pointed out allocative distortions and could have initiated a change in the statutory conditions. This is further evidence that personal preferences of some representatives were crucial in this process (thesis (c)). In addition, systematic business-damaging behaviour is no exclusion criterion for an innovation (thesis (d)). To prove this, one example has to be given; and we just did so. Though the innovation might be disastrous from the perspective of a health insurance fund, all circumstances corresponded to each other (particularly the preferences) in that the innovation was evaluated as socially desirable (thesis (d)).

NOTES

1. I would like to thank Frank Engelmann for his helpful comments. The first translation of the German original (Hellbrück 2003) was made by some busy students: Christian Haas, Patricia Wlodarczak, Dirk Enskat, and Ina Wunderlich; nevertheless, I am responsible for

the remaining errors. This work reflects solely the opinion of the author. The chapter relates to the developments up to May 2001.

2. Statement of Albrecht Dietz, a 'Schumpeter' entrepreneur.
3. 'GKV' is the abbreviation for statutory health insurance.
4. In Germany we distinguish various types of health insurance funds (§§143–171 SGB V 1997): Allgemeine Ortskrankenkassen (AOK), Betriebskrankenkassen (BKK), Innungskrankenkassen (IKK), See-Krankenkassen, Landwirtschaftliche Krankenkassen, Bundesknappschaft, Ersatzkassen. Each health insurance fund is a member of exactly one type which is determined by law.
5. The date given shows the time of the publication in the federal law paper. In most cases, the day of publication and the date of introduction and enforcement are not the same.
6. Benefits in kind are one principle of the German statutory health system. Everybody should pay according to his abilities and everybody should get equal access to the health care system and equal health care. To accomplish this, benefits in kind are seen as fundamental; reimbursements would break the principle as healthier people would not pay anymore according to their abilities.

REFERENCES

Adler, A., I. Stratton, H. Neil and J. Yudkin (2000), 'Association of systolic blood pressure with macrovascular and microvascular complications of type 2 diabetes (UKPDS 36): prospective observational study', *British Medical Journal*, **321**, 412–19.

Ahrens, H.J. (1997), 'Ökonomische Anreizsysteme – Herausforderungen und Chancen', in AOK-Bundesverband (ed.), *AOK im Dialog; Qualität und Wirtschaftlichkeit – Neue Wege gemeinsamer Verantwortung*, Bonn, pp. 49–54.

Ahrens, H.J. (2001), Pressekonferenz zu AOK im Dialog 'Weiterentwicklung des Risikostrukturausgleichs', Berlin, 15 March 2001, AOK-Bundesverband.

Andersen, H. and J. Schwarze (1999), 'Kassenwahlentscheidungen in der GKV', *Arbeit und Sozialpolitik*, **53**, 10–23.

Ärzte-Zeitung (15 September, 1998): 'Endlich Klarheit für die Behandlung von Typ-II-Diabetikern in der Praxis'.

Ärztliche Zentralstelle Qualitätssicherung (1998), 'Checkliste "Methodische Qualität von Leitlininen" 1. Version: Gültigkeit: 1.2.1998–31.1.1999', *Deutsches Ärzteblatt*, **95**, B-2014-B-20116.

Becker, J. (1999), 'Drei-Klassen-Medizin darf es nicht geben', *Gesundheit und Gesellschaft*, **2**, 44–5.

Bertram, B. (1999), 'Zusammenarbeit von Hausarzt und Augenarzt in der Diabetikerbetreuung. Kommunikation unerläßlich', *Deutsches Ärzteblatt*, **96**, B-2450-B-2454.

Bundesministerium für Gesundheit (2000), 'Begründung zum Entwurf eines "Gesetzes zur Strukturreform der gesetzlichen Krankenversicherung" im Jahr 2000'.

Hellbrück, R.P. (1997), *Qualität und Ausgaben in der medizinischen Versorgung – Von Qualitätssicherung und Kosteneffizienz zu mehr Wettbewerb im Gesundheitswesen?*, Berlin: Duncker & Humblot.

Hellbrück, R.P. (2000), 'EDV-gestütztes Qualitätsmanagement in Praxisnetzen', *Das Gesundheitswesen*, **62**, 511–15.

Hellbrück, R.P. (2003), 'Entstehung und Ausbreitung geschäftsschädigender

Innovationen: ein Fallbeispiel', in Kurt Dopfer (ed), *Studien zur Evolutorischen Ökonomik Band VII*, Berlin: Duncker & Humblot, pp. 219–41.

Henkel, H. (1999), 'Selbstverwaltung ist ein Modell mit Zukunft', *Gesundheit und Gesellschaft*, **2**, 42–3.

Hesse, G. (1990), 'Evolutorische Ökonomik oder Kreativität in der Theorie', in U. Witt (ed.), *Studien zur Evolutorischen Ökonomik I*, Berlin: Duncker & Humblot, pp. 49–73.

Jacobs, K., P. Reschke, D. Cassel amd J. Wasem (2001), *Zur Wirkung des Risikostrukturausgleichs in der gesetzlichen Krankenversicherung: Eine Untersuchung im Auftrag des Bundesministeriums für Gesundheit. Endbericht*, Berlin, Duisburg, Greifswald: IGES, Gerhard-Mercartor-Universität Duisburg, Ernst-Moritz-Arndt Universität Greifswald, 15 February.

Landgraf, R. et al. (1999), 'Diskussionsentwurf Regelungsbedürftige Vertragsinhalte von Diabetesvereinbarungen – eine Initiative des DQI-Ausschusses der DDG', *Diabetes und Stoffwechsel. Zeitschrift für angewandte Diabetologie*, **8** ii-vi.

Laschet, M. (1998), 'Erstmals flächendeckende und optimale Diabetikerversorgung in Bayern', *Bayerisches Ärzteblatt*, **53** (8).

Lauterbach, K. and W. Wille (2001), *Modell eines fairen Wettbewerbs durch den Risikostrukturausgleich. Sofortprogramm 'Wechselkomponente' und 'solidarische Rückversicherung' unter Berücksichtigung der Morbidität. Abschlußbericht*, expert's opinion commissioned by Verband der Angestellten-Krankenkassen e-V. (VdAK), Arbeiter-Ersatzkassenverband (AEV), AOK-Bundesverband (AOK-BV) and IKK-Bundesverband (IKK-BV); obtainable at www.vdak.de

Mehl, E., S. Becker-Berke and G. Müller-de-Cornejo (2000), *Einführung eines Disease-Managements am Beispiel Diabetes*, Bonn: KomPart.

Meierjürgen, R. (1994), 'Gesundheitsförderung und Krankenkassenwettbewerb. Die Auswirkungen des Gesundheitsstruktur-Gesetzes', *Arbeit und Sozialpolitik*, **48**, 58–64.

Müller, M., S. Richard and K. Schönbach (1999), 'Erste Jahresbilanz zeigt: Kombiniertes Budget hat sich bewährt', in *Die BKK*, pp. 585–90.

Nachtigall, G. (1997), 'Rationale Medizin – Ein Beitrag zur Zukunftssicherung der sozialen Krankenversicherung', in AOK-Bundesverband (ed.), *AOK im Dialog; Qualität und Wirtschaftlichkeit – Neue Wege gemeinsamer Verantwortung*, Bonn, pp. 13–18.

Robra, B. et al. (1996), *Krankenhausfallanalyse. Die stationäre Versorgung von Versicherten der AOK*, Magdeburg and Sankt Augustin: Asgard-Verlag Dr Werner Hippe KG.

Rürup, B. (2001), *Die Reform des Risikostrukturausgleichs im Rahmen der Vorstellungen der 'Fünf Weisen' zur Gesundheitspolitik*. Berlin: AOK-Kongress: Reform des RSA, 15 March.

Scherbaum, W. (1997), 'Schnittstellenmonitoring durch Qualitätsindikatoren: Neue Konzepte zur Verbesserung der Versorgung von Diabetikern', in AOK-Bundesverband (ed.), *Qualität und Wirtschaftlichkeit – Neue Wege gemeinsamer Verantwortung*, Bonn, pp. 33–47.

SGB IV, 2000, Sozialgesetzbuch IV vom 23.12.1976 (BGBl. fI S. 3845), zuletzt geändert durch Gesetz vom 22.12.1999 (BGBl. I S 2601) und 20.12.1999 (BGBl. I S. 2), 2000.

SGB V 1993, Sozialgesetzbuch V – Gesetzliche Krankenversicherung – vom 20. Dezember 1988, BGBl. I S. 2477 zuletzt geändert durch das Gesundheitsstrukturgesetz *vom 21. 12. 1992*, BGBl. I S. 226. 1992.

SGB V 1997, Sozialgesetzbuch V – Gesetzliche Krankenversicherung – vom 20. Dezember 1988, BGBl. I S. 2477 zuletzt geändert durch das 1. Und 2. GKV Neuordnungsgesetz vom 23.6.1997 (BGBl I S. 1518 u. S. 1520).

SGB V 2000, Sozialgesetzbuch V – Gesetzliche Krankenversicherung – vom 20. Dezember 1988, BGBl. I S. 2477, Artikel 1), zuletzt geändert durch Gesetz vom 21.7.1999 (BGBl. I S. 1648), 22.12.1999 (BGBl. I S. 2534), 22.12.1999 (BGBl. I S. 2626) und 22.12.1999 (BGBl. I S. 2657), 2000.

SGB V 2000, Sozialgesetzbuch V – Gesetzliche Krankenversicherung – vom 20. Dezember 1988, BGBl. I S. 2477, Artikel 1), zuletzt geändert durch Gesetz vom 21.7.1999 (BGBl. I S. 1648), 22.12.1999 (BGBl. I S. 2534), 22.12.1999 (BGBl. I S. 2626) und 22.12.1999 (BGBl. I S. 2657), 2000.

SGB V 2001, Sozialgesetzbuch V Gesetzliche Krankenversicherung [SGB V] vom 20.12.1988 (BGBl. I p. 2477, Artikel 1), zuletzt geändert durch Gesetz vom 21.12.2000 (BGBl. I S 1971), 2001.

Tuschen, K. and M. Quaas (1995), *Bundespflegesatzverordnung Kommentar mit einer umfassenden Einführung in das Recht der Krankenhausfinanzierung*, Stuttgart, Berlin, Cologne: W. Kohlhammer.

13. Applying evolutionary economics to public policy – the example of competitive federalism in the EU

Wolfgang Kerber

1. INTRODUCTION

One of the major problems of evolutionary economics is its difficult and unclarified relationship to public policy questions.[1] Often the problem arises that evolutionary reasonings can be used rather well for a sound critique of a wide range of policy recommendations. But due to the evolutionary argument of the openness of economic processes and the resulting Hayekian knowledge problem it seems often very difficult to derive positive policy proposals from evolutionary reasonings – leading to the danger of a general retreat from policy discussions. In this chapter it is suggested that evolutionary economics should take a pragmatic approach to economic policy questions:

1. Evolutionary economics should be pragmatic in a methodological sense, i.e. that in an ever-changing world economic policy can and has to be made despite the impossibility of eliminating all uncertainties in regard to its effects.
2. Evolutionary economics should not restrict itself to theoretical and basic research but should also do research about the application of evolutionary reasonings to the solving of real-world problems including participation in policy discussions.
3. For applying evolutionary arguments to policy questions we have to find a pragmatic way to combine evolutionary with neoclassical arguments, which to a certain degree will remain indispensable for many real-world problems.

Instead of discussing these demands on evolutionary economics on a methodological or theoretical level, I would like to show in regard to a specific, hotly discussed policy question, how evolutionary economics can be productively applied to economic policy. The policy problem is the question of the future institutional development of the EU in regard to centralization and decentralization. The allocation of competencies to the EU level on one hand and on the national level of the EU member states on the other hand is one of the most important problems in the process of European integration. From an economic point of view the theory of fiscal federalism offers criteria for the optimal vertical allocation of competencies. In this chapter I will argue that the perspective of evolutionary economics will provide crucial additional arguments in favour of a greater decentralization of competencies, because from an evolutionary perspective a more decentralized system will be characterized by more innovativeness and adaptability than a more centralized federal system. On the theoretical level, the implications will be that the originally neoclassical theory of fiscal federalism has to be supplemented by evolutionary reasonings in regard to the innovation and diffusion of public policies. This will lead to the proposal of an evolutionary concept of competitive federalism as the appropriate theoretical basis for deciding on the vertical allocation of competencies in the EU.

The chapter is structured as follows: In section 2 a short introduction is given into the problem of centralization and decentralization in the EU. Section 3 presents a short overview of the well-established neoclassical theories of federalism and interjurisdictional competition before they are critically examined from an evolutionary perspective in section 4. Particularly important is section 5, in which both explicit and implicit evolutionary contributions to the theory of federalism and interjurisdictional competition are presented. These reasonings are used for the sketching of a pragmatic approach to competitive federalism (and the problem of the appropriate vertical allocation of competencies in a federal multilevel system) in section 6, which entails both neoclassical and evolutionary criteria. In section 7 some brief implications are deduced for our policy problem of centralization and decentralization in the EU, before in section 8 some general conclusions are drawn as to how policy questions should be dealt with from the perspective of evolutionary economics.

2. THE POLICY PROBLEM: CENTRALIZATION VERSUS DECENTRALIZATION WITHIN THE EU

The problem of the future institutional development of the European Union is one of the most important topics in economic policy in Europe. The specific problems of the enlargement of the European Union and the inevitable reform of European institutions and decision processes (European Commission, majority decisions etc.) are well known. But at least as important as these topics is the question how centralized or decentralized the European Union should be in the long run.

The debate on centralization and decentralization in the EU is characterized by the tension between two tendencies:

1. There can be no doubt that the large efforts of the EU to complete the European internal market by breaking up many barriers to national markets and to introduce competition in many industries, which for decades were monopolized in the member states (as e.g. telecommunication and energy markets), were a huge success. In that respect the policies of the European Commission (internal-market programme) and also the European Court of Justice ('Cassis de Dijon' judgment) to enforce the four basic freedoms (freedom of goods, services, labour, and capital) by removing national non-tariff barriers to trade were very helpful. This was carried out partly by introducing the principle of mutual recognition of national regulations and partly by (minimum) harmonization of regulations. To some degree also European Monetary Union with the introduction of the Euro as single currency can be seen in this perspective of promoting the European internal market. Consequently, many efforts on the EU level that simultaneously implied a pushing back of the competencies of the member states, were important for enforcing competition of European markets.
2. But the observed tendencies to centralization in the EU are also evaluated very critically both by European citizens and politicians on one hand and by economists and legal scholars on the other. Increasing dangers of intransparency and lack of monitoring by the citizens, bureaucratization, and mounting rent-seeking problems are suggested (Vaubel 1995, 1997). There are widespread preferences in the European population for a high degree of decentralization that limit considerably the acceptance of additional shiftings of competencies to the European level. The increasing heterogeneity within the EU – due to the enlargement by mostly much less developed Middle and East European countries – will reinforce this problem. So the introduction of the principle of subsidiarity in the Treaty of Maastricht can be seen as an important political sign against too quick and often too unreflective tendencies of centralization and harmonization in the EU.

But the problem of the best vertical allocation of competencies between the EU and the member states is still unsolved. How is it possible to maintain a high degree of decentralization and heterogeneity within the EU without impeding the achievement of the aim of European integration? This has remained an open question both in public and academic discussions.

Neither political scientists, legal scholars nor economists have developed convincing elaborated concepts of how European integration can be realized without giving up decentralization and variety to a large degree. To answer this question a careful balancing of the advantages and disadvantages of centralization and decentralization of competencies is required.

3. ECONOMIC THEORIES OF FEDERALISM AND INTERJURISDICTIONAL/REGULATORY COMPETITION AS A POSSIBLE ANSWER

From a theoretical perspective, the problem of centralization and decentralization in the EU can be conceived as the question of how the competencies of the state should be allocated within a federal multilevel system of jurisdictions (with the levels EU, the member states, regions, and municipalities). For solving this problem of the optimal vertical allocation of competencies, we can use the criteria of the well-established economic theory of fiscal federalism, which has been developed in the public finance literature since the 1960s.[2] From this perspective, policies which attempt to achieve aims of macro-economic stabilization or redistribution should be allocated to the central federal level. For the efficient provision of public goods and their financing by taxes several criteria have been developed, on which the decision for a centralized or decentralized provision depends: regional scope of the utility of public goods (spillover effects, interregional externalities), economies of scale in regard to the provision of public goods, the extent of regional homogeneity/heterogeneity of preferences of the citizens, and decision and transaction costs, which might vary in differently structured federal systems.

But two central problems, which are important for the current discussion in regard to the EU, have not been investigated in this traditional theory of fiscal federalism:

1. One is the problem of competition between states, regions, or municipalities (interjurisdictional competition). If mobility of persons, firms, and production factors (particularly capital) between jurisdictions exists to some extent, processes of interjurisdictional competition for these mobile resources emerges in federal systems. Therefore the issue of the positive or negative effects of these competition processes arises. Since the removal of all mobility barriers is one of the central aims of the EU, this is particularly important for the European discussion.
2. The theory of fiscal federalism neglected the problem of the appropriate vertical allocation of legal rules and regulations – due to its focus

on public goods and taxation. Implicitly it was assumed that the legal framework was the task of the central (national) level. But within the EU it has become a crucial question, to what extent legal rules and regulations have to be centralized/harmonized or can also remain on a more decentralized level. This also raises the problem of the extent and effects of processes of regulatory competition.

The long-existing reluctance to integrate interjurisdictional competition into the economic theory of federalism is surprising, because through Tiebout's theory of the competitive provision of local public goods, a well-formulated model for interjurisdictional competition existed from the 1950s, leading to a broad theoretical and empirical literature based upon Tiebout's approach (Tiebout 1956, Dowding, John and Briggs 1994). But only since the 1990s have the issue of interjurisdictional and regulatory competition (also called systems competition, locational competition, competition among governments) been discussed broadly. This encompassed general studies on competitive federalism (in contrast to cooperative federalism), the problem of tax competition, and the specific European discussion on the advantages and disadvantages of harmonization or competition of regulations within the EU.[3] All these discussions are deeply influenced by the dispute between two opposing views, being either extremely optimistic or extremely pessimistic in regard to the effects of interjurisdictional or regulatory competition.

The proponents of interjurisdictional competition argue that it would induce the governments of these jurisdictions to offer bundles of public goods, regulations, and taxes that better fulfil the preferences of the citizens, because interjurisdictional competition restricts the discretionary scope of governments, leading to a more efficient provision of public goods and less redistribution due to rent-seeking activities. Furthermore, interjurisdictional competition will lead to more innovations in regard to the public services of the jurisdictions – an argument to which we will later come back in more detail. In contrast to that, the opponents of interjurisdictional competition show that there are sound arguments why interjurisdictional competition can suffer from considerable market failures implying inefficient outcomes and therefore considerable welfare losses (Sinn 1997). In theoretical models it has been attempted to show, for example, that tax competition might lead to an under-provision of public goods and/or to an inefficiently low degree of redistribution. But the overall results of the theoretical models in regard to the positive or negative effects of tax competition depend very much on the specific assumptions of the models. The same is true for the empirical literature. Empirical studies of Switzerland, however, which due to its far-reaching competencies for their regional units ('Kantone') can be seen as a kind of a model for competitive federalism, show that no systematic negative effects can be observed (Feld 2000).

Closely linked to this dispute about interjurisdictional competition is the discussion about the advantages and disadvantages of regulatory competition.[4] In Europe, this question has been much discussed in the context of the introduction of the principle of 'mutual recognition' of national regulations by the European Court of Justice ('Cassis de Dijon' judgment). This transition to the so-called 'rule of origin', which implies that it is sufficient for firms that their products fulfil the requirements of the regulations in their home country in order to export freely to all other member states of the EU, can lead to an indirect form of competition among the regulations of different member states, because within the EU firms with different product regulations compete with one another (Sun and Pelkmans 1995). In the US, competition among the corporate laws of the federal states is known as a famous example of regulatory competition. Similar to the discussion on interjurisdictional competition, the proponents and opponents of the concept of regulatory competition hold different opinions, whether the positive effects in form of restrictions for rent-seeking activities and more legal innovations are more important than potential problems of regulatory competition, particularly in form of 'race to the bottom' problems. Here too neither the theoretical models nor the few empirical studies have come up with clear results. For the well-studied competition among corporate laws within the US, however, most experts have come to the conclusion that the positive effects of this regulatory competition are much larger than the negative ones (Romano 1998).

Although much research work has been done on the question of the appropriate vertical allocation of competencies in a federal multilevel system of jurisdictions including the analysis of interjurisdictional and regulatory competition, which might emerge in decentralized systems, a consistent, integrated theory of (competitive) federalism that can give a well-founded orientation for the future development of the EU has not been developed yet. In the following, the theoretical foundations of the central arguments in the economic theories of federalism and interjurisdictional/regulatory competition are critically analysed.

4. CRITIQUE OF NEOCLASSICAL ARGUMENTS IN FEDERALISM THEORY FROM THE PERSPECTIVE OF EVOLUTIONARY ECONOMICS

The traditional economic theory of fiscal federalism can be characterized as a typical neoclassical equilibrium approach, which normatively is based upon Paretian welfare theory. The dominant criteria for the vertical allocation of competencies, regional scope of the utility of public goods (spillover effects/externalities), economies of scale-effects and the extent of regional homogeneity/heterogeneity of preferences, can be consistently deduced from the neoclassical theories of public goods and taxation – as well as the dominant aim of efficient allocation follows from Paretian welfare theory. The same is true for most approaches to interjurisdictional and regulatory competition. Tiebout's model of the competitive provision of local public goods was the exact transfer of the model of perfect competition to the market for local public goods.[5] Most of the theoretical discussion about interjurisdictional competition (and, particularly, tax competition) as well as regulatory competition are such welfare-theoretic neoclassical analyses. This implies that the outcome of interjurisdictional and regulatory competition is compared with the perfect theoretical solution of allocative efficiency. And according to market-failure theory, any allocative inefficiency and therefore any deviation from the optimal outcome of the perfect competition model leads to the diagnosis of a failure of interjurisdictional or regulatory competition. Thus it seems to be the obvious conclusion that interjurisdictional (or regulatory) competition, and therefore also competitive federalism, is no viable approach, leading to the policy recommendations of the centralization of competencies or the harmonization of regulations.

One kind of fundamental critique to this neoclassical market-failure argumentation is the well-known critique of Demsetz (1969), comparing situations in the real world with the fictitious approach of the model of perfect competition ('nirvana approach'). This method leads to the diagnosis of ubiquitous market failure and therefore the suggestion of ubiquitous state intervention or the entire abolishment of competition. Rather, a more differentiated methodological approach along the lines of Demsetz's concept of 'comparative institutional analysis' seems to be appropriate:

1. After the diagnosis of some kind of inefficiency in regard to interjurisdictional/regulatory competition, firstly, it is necessary to examine whether these problems of market failure might not be reduced or even eliminated by modifications of the institutional framework for these competition processes, because it is well known that many problems of market failure can be traced back to defective institutional arrangements (or property rights structures). This raises the crucial issue, what kind of institutional framework (sets of rules) is necessary for the proper working of interjurisdictional/regulatory competition and competitive federalism in general. In most neoclassical studies this import dimension of the problem is not discussed at all.

2. But even if we do not succeed in eliminating or reducing the allocative inefficiencies by changing the institutional framework, these disadvantages of decentralized federal systems have to be compared with the real disadvantages of the centralization of competencies or the harmonization of regulations. In that respect also the disadvantages of the institutional alternatives 'centralization'/'harmonization' have to be studied, before well-founded policy recommendations can be given. For their analysis political-economic models are appropriate. From the perspective of economic policy, this is the well-known problem of weighing market failure against state failure.

Despite its fundamental character, this first kind of critique of neoclassical welfare-theoretic reasonings about the working of decentralized federal systems is primarily based upon argumentations from institutional economics and political-economic literature.[6] The main critique from the perspective of evolutionary economics can start from basic ideas of Schumpeterian and Hayekian thinking, which emphasise the importance of innovations and knowledge problems. Our argumentation begins with the knowledge problems from the perspective of Hayek.[7] In the traditional theory of fiscal federalism it is – explicitly or most often implicitly – assumed that the policy makers on the central level of a federal system have perfect knowledge of which combination of public goods, taxes and regulations are most suitable for fulfilling the preferences of the citizens and therefore ensuring efficiency. If we make the assumption of an 'omniscient dictator' (Breton 1996) on the central level (and exclude knowledge problems), and combine this with the additional assumption of a 'benevolent dictator' (and therefore exclude also rent-seeking problems), it is not surprising that centralized solutions seem to be superior to decentralized solutions. But reality is different. Starting from basic ideas of Hayek we can distinguish two fundamental knowledge problems that are of great importance for our problem of the appropriate extent of centralization and decentralization in the EU.

In the discussion about federalism, it is often argued that policy makers on lower-level jurisdictions have a better knowledge about the specific problems of their citizens, and are therefore better able to solve these problems. Theoretically, this problem can be characterized with the Hayekian notion of 'dispersed knowledge' about the particular circumstances of time and space (Hayek 1945) or as the problem of 'local knowledge'. Thus the Hayekian argument about the impossibility of the centralization of all relevant knowledge in society, which he developed as a critique of the concept of a centrally planned economy, can also be applied to the provision of public goods and regulations by jurisdictions. If it is true that the knowledge about the specific regional and local problems is to a considerable extent local knowledge, which cannot be centralized, then decentralized federal systems are able to use more of this relevant local knowledge than more centralized systems. But to be able to use this knowledge, lower-level jurisdictions have to have competencies for deciding freely on their policies. Another variant of this 'local knowledge' argument uses reasonings from public choice theory. It is maintained that a greater decentralization increases the capability of citizens to monitor the decisions of politicians leading to less welfare losses due to rent-seeking activities.

At least as important as the problem of decentralized knowledge is the general problem that there is no perfect knowledge of what kind of public goods and what kind of regulations are the best solutions for the problems of the citizens. In neoclassical theories of public goods and regulations, it is implicitly assumed that the knowledge about the optimal solution in terms of the provision (and production) of public goods, of regulations, and taxation already exists. But just as nobody – not even scientists – knows the optimal solution for building cars or other private goods, we also cannot assume that we already know the best way how jurisdictions can provide security, establish systems of higher education, organize their judicial system, or fulfil the cultural preferences of their citizens. Neoclassical theories, however, always presuppose that the optimal public good and the optimal way for its production are already known. But there are no good reasons why we should assume that governments are better informed about the best solutions for public-good problems or regulatory problems than private firms are in regard to private goods. Rather in both cases, the problem solutions which are offered by jurisdictions and private firms can only be seen as fallible hypotheses about what the best problem solutions might be. The Hayekian knowledge problem implies that we have to accept that the knowledge of the policy makers can always be only fallible knowledge that can be more or less wrong. Therefore innovative improvements of these solutions are always possible.

In respect of private goods, it is the task of market competition to help to solve this knowledge problem. In competition firms experiment with different problem solutions (innovations), test them on the market, and learn from their experiences and those of their competitors. Therefore Hayek (1948, 1978) rejected the neoclassical concept of market competition, because it presupposes that the firms already know what the best products or production technologies are. In his notion of 'competition as a discovery procedure', which conceives competition as a process of parallel experimentation, knowledge about the best products or production technologies is the central outcome of market competition – and not a precondition. This implies that all theoretical approaches which use this neoclassical concept of competition for analyzing the effects of interjurisdictional or regulatory competition (as the Tiebout model and most of the literature do) fail to grasp a crucial part of the problem, i.e. that the knowledge problem cannot be assumed to be solved, rather that its solving is one of the central tasks that have to be tackled with by federal multilevel systems and interjurisdictional/regulatory competition.

Thus a theory that wants to give well-founded policy recommendations about the appropriate degree of centralization or decentralization of public policies in a multilevel system of jurisdictions (like the EU) has to take this knowledge problem seriously. From this perspective one question arises that has not been addressed in the traditional theory of fiscal federalism or in neoclassical theories of interjurisdictional or regulatory competition: How can new knowledge about the improvement of public goods and regulations be produced? Or: What do we know about innovation and technical progress in regard to all of those public services that jurisdictions provide to their citizens? It is a fundamental deficit of the traditional literature in public finance that the dimension of innovation in the public sector has not been taken into account in a systematic way. The neoclassical approaches to fiscal federalism as well as the neoclassical theories of interjurisdictional and regulatory competition do not ask for the effects of different degrees of centralization or decentralization on the innovation of public goods and regulations. But since in the public sector product and process innovations are as important as in the private sector, it is necessary to ask for the capability of federal multilevel systems of jurisdictions to generate innovations and to adapt quickly to exogenous change. This introduction of the innovation perspective opens the door for applying arguments from evolutionary economics to the analysis of the advantages and problems of competitive federalism.

5. EVOLUTIONARY CONTRIBUTIONS TO THE THEORIES OF FEDERALISM AND INTERJURISDICTIONAL/REGULATORY COMPETITION

The discussion about centralization and decentralization does not consist only of neoclassical arguments as they were shown in the last section. Also, important arguments emerged which cannot be derived from the neoclassical theory of fiscal federalism. A crucial part of them can be traced back to basic concepts of evolutionary economics.[8] Some of these arguments refer explicitly to evolutionary economics, whereas other arguments have been developed independently of evolutionary thinking, but can be interpreted as evolutionary.

5.1 Explicit Evolutionary Arguments: Competition and Decentralization as Processes of Experimentation

Particularly in the discussion about systems competition, interjurisdictional and regulatory competition, a number of authors, who are relatively optimistic about the potential positive effects of these competition processes, base their more positive assessment explicitly on evolutionary reasonings.[9] The starting point of their argumentation is the Hayekian knowledge problem and his critique of neoclassical concepts of competition, as was shown in the last section. They suggest using evolutionary concepts of competition (Schumpeter, Hayek) for analysing the effects of interjurisdictional and regulatory competition. Particularly, Hayek's concept of 'competition as a discovery procedure' has been applied to show that interjurisdictional and regulatory competition can be characterized also as an evolutionary process of variation and selection of policies and institutions/legal rules, in which new knowledge is generated of how the jurisdictions can improve their bundles of public goods, regulations and taxes.[10] From this evolutionary perspective decentralization and interjurisdictional/regulatory competition can lead to advantages in the form of innovations, which were not seen from a purely neoclassical point of view. What would a more detailed application of this argument of the innovative effects of experimentation to federalism look like?[11]

Starting from the Hayekian knowledge problem, jurisdictions have only fallible hypotheses about the best bundles of public goods, legal rules and taxes. In their endeavour to attract mobile individuals, firms and production factors, they will experiment with different bundles of public goods, legal rules and taxes. The resulting competition process can be seen as a process of experimentation, in which the mobile factors have the task of deciding on the relative quality of the public services of the competing jurisdictions. The basic idea is that in this process of variation and selection the superior hypotheses about the best and/or cheapest way in which jurisdictions can offer public services will be sifted out. Since successful jurisdictions will flourish, and their less successful competitors will suffer from losses of mobile resources, there will be incentives for the latter to attempt to catch up with the leading jurisdictions, either by imitation (mutual learning) or by innovating themselves. In that respect, an evolutionary conceptualization interprets interjurisdictional (or regulatory) competition as a 'discovery procedure', in which new knowledge is generated and spread, or, to put it in Schumpeterian terms, as a dynamic process of innovation and imitation, in which technical progress in the form of product and process innovations in regard to public goods and legal rules is created. Of course, the appropriate working of those competition processes depends on a number of conditions.

If we apply this evolutionary concept of interjurisdictional/regulatory competition to a federal multilevel structure of jurisdictions (as, for example, the EU, member states, regions, and municipalities), those competition processes emerge on each jurisdictional level. Since the vertical delimitation of competencies between the different federal levels defines the policies, which the jurisdictions can use to compete with other jurisdictions on the same level, this vertical allocation of competencies determines the action parameters of the competing jurisdictions. The positive innovative effects of interjurisdictional competition can emerge only in regard to those policies on which the respective jurisdictions can decide freely. Therefore the vertical allocation of competencies determines on which levels innovation of new policies and therefore experimentation and mutual learning are possible.

What does more or less centralization imply for the extent of this positive innovation effect due to interjurisdictional competition? Each shifting of competencies to a higher jurisdictional level (or each harmonization) eliminates competition among lower-level jurisdictions, and therefore discards the advantages of experimenting with policy innovations. Vice versa, the shifting of tasks to lower-level jurisdictions increases the scope of interjurisdictional competition, leading to additional processes of parallel experimentation. If competencies are allocated to the central level or a complete harmonization (of regulations) takes places, interjurisdictional (or regulatory) competition is completely eliminated and the positive innovative effects of experimentation and mutual learning cannot emerge.[12] Consequently, it can be suggested that the extent of centralization and decentralization has a crucial impact on the extent of variation selection processes and the capability of a federal system in creating and spreading innovations in regard to the performance of jurisdictions. Since evolutionary innovation economics has shown that heterogeneity and variety is a positive resource for the innovation capability of systems (Röpke 1977; Metcalfe 1998), variety within a decentralized federal system can be expected to enhance the long-term development of the performance of jurisdictions.

But the application of these arguments to the analysis of particular processes of interjurisdictional or regulatory competition requires a more differentiated approach in regard to the transmission mechanisms of innovation and imitation of policies. It is necessary to distinguish between different types of interjurisdictional (or regulatory) competition in depending on different assumptions in regard to mobility (Kerber 2000a, Kerber and Budzinski 2003, Heine 2003). Advantages from mutual learning due to parallel processes of experimentation can even emerge, if there is no mobility of goods, services, individuals, firms or production factors at all. If the citizens of different jurisdictions can observe the performance of policies in other jurisdictions, e.g. the German population can observe the labour-market policies and their relative success and failure in other countries, they can use this information as a benchmark for the evaluation of the performance of their own government in regard to domestic elections as well as the domestic government can learn from the positive and negative experiences in other countries. Therefore parallel experimentation processes with mutual learning are possible without any direct interjurisdictional competition in the form of gains and losses due to the migration of individuals, firms and production factors and not even through an indirect interjurisdictional competition via international trade. Only the mobility of information is necessary for this so-called yardstick competition.[13] Consequently, pure decentralization within a federal system can already lead to these positive innovation effects, even if interjurisdictional competition does not work – for example, due to relatively high migration costs.

But if additionally to that there is also considerable mobility of goods and services or even of firms and production factors, interjurisdictional competition processes emerge, which increase the pressure on governments to offer attractive bundles of public goods, regulations and taxes. It depends crucially on the specific conditions of mobility, and therefore also on the institutional framework, what type of interjurisdictional or regulatory competition processes arises. If, for example, firms can choose directly between legal rules of different countries without having to migrate to another jurisdiction (choice of law), regulatory competition among jurisdictions in regard to these particular legal rules can be very intensive, as in the case of e.g. competition among corporate laws in the US.

5.2 Implicit Evolutionary Arguments in Theories of Federalism and Regulatory Competition

After these explicit evolutionary contributions, it will be shown that this evolutionary argument about the innovation advantages of experimentation and variety has been used by many authors in the discussion about federalism, centralization/decentralization and interjurisdictional/regulatory competition without explicit reference to evolutionary economics. This argument was partly used as a – theoretically not integrated – additional argument in economic discussions about federalism or as an important argument in isolated discussions about special problems, which have gained almost no broad attention.

Oates – as one of the most important economists working on fiscal federalism – had already mentioned the additional advantages of experimentation with public policies, which are possible in a decentralized federal system, in his classical standard book *Fiscal Federalism* (Oates 1972), although he did not integrate this effect into his consequently elaborated welfare-theoretic neoclassical approach to federalism. The same is true for other new contributions to federalism as, for example, Breton's *Competitive Governments* (1996, p. 233), who, for example, used the external benchmark mechanism of Salmon (1987), which goes back to the theory of rank-order tournaments and is linked to the concept of yardstick competition.[14] Thus the importance of the innovation dimension of public policies and its reference to federalism is increasingly emphasized in economic theories of federalism.

Oates (1999) took the opportunity in his comprehensive survey article on fiscal federalism in the *Journal of Economic Literature* to stress the advantages of experimentation in decentralized federal systems and claims the necessity of an entire research programme for the study of innovation and imitation processes of public policies in federal systems. After the diagnosis of the problem of imperfect knowledge about appropriate public policies, he develops the perspective of federalism as 'laboratory federalism'. 'In a setting of imperfect information with learning-by-doing there are potential gains from experimentation with a variety of policies for addressing social and economic problems. And a federal system may offer some real opportunities for encouraging such experimentation and thereby promoting "technical progress" in public policy' (Oates 1999, 1132).

It is particularly remarkable that Oates, who in the first part of his survey article argues consistently within a neoclassical welfare-theoretic framework, assesses the advantages of decentralized experimentation in some cases as so large that they can dominate neoclassical arguments for centralization. As an example, he uses redistribution policy. First, he repeats the neoclassical argument of traditional federalism theory that redistribution policies, aiming to help the poor, should be allocated to the central level, because in the case of decentralized redistribution policies a 'race to the bottom' problem should be expected due to the mobility of the rich and poor between lower-level jurisdictions, leading to an inefficient low level of redistribution. Although Oates does not deny this argument, he is in favour of a decentralized redistribution policy (Oates 1999, 1131), because he estimates the advantages of decentralized experimentation with different redistribution policies as so high that they overcompensate potential negative effects of 'race to the bottom' problems.

But these implicitly evolutionary arguments have been developed without an explicit reference to the established literature on evolutionary economics. Oates neither uses Hayek as a reference for the knowledge problems he wants to alleviate by his 'laboratory federalism' nor does he apply an evolutionary concept of interjurisdictional competition, which he could have used for integrating experimentation and innovation, imitation processes in regard to public policies. On the contrary, his critical reasonings about interjurisdictional competition – in another section of his article (1999, 1134) – are purely neoclassical in the Tieboutian tradition. Therefore the theoretical perspective to integrate his implicitly evolutionary 'laboratory federalism' argument about the advantages of experimentation by applying an explicitly evolutionary concept of interjurisdictional (or regulatory) competition (instead of a neoclassical concept of interjurisdictional competition) into an integrated theory of federalism, which includes both interjurisdictional competition and the innovation dimension, has not been elaborated in his broad survey article by Oates.

But Oates (1999, 1133) develops a clear perspective for applying innovation economics to the problem of the creation and spreading of new public policies and linking it to his concept of 'laboratory federalism'. He mentions a number of studies of political scientists, who analysed horizontal and vertical diffusion processes of successful policy innovations within the US federal system.[15] He also applies typical arguments from innovation economics to federalism. Is it possible that in a decentralized federal system the positive information externalities from new public policies might lead to free-rider problems and therefore to an underprovision of experimentation (appropriability problem of innovations)?[16] Should this problem be addressed by subsidizing experimentation on lower jurisdictional levels? Or should the central government undertake limited experiments without committing the nation to an untested and risky policy measure' (1133)? But Oates also sees 'that relatively independent efforts in a large number of states will generate a wider variety of approaches to public policy than a set of centrally designed experiments' (1133). Thus the question is raised whether experimentation should be organized 'top-down' or allowed to develop 'bottom-up'. A very interesting simulation model of the effects of decentralized experimentation was presented by Kollman, Miller, and Page (2000). In their model innovation and imitation of policies is analysed for different cases of centralized and decentralized political decision making. Their simulation results suggest a trade-off between the advantages of experimentation and the advantages of the potential larger ability of the central level to solve problems.

Although Oates primarily uses arguments from neoclassical approaches to innovation economics, it has to be seen as considerable progress that he opens up the perspective of applying innovation economics systematically to federalism and therefore to the problem of centralization and decentralization. 'More generally, we need a lot more work on the implications of fiscal decentralization for both the amount of policy experimentation and innovation' (1999, 1134).

The problems of the advantages and disadvantages of centralization and decentralization are also discussed in regard to the legal system. Particularly within the EU, the question increasingly arises whether legal rules should be harmonized with the long-term perspective of a uniform European law or whether there also might be advantages from the diversity of legal rules. In this discussion on uniformity vs diversity of law, legal scholars also developed the argument that a decentralized legal system, which allows for variety and experimentation with new legal rules, can have considerable advantages in comparison to an entirely centralized, uniform legal system.[17] Also, in regard to legal rules – as institutional solutions for solving transaction and cooperation problems – it cannot be assumed that the best legal solutions have already been found. And from an evolutionary perspective, a permanent stream of new problems emerge, which require a high adaptability of the legal system. Consequently, searching for legal innovations is necessary. Therefore a decentralized legal system (legal federalism), in which parallel processes of experimentation with legal innovations, mutual learning and a quick correction of inappropriate legal solutions are possible, might be much more innovative in the long run than a centralized legal system. This can be true, in particular, if it also allows for competition among legal rules (regulatory competition).

One famous example of regulatory competition was already mentioned in section 3 – competition among corporate laws in the US.[18] The federal states have the competence in corporate law in the US. Since within the US, the so-called 'incorporation theory' determines that the federal states mutually each accept the corporate law of the others, firms have the choice to incorporate in any of the federal states without having any restrictions in regard to their location within the US. So firms can choose freely between the corporate laws of 50 federal states. This situation has led to an intensive regulatory competition between the corporate laws of the federal states, which it has been possible to observe for decades. The incentives of the states are 'franchise taxes', which incorporated firms have to pay.[19] In the US, there have been many studies of this regulatory competition among corporate laws, focusing on the question whether it has led to a negative 'race to the bottom' or to a positive 'race to the top'. Although there are adherents of both claims, nowadays most scholars hold the opinion that the positive effects prevail. Particularly interesting is that this regulatory competition can be primarily described as a dynamic process of innovation and imitation of new legal rules leading to a step-by-step improvement of the corporate laws. Therefore in this special discussion about the evolution of US corporate laws, evolutionary arguments from innovation economics were applied to regulatory competition. These arguments encompassed the advantages of experimentation with different legal rules, but also Schumpeterian argumentation patterns on dynamic processes of innovation and imitation, path-dependency argumentations due to critical-mass phenomena and dynamic economies of scale-effects (Romano 1985, Heine 2003).[20]

6. COMPETITIVE FEDERALISM FROM THE PERSPECTIVE OF NEOCLASSICAL AND EVOLUTIONARY ECONOMICS

What are the consequences for the development of an integrated theory of federalism, which can give a better basis for answering the question of centralization and decentralization within the EU?

6.1 Knowledge, Competition, and Innovation in Federalism Theory

The traditional theory of fiscal federalism is based upon a static neoclassical approach, in which the knowledge problem in regard to the appropriate public goods and regulations is assumed to be already solved. Contrary to that, an appropriate theory of federalism has to take this knowledge problem seriously, which also implies the systematic taking into account of the innovation dimension in regard to public goods and regulations. Therefore the capability of a federal multilevel system of jurisdictions in generating and spreading new problem solutions (public goods, regulations) and therefore helping to solve the knowledge problem is a crucial criterion for the evaluation of alternative options for the vertical allocation of competencies. From the evolutionary perspective, a more decentralized system is better able to exploit both the decentralized local knowledge and the advantages that accrue from decentralized experimentation of lower-level jurisdictions with policy innovations and their mutual learning by imitation (diffusion of policies). Therefore a federal multilevel system of jurisdictions also has to be seen as a system of innovation. In addition to that, from an evolutionary point of view the main perspective changes from a 'top-down' to a 'bottom-up' approach.

Since neoclassical concepts of interjurisdictional and regulatory competition cannot take innovation effects into account, evolutionary concepts of competition based upon Hayekian and Schumpeterian approaches should be applied. Due to the positive effects of interjurisdictional/regulatory competition on innovations, and the considerable knowledge problems of centralized decisions, allowing interjurisdictional and regulatory competition is a much more interesting policy option from an evolutionary perspective than from a purely neoclassical point of view. As a consequence, it is suggested that one integrate systematically interjurisdictional and regulatory competition processes within a federal multilevel structure of jurisdictions – leading to the perspective of an integrated concept of competitive federalism. Of course, interjurisdictional and regulatory competition can only be permitted if they work satisfactorily in comparison to alternative institutional solutions. But similar to private goods, the provision of the public services of jurisdictions should also be controlled by competition as far as possible (application of the market paradigm). The resulting reduction (or even loss) of the monopoly power of jurisdictions in regard to individuals, firms and production factors, which leads to competition among public policies, is another basic change of perspective, which gains weight from an evolutionary point of view.

6.2 Centralization and Decentralization: Neoclassical and Evolutionary Criteria

The consideration of evolutionary arguments might change the relative importance of neoclassical criteria for the vertical allocation of competencies. But also most evolutionary economists would not deny that the neoclassical criteria such as spillover effects (externalities), economies of scale-effects, and heterogeneity of preferences are relevant criteria for deciding on the optimal degree of centralization or decentralization. They would also not deny that interjurisdictional and regulatory competition might fail, for example, due to 'race to the bottom' problems or to the lack of incentives. Therefore the methodological problem arises that both neoclassical and evolutionary arguments are relevant without having a common theoretical basis. But for scholars dealing with policy questions, this is not an unusual situation. Many policy problems are characterized by the fact that one theoretical approach is not sufficient to grasp the complexity of the problem in a satisfactory way. This leads to the consequence of the simultaneous application of different theoretical approaches and implies a careful assessment of the relative importance of arguments from different theoretical approaches, each of which can explain only a part of the complex problem. Therefore the pragmatic method I want to suggest also for the issue of centralization and decentralization is the simultaneous application of both neoclassical and evolutionary arguments.

Additionally, a comprehensive theory of federalism needs an institutional economics approach by applying the principle of 'comparative institutional analysis'. From that perspective, the issue of centralization and decentralization can be conceived as the problem of what the institutional structure of a multilevel system of jurisdictions should look like. Theoretically, this would entail both the vertical allocation of competencies within this multilevel system of jurisdictions and the necessary set of institutional arrangements (in the form of metarules), which are necessary for solving conflicts and ensuring the working of the multilevel system of jurisdictions as a whole. For the vertical allocation of competencies, it is suggested that the already existing catalogue of (up to now predominantly neoclassical) criteria is extended by additional evolutionary criteria. In that respect, particularly important are the innovation advantages of experimentation (and variety), but also the Hayekian problem of the use of decentralized knowledge, dynamic economies of scale and the problem of path dependencies – as additional evolutionary arguments.[21] In the same way it is necessary to examine the working of any interjurisdictional or regulatory competition processes which might emerge in decenteralized federal systems, in order to recognize potential market failures and reduce or eliminate them by establishing appropriate sets of rules for interjurisdictional or regulatory competition. But from the perspective of evolutionary economics these analyses should not only be made in regard to neoclassical static efficiency but also in regard to dynamic efficiency in the tradition of the Schumpeterian approaches. And as in other fields of public policy, in federalism also trade-off problems between static and dynamic efficiency cannot be excluded.

But up to now, no elaborated theory of competitive federalism exists which encompasses both neoclassical and evolutionary analyses of the effects of federal multilevel systems of jurisdictions. Therefore much research work needs to be done, particularly in regard to the application of evolutionary innovation economics to the provision of public goods and regulations by jurisdictions. But first studies about the problem of centralization and decentralization of regulations and regulatory competition show that no simple solutions can be expected. It seems rather to depend very much on the specific kind of legal rules/regulations and on the specific institutional preconditions whether decentralization and/or regulatory competition might be an appropriate solution.[22] Therefore for future research, a double strategy seems to be most suitable. Although on one hand a general theory about the design of federal multilevel systems of jurisdictions should be developed, the specific problems in different fields of public goods, policies, and regulations seem to be so heterogeneous that on the other hand profound special studies also have to be made in each of these fields for answering the question of the particular optimal degree of centralization and decentralization.

7. CONSEQUENCES FOR EUROPEAN INTEGRATION: COMPETITIVE FEDERALISM INSTEAD OF CENTRALIZATION

There is a large uncertainty about the final state of the European Union, after the process of European integration is finished. The danger is that the traditional idea of the nation state, in which nearly all kind of economic policies are 'naturally' allocated to the central (i.e. national) level, will be simply transferred to the EU, implying that the EU is seen as a new 'nation state' in the traditional sense. From this perspective, it seems evident that in the long run the central European level should have the same competencies for public policies as the traditional nation states had in the past. This would lead to a much stronger centralization of competencies and harmonization than it is being discussed now. Within the European Union not much scope would remain either for decentralization or variety. It can be suggested that this is also a consequence of the lack of alternative concepts of European integration that do not equate European integration with uniformity and harmonization.

The concept of competitive federalism is an alternative concept for European integration that aims at the development of an institutional structure for a federal multilevel system of jurisdictions in Europe, which attempts to combine integration with decentralization and the potential for maintaining variety.[23] If we understand integration – in the tradition of the judgment of the European Court of Justice – as the removal of barriers to the mobility of individuals, firms, goods, services and production factors ('basic freedoms') within the EU, and want to pursue the aim of as much decentralization as possible (principle of subsidiarity), then both aims can only be attained simultaneously within a multilevel system of jurisdictions that is based upon the concept of competitive federalism (Kerber 2000b). The crucial contribution of evolutionary economics to this reasoning is that evolutionary arguments about the necessity, mechanisms and determinants of innovation processes in regard to the provision of public goods and regulations are very important for the elaboration of the long-term advantages of a higher degree of decentralization within the EU – in comparison to purely neoclassical arguments.

It is not possible here to elaborate on specific argumentations and draw conclusions about the appropriate vertical allocation of competencies in the EU from this perspective. But a few general implications can be briefly sketched:

1. Heterogeneity in regard to policies and regulations within the EU should not only be seen as potential causes for impeding the internal market and distortions of competition, but also as a positive resource for innovation for the whole EU. Therefore policies aiming at 'levelling the playing field' are problematic in order to maintain the innovation capability of the EU.
2. Competition among member states, regions, and municipalities should not be seen primarily as a danger for European integration, but instead

as an opportunity to extend the principle of competition (as a core principle of the EU) also to the provision of many public goods and regulations – as far as this is possible. In that respect, the concept of competitive federalism opens up the perspective for the introduction of an internal market for competing jurisdictions as location for individuals, firms, and production factors (internal market for public goods and regulations).

3. From the perspective of competitive federalism, the EU has to fulfil the task of providing the institutional framework for ensuring the working of the federal multilevel system of jurisdictions as a whole. For example, even if the competencies for specific public policies, as e.g. labour-market regulations or social policy, are allocated to the member states, a set of metarules for the solving of conflicts (delimitation of these national competencies) and problems (e.g. in regard to free-rider problems due to migration) will be necessary. Therefore decentralization of competencies in a European multilevel system also requires the fulfilment of important tasks on the European level. But the European Union should limit its activities – beyond specific tasks that should be allocated entirely on the central level – more to the provision of an institutional framework, within which the jurisdictions on different levels can provide public services to European citizens.

8. PUBLIC POLICY AND EVOLUTIONARY ECONOMICS: SOME CONCLUSIONS

One of the most important insights of evolutionary economics is that both the complexity of human society and the permanent dynamic change due to the emergence of novelties lead to fundamental limitations of our knowledge about the world and its functioning. Therefore from an evolutionary perspective the Hayekian knowledge problem is a crucial problem that cannot be ignored. It rather has to be the starting point for all reasonings about our options to influence economic processes, and therefore for all questions of public policy.

Our inevitable ignorance about the best policy solutions, however, should not prevent evolutionary economists from making positive policy recommendations, although we cannot foresee for sure what the exact effects of these policy options are. Two reasons can be given for this conclusion:

1. In a changing world, in which nobody can foresee the future, actions and policies of individuals, firms, and states have always to be based

upon uncertain, fallible knowledge. Therefore any requirement of perfect foresight of the effects of policies is not compatible with an evolutionary view of the world. So evolutionary economists especially should take a pragmatic attitude in regard to the knowledge base that is deemed as necessary for carrying out policies.[24] This argument, however, does not deny that often a careful analysis will come to the conclusion that many policies should not be made all due to the lack of knowledge about their effects.
2. In specific policy discussions many arguments from different theoretical approaches are brought in. Although evolutionary arguments do not seem to be as exact as e.g. neoclassical arguments, they are a very valuable complement, and also a corrective to other arguments. Being too scrupulous and reluctant in policy discussions due to the insight into one's own ignorance only leaves the ground to other theoretical approaches that have not solved the knowledge problem either – but are not aware of it and therefore pretend to know the right solutions.

In addition to that, evolutionary economics open up the perspective to do systematic research on the question how we should deal with the problem of our always fallible and deficient knowledge about the effects of policies. One answer is well known: the substitution of discretionary, interventionist policies by rule-oriented policies – such as Hayek's demand for a 'rule of law' and the claim of the Freiburg School of Law and Economics (Ordoliberalism) for a stable institutional framework for the market economy ('Wettbewerbsordnung', 'Ordnungspolitik') – can be seen also as the demand for a specific *form* of economic policy that economizes on the amount of knowledge that is necessary for public policy (Eucken 1952, Hayek 1973). The second answer is that public policy should be institutionalized in such a way that new knowledge about appropriate public policies is endogenously generated – implying both the production of appropriate policy innovations and the fast discovery and elimination of wrong policies. This is perfectly in line with Oates' concept of federalism as 'laboratory federalism'. Since evolutionary economics has comparative advantages in doing research on innovation, learning, and change, it should develop concepts of how public policy could be organized as a systematic, innovative, searching process in regard to how jurisdictions can improve their public policies.

The concept of competitive federalism can be seen as an application of this general idea. The establishment of a federal multilevel system of jurisdictions with as much decentralization and interjurisdictional and regulatory competition as is feasible, implies the implementation of a whole set of processes of experimentation with public policies on different jurisdictional levels – including the sifting out of superior policies, mutual learning by imitation, and the elimination of erroneous policies. Since competitive federalism can also be seen as a concept for implementing an innovation system in regard to the provision of public goods and regulations, evolutionary economics might contribute considerably to the development of an integrated concept of competitive federalism. In particular, the investigation of the knowledge-generating effect of decentralized experimentation with new policies, including the creation of policy innovations and the often difficult process of policy diffusion, might be an interesting issue for applying evolutionary analyses. Therefore the question of 'centralization vs decentralization' is a promising candidate for the application of evolutionary economics. Vice versa, it has become evident that the main advantages of decentralization, and therefore of federalism in general, only become clearly apparent from the perspective of evolutionary economics.

NOTES

1. See, e.g., Koch (1996), Wegner (1996, 1997), Slembeck (1997), Meier and Slembeck (1998), Witt (2003), and the contributions in Pelikan and Wegner (2003).
2. See Oates (1972, 1999) and Breton (1996).
3. See, e.g., Oates and Schwab (1988), Siebert and Koop (1990), Sinn (1990, 1997, 2003), Kenyon and Kincaid (1991), Sinn (1992), Vanberg and Kerber (1994), Frey and Eichenberger (1995), Streit and Mussler (1995), Sun and Pelkmans (1995), Bratton and McCahery (1997), Kerber (1998, 2000b), Streit and Wohlgemuth (1999), Feld (2000), Kollman, Miller and Page (2000), Van den Bergh (2000), Wellisch (2000), Esty and Geradin (2001), Besley and Coate (2003).
4. See, in particular, Siebert and Koop (1990), Hauser and Hösli (1991), Woolcock (1994), Sun and Pelkmans (1995), Streit and Mussler (1995), Sinn (1997), Gatsios and Holmes (1998), Kerber (2000b), Van den Bergh (2000), Esty and Geradin (2001), Heine and Kerber (2002), Kerber and Budzinski (2003), Marciano and Josselin (2003).
5. The assumptions of Tiebout's model are nearly identical to the assumptions of the perfect competition model, e.g. in regard to the homogeneity of public goods and jurisdictions, perfect market transparency, and atomistic structure of the jurisdictions.
6. See, e.g., Brennan and Buchanan (1980), Besley and Coate (2003), and Wilson and Wildasin (2004).
7. See Hayek (1945, 1978, 1996) and Wegner (1996).
8. As examples for arguments from political science, see Inman and Rubinfield (1997) and Weingast (1995).
9. See, e.g., Vihanto (1992), Vanberg and Kerber (1994), Frey and Eichenberger (1995), Streit (1996), Kerber (1998, 2000a), Streit and Wohlgemuth (1999), Heine and Kerber (2002), Wohlgemuth (2002); for a comparison of neoclassical and evolutionary approaches to systems competition, see Windisch (1998). For an integrated evolutionary concept of competition, which encompasses both Schumpeterian and Hayekian arguments, see Kerber (1997).
10. These considerations are also directly linked to the general Hayekian approach of cultural evolution, which suggests that a process of variation and selection of rules might lead to the development of superior rules and institutions (Hayek 1973; Vanberg 1992).
11. For the following, see in more detail Kerber (1998, 2000a); for the general advantages of experimentalism from the perspective of economic policy, see also Okruch (2003).

12. Please note that sequential experimentation processes, in which particular policies are implemented, and after evaluation maintained or modified, are possible also on the central level. The advantage of decentralised competencies is that here parallel experimentation processes and simultaneous mutual learning are possible, which can be expected to lead to a much faster growth of knowledge.
13. See, e.g., Besley and Case (1995), Bodenstein and Ursprung (2005) and for a short overview Schnellenbach (2004); the basic ideas go back to Salmon (1987).
14. It would be worthwhile to analyse the widespread concept of yardstick competition in regard to its implicit evolutionary character, which cannot be done here.
15. See for this mainly empirical political science literature on the diffusion of policy innovations, e.g., Walker (1969), Gray (1973, 1994), Canon and Baum (1981), Berry and Berry (1991), Berry (1994), Nice (1994), Rogers (1995), Sparer and Brown (1996), Mintrom (1997), and Clark (2000).
16. See in more detail Rose-Ackerman (1980), Mukand and Rodrik (2002), Strumpf (2002).
17. See, e.g., Kötz (1986, p. 9), Behrens (1986, p. 26), Parisi and Ribstein (1998, p. 238); for advantages of experimentation in regulatory competition, see Streit and Mussler (1995), Ogus (1999), Kerber (2000a), Van den Bergh (2000), Kerber and Budzinski (2003); from a more critical perspective, see Kieninger (2002). The basic ideas of 'laboratory federalism' stem from early legal scholars in the US (see Oates 1999, p. 1132).
18. See, e.g., Romano (1985, 1998), Bebchuk (1992), and Easterbrook and Fischel (1996).
19. See Romano (1985). Delaware, for example, which is the market leader in this market for corporate law, is financing a considerable part of its budget by this franchise tax.
20. Recently, this US debate on the effects of regulatory competition between corporate laws has become relevant in regard to the EU. The so-called 'Centros' decision of the European Court of Justice of 1999 has triggered off an intensive discussion among legal scholars, of whether the 'Incorporation theory' should also be implemented within the EU. Contrary to the present situation, this would imply the mutual recognition of corporate laws and open up the long-term perspective that in the future firms in Europe might choose also freely between the corporate laws of different European countries leading to regulatory competition among the corporate laws of the member states of the EU (Wouters 2000, Heine and Kerber 2002). For an analysis of the workability of this regulatory competition in regard to potential path dependencies see Heine and Kerber (2002), who apply explicitly evolutionary concepts of innovation economics (technological paradigms of Dosi) to legal evolution and regulatory competition.
21. For preliminary catalogues of criteria for the vertical allocation of competencies in regard to regulations, see Grundmann and Kerber (2002), Kerber and Heine (2002), Van den Bergh (2002) and Kerber and Grundmann (2006).
22. See, for example, Grundmann and Kerber (2002) for an application on the problem of centralization and decentralization of contract law in the EU, Van den Bergh and Camesasca (2001, pp. 125–65) and Kerber (2003b) in regard to competition law, and Heine and Kerber (2002) and Heine (2003) in regard to corporate law.
23. For attempts to apply competitive federalism to the EU, see e.g. Kirchner (1998), Frey and Eichenberger (1999), and Kerber (2000b, 2003a).
24. For a plea for a more pragmatic view of economic policy (with explicit reference to Dewey and additional literature), see Okruch (2003).

REFERENCES

Bebchuk, L.A. (1992), 'Federalism and the corporation: the desirable limits on state competition in corporate law', *Columbia Law Review*, **105**, 1435–510.

Behrens, P. (1986), 'Voraussetzungen und Grenzen der Rechtsfortbildung durch Rechtsvereinheitlichung', *Rabels Zeitschrift für ausländisches und internationales Privatrecht*, **50**, 19–34.

Berry, F.S. (1994), 'Sizing up state policy innovation research', *Policy Studies Journal*, **22**, 442–56.
Berry, F.S. and W.D. Berry (1991), 'Specifying a model of state policy innovations', *American Political Science Review*, **85**, 573–9.
Besley, T. and A. Case (1995), 'Incumbent behavior, tax-setting, and yardstick competition', *American Economic Review*, **85**, 25–45.
Besley, T. and S. Coate (2003), 'Centralized versus decentralized provision of local public goods: a political economy analysis', *Journal of Public Economics*, **87**, 2611–37.
Bodenstein, M. and H.W. Ursprung (2005), 'Political yardstick competition, economic integration, and constitutional choice in a federation', *Public Choice* (forthcoming).
Bratton, W.W. and J.A. McCahery (1997), 'The new economics of jurisdictional competition: devolutionary federalism in a second-best world', *The Georgetown Law Journal*, **86**, 201–78.
Brennan, G. and J.M. Buchanan (1980), *The Power to Tax: Analytical Foundations of a Fiscal Constitution*, Cambridge, MA: Cambridge University Press.
Breton, A. (1996), *Competitive Governments: An Economic Theory of Politics and Public Finance*, Cambridge, MA: Cambridge University Press.
Canon, B.C. and L. Baum (1981), 'Patterns of adoption of tort law innovations: an application of diffusion theory to judicial doctrines', *American Political Science Review*, **79**, 178–94.
Clark, J. (2000), 'Policy attributes and state policy innovation', *Southeastern Political Review*, **28**, 3–25.
Demsetz, H. (1969), 'Information and efficiency: another viewpoint', *Journal of Law and Economics*, **12**, 1–22.
Dowding, K., P. John and S. Biggs (1994), 'Tiebout: "A Survey of the Empirical Literature"', *Urban Studies*, **31**, 767–97.
Easterbrook, F.H. and D.R. Fischel (1996), *The Economic Structure of Corporate Law*, Cambridge, MA: Harvard University Press.
Esty, D.C. and D. Geradin (eds) (2001), *Regulatory competition and Economic Integration: Comparative perspectives*, Oxford: Oxford University Press.
Eucken, W. (1952), *Grundsätze der Wirtschaftspolitik*, Tübingen: Mohr Siebeck.
Feld, L. (2000), *Steuerwettbewerb und seine Auswirkungen auf Allokation und Distribution:Eine empirische Analyse für die Schweiz*, Tübingen: Mohr Siebeck.
Frey, B.S. and R. Eichenberger (1995), 'Competition Among Jurisdictions: The Idea of FOCJ', in L. Gerken (ed.), *Competition Among Institutions*, Basingstoke and London: Macmillan, pp. 209–29.
Frey, B.S. and R. Eichenberger (1999), *The New Democratic Federalism for Europe*, Cheltenham, UK and Northampton, MA, USA: Edward Elgar.
Gatsios, K. and P. Holmes (1998), 'Regulatory Competition', in P. Newman (ed.), *The New Palgrave Dictionary of Economics and the Law*, vol. 3, London and Basingstoke: Macmillan, pp. 271–5.
Gray, V. (1973), 'Innovation in the states: a diffusion study', *American Political Science Review*, **67**, 1174–85.
Gray, V. (1994), 'Competition, emulation, and policy innovation', in L.C. Dodd and J. Calvon (eds), *New Perspectives on American Politics*, Washington, DC: CQ Press, pp. 230–48.
Grundmann, S. and W. Kerber (2002), 'European system of contract laws. A map for combining the advantages of centralised and decentralised rule-making', in

S. Grundmann and J. Stuyck (eds), *An Academic Greenpaper on European Contract Law*, The Hague/London/New York: Kluwer Law International, pp. 295–342.

Hauser, H. and M. Hösli (1991), 'Harmonization of Regulatory Competition in the EC (and the EEA)?', *Aussenwirtschaft*, **46**, 497–512.

Hayek, F.A.v. (1945), 'The use of knowledge in society', *American Economic Review*, **35**, 519–30.

Hayek, F.A.v. (1948), 'The meaning of competition', in F.A.v. Hayek, *Individualism and Economic Order*, Chicago: University of Chicago Press, pp. 92–106.

Hayek, F.A.v. (1973), *Law, Legislation and Liberty. Vol. 1: Rules and Order*, Chicago and London: University of Chicago Press.

Hayek, F.A.v. (1978), 'Competition as a discovery procedure', in F.A.v. Hayek, *Studies in Philosophy, Politics and Economics*, Chicago: Chicago University Press, pp. 66–81.

Hayek, F.A.v. (1996), 'Die Irrtümer des Konstruktivismus und die Grundlagen legitimer Kritik gesellschaftlicher Gebilde', in F.A.v. Hayek, *Die Anmaßung von Wissen* (ed. W. Kerber), Tübingen: Mohr Siebeck, pp. 16–36.

Heine, K. (2003), *Regulierungswettbewerb im Gesellschaftsrecht: Zur Funktionsfähigkeit eines Wettbewerbs der Rechtsordnungen im europäischen Gesellschaftsrecht*, Berlin: Duncker & Humblot.

Heine, K. and W. Kerber (2002), 'European corporate laws, regulatory competition and path dependence', *European Journal of Law and Economics*, **13**, 43–71.

Inman, R.P. and D.L. Rubinfeld (1997), 'The political economy of federalism', in D. Mueller (ed.) *Perspectives on Public Choice: A Handbook*, Cambridge, MA: Cambridge University Press, pp. 73–105.

Kenyon, D.A. and J. Kincaid (eds) (1991), *Competition Among States and Local Governments: Efficiency and Equity in American Federalism*, Washington; DC: Urbane Institute Press.

Kerber, W. (1997), 'Wettbewerb als Hypothesentest: eine evolutorische Konzeption wissenschaffenden Wettbewerbs', in K.v. Delhaes and U. Fehl (eds), *Dimensionen des Wettbewerbs: Seine Rolle in der Entstehung und Ausgestaltung von Wirtschaftsordnungen*, Stuttgart: Lucius & Lucius, pp. 29–78.

Kerber, W. (1998), 'Zum Problem einer Wettbewerbsordnung für den Systemwettbewerb', *Jahrbuch für Neue Politische Ökonomie*, **17**, 199–231.

Kerber, W. (2000a), 'Rechtseinheitlichkeit und Rechtsvielfalt aus ökonomischer Sicht', in S. Grundmann (ed.), *Systembildung und Systemlücken in Kerngebieten des Europäischen Privatrechts. Gesellschafts-, Arbeits- und Schuldvertragsrecht*, Tübingen: Mohr Siebeck, pp. 67–97.

Kerber, W. (2000b), 'Interjurisdictional competition within the European Union', *Fordham International Law Journal*, **23**, S217–49.

Kerber, W. (2003a), 'Wettbewerbsföderalismus als Integrationskonzept für die Europäische Union', *Perspektiven der Wirtschaftspolitik*, **4**, 43–64.

Kerber, W. (2003b), 'An international multi-level system of competition laws: Federalism in Antitrust', in J. Drexl (ed.), *The Future of Transnational Antitrust – From Comparative to Common Competition Law*, Berne, The Hague, London, Boston, MA: Staempfli/Kluwer, pp. 269–300.

Kerber, W. and O. Budzinski (2003), 'Towards a differentiated analysis of competition of competition laws', *ZWeR – Journal of Competition Law*, **1**, 411–48.

Kerber, W. and K. Heine (2002), 'Zur Gestaltung von Mehr-Ebenen-Rechtssystemen aus ökonomischer Sicht', in C. Ott and H.-B. Schäfer (eds),

Vereinheitlichung und Diversität des Zivilrechts in transnationalen Wirtschaftsräumen, Tübingen: Mohr Siebeck, pp. 167–94.
Kerber, W. and S. Grundmann (2006), 'An optional European contract law code: advantages and disadvantages', *European Journal of Law and Economics* (forthcoming).
Kieninger, E.-M. (2002), *Wettbewerb der Privatrechtsordnungen im Europäischen Binnenmarkt*, Tübingen: Mohr Siebeck.
Kirchner, C. (1998), 'The principle of subsidiarity in the Treaty of European Union: a critique from the perspective of constitutional economics,' *Tulane Journal of International and Comparative Law*, **6**, 291–308.
Koch, L.T. (1996), *Evolutorische Wirtschaftspolitik*, Tübingen: Mohr Siebeck.
Kollman, K., J.H. Miller and S.E. Page (2000), 'Decentralization and the search for policy solutions', *Journal of Law, Economics, & Organization*, **16**, 102–28.
Kötz, H. (1986), 'Rechtsvereinheitlichung – Nutzen, Kosten, Methoden, Ziele', *Rabels Zeitschrift für ausländisches und internationales Privatrecht*, **50**, 1–18.
Marciano, A. and J.-M. Josselin (eds) (2003), *From Economics to Legal Competition*, Cheltenham, UK and Northampton, MA, USA: Edward Elgar.
Meier, A. und T. Slembeck (1998), *Wirtschaftspolitik. Kognitiv-evolutionärer Ansatz*, second edition, Munich/Vienna: Oldenbourg.
Metcalfe, J.S. (1998), *Evolutionary Economics and Creative Destruction*, London and New York: Routledge.
Mintrom, M. (1997), 'Policy entrepreneurs and the diffusion of innovation', *American Journal of Political Science*, **41**, 738–70.
Mukand, S. and D. Rodrik (2002), 'In search of the Holy Grail: policy convergence, experimentation, and economic performance', unpublished manuscript, John F. Kennedy School of Government, Harvard University.
Nice, D.C. (1994), *Policy Innovation in State Government*, Ames, IO: Iowa State University Press.
Oates, W.E. (1972), *Fiscal Federalism*, New York: Harcourt Brace Jovanovich.
Oates, W.E. (1999), 'An essay on fiscal federalism', *Journal of Economic Literature*, **37**, 1120–49.
Oates, W.E. and R.M. Schwab (1988), 'Economic competition among jurisdictions: efficiency enhancing or distortion inducing?', *Journal of Public Economics*, **35**, 333–54.
Ogus, A. (1999), 'Competition between national legal systems: a contribution of economic analysis to comparative law,' *International and Comparative Law Quarterly*, **48**, 405–18.
Okruch, S. (2003), 'Knowledge and economic policy: a plea for political experimentalism', in P. Pelikan and G. Wegner (eds), *The Evolutionary Analysis of Economic Policy*, Cheltenham; UK and Northampton, MA, USA: Edward Elgar, pp. 67–95.
Parisi, F. and L.E. Ribstein (1998), 'Choice of law', in P. Newman (ed.), *The New Palgrave Dictionary of Economics and the Law*, vol. 1, London and Basingstoke: Macmillan, pp. 236–41.
Pelikan, P. and G. Wegner (eds) (2003), *The Evolutionary Analysis of Economic Policy*, Cheltenham; UK and Northampton, MA, USA: Edward Elgar.
Rogers, E. (1995), *Diffusion of Innovations*, fourth edition, New York: Free Press.
Romano, R. (1985), 'Law as a product: some pieces of the incorporation puzzle', *Journal of Law, Economics, and Organization*, **1**, 225–83.
Romano, R. (1998), 'Competition for state corporate law', in P. Newman (ed.), *The*

New Palgrave Dictionary of Economics and the Law, vol. 1, London and Basingstoke: Macmillan, pp. 364–70.
Röpke, J. (1977), *Die Strategie der Innovation*, Tübingen: Mohr Siebeck.
Rose-Ackerman, S. (1980), 'Risk taking and reelection: does federalism promote innovation?', *Journal of Legal Studies*, **9**, 593–616.
Salmon, P. (1987), 'Decentralisation as an incentive scheme', *Oxford Review of Economic Policy*, **3**, 24–42.
Schnellenbach, J. (2004), *Dezentrale Finanzpolitik und Modellunsicherheit: Eine theoretische Untersuchung zur Rolle des fiskalischen Wettbewerbs als Wissen generierender Prozess*, Tübingen: Mohr Siebeck.
Siebert, H. and M.J. Koop (1990), 'Institutional competition. A concept for Europe?', *Aussenwirtschaft*, **45**, 439–62.
Sinn, H.-W. (1990), 'The limits to competition between economic regimes', *Empirica – Austrian Economic Papers*, **17**, 3–14.
Sinn, H.-W. (1997), 'The selection principle and market failure in systems competition', *Journal of Public Economics*, **88**, 247–74.
Sinn, H.-W. (2003), *The New Systems Competition*, Malden, MA: Blackwell.
Sinn, S. (1992), 'The taming of Leviathan: competition among governments', *Constitutional Political Economy*, **2**, 177–96.
Slembeck, T. (1997), 'The formation of economic policy: a cognitive-evolutionary approach to policy-making', *Constitutional Political Economy*, **8** (3), 225–54.
Sparer, M.S. and L.D. Brown (1996), 'States and the health care crisis: the limits and lessons of laboratory federalism', in R.F. Rich and W.D. White (eds), *Health Policy, Federalism, and the American States*, Washington, DC: Urban Institute Press, pp. 181–202.
Streit, M.E. (1996), 'Systemwettbewerb im europäischen Integrationsprozess', in U. Immenga, W. Möschel and D. Reuter (eds), *Festschrift für Ernst-Joachim Mestmäcker: zum siebzigsten Geburtstag*, Baden-Baden: Nomos, pp. 512–35.
Streit, M.E. and W. Mussler (1995), 'Wettbewerb der Systeme und das Binnenmarkt programm der Europäischen Union', in L. Gerken (ed.), *Europa zwischen Ordnungswettbewerb und Harmonisierung*, Berlin: Springer, pp. 75–107.
Streit, M.E. and M. Wohlgemuth (eds) (1999), *Systemwettbewerb als Herausforderung an Politik und Theorie*, Baden-Baden: Nomos.
Strumpf, K.S. (2002), 'Does government decentralization increase policy innovation?', *Journal of Public Economic Theory*, **4**, 207–41.
Sun, J.-M. and J.J. Pelkmans (1995), 'Regulatory competition in the single market', *Journal of Common Market Studies*, **33**, 67–89.
Tiebout, C.M. (1956), 'A pure theory of local expenditures', *Journal of Political Economy*, **64**, 416–24.
Vanberg, V. (1992), 'Innovation, Cultural Evolution, and Economic Growth', in U. Witt (ed.), *Explaining Process and Change. Approaches to Evolutionary Economics*, Ann Arbor, MI: University of Michigan Press, pp. 105–21.
Vanberg, V. and W. Kerber (1994), 'Institutional competition among jurisdictions: an evolutionary approach', *Constitutional Political Economy*, **5**, 193–219.
Van den Bergh, R. (2000), 'Towards an institutional legal framework for regulatory competition in Europe', *Kyklos*, **53**, 435–66.
Van den Bergh, R. (2002), 'Forced harmonization of contract law in Europe: communication from the Commission on European Contract Law', in S. Grundmann and J. Stuyck (eds), *An Academic Greenpaper on European Contract Law*, The Hague, London, New York: Kluwer Law International, pp. 249–68.

Van den Bergh, R.J. and P.D. Camesasca (2001), *European Competition Law and Economics: A Comparative Perspective*, Antwerp: Intersentia.
Vaubel, R. (1995), *The Centralisation of Western Europe: The Common Market, Political Integration, and Democracy*, London: Institute of Economic Affairs.
Vaubel, R. (1997), 'The constitutional reform of the European Union', *Constitutional Political Economy*, **7**, 317–24.
Vihanto, M. (1992), 'Competition between local governments as a discovery procedure', *Journal of Institutional and Theoretical Economics*, **148**, 411–36.
Walker, J.L. (1969), 'The diffusion of innovation among the American states', *American Political Science Review*, **63**, 880–99.
Wegner, G. (1996), *Wirtschaftspolitik zwischen Selbst- und Fremdsteuerung – Ein neuer Ansatz der Wirtschaftspolitik*, Baden-Baden: Nomos.
Wegner, G. (1997), 'Economic policy from an evolutionary perspective', *Journal of Institutional and Theoretical Economics*, **153**, 485–509.
Weingast, B.R. (1995), 'The economic role of political institutions: market-preserving federalism and economic development', *Journal of Law, Economics and Organisation*, **11**, 1–31.
Wellisch, D. (2000), *Theory of Public Finance in a Federal State*, Cambridge, MA: Cambridge University Press.
Wilson, J.D. and D.E. Wildasin (2004), 'Capital tax competition: bane or boon', *Journal of Public Economics*, **88**, 1065–91.
Windisch, R. (1998), 'Modellierung von Systemwettbewerb: Grundlagen, Konzepte, Thesen', *Jahrbuch für Neue Politische Ökonomie*, **17**, 121–54.
Wohlgemuth, M. (2002), 'Evolutionary approaches to politics', *Kyklos*, **55**, 223–46.
Woolcock, S. (1994), *The Single European Market: Centralization or Competition Among National Rules?*, London: Royal Institute of International Affairs.
Wouters, J. (2000), 'European company law: Quo Vadis?', *Common Market Law Review*, **37**, 257–307.

14. Can evolutionary economics make a billion $ difference for 60 per cent of the world's poor in Asia?

Hans-Peter Brunner*

1. THE POWER OF THE EVOLUTIONARY APPROACH

The first issue of the *Journal of Evolutionary Economics* (1991) featured prominent academics in the field, such as Dosi, Boulding, and Eliasson among others, presenting and discussing key elements of an 'evolutionary approach'. The key notions elaborated constitute a possible evolutionary approach to economic development. They are: irreversibility (history and path dependence); institutions; population; restructuring and 'creative destruction'; disequilibrium and multiple equilibria; information and learning; innovation and entrepreneurship; non-average behaviour by economic agents; and, positive feedback mechanisms, linkages, and externalities. The discussion in this and other parts of the literature (Witt, 1992; Silverberg, 1994) does not provide a clear manifesto of evolutionary economics. The ability to differentiate evolutionary economics from neoclassical or other types of economic approaches is, however, considered of less importance when compared to the fruitfulness of such concepts in theoretical and empirical exploration of economic development phenomena (Adams, 1993; Witt, 2001b). The argument is not that neoclassical economics is wrong or unnecessary but that there are demonstrable advantages in using institutional and evolutionary concepts. 'Fruitfulness' means making a difference based on the evolutionary explanation of economic phenomena. Does the evolutionary approach have the power to make a difference, that is, to make a real and measurable difference, to people's lives, in the poor, developing economies of Asia?

This chapter explores and explains how key evolutionary concepts are being applied in field cases to the poorest of the developing economies in

Asia, Nepal and the Indian state of West Bengal. This chapter does not intend to present complete institutional economics and evolutionary mathematical models. For those I refer to the literature (for example Allen and Brunner, 2001; Adams, Brunner and Raymond, 2003; Brunner and Allen, 2005). Rather it is the key institutional and evolutionary concepts that can lead to novel solutions to empirical issues encountered in development practice. Concepts are embedded in analytical methods. Method can be mapped onto an evolutionary spectrum, as I will do in section 4 of the chapter. The spectrum starts with 'simple' neoclassical methods with restrictive assumptions and extends to 'complex' adaptive-learning models. Even simple methods can help explore key institutional and evolutionary concepts to act on in practice. For example in the Nepal case, we used a neoclassical CGE model, which was modified to consider transaction-cost reductions in the financial sector as the drive for economic change. The Nepal information-economics issues were then examined from a different angle with a dynamic game-theoretic model. Finally we progressed along the evolutionary spectrum with the application of an evolutionary spatial and non-linear feedback-loop model in the example of West Bengal. This because the issue we felt required higher complexity of analysis, and furthermore because we had the luxury and money to accumulate the requisite quality and quantity of data to test such a model. Models are always, and to a degree, partial representations of the cloud of reality they depict. Knowledge is really about knowing what simplifications can be made in practice without compromising on results. Models should be detailed enough to capture all the important causal real-world relationships that explain outcomes of development. Policy actions spring from fruitful analysis of underlying causes of underdevelopment.

Do evolutionary actions lead to significantly different outcomes from actions that may have been taken, or not taken, on the basis of, let us say, neoclassical concepts and empirical approaches in a field of analysis? Two Asian Development Bank (ADB) investment examples illustrate that, indeed, evolutionary concepts when embedded appropriately in a variety of methods, have the power to make a big difference for economic development in Asia and in the effectiveness of resource use by the ADB and its borrowers. Making institutional and evolutionary economic analysis policy-relevant also means relating different methods and concepts to the methodological and concept frameworks of decision makers, who are still largely steeped in neoclassical economics. The West Bengal example shows how an essentially evolutionary analysis can be related back to traditional, simple decision models of cost-benefit analysis.

2. DEVELOPING COUNTRY SYMPTOMS OF POOR INSTITUTIONS – THE CASE OF THE FINANCIAL SECTOR IN NEPAL

The Concept of Irreversibility

Factors of production are not fungible. A factor is tied up with other factors, and thus increases its marginal contribution beyond what it could contribute on its own. Once factors are tied together they lose value if separated. Factors are up tied in two ways: they are tied through a specific technology and they are connected in an institutional context. They are contextual. A simple example is cultivation where labour, animal power, and land come together when a farmer uses a bullock-drawn plough to prepare a wheat-field. The institutional web includes the specifics of land tenure, input markets, irrigation rights, and credit institutions. A more complicated example would be the organisation of a financial sector or a national airline. In the words of Caballero and Hammour (2000, p. 7) 'relationship specificity forms the underpinning of what *institutional arrangements* are about; technological specificity forms the underpinning of what *restructuring* is about. Most of the time, both are present simultaneously and interact in important ways.'

Simply put, in a developing economy the productive factors, land, labour and capital, can either remain in autarchy, or they can enter into joint production through institutionalised co-operation. Institutions help to ensure that factors in a joint production arrangement will get their commensurate share of returns. When they do not, as is often the case in developing economies like Nepal, or India, one or the other factor will stay in a situation of autarchy; that is, it will be withdrawn in whole or in part because of the absence of incentives or rewards for participation. This means, for example, subsistence jobs for labour will prevail or that a self-employed informal sector will predominate. It may mean capital moving abroad, or being diverted into consumption, rather than employed to put labour and land jointly to work in high-yield activities.

Institutional Economics

The institutional environment as encountered in most developing economies discourages factor co-operation. This is because the hold-up problem is not resolved, so that co-operating factors are encouraged to pre-commit. Institutions solve the hold-up problem by guaranteeing ex ante the effective distribution of the various factors' returns at the margin. These ex-ante controls may be supported by ex-post mechanisms insuring compliance with customary practices or legal requirements; using the term very broadly, implicit or explicit contract enforcement is part and parcel of a working set of institutions. Strong institutions prevent the appropriation of returns attributed to one factor by another factor. For example, only when capital is not appropriated by another factor, let us say labour, through excessive market regulation in favour of labour, is it assured a return commensurate with what is obtainable in international capital markets. When capital can be assured its share of return it will co-operate with labour to invest in job creation, and it will tie itself to the other factors with efficient technologies.

Irreversibility and a weak institutional environment lead to the following phenomena. There is reduced co-operation and at least one factor loses out relatively, and usually it is labour, although all factors are likely to lose when institutional co-ordination does not function. The poor institutional environment in Nepal's financial sector combines bad corporate governance arrangements with a lack of disclosure rules, accounting standards, and bankruptcy procedures. This network of procedures and incentives leads to a severe restriction on movements of capital to the more efficient sectors of the economy and to resource underutilisation and misallocation. The intermediation mechanism of financial institutions has largely not come into being and credit remains directed to short-term commercial and construction finance, predicated on reputation or social ties. Caballero and Hammour (2000) voice a generalisation that fits Nepal well, when they remark, 'The poor institutional framework is the result of a combination of under-development of contracting and regulations and of overly powerful political interest groups who have tilted the institutional balance excessively in their favour (p. 10).'

To counter the co-operation failure, Nepal has pursued a policy of directed lending where large portions of private loanable funds are directed according to a government formula to the so-called deprived sections at low, mandated rates. The chief targets are, in principle, small businesses, marginal farmers, and impoverished women. Most banks choose not to engage in such loans because of high transaction costs, and simply follow the legal alternative of pushing money to microcredit wholesalers. Moreover, the quota system of directed lending leads financial institutions to see this lending as a tax on their turnover and profits. Efforts at risk management and evaluation of borrowers are diminished with the effect of high non-performing loans. The deprived sections see directed lending as a give-away. It has become the ideal target for rent seekers inside and outside the system. Ultimately, the intent of lending to poorer sections of the economy is undermined. Directed lending in Nepal has increasingly favoured those with some clout and good connections to avail of money give-aways.

Capital deployment in Nepal is being held up by financial-sector failures. In this instance, capital is the appropriated factor, which gets a lower rate of return than it should at the margin. Because two public-sector banks control about two-thirds of the banking sector's assets, it has been easy for officials to command funds to cover government deficits and borrowing needs. It has been simple, too, for the public-sector firms to cover their losses by borrowing from public-sector commercial and investment banks. There is thus the paradox that private banks are awash in loanable funds but cannot pursue long-term lending in an atmosphere of reliable information disclosure, secure contract enforcement, and prudential regulation, while public institutions, whose assets have been raided by government and politicians, are insolvent. A consequence is that capital in Nepal has been reluctant to tie itself efficiently to labour and land, applying efficient technologies in commerce, manufacturing, or farming. Productivity remains extremely low in all sectors and Nepal's 2001 per-capita income of $235 earns membership in the club of the world's poorest countries.

Ideally, small, but growing, amounts of credit would mobilise large pools of underutilised labour and set off a growth process, but distortions in the financial sector make this infeasible. Compared to the more capital-abundant, wealthier countries, efficient investment in Nepal ought to take the form of encouraging labour-intensive technologies but this is not happening in urban or rural areas. Theoretical and empirical work at the ADB shows in Nepal's case that financial-sector distortions and institutional weakness have led to excessive capital invested in inefficient sectors of the economy, mainly capital-intensive production in public-sector enterprises and government services. Financial-sector repression leads to unemployment, impedes economic growth, and increases poverty.

Distortions also characterise rural lending institutions in Nepal. Despite the nationwide system of branches of the state-owned Agricultural Development Bank of Nepal (ADBN), offering low, subsidised loans, informal money lending is pervasive. A key finding that has emerged in Nepal is that informal and formal lenders offer borrowers differentiated bundles of loans and services because of their differing opportunity costs of funds, command of information, and the weight of transaction costs, including under-the-table payments to formal agents (Adams et al., 2003). This approach applies deep institutional analysis to explain the common observation that despite the appearance that formal interest rates are well below those of the money lenders, the informal sector is not displaced by formal lending. The explanation is that when the full costs of a formal loan, including transportation, lost time, documentation, and bribes, are estimated, they converge upwards to the rate charged by the informal lenders, who incorporate similar charges into their quoted interest rates.

Beck (1997) demonstrates that the emergence of formal and informal financial markets occurs largely because of informational asymmetries between lenders and borrowers. Gupta and Chaudhuri (1998) investigate the effects of bribery in the formal sector. Morduch (1999) validates the presence of variant informal and formal client risks and information costs. Stiglitz and Weiss (1981), Broecker (1990), and Hannan (1997) investigate the impact of information problems on interest rates and competition. Dell'Ariccia (1998) employs a model of spatial competition in banking to analyse the effects of product differentiation and information asymmetries in determining barriers to entry. None of these studies treats in one rigorous framework the principal features observed to typify South Asian rural credit markets: spatial segmentation, information lacunae, transaction costs, heterogeneous informal and formal agents, and moderately disparate bundles of services or loan 'products'. The Nepal work integrates each of these facets into a competitive model of development finance with heterogeneous credit services, with an emphasis on how adverse selection problems associated with information asymmetries can evolve from differences in credit services. This decidedly institutional approach hinges on the existence of information barriers across geography and customer segments.

The main features of rural finance are now well known. Most borrowers are remote from formal sources of credit whereas informal sources are readily accessible. Travel burdens add to the formal-sector transaction costs. Informal lenders have good knowledge about individual credit histories in their circles of clients, while formal agents rely upon irrelevant templates and place costly documentation encumbrances on potential borrowers. Further, informal credit agents can tailor the attributes of a loan to the length of a crop-growing season, offer a balloon payment after harvest, and permit use of funds for consumption or weddings; the regulation-bound formal agent can normally not make these accommodations. With respect to enforcement, money-lenders and their ilk have immediate recovery or punishment capabilities and can display flexibility when necessary. Contrariwise, in Nepal, for example, as against tens of thousands of defaults to the Agricultural Development Bank, only a handful of cases have been brought to adjudication (Adams and Brunner, 1997). For the borrower, the total loan experience entails a choice between one bundle of services or 'product' and another, and a comparison to the associated total costs. In brief, the informal loan 'product' is differentiated from the formal loan 'product'.

Although the perspectives of the informal and formal lenders differ, the costs of determining the creditworthiness of clients, in order to address the hidden information problem; monitoring loan use, to address the moral-hazard problem; and, securing collection, to address the enforcement problem, are high, while most loans are small and short-term. Levine (1997) offers conditions for formal financial market viability, but in practice agricultural lending is very commonly non-viable for private-sector credit institutions. Consequently, the formal credit sector is severely constrained in its ability to meet the requirements of rural development, at least with current institutional arrangements, in-built incentives, and poor information systems. The common response of governments and international donors has been to offer subsidised credit, set credit quotas by type of loan, peg an array of interest rates, and target special groups such as women or the poor. The outcome has usually been very low or even negative rates of social return on the one hand, and ultimate insolvency for the institutions on the other.

What institutional analysis offers, in conjunction with careful measurement of true transaction costs and informational asymmetries, is not only an understanding of the workings of the informal and formal mechanisms, but the hope of appropriate institutional design that can improve loan delivery and recovery from formal agencies.

The system's institutional and incentive failures are associated with use of extremely primitive technologies and resistance to the adoption of new skills and tools, oftentimes out of a misguided sense, shared by management and labour, that their jobs are at risk. Nepal's financial system operates largely on a manual basis. This leads to costly and cumbersome procedures as well as poor service delivery. Payment and settlement systems are not fully computerised and no electronic funds transfers are possible. It may take up to 30 days to have a cheque cleared if it was issued outside Kathmandu and as a result, the economy is largely 'cash and carry' based. Moreover, the absence of information technologies in all areas of the financial sector makes information collection costly and unreliable, and hinders effective monitoring and supervision. Nepal's ADBN, for instance, is at least three years behind in generating credible income statements and balance sheets.

Development Policy Responses

Understanding irreversibility consequences for an economy and the role of institutions in an evolutionary frame leads to sound policies for financial-sector reform. Furthermore, there are several ways of estimating the sizeable benefits that accrue from comprehensive reforms, buttressed by the parallel adoption of modern technologies. The use of a modified Computable General Equilibrium (CGE) model (Bhattarai, 1999) such that change is driven by a reduction in transaction costs, demonstrates that continuing down the path of rapid and comprehensive financial-sector reform in Nepal will release extra resources for savings and investment. 'Comprehensive reform' means mutually reinforcing institutional and legal developments involving the Ministry of Finance, Central Bank (Nepal Rastra Bank), the Nepal Stock Exchange, commercial banks, joint-venture banks, multinational banks, finance companies, and rural development banks, including the Agricultural Development Bank of Nepal, co-operatives, and NGOs.

Financial reform has a widespread effect on informal credit markets in the rural sector. Nepal's rural credit market is dominated by the informal sector. In repression, access of rural firms or households to financial institutions is limited and the local money-lenders charge rates of interest that may reflect market power. Increased competition with formal-sector financial institutions will, over time, increase lending-flows and offer lower rates. The opening of rural savings windows by formal agencies will enhance savings-flows throughout the financial system, raising Nepal's aggregate savings rate.

In addition to the pro-poor effects on employment and income generation through more efficient capital allocation, the introduction of technologies will increase transparency and reduce rent-seeking opportunities of individuals through monopolisation of information. Access to information is often excessively priced for the poorest segment of the population. The use of information technologies also allows for a more efficient franchising and distribution system, and greater bargaining power for the original producer against traditional intermediaries who often collect excessive margins at the expense of the original producer.

In sum, the institutional immaturity of Nepal's financial sector has produced the effects that arise from factor appropriation, in this case capital: reduced co-operation with the other factors, labour and land, investment tilted towards capital-intensive and unproductive projects; resulting under-employment and poverty; and, chronic formal and informal credit market segmentation. While the methods used in the analysis of factor appropriation of returns are on the 'simple' side of the evolutionary spectrum, the empirical application of institutional and evolutionary concepts to Nepal's financial sector problems makes a real and measurable difference.

The ADB has responded to the technological and institutional challenge in the financial sector in Nepal. A series of technical assistance projects amounting to over $10 million are aimed at improving financial and corporate governance. This means improving disclosure standards, training the accounting and auditing professions, updating and completing the legal framework of the financial sector, and training the judiciary and attorneys in commercial law and enforcement of contracts in the market framework. It means modest investment of $10 to $20 million in the information infrastructure of the financial sector, including an electronic payment system, interbank settlements, automated teller machine connections, management information systems, company information systems, and associated training and marketing, among other things. None of this would have been conceived in this manner as a response to the co-operation and co-ordination problem, without the power of evolutionary and institutional analysis.

An important further point, which draws on the evolutionary tradition, is that institutional changes must move hand in hand, and in fact lead, technological innovations. The aforementioned reforms in institutional designs and incentives must be reinforced by the introduction of computers, information systems, and a nationwide information and communications grid. Beginning in 2001, with ADB technical assistance, Nepal's private banks have undertaken an initiative to create an initial hub for payment clearances. Long-term studies demonstrate large economic returns from a national system that will embrace the public-sector banks, as they advance to privatisation, the rural banks, and microfinance institutions. E-commerce, reduced telecommunications costs, and other advantages are understood to be part of this bundle of services.

3. TECHNOLOGY RESTRUCTURING AND POPULATION DYNAMICS – BRINGING THE ENTREPRENEUR BACK: THE CASE OF TRADE AND TRANSPORT IN WEST BENGAL

Evolutionary Concepts of Population Restructuring and 'creative destruction'

Modern economies are essentially evolutionary economies. They are in a state of constant disequilibrium. Technology creation and diffusion through learning is an essential feature. Entrepreneurs learn about new technologies and are able to embody them in new ways in productive and service activities. In the words of Caballero and Hammour, technological specificity forms the underpinning of what restructuring is about. Resource re-allocation is made in a market arrangement, constrained and regulated by societal institutions. That arrangement allows for effective creative destruction where new firms using the newest techniques are continuously created, and outdated units are destroyed as their sales fall, their prices become uncompetitive, and their inputs are bid away by succeeding firms. Murrell (1990) argued strongly that the lack of creative destruction and learning processes led to the rapid technological demise of the Eastern bloc. The Eastern bloc was notoriously inefficient in restructuring production factors from less productive uses into increasingly productive units.

It lacked the institutional mechanisms for competitive selection in a fluid market and information environment. In Nepal, the institutional environment has been shown crucial for the efficiency of restructuring transactions on a short to medium-term time-scale. Recent empirical work in transformation and developing countries has confirmed the applicability of the creative destruction concept, and the use of effective restructuring processes for entrepreneurial learning, new employment, wealth creation, and economic growth (Kornai, 2000; Brunner, 2001).

In the long term, the self-generating potential of an economy reforms business organisations and increases the knowledge potential. Growth is the result of these processes that move production constraints. Macroeconomic effects emerge from the micro-economic effects of institutional and firm interaction as part of a sector population. Selection forces and transition processes elevate an economy on a macro-economic level. The interaction of firm-level process with aggregate economic performance has not been adequately studied by evolutionary economists. Dopfer (2001) aptly describes the nested hierarchy and systemic 'complexification' from the 'subject level' of a firm, to the 'plurality level' of many sector populations of firms at the economy level.

(Positive) Feedback and Externalities

The process of creative destruction is most effective for economic development and growth when it allows the exploitation of positive externalities, involving increasing returns, agglomeration effects, and non-linearity or network effects. Increasing returns are prominent in knowledge-intensive sectors, but not only there. The winner-take-all literature relates to this, when it shows the urgency for market players to corner market-share for dominance through monopolistic competition. Agglomeration effects are prominent in spatial models, where productivity increases relate to a spatial convergence of resources in a critical mass. Overcrowding in mental or physical space can however lead to negative agglomeration and environmental effects, as many inhabitants of ugly, polluted megalopolises can attest. Network effects play a prominent role for entrepreneurs who produce network goods, where the utility to consumers rises with the increased and more geographically widespread use of the product, or by services delivered through an infrastructure.

Non-average Behaviour by Economic Agents

Firms exist of course not in the abstract but are real, run by entrepreneurs and helped by people. Variety, for example reflected in differences in product and service-unit costs, is constantly recreated in an evolving economy at the subject or firm level. However to evolve, modern models of circular and cumulative causation define the macro-environment in terms of frequency of adoptions of a product and service by a sector population (Dopfer, 2001, p. 34). A change in relative frequencies of varieties present in a population comes about through frequency-dependency effects. Members of a firm population exert an effect on each other (Witt, 2001a, p. 55). Firm behaviour is correlated, and even more so in geography when firms which are physically close are more likely to adapt to and learn from each other's behaviour. In that process, variety is reduced as at the subject level, firms want to imitate best practice, if they learn of such practice. (Tacit) information transfer is incomplete, and levels of know-how and capabilities of firms to innovate and imitate are inherently different. In the market, a selection process works on firm populations. Firms with better products and services (unit price per quality) win market share at the cost of others, and some firms are driven out of business, or at times new firms enter with new knowledge, translated into products and services. The circular and cumulative interplay of creation of non-average behaviour, with co-ordination when learning and imitation come into play, and with market selection, provides the engine of transformation. The processes in their interplay require the theoretical link of micro- with macro- level analysis in a nested hierarchy, as variety and its frequency distribution is a concept at the macro level, and regeneration of variety is one at the micro level.

People learn and carry know-how, and are motivated to innovate. To do so they converge on a distinct place in time and on bricks-and-mortar facilities. Firm-level heterogeneity in plant-level productivity and competitiveness is in good part driven by firm-specific locational and disturbance factors (Haltiwanger, 2000). Firm facilities are served by infrastructure; for example, roads connect to the factory and help move people and goods in and out. It is an important question why firms locate and invest in space when they are supposed to attract the most productive resources, and combine them under management for a competitive service or product to be sold in the domestic and foreign market. Surely firms will locate only in places where they have cost-effective access to resources, markets, know-how and so on. Governments are often in the business of providing the public goods of access and location, learning, and know-how to make sure the process of creative destruction is tilted towards the creative side. Generally, research shows that firms locate most productively where they have the best access to inputs and to markets on a per quality adjusted service or product unit/kilometre measure related to time. This depends also on the institutional arrangements for exchange and regional or international trade. One could of course say that knowledge-intensive services and products are less geography- and infrastructure-dependent. Still they are even more people-dependent, and qualified people want to live and work in an attractive location. Also, high-tech products tend to be more time-sensitive in delivery to customers, and even if roads may not be necessary for their transport, these services or products would have to be moved out and around, and across borders by electronic means or by air.

Development-policy Responses

Here is a brief summary of a partial application of the ideas just described as this chapter does not intend to present the complete evolutionary mathematical model (for the model refer to Brunner and Allen, 2005). The question that was addressed by this ADB work concerned the probable impacts of a large transportation infrastructure project for West Bengal. Transport consultants gathered detailed data concerning the flows of goods through the region, and explored the possible changes in costs that might result from the proposed infrastructure development. This relatively complex model is driven again by the change in transaction or transport costs, as was the 'simple' model in the case of Nepal's financial sector. Further, the model used here set out to explore the spatial economic impacts of these changes. The transportation consultant supplied the flows of goods and commodities between 46 economic zones (i, j . . .), along the transport-infrastructure grid of West Bengal. This was provided in the form of a matrix of origin and destination flows by volume and by value, for 24 different sectors.

The provision of these data concerning flows and costs for the region allowed a much simpler version of a general model described in Allen and Brunner (2001). In fact the key piece of information that is needed to drive the model is the actual cost of transporting goods between the zones, and the manner in which this will be changed by any particular transportation investment project. It is these changes in cost that will affect the prices charged at the points of consumption, and will therefore confer an economic benefit on consumers. This can then be run 'through' the simplified model, demonstrating where the multipliers will lead to increased production, and in turn how this will create employment and increased incomes. See Figure 14.1.

From the view of spatial structure, variables in the modelling framework are disaggregated into those of different regions and sectors. The spatial structure that exists is generated by the interactions among regions and sectors. The interactions in spatial structure strengthen their non-linearities and feedback features. Therefore, the spatial structure of the

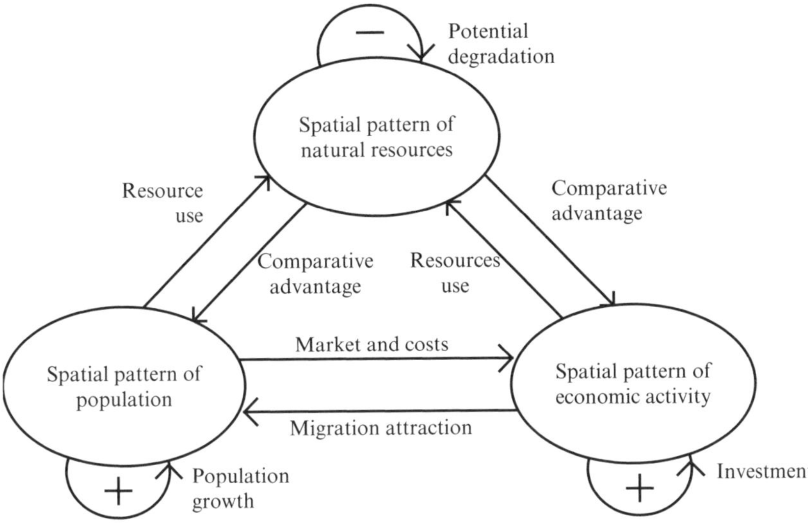

Figure 14.1 Basic modelling framework

system is not taken as being fixed necessarily, but instead as being the result of an ongoing evolutionary process. Most importantly, it introduces three behaviours through the use of 'attractiveness' which are the demand attractiveness, migration attractiveness and investment attractiveness. These are the mechanisms by which small differences in price, incentives and productivity can be amplified through self-reinforcing processes, eventually leading to a spatial restructuring of the system. Economic incentives and investment attractiveness create the opportunity of employment, increase the vacancies and raise labour productivity, leading to increases in employment levels and wages. The improved income-earning opportunity will alter relative economic conditions among the regions and increase migration of the workforce, which in turn will alter relative investment behaviour of sectors.

The model considers how the lower prices of delivery result in consumers spending their gains on extra consumption that, in turn, generates more jobs. The model therefore responds to the reduced prices by examining how much the different income classes are affected and how they may choose to spend the resulting income. Savings will affect income groups differently, as those that spend more save more in absolute terms, but the poor will be able to buy more food, and also if jobs available in the industrial and service sectors increase, then this will also increase the income of some of the poor.

The model uses three sectors (k) for its operation: agriculture, industry and services. One of the first steps therefore was to aggregate the data concerning transport into these categories.

The flows of goods are generated by the fact that the spatial distribution of demand does not coincide with that of supply. For example, the city of Calcutta clearly requires large quantities of food, but has no agricultural land available to produce it. The cost of transportation, however, acts as a 'net loss' to the 'utility' of consumers, since they must pay for it, but only because they want the goods that it brings.

The model allows us to follow the manner in which the increased demand from each point falls onto the different zones of production and leads to the possibility of increased production. This in turn requires jobs to be created and filled, which means that people must be available to fill them. The demographic increase in each zone provides a growing number of people seeking jobs, but this may be insufficient in some zones, and too great in others. The actual growth of active, filled jobs therefore reflects the changing distribution of population between the zones, and the migratory flows that tend to reflect the job opportunities. Moreover, different wage levels available in the sectors will also allow growth in a higher-paying sector at the expense of a lower-paying one. Another factor that is important is the availability of land for economic activities. For example, clearly there is a very large demand for agricultural products in Calcutta, but there is no space to make fields and grow crops and so instead, jobs are not created and filled (despite the demand) and food is transported into the city.

The model takes into account these different factors, and calculates where economic growth will occur, by sector and zone. This allows us to track the changes in employment for the 33 different spatial zones in West Bengal, and to use this as a base for a comparison with the changes that occur when different transport infrastructure projects are implemented. The model runs these mechanisms over the 33 different spatial zones, and also for the different sectors of the economy. Population is attracted to places of perceived employment opportunity and this allows vacancies to be transformed into jobs. This increases the local income, and hence the demand emanating from the zone.

The non-linear dynamic model will generate changes resulting from the reduced prices of goods in different zones, adjusting supply and demand arriving at each zone to equality, and changing the distribution of jobs to reflect the relative locations of the demand and of transportation costs. By running the model with no modifications in the transportation-matrix costs, we can generate a 'base scenario'. This can then be compared with a run in which the costs of transportation have been changed as a result of some investment in an infrastructure project.

The model can then compare various differences between the two simulations. First, there is the amount of 'extra income' available for spending in any particular zone. This can further be broken down into that arising for the poor, medium and rich income-groups. In addition however, we can see the difference in the distribution of jobs over time. This changes the income distribution within each zone and changes the proportions of the different income groups. It also changes the overall income generated in a zone, and hence contributes to the benefits.

The data supplied were the comparative transportation costs in 2015, with or without the project, and again in 2025 with and without the project. The 'with or without' differences reveal the spatial distribution of consequences of the project, the impacts on employment, and on the different income groups of the zone. For 2015, the overall gain is some 40 000 jobs. These extra jobs can immediately translate into a gain for the poor of each zone. This is because these are 'new jobs' in addition to those that would have existed without the infrastructure investment. For decision-making purposes, when we take out these results from the evolutionary model into the simple conceptual frame of a cost-benefit analysis, we can find a difference in results resulting from the use of a more complex model. If we multiply the 40 000 by the average wages per job, then we find about 600 million Rs per year. In addition to this, there are the effects on external trade, and also the savings in consumption costs as a result of the cheaper transportation. These two effects add up to a nominal consumer surplus for 2015 of about 19 billion Rs. For 2025, the extra jobs generated are estimated at about 117 000, which are worth about 1.7 billion Rs. The consumer surplus attributed to investment multiplies to 50 billion Rs. by 2025.

Interpolating the continuing growth of the investment benefits between the first investment year 2002, and 2025 (a gestation period of some 20 to 30 years is normal in large infrastructure projects), one gets a cost/benefit stream as shown in Table 14.1. The stream is discounted at 12 per cent, and results in a net present value (NPV) of about 28.9 billion Rs. In the table, I have separated out the benefit stream calculated for the poorer section of West Bengal's population. As a percentage, a share of 21.5 per cent of the overall benefit stream accrues to the poor.

What difference does the evolutionary approach employed make to the outcome? We would know, had a conventional cost-benefit model been used in parallel. In fact, the transportation consultant used a conventional linear trade, transport and logistics model, as outlined in Figure 14.2. Linear traffic forecasts induce transport-cost savings (consumer surplus). In addition, a reduction in transport logistics costs induces demand for both domestically consumed and internationally traded goods. The latter

Table 14.1 Corridor evaluation level

Corridor evaluation level	Rs million in 2000 prices	
Year	Cost/benefit	Benefits to poor
2002	−3500	
2003	−4000	
2004	−3500	
2005	−3500	
2006	1700	357
2007	2140	449
2008	2690	565
2009	3390	712
2010	4270	897
2011	5370	1128
2012	6770	1422
2013	8520	1789
2014	10720	2251
2015	13500	2835
2016	14573	3060
2017	15731	3303
2018	16981	3566
2019	18330	3849
2020	19786	4155
2021	21359	4485
2022	23056	4842
2023	24888	5226
2024	26865	5642
2025	29000	6090
NPV	**28907**	
Sum of benefits	**298544**	**56624**
%poor of benefits		**21.5%**
EIRR + 25.07%	($0.15)	

results were obtained by simply using price elasticities of demand. Since this linear model relates trade generated to single (not multiple) geographic zones and thus to individual investment projects only, it did not estimate the cumulative effects as well as the multiplier effects that result from a series of investments along a trade corridor. All this model generates is first-round cost (time) savings and demand changes.

The calculation of the benefits related to the individual investment components yield, as is shown in Table 14.2, considerably lower total benefits. These are on aggregate still good investment projects. However a

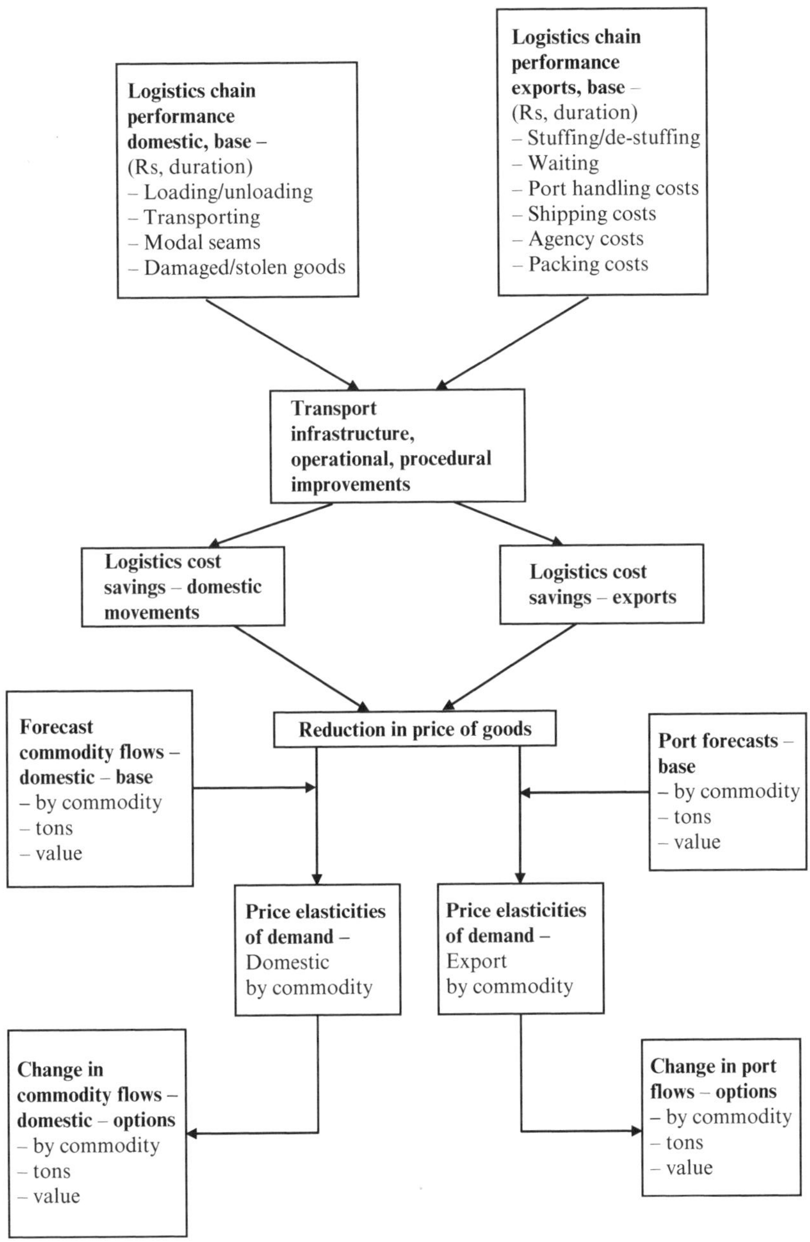

Figure 14.2 Estimating trade impacts from corridor improvements

Table 14.2 Individual project evaluation level (on constant annuity payments, scenario A)

	Rs. Million at 2000 prices		
Component	Cost	NPV	EIRR
Haldia-Uluberia	−5200	8000	27.9
Uluberia- Joka	−7500	−2458	6.2
Raiganj-Islampur	−2000	2600	25.8
Shantipur	−800	1800	30.7
Sum	−15 500	9942	

decision maker using the output of these individual projects would conclude that it was wise to not invest in the lowest-return project, so as not to lower the average return on investment. This however has the effect that one corner-stone project along the entire transport and trade chain is eliminated, with dramatic effects, as the largest part of the multiplier gains are lost. The evolutionary model did take into account the multiplier gains that accrue to the whole system by combining the four investments in one model, and achieving a combined EIRR on combined investment of some 20 billion Rs. This is an extra NPV of $500 million (which is equivalent to $5 billion in nominal benefits, with an estimated 21 per cent going to the poor)!

As significant as the differences between the use of an evolutionary and a neoclassical approach turned out to be, it should be noted here that the evolutionary model was much less of an evolutionary model than would be ideally wanted. Although the model used increasing returns from investment, and was based on geography and positive agglomeration and network effects, it fell short in not modelling behavioural differences among actors, such as employers along the trade corridor. The model lacks in reality because it cannot generate learning among actors, and it does not allow for qualitative systems-change based on actors' creativity and on a selection process taking hold. Such a model extension has been proposed by Allen and Brunner (2001) and Brunner and Allen (2005). Would such an extension be worthwhile, given the already large gain from using a simpler non-linear dynamics model? Let us now discuss the issue of geography and modelling. How close to reality can (or should) we get without getting lost in the complexities?

4. ISSUE IN EVOLUTIONARY ECONOMICS: GEOGRAPHY AND MODELLING – HOW CLOSE TO REALITY CAN WE GET WITHOUT GETTING LOST IN THE COMPLEXITIES?

Understanding reality and gaining knowledge about a problem require us to reduce the real complexity of any particular situation to a simpler, more understandable system by making specific simplifying assumptions or by undertaking institutional analysis that reifies many acts of behaviour into non-random patterns. The hope is that there exists a representation that, while being sufficiently simple to be understood, remains sufficiently representative of reality to be useful. These assumptions and reifications have been discussed elsewhere (Allen, 1988, 1993, 1994, 1997, 1998) and we shall briefly summarise them here in Figure 14.3.

We use assumptions, simplifications, and reifications in order to reduce social and economic complexity to manageable proportions. These are:

1. That we can define a boundary between the part of the world that we want to 'understand' and the rest. In other words, we assume first that there is a 'System' and an 'Environment'.
2. That we have rules for the classification of objects that lead to a relevant taxonomy for the system components, which will enable us to understand what is going on. This is often decided entirely intuitively.
3. The third assumption concerns the level of description below that which we are trying to understand, and assumes all phenomena are either all identical to each other and to the average, or have a diversity that is at all times distributed 'normally' around the average.
4. That the individual behaviour of sub-components can be described by *average interaction parameters*.

The crucial difference that marks out evolutionary (complex) systems concerns assumption 3. This assumes that all firms of a given type, 'x' say, are either identical, equal to the average type; or have a diversity that remains normally distributed around the average type. This means that for such models 'sectors' or statistical aggregates of 'firms' are used as variables reflecting the 'average properties' of the included firms. But in reality, the microdiversity of behaviours among individual firms in any particular part of the system is the result of the history of local dynamics occurring in the system. This local history concerns the local mechanisms by which knowledge, skills, techniques and heuristics are passed on to new individuals over time. The existence of microdiversity will necessarily lead to an evolutionary learning process of economic development. If there are firms

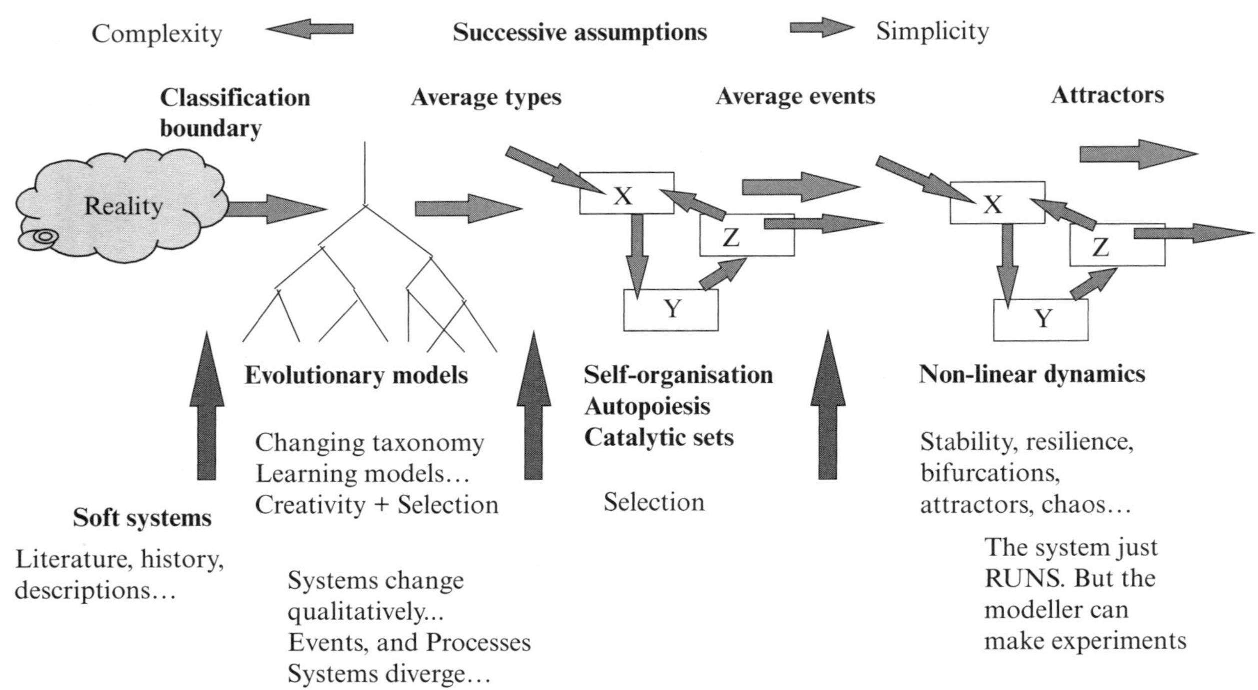

Figure 14.3 *Assumptions made in reducing complexity to simplicity, in order to obtain understanding, and predictability – providing the assumptions hold*

with higher and lower productivity then the higher ones will be gradually amplified, while those with lower productivity are suppressed, and the 'average' for the whole population of firms increases productivity (Allen and McGlade, 1987; Brunner, 1994; Caballero and Hammour, 2000). This is the mechanism by which adaptation takes place. This demonstrates the vital part played by exploratory, non-average behaviour, and shows that, in the long term, evolution selects for firms with the ability to learn, rather than for populations with optimal, but fixed, behaviour. Economic transformation therefore should really be modelled by these fully evolutionary models.

As mentioned before, models are always, and to a degree, partial representations of the cloud of reality they depict. Models should be detailed enough to capture all the important causal real-world relationships that explain outcomes of development. Evolutionary complexity, however, reduces predictability as non-linear causal relationships, externalities, network effects, and geography lead to multiple equilibria. Outcomes are path-dependent, in part matter of chance. In arguing with Krugman (1997) on the utility of complex models, one needs to show that complex and realistic approaches yield results which formalised models in a simple setting cannot. The West Bengal example shows that models that are complex, and even those that may take into account heterogeneity of actors, can be tested for results. Yet even simple models as applied to the analysis of the financial sector in Nepal, once enriched with institutional concepts such as transaction costs, yield significant power to make a big difference for economic development in Asia and in the effectiveness of resource use by the ADB and its borrowers.

5. EVOLUTIONARY AND INSTITUTIONAL ECONOMICS AS A HOUSEHOLD TOOL IN MULTILATERAL DEVELOPMENT-AGENCY ECONOMICS

Models have to incorporate sufficiently realistic assumptions in order to be reliable and useful. The parsimonious rendering of a society or economy in terms of a set of reified institutions must render the essential features of ongoing interactions of thousands of disparate individual actors, be they consumers, farmers, or firms. Otherwise one falls into the trap of the drunkard who looks for his watch under the street-lamp, because that is where there is light. While simple non-linear, dynamic models may appear to predict perfectly the future path of the system, this seemingly solid piece of knowledge is only as good as the assumptions that underlie it (Allen, 1999). Making an unrealistic prediction may actually be misleading, and thus much worse than knowing outcomes only with some probability. Knowledge is really about knowing what simplifications can be made without compromising on results. It is also about knowing the limits to knowledge. Complex, self-organising systems, and the human society and economy, can only be grasped up to a point, but we are fortunate that in most cases, whether we are farmers, entrepreneurs, policy makers, or international development economists the artificial constructions of models embedded in institutional systems are sufficient to permit self-correcting policy recommendations, including on specific projects.

With these caveats in mind, the chapter shows an evolutionary approach, if widely used, can make billions of dollars of difference in incomes for the 60 per cent of the world's poor who reside in Asia. The case studies in Nepal and West Bengal show very large incremental impacts of well-conceived projects on such key indicators as per-capita incomes, employment, and poverty reduction. Decisions are being based sometimes on one approach or another, and sometimes on a combination of approaches. The choice of analytical method and of concepts not only helps in selecting the best use of funds by international agencies, but facilitates institutional designs more likely to lead to desirable outcomes. The evolutionary-economics profession should stand by its theoretical models and by the concepts derived from them, and get involved in the practice of these models. The practice requires us at times to couch institutional and evolutionary concepts in simple, even neoclassical terms for a decision maker, as the two ADB cases illustrate.

What practical steps would make use of institutional analysis and evolutionary modelling as methods more common in the development profession, and hence more familiar to development policy makers? There are several concrete measures. The first is to propose appropriate measures of economic and social targets. Traditionally, the construction of economic aggregates has fallen short of the measures appropriate from an evolutionary and institutional perspective. This situation serves as an obstacle to applied work. Hard work needs to go into the collection of appropriate data and information that make the parameters and variables used in evolutionary models measurable and communicable. It may be necessary to use fieldwork to compensate for the absence of relevant data. In the Nepal and Bengal projects, teams spent many person-days in the field gathering baseline information on such normally unmeasured variables as transaction costs, prevalence of corruption, the implicit cost burdens on borrowers, actual transport costs, and so forth.

Second, we need to look at the regional distribution and population distribution of economic effects. The spatial and social dimensions of projects are rarely estimated. The frictions associated with transaction costs and information costs have a strong impact on locational and distributional outcomes. Quality needs to be considered alongside quantity. With respect to financial services, this means lowering transaction and information costs for both lenders and borrowers. Selection processes for firms would be modelled on quality unit cost as the selection criterion. Population-model parameters would be calibrated on sector entry- and exit-rates, concentration-ratios, and changes in firm concentration. Learning parameters and variables would be incorporated on the basis of entrepreneurial response and adjustment rates.

Third, there is a need for expanded training of the staff of development agencies and client governments. For example, because of budget constraints, United States Agency for International Development (USAID) economists working in overseas posts have not had in-service training for over a decade. In 2000, a workshop was conducted to update economic-growth officers on the approaches of institutional and evolutionary economics (USAID 2000). Economists can engage in co-operative, network arrangements within the academic community to connect with practitioners. Very few development practitioners take the time, or have the budget and incentives, to participate in academically oriented conferences. Some may be discouraged by the lack of relevance of much academic dialogue. Thought needs to be devoted to building bridges with practitioners. The evolutionary-economics associations throughout the world can play a role in facilitating cross-fertilisation. Exchange of knowledge, diffusion of empirical work, and concentration of effort in tandem with practitioners will help remove the obstacles to applied work which exist in the academic community.

Fourth, evolutionary and institutional economists should make strong efforts to connect to development banks and to the consulting firms that provide expertise for their projects. Most institutionalists are well prepared to provide evolutionary types of analysis for the practitioners in the multilateral agencies and to liaise with the financial, development and business communities in overseas assignments.

NOTES

* The author alone in his personal capacity, not the Asian Development Bank, is responsible for the article's content. The author thanks the participants of the Wartensee seminar and is particularly grateful to Kurt Dopfer and John Adams as well as an anonymous referee for their helpful comments. The usual disclaimer applies.

REFERENCES

Adams, John (1993), 'Institutions and economic development: structure, process, and incentive', in Marc R. Tool (ed.), *Institutional Economics: Theory, Method, Policy*, Boston, MA: Kluwer Academic, pp. 245–69.

Adams, John and Hans-Peter Brunner for Asian Development Bank (1997), *Project Performance Audit: Fifth Agricultural Credit in Nepal*, ADB, PPAR, NEP 181054.

Adams, John, Hans-Peter Brunner and Frank Raymond (2003), 'Interactions of informal and formal agents in South Asian rural credit markets: an analysis of information asymmetries and adverse selection with heterogeneous credit services', *Review of Development Economics*, **7** (3) (August), 431–44.

Allen, Peter (1988), 'Evolution: why the whole is greater than the sum of its parts', in W. Wolff, C.J. Soeder and F.R. Drepper (eds), *Ecodynamics*, Berlin: Springer.

Allen, Peter (1993), 'Evolution: persistent ignorance from continual learning', in R. Day and P. Chen (eds), *Nonlinear Dynamics and Evolutionary Economics*, Oxford: Oxford University Press, Chapter III, 8, pp.101–12.

Allen, Peter (1994), 'Evolutionary complex systems: models of technology change', in Loet Leydesdorff and Peter Van den Besselaar (eds), *Evolutionary Economics and Chaos Theory*, London: Pinter.

Allen, Peter (1997), *Cities and Regions as Self-Organising Systems: Models of Complexity*, London: Gordon and Breach.

Allen, Peter (1998), 'Selbstorganisation', in F. Scheiter and G. Silverberg (eds), *Modelling Complex Economic Evolution*, Berlin: Duncker & Humblot.

Allen, Peter (1999), 'Knowledge, ignorance and the evolution of complex systems', paper prepared for 'Evolutionary Economics' Meeting, Brisbane.

Allen, Peter (2001), 'Knowledge ignorance and the evolution of complex systems', in J. Foster and S. Metcalfe (eds), *Frontiers of Evolutionary Economics: Competition, Self-Organisation and Innovation Policy*, Cheltenham UK and Northampton, MA, USA: Edward Elgar.

Allen, Peter and Hans-Peter Brunner (2001), 'A sub-regional development approach – transport, international trade, and investment modeled in space', electronic copy on SSRN http://papers.ssrn.com/paper.taf?abstract_id=258429

Allen, Peter and J.M. McGlade (1987), 'Evolutionary drive: the effect of microscopic diversity, error making and noise', *Foundations of Physics*, **17** (7) (July), 723–8.

Beck, T. (1997), 'Banking at the margin: why do formal and informal intermediaries coexist?', working paper, University of Virginia.

Bhattarai, Keshab (1999), 'Welfare and distributional impacts of financial liberalization in Nepal', working paper, University of Warwick.

Boulding, Kenneth (1991), 'What is evolutionary economics?', *Journal of Evolutionary Economics*, **1** (1), 9–17.

Broecker, T. (1990), 'Credit-worthiness tests and interbank competition', *Econometrica*, **58** (2), 429–52.

Brunner, Hans-Peter (1994), 'Technological Diversity, Random Selection in a Population of Firms, and Technological Institutions of Government', in Loet Leydesdorff and Peter Van den Besselaar (eds), *Evolutionary Economics and Chaos Theory*, London: Pinter.

Brunner, Hans-Peter (2001), 'East German international trade during transition as reflection of the dynamics of competitiveness,' *Eastern Economic Journal*, **27** (3) (Summer), 287–308.

Brunner, Hans-Peter and Peter M. Allen (2005), *Productivity, Competitiveness and Incomes in Asia: An Evolutionary Theory of International Trade,* Cheltenham, UK and Northampton, MA, USA. Edward Elgar.
Caballero, Ricardo and Mohammad Hammour (2000), 'Institutions, restructuring, and macroeconomic performance', NBER Working Paper 7720, May.
Dell'Ariccia, G. (1998), 'Asymmetric information and the market structure of the banking industry', Working Paper WP/98/92, International Monetary Fund.
Dopfer, Kurt (2001), 'Evolutionary Economics: Framework for Analysis', in Kurt Dopfer (ed.), *Evolutionary Economics – Program and Scope*, Boston, MA and Dordrecht: Kluwer Academic.
Dosi, Giovanni (1991), 'Some thoughts on the promises, challenges and dangers of an "evolutionary perspective" in economics', *Journal of Evolutionary Economics*, **1** (1), 5–7.
Eliasson, Gunnar (1991), 'Deregulation, innovative entry and structural diversity as a source of stable and rapid economic growth', *Journal of Evolutionary Economics*, **1** (1), 49–63.
Gupta, M. and S. Chaudhuri (1998), 'Formal credit, corruption and the informal credit market in agriculture: a theoretical analysis', *Economica*, **65**, 100–111.
Haltiwanger, John (2000), 'Aggregate growth: what have we learned from microeconomic evidence?', working paper, University of Maryland.
Hannan, T. (1997), 'Foundations of the structure-conduct-performance paradigm in banking', *Journal of Money, Credit and Banking*, **23** (1), 68–84.
Kornai, Janos (2000), 'Ten years after "The Road to a Free Economy": the author's self-evaluation', paper for the World Bank 'Annual Bank Conference on Development Economics', Washington, DC, April.
Krugman, Paul (1997), *Development, Geography and Economic Theory*, Cambridge, MA: MIT Press.
Levine, Ross (1997), 'Financial development and economic growth: views and agenda', *Journal of Economic Literature*, **35** (2) (June), 688–726.
Morduch, J. (1999), 'The microfinance promise', *Journal of Economic Literature*, **37**, 1569–1614.
Murrell, Peter (1990), *The Nature of Socialist Economies*, Princeton, NJ: Princeton University Press.
Silverberg, Gerald (1994), 'Evolution, Formal Models of Economic', in Geoffrey Hodgson, Warren Samuels and Marc Tool (eds), *The Elgar Companion to Institutional and Evolutionary Economics*, two Vols, Aldershot, UK and Brookfield, US: Edward Elgar.
Stiglitz, J. and A. Weiss (1981), 'Credit rationing in markets with imperfect information', *American Economic Review*, **71**, 393–410.
United States Agency for International Development (USAID) (2000), *Economic Growth Officers Training Workshop*, folio, Charlottesville, VA, 26 November–1 December.
Witt, Ulrich (1992), 'Evolutionary concepts in economics,' *Eastern Economic Journal*, **18** (4), 405–19.
Witt, Ulrich (2001a), 'Evolutionary economics: an interpretative survey', in Kurt Dopfer (ed.), *Evolutionary Economics – Program and Scope*, Boston, MA and Dordrecht: Kluwer Academic.
Witt, Ulrich (2001b), 'The evolutionary perspective on economic policy making – does it make a difference?', Papers on Economics and Evolution no. 0101, Max-Planck-Institute, Jena.

Index